Stealing Scenes in NYC
by nick migliore

To my parents.
Photos, copy, and design by Nick Migliore
candidpicsny@gmail.com

ISBN: 978-1-7358551-0-3

Copyright © 2020 by Nick Migliore

All rights reserved including the right of reproduction in whole or in part or in any form.

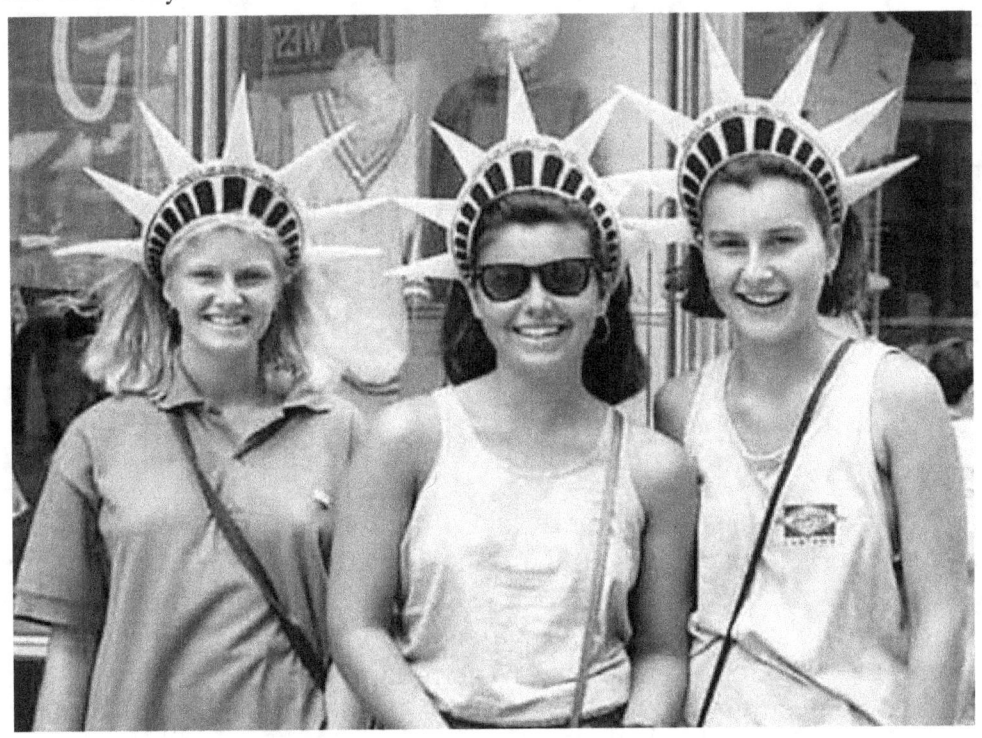

An important message to tourists

If you are looking through this book, please don't be alarmed by the many pictures of violent street crime. Most of these shots were taken decades ago, when the city was indeed a dangerous place. Today New York City is the safest large city in America, so relax and enjoy yourself.

Table of Contents

About this Book
Foreword
Introduction 4
1. The Main Library 6
2. Lovers & other strangers 12
3. The subway 18
4. Five short stories 24
5. Taking it easy 32
6. The angels 36
7. Lunch 40
8. Five more stories 44
9. Construction workers 50
10. When buses pull up 56
11. Times Square 58
12. The tourists 72
13. Four more stories 76
14. The Deuce 84
15. Interesting characters 100
16. Two more stories 106
17. The homeless 114
18. Stacks 124
19. City critters 127
20. The little man 134
21. Five more short stories 136
22. The future 146
23. End piece 150

About this book

  The pictures in this book were taken mostly from 1962 to the present. They are all of real people, in actual events, none of them are staged. Photoshop was used to perform typical darkroom tasks, such as cropping, dodging and burning, spotting, etc. However, in no case was the substance or spirit of a picture altered. All of the short stories are true. However, many of them happened decades ago. So some of the details could be inaccurate.

Foreword

    I was standing on the corner of 6ave and 23st. It`s one of my favorite places for taking pictures in New York. It`s a very busy corner with an eclectic mix of people. There are lots of hipsters and artsy types, plus tons of models and media people. There`s also a large Gay presence, as well as many blind folks for some reason. I usually get a lot of good shots when I work this corner.

    Suddenly, I could sense that someone was right behind me. I turned around and standing just inches from me was a young black woman with seething anger in her eyes! I was scared because she was too close for comfort, she was within stabbing range. I took a step back and placed my left hand on my camera bag. I wanted to use it as a shield, just in case. She looked at me with burning hatred. She was in her mid- 20`s, with long dreadlocks and African style dress. She looked to me like a Rastafarian. She hissed at me "I know what you`re doing here, you ugly old man, you evil, ugly old man! I see you here all the time. "What am I doing" I asked. "Don`t act so innocent, you White Devil, I know what you`re up to, always on this corner, stalking your victims like a viper"." You don't fool me, I know who sent you. I know what you`re doing with that cursed machine that you point at people." "What am I doing?" I repeated" "You`re stealing souls" she said. "No I`m not" I said "I`m just taking pictures". "Liar" she sneered, I have put a Voodoo curse on you, I hope you get a heart attack!" "I hope you get Ebola" I replied. That threw her off balance, she was not expecting that, I saw an opening. "I`ve been baptized, I said, "your curse won`t work on me". She gave me a smile that did not include her eyes. "I have other tricks up my sleeve" she said. "So do I" I replied, as I raised the camera and pointed it right at her face! She shrieked in terror and covered her face with her hands, like a vampire facing a cross! She backed off and started to run, as she ran off, I yelled after her "I got it, I got your soul".

Introduction

The year was 1962, it was a rainy Saturday afternoon in Brooklyn. I was 14 at the time, moping around the house, nothing to do. I was getting on my mother's nerves. "Nicholas," she said "Why don't you go to the basement and go through all the books down there, maybe you'll find something that you'd like." The basement had the musty smell of a used bookstore. There were hundreds of volumes stored in cardboard boxes. I started to go through them. At first, they seemed to be mostly about women's interests, cooking, gardening, rearing children, etc. As I dug deeper, the subject matters became more eclectic. I was surprised to find that my mother was interested in art history, classical music, and photography.

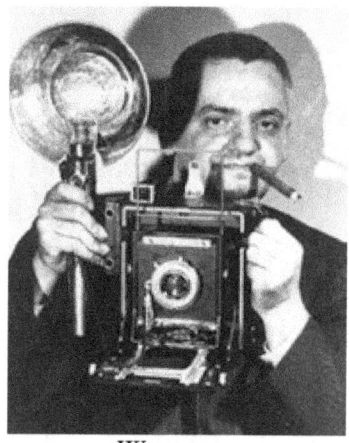

Weegee

One of these photography books caught my eye. It was entitled Naked City, by some guy named Weegee. It was a book of photographs of ordinary New Yorkers, from what seemed like long ago. I was mesmerized by this book right from the start. I would lay on my bed at night and go through it over and over, wondering how this guy Weegee, always seemed to be at the right spot, at the right time, to get these amazing pictures. There was a shot of a mafia rubout, where the victim is lying near a pail of bocce balls. Another picture showed poor immigrant kids sleeping on a fire escape, on a hot summer night, and the most moving of all, was the image of an old lady and her granddaughter, crying hysterically as they watch their entire family burn to death in a tenement fire.

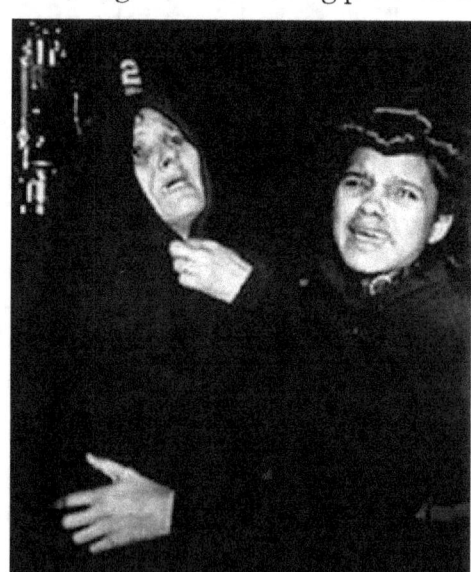

This guy Weegee (his real name was Arthur Fellig) was a real character, a cigar chomping, fedora wearing, press photographer, right out of one of those gangster movies from the thirties and forties. He used one of those old 4 x 5 speed graphic cameras that only took one shot at a time. This book would have a profound influence on me. I wanted to be just like Weegee, roaming the streets, looking for shots. There were just a few obstacles in my way. First, I didn't even own a camera and second, I knew nothing about photography. I had a friend named Danny who was an amateur photographer. I went to him for advice. He sold me a used camera plus an entire darkroom. He also taught me how to develop prints from scratch. I'll never forget the first time I saw an image slowly appear on a sheet of white paper. It was pure magic. I was hooked.

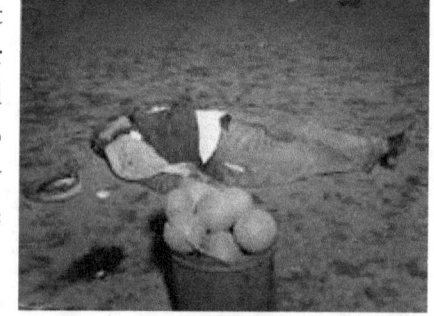

I began roaming the streets of my Brooklyn neighborhood, taking pictures of my friends and strangers alike, but I was unhappy with the results. My pictures were nothing like Weegee's, they weren't exciting, or funny, or action packed. They were boring, just like my neighborhood. We didn't even lock our doors during the daytime. I showed my pictures to an older relative of mine. After looking at them, he said that there wasn't one in the whole pile that was halfway decent. It was like a knife going into my heart.

It was my friend Danny who suggested that I 'go into the city' if I was looking for action, you'll find plenty there, especially in Times Square. No sooner did these words leave his lips then he tried to take them back. "Forget what I just said, Nick, It's too dangerous there. You're too young and scrawny; they'll just steal your camera." "Yeah, you're probably right," I said. I couldn't wait to get to Times Square.

First, I wanted to buy a new camera. The one that Danny sold me was too slow to operate. I started to do some research about the new Japanese cameras that were coming on the market. I settled on a Yashica range finder, it was over 200 dollars, a lot of money back then. I had a part time job, so the money was no problem. I took the subway into the city (my first time alone) and went to Willoughby Peerless, a large camera store on 32nd St. I walked into the store and approached one of the salesmen behind the counter, who looked like one of my uncles. He said to me, "Hello young man, what can I do for you?" I said, "I want to buy a Yashica rangefinder camera." "Whoa, do you know they cost over $200?" I said, "Yeah, I know." "You have $200 on you?" "Sure." "How old are you?" "14." "Where did you get $200 from?" "I robbed a bank." "Oh, a wise guy. Well, for your information we don't sell anything to people under 16, unless their parents are with them." "No problem." – I said, "I'll go to Olden's (that was their competitor right down the block) and you'll lose a customer for life." "Ok kid, you win, but if anyone else asks your age, tell them you are 16."

He handed me the camera. It fit my grip perfectly. It was black with chrome trim. It was so sexy, like a miniature sports car for the hands. I couldn't wait to use it. At the first garbage basket, I threw the box away. Suddenly, this guy grabs the empty box, and takes off with it. He was a con artist who would put a brick into the empty box, rewrap it, and then sell it to some unsuspecting tourists. I loaded the camera with film and began walking up 34th St. towards 5th Ave. As I passed the Empire State Building, I thought to myself 'Imagine someone jumping off that thing.' Twenty years later, somebody would, a guy in a parachute, and I would be there to catch it on film. Thus began my 50 years of wandering around the city, camera in hand.

- Nick Migliore

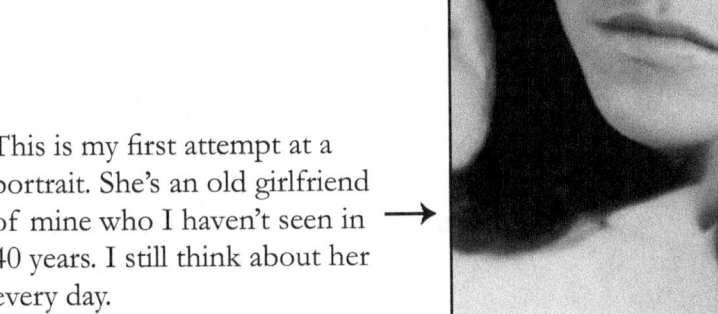

This is my first attempt at a portrait. She's an old girlfriend of mine who I haven't seen in 40 years. I still think about her every day.

Nancy

Chapter 1 — *The Main Library*

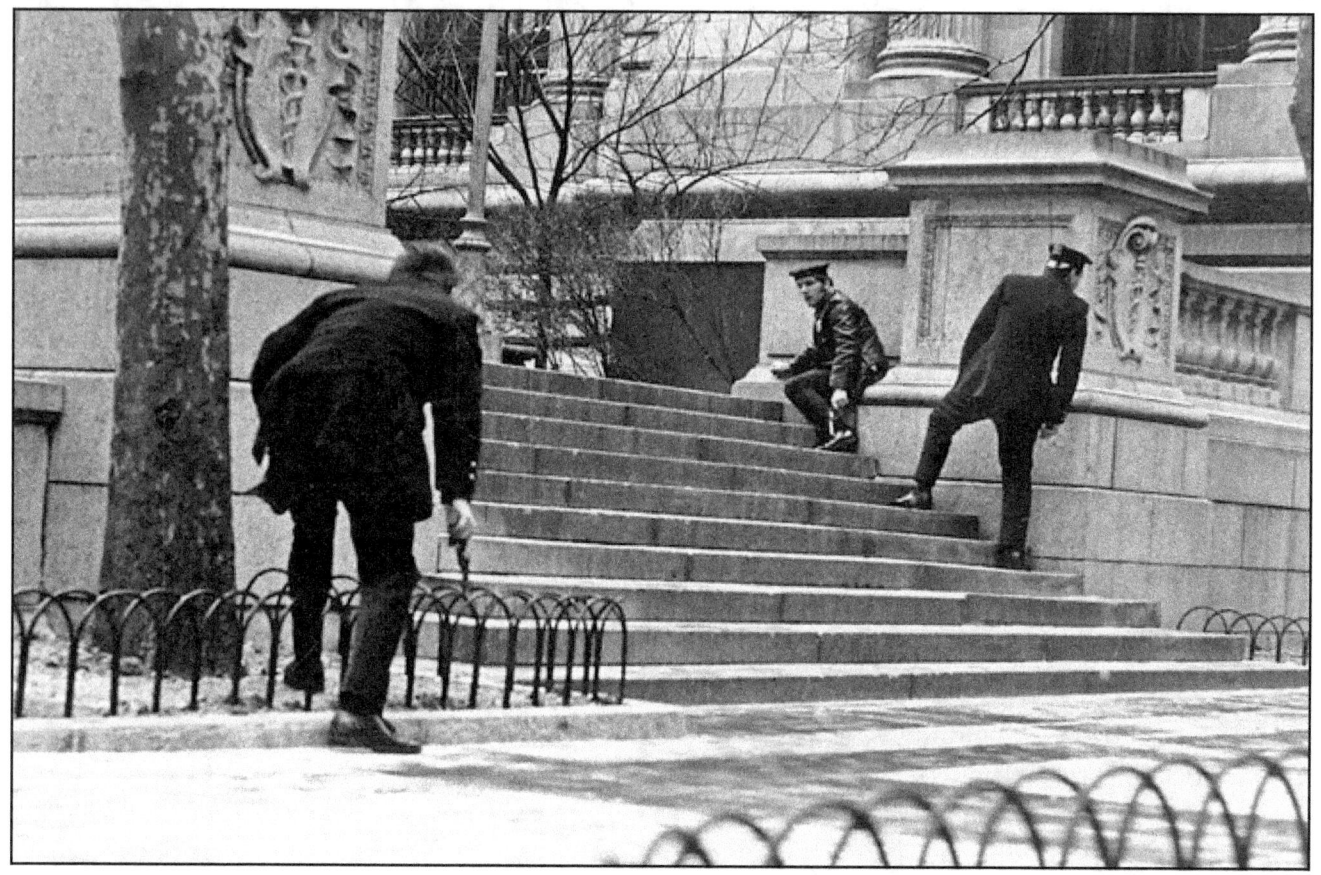

I was 14 when I took this picture. When my father saw it, he confiscated my camera.

Hunting for easter eggs

I had just bought a brand new camera. It was my first time shooting in Manhattan. I was walking up Fifth avenue, near the main library. All of a sudden, police cars came screeching down 42nd street and pulled up onto the sidewalk, in front of the main library. The cops jumped out of their cars with their guns out. They took cover in front of the library as if they were looking for someone. They all had their hats turned backwards (so their visors wouldn't block their vision.) I ran to the corner and started sneaking up behind them to get a good shot. I heard on their radio that there was a man with a gun, and shots had been fired. I thought to myself, maybe being here isn't such a good idea. Suddenly, someone grabbed me from behind, I turned around, it was another cop. He had his gun out and his hat turned backwards.

He said, "Who are you?" I said, "Nick." "What are you doing here?" "Taking pictures." "How old are you?" "14." "Where are you from?" "Brooklyn." "Nick, go back to Brooklyn, you don't belong here. Don't you see it's dangerous here?"

He took me by the shoulder and shoved me towards the police car that was parked on the sidewalk. "Get behind that car and stay there," he said. I watched as they continued to search the main library, taking pictures now and then. When it looked like the danger was over, I moseyed over to them, but they were looking for something on the ground (probably drugs.) I said to them, "What are you looking for?" The cop looked at me and said, "Easter eggs."

I never made it to Times Square that day. Instead I headed home to develop the film that I just shot. I had a darkroom set up in the attic, so I had the prints in few hours. I couldn't wait to show them to my parents. Around 7 p.m. I could hear my father coming in the door. I ran down the stairs to greet him. The prints were still damp. I put them on the kitchen counter. "I just took them today with my new camera dad, what do you think?"
My father hit the ceiling.
- "What the hell are you doing around cops with their guns out? What the hell are you doing in the city? Why do they have their guns out? What's going on?"
- "They were looking for some guy about something or other..." I said.
- "No, I don't like this at all. Where the hell is your common sense? If you saw cops with their guns out, you should have run the other way."
My mother said to him, "Nicky, calm down."
- "Don't tell me to calm down, it's that damned book of yours that put all this crap into his head in the first place. No, I don't like this at all." My father was no fool.
He looked at the pictures again, and said:
- "They were looking for someone with a gun, weren't they?"
- "Yeah, but it was a false alarm."
- "But you didn't know that! Suppose there was a gun fight, and suppose the bullets started flying, and suppose you got hit by a stray shot!"
- "Suppose, suppose, suppose!" I said.

My father got into my face and said, "Don't get sassy with me mister, I'll slap your damned face." He was beet red, his lips were quivering. I've never seen him so mad in my life. My father never hit me, but I thought this time he might.
- "You've shown me that you're not mature enough to be doing this, no common sense, I want that camera."
- "What!" I said, "It's mine, I paid for it myself."
- "I don't care, if you live under my roof, you

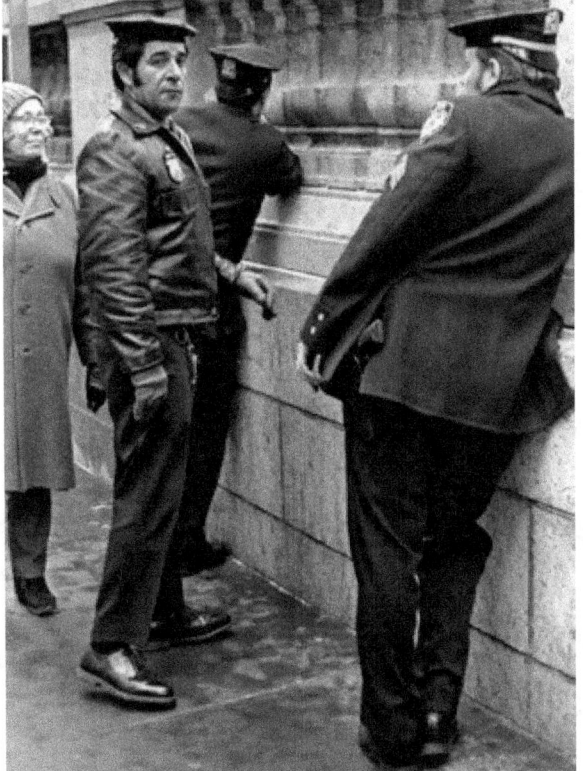
'Hey kid, didn't I tell you to scram'

obey my rules, period! End of discussion! Now, give-me-the-camera!" I gave him the camera.

It took about a week of walking around with a long face before he finally gave me the camera back. I had to promise not to do anything stupid again. I wouldn't show him any of my action shots again, until I was 21 and under my own roof.

I enjoyed my first trip to Manhattan so much that I would repeat it thousands of times over the next 50 years. I also developed an interest in covering police action, and crime in general. Without realizing it, I would be exactly in the right time, and place, to cover both. New York was a about to enter a long dark period of ever rising crime rates, and at the helm, was a very handsome, but very ineffectual mayor, John Lindsey.

The Main Library is one of the focal points of Midtown Manhattan. There are plenty of places to sit and relax and watch the passing scene.

'God is great'

Years ago, I made this shot into a postcard. I was in a store trying to make a sale, the owner looked at this card and smiled, then he kissed it, then he let his wife and daughter kiss it. I asked him why he kissed that particular card. He explained that he was a Muslim, and that the writing on the wall, behind the musician, was Arabic for "God is great." It was a term that was to become all to familiar to New Yorkers years later. ↓

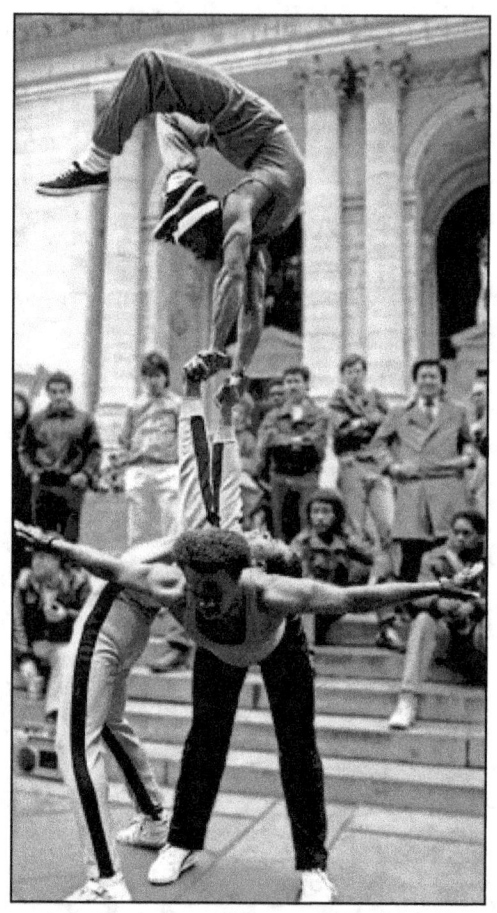

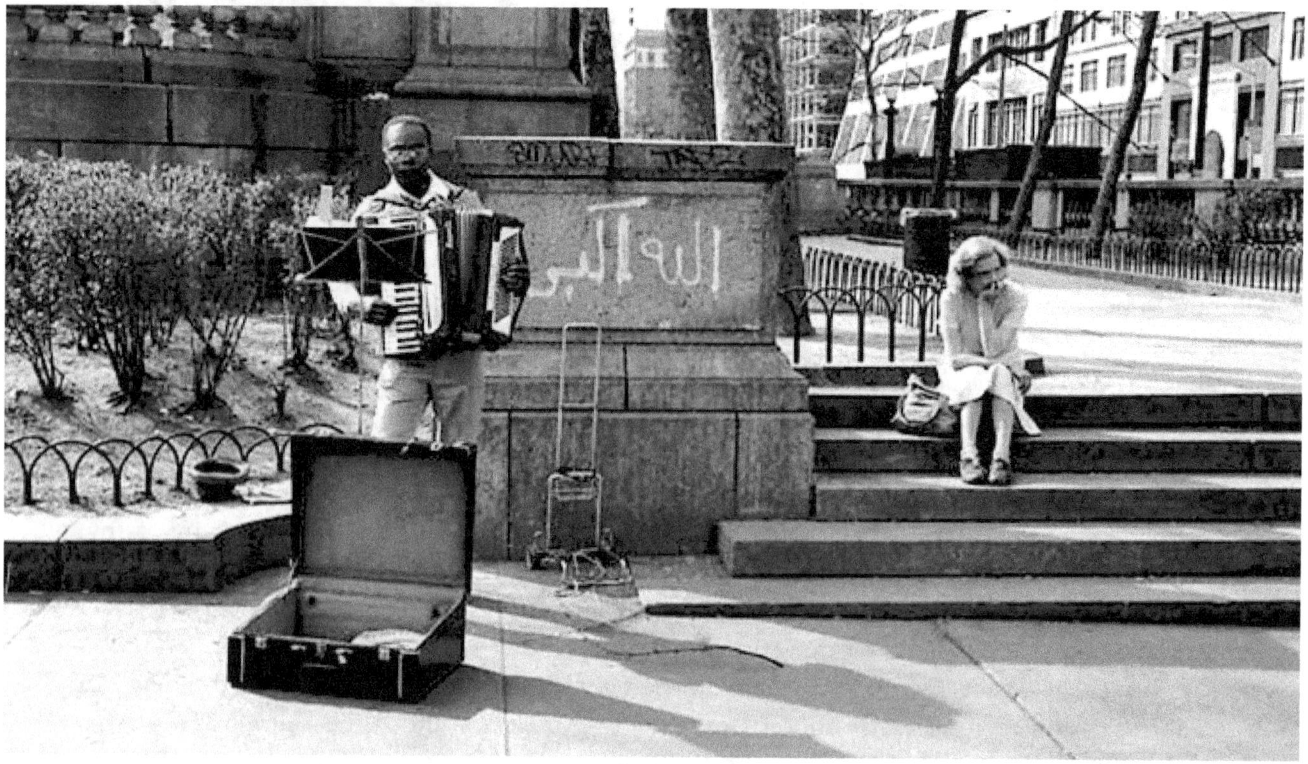

Amazing African acrobats.

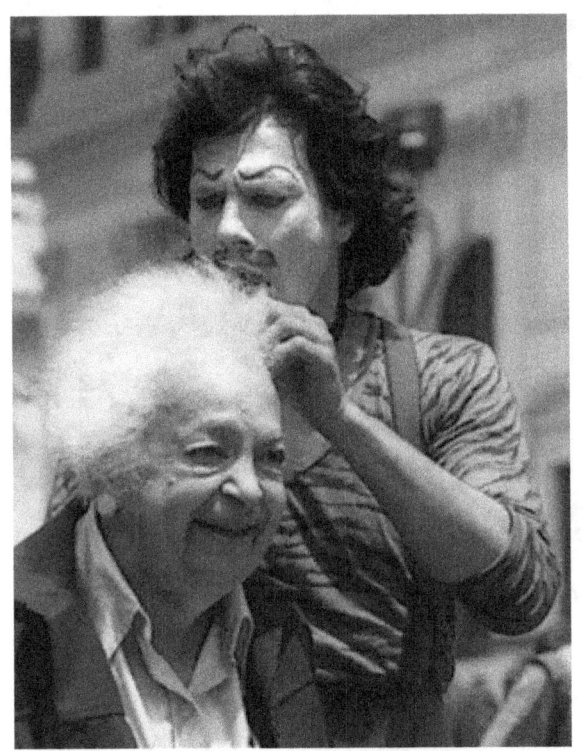
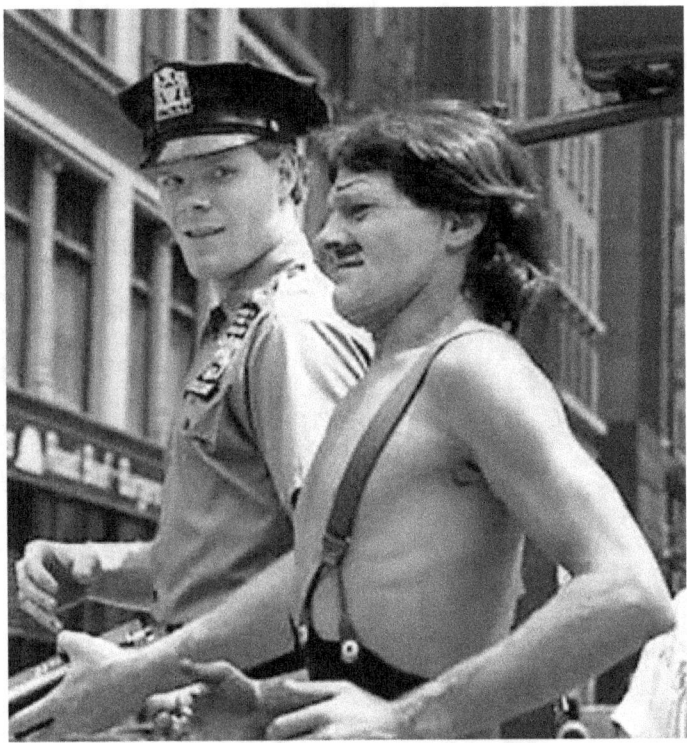
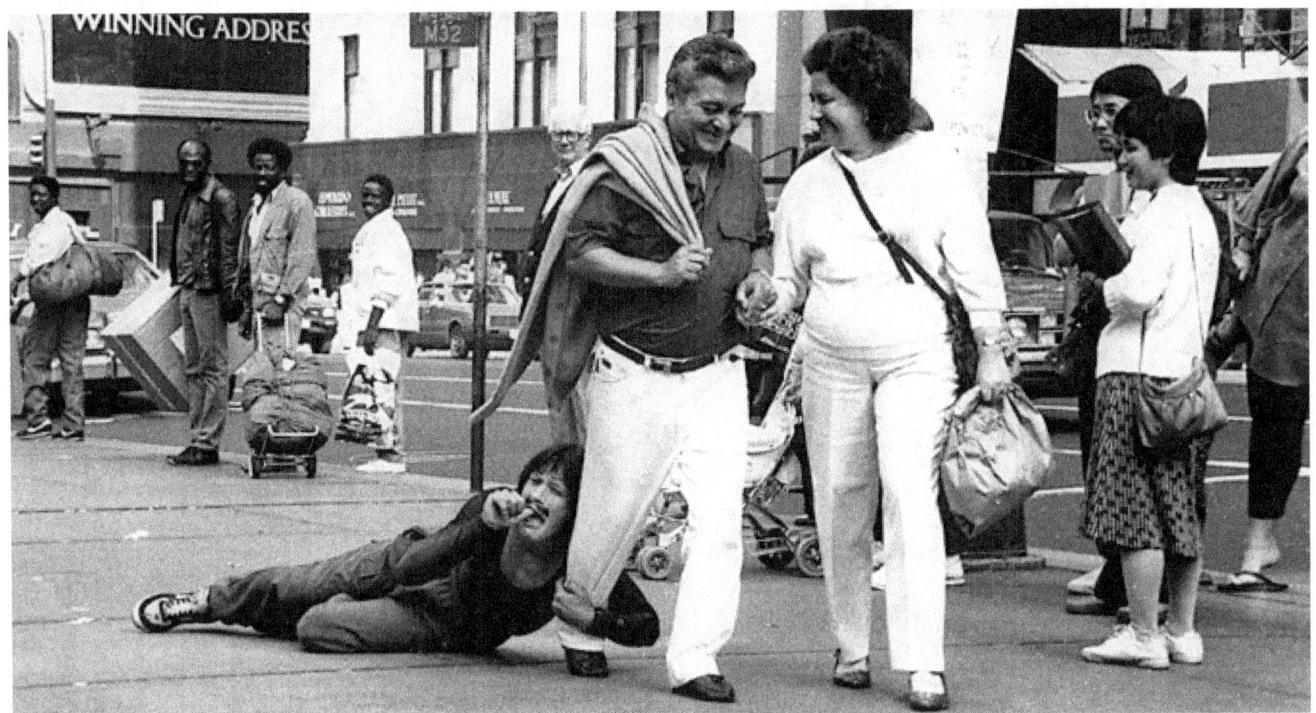

The mimes

The mimes are considered by many to be France's greatest gift to Western Civilization, others just hate them. The steps of the Main Library make a perfect makeshift grandstand for office workers on their lunch breaks, along with many tourists. The ensuing show can sometimes be hilarious, as passersby are made complete fools of, for the amusement of the crowd. And absolutely no one is immune from their barbs.

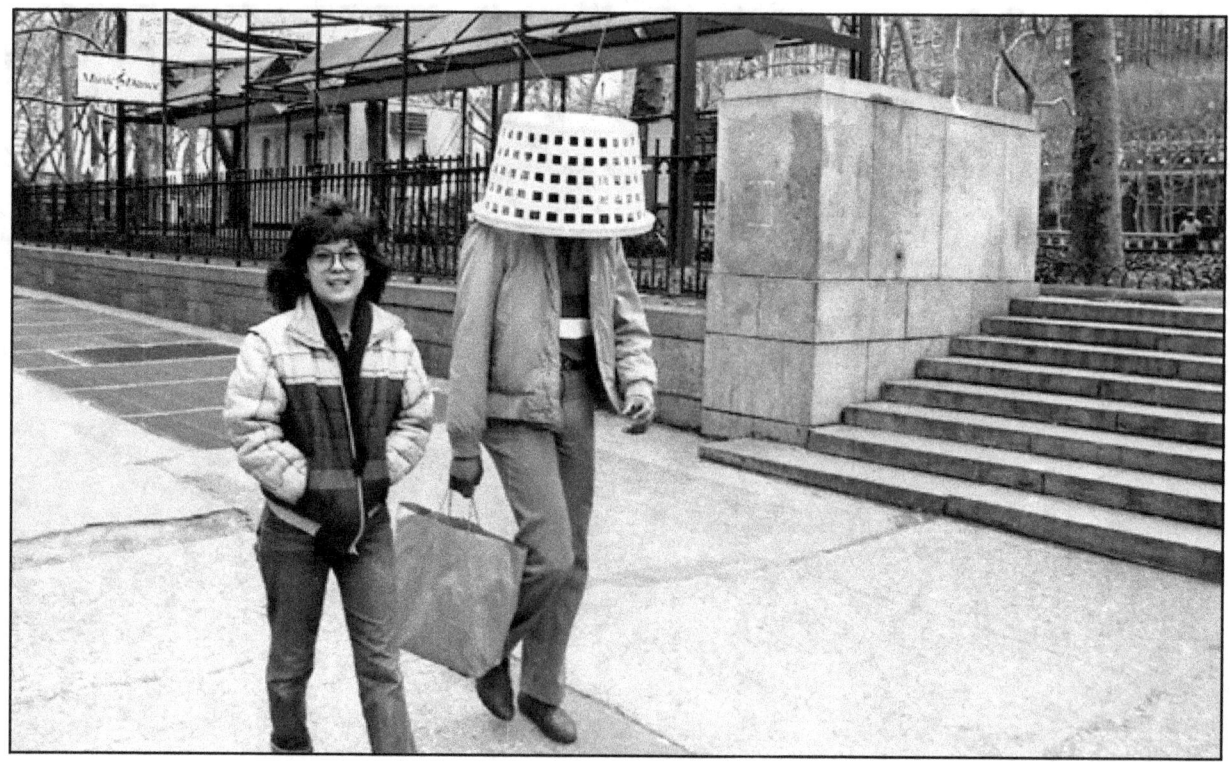

One of the first things I noticed about Manhattan was that there were a lot more weirdos than in Brooklyn.

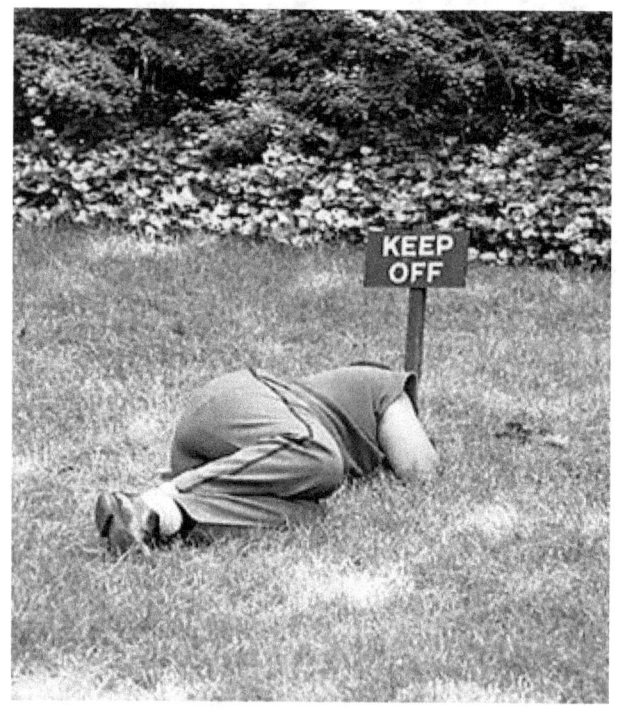

Stick-it to the man

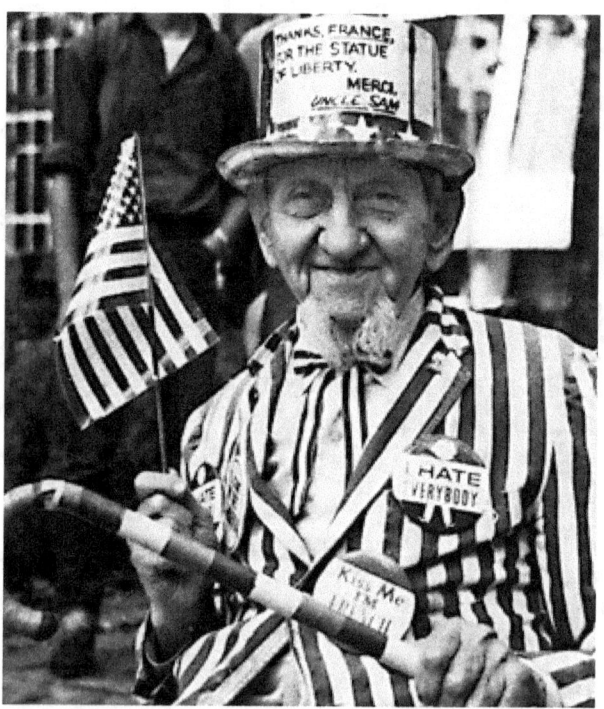

Uncle Sam was a regular fixture in Bryant Park

That was the battle cry during the 1960s, when everybody was revolting against everything. Showing contempt for authority was cool, even in petty little ways.

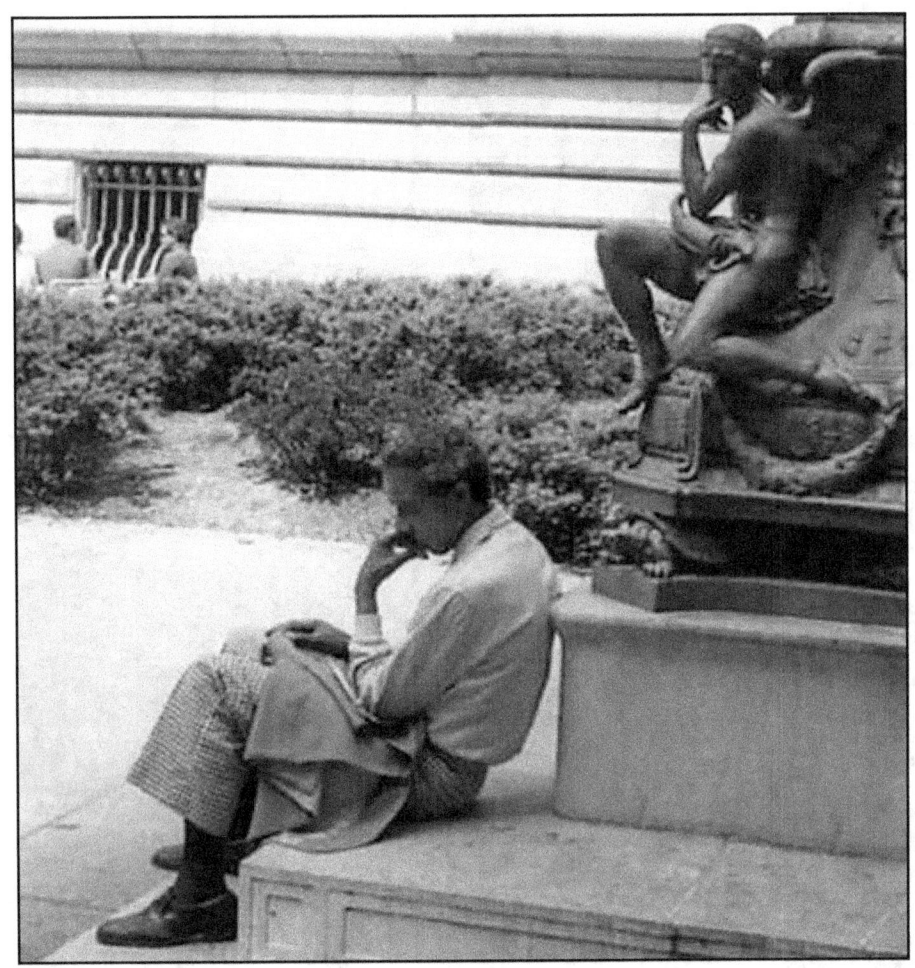

The thinkers

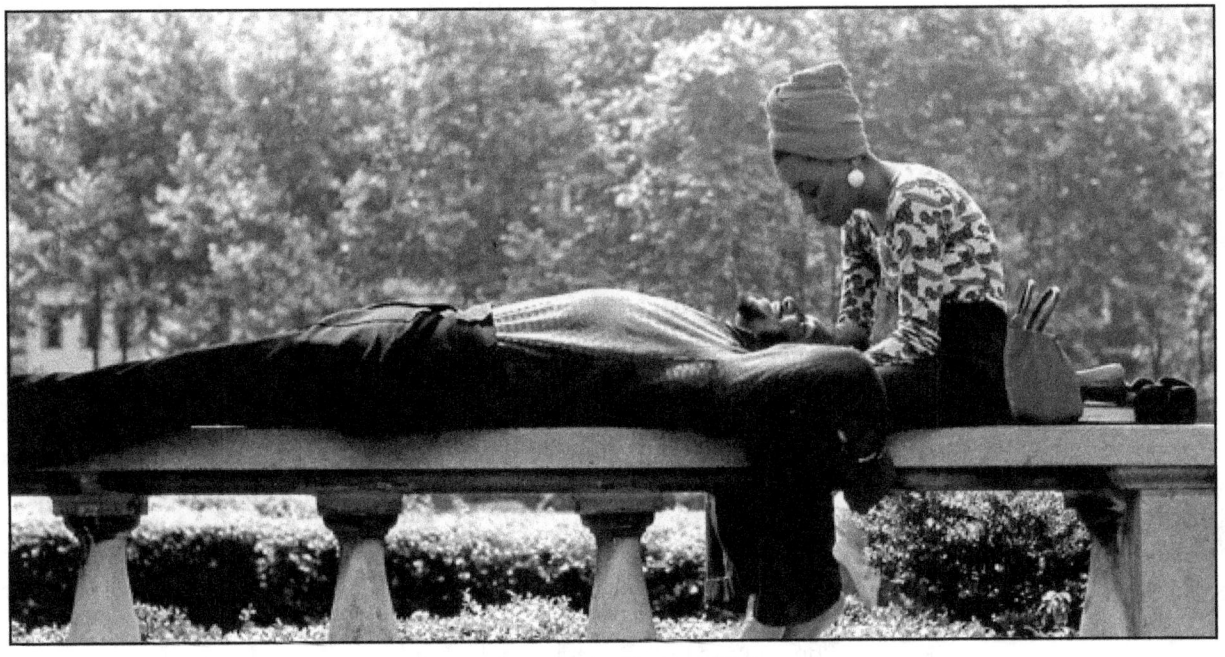

Lovers in Bryant Park.

Chapter 2 — *Lovers and other strangers*

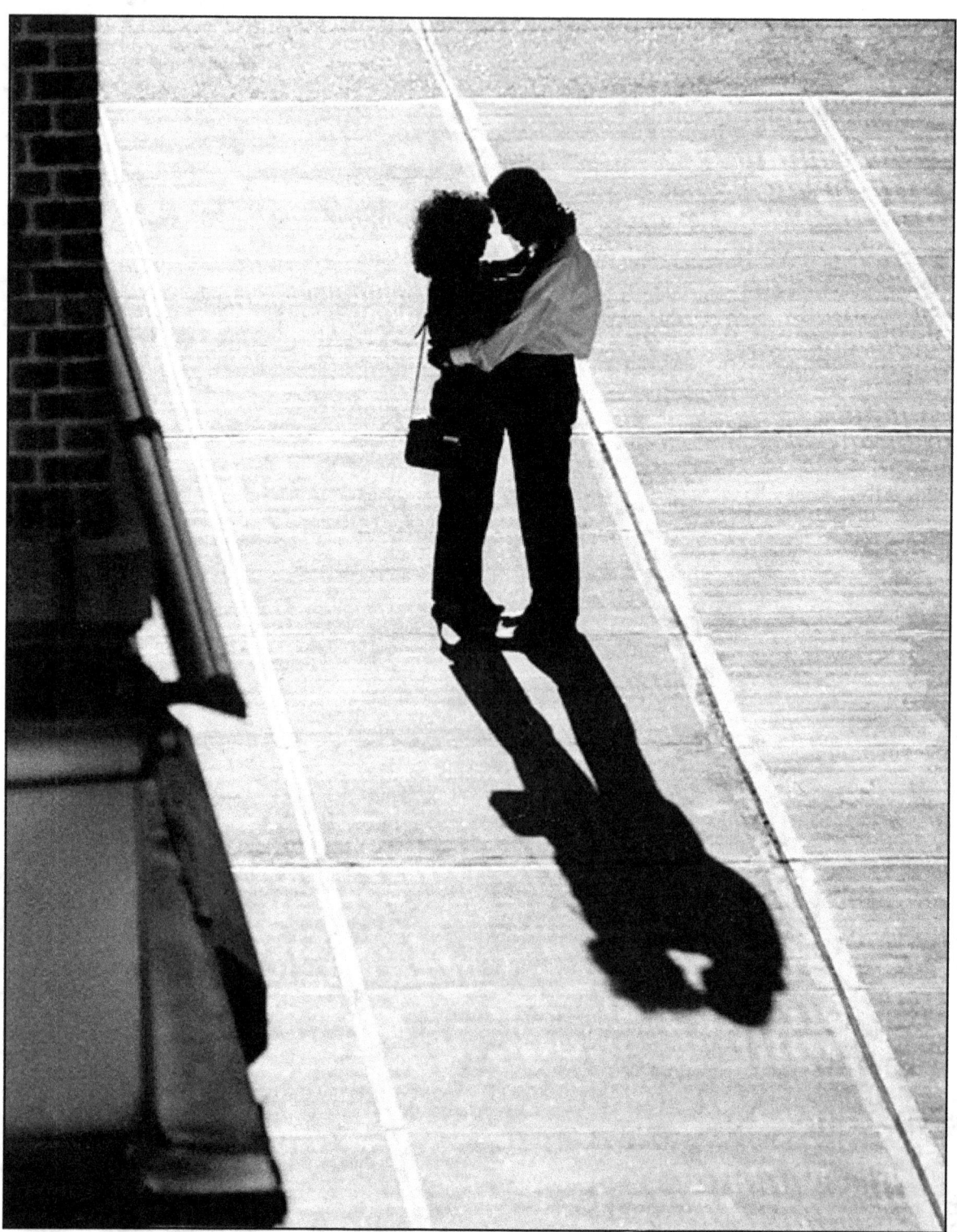

The view from my kitchen window.

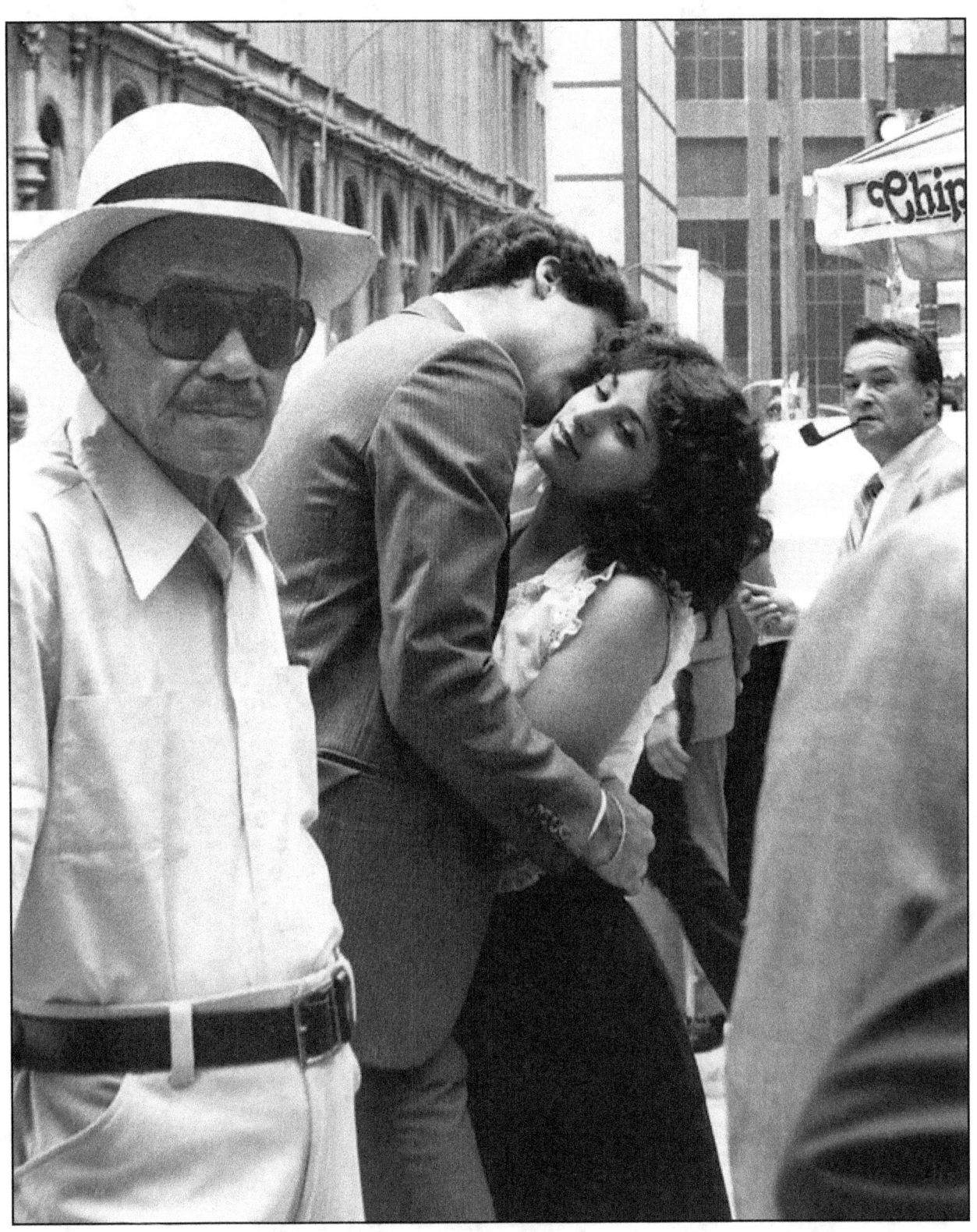
This girl was gorgeous, she reminded me of Sophia Loren.

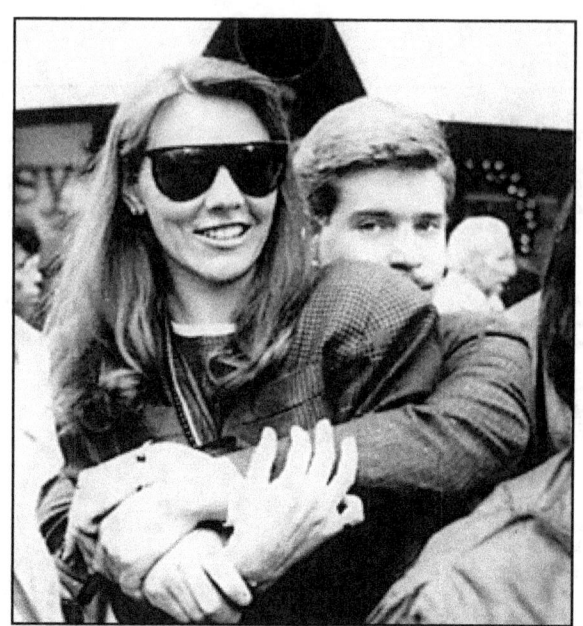 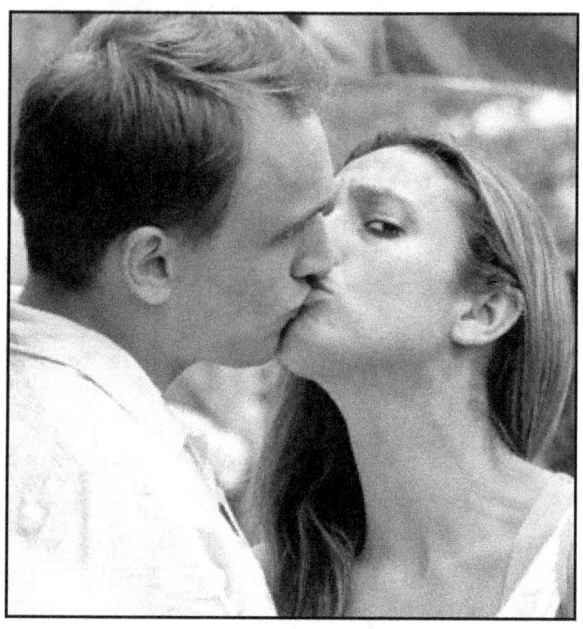

Hard learned lessons about women

1. Avoid women who wear combat boots. **2.** Avoid nurses. They spend their whole day taking care of other people. When they get home, they don't want to do a thing. You're lucky if you can get a cup of coffee out of them. **3.** Avoid women with aliases – at all costs. I dated three women with aliases. What are the odds of that happening? If a woman has multiple identities, she's usually up to no good, or is trying to hide a shady past. **4.** Avoid beautiful women who are too easy. They usually have needs that require large amounts of your cash to satisfy. And when your money is gone, they're gone.

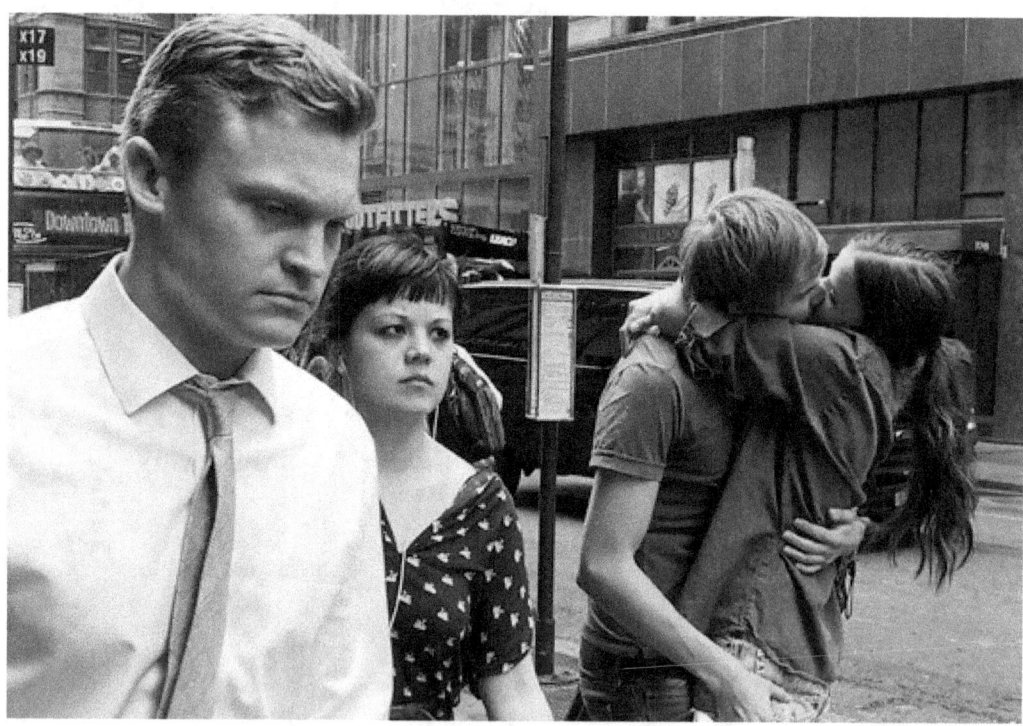

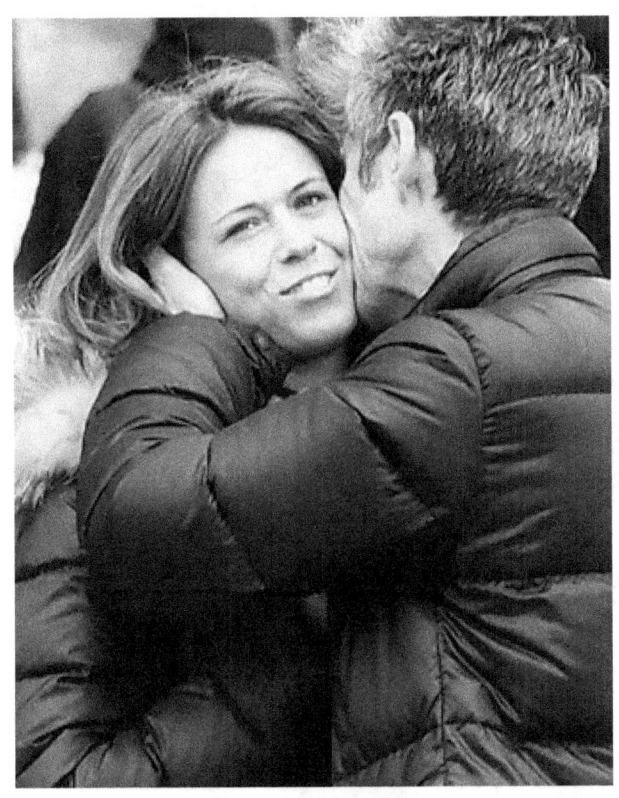
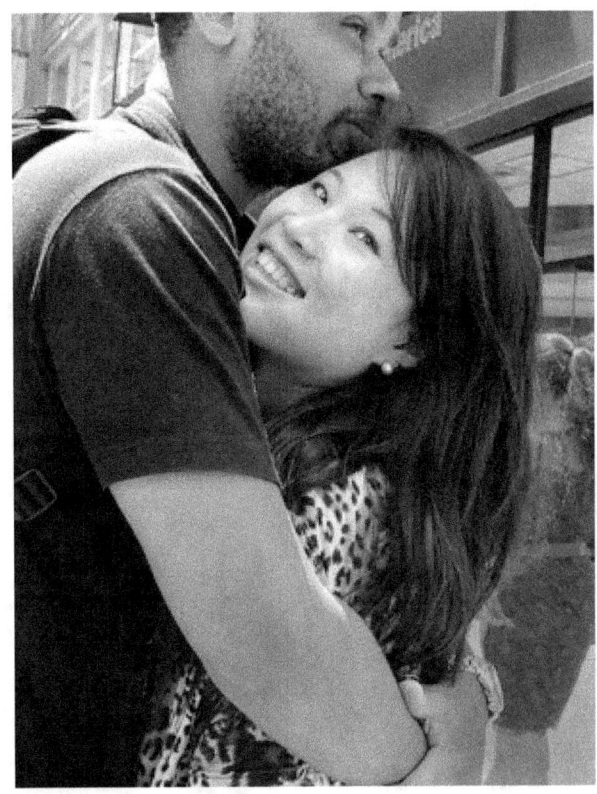
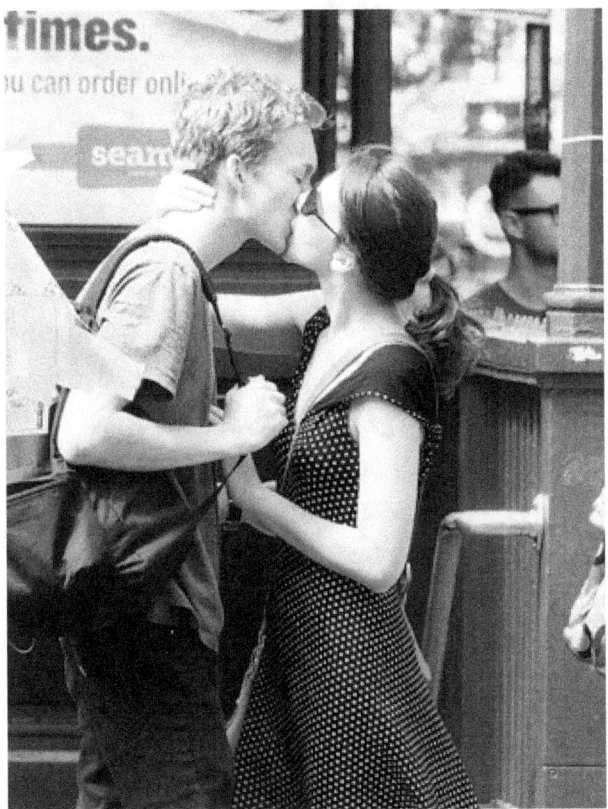
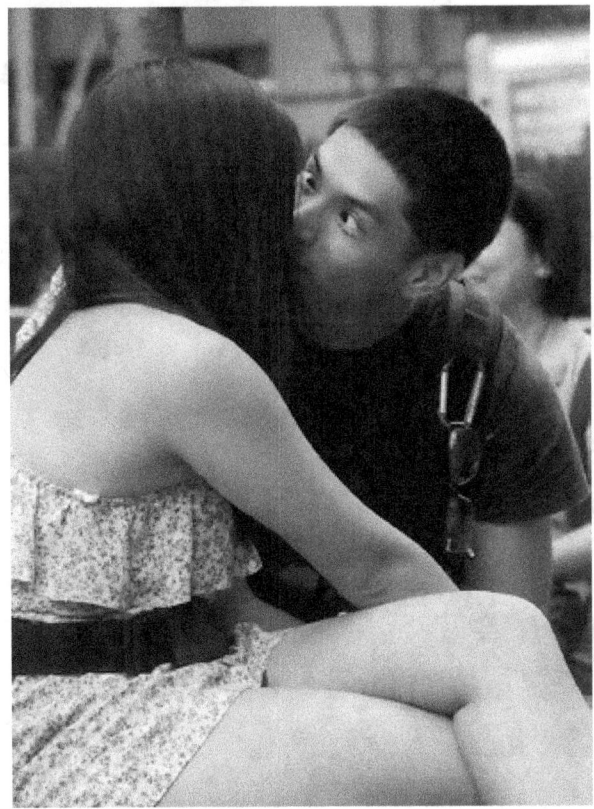

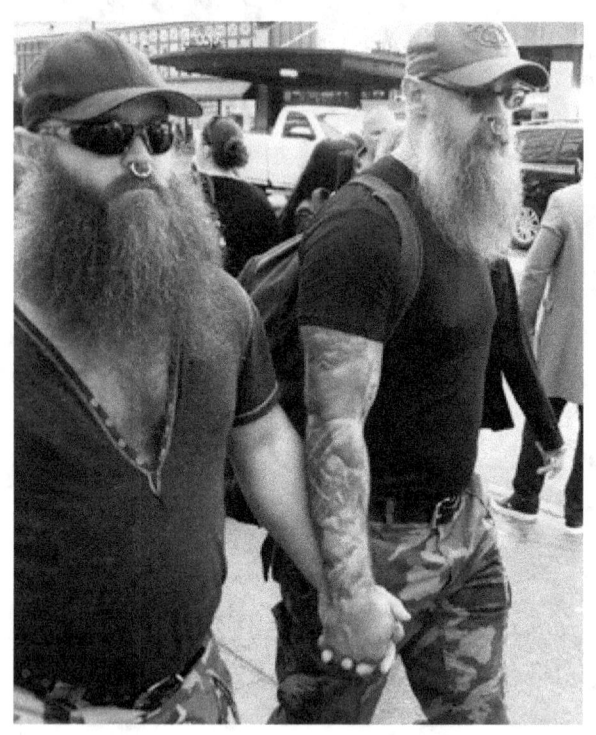
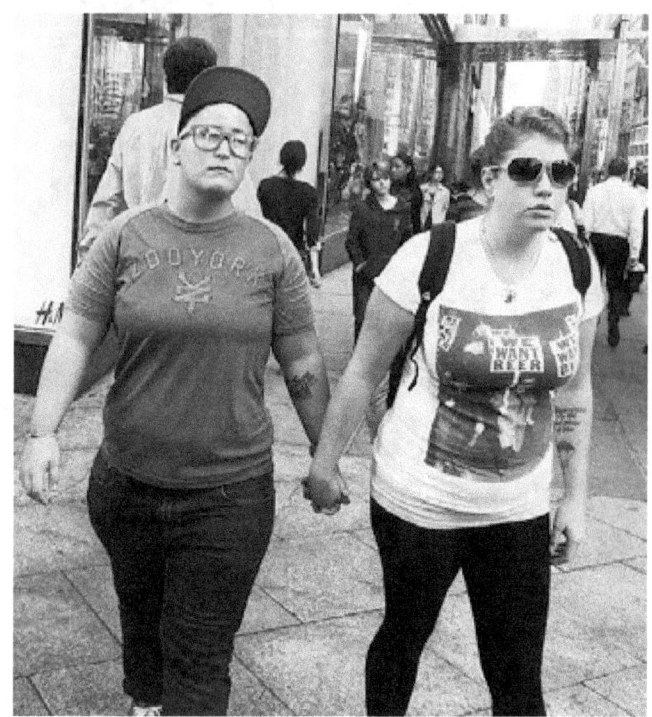

Out of the Closet!

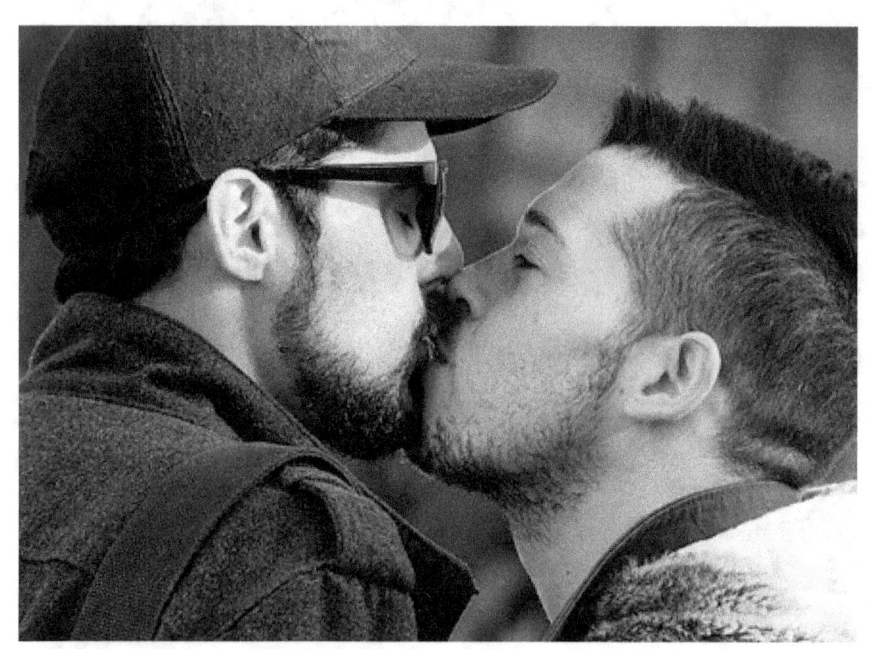

For years, scenes like this would only be seen in the gay sections of New York City. Now they happen everywhere. About time.

The one that got away

I was lying on a park bench in Columbus Circle. I was pretending to be asleep. My camera was hidden beneath a newspaper. Through my half-opened eyes, I was watching two cops who where behaving strangely. It seemed to me that they were enjoying each others company a little too much. It was obvious that the female officer was allowing herself to be maneuvered into this little niche at the rear of the monument. From here they couldn't be seen, except by me, but I was asleep. They stood there talking, very close to one another. It looked to me like they were going to kiss. I knew my timing had to be exact. Too soon, and I would spook them, too slow, and I would miss the shot.

He took one last look around to see if anyone was watching. He was going in for the kill. He puts his arms around her. Their lips were just inches apart. I raised the camera to my eye...and then she saw me. She backed off in a flash, and pushed him away...it was all over, I blew it. Of all the shots that I've missed over the years, (and there have been many) it's this one, that I regret the most.

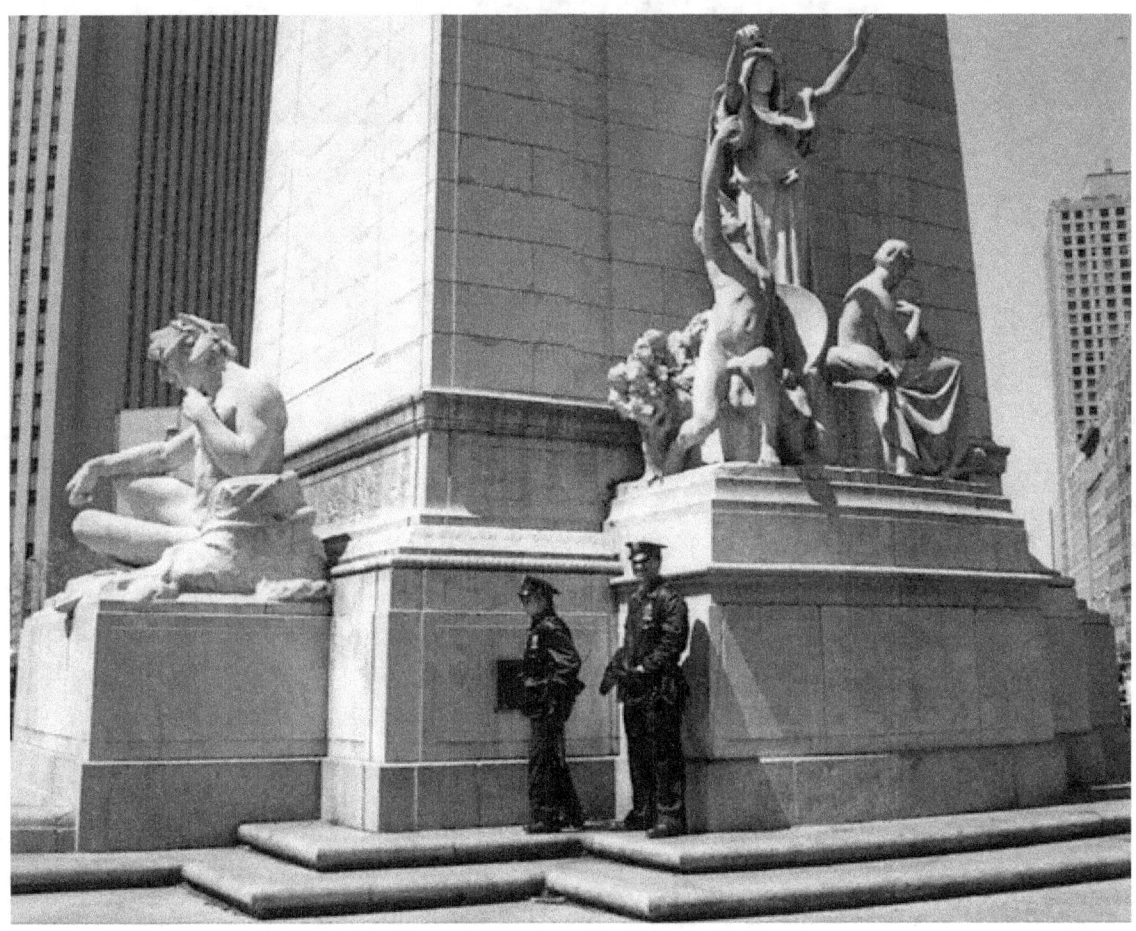

Chapter 3

The subway

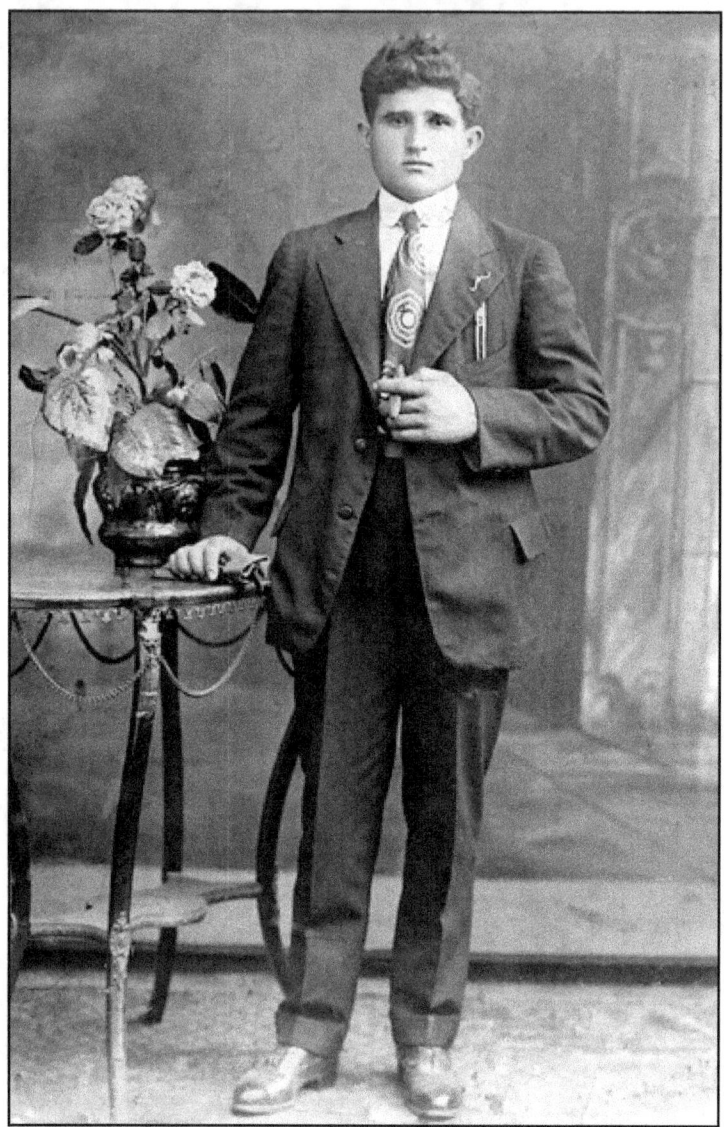

It was men like this who built the subways.

It was mostly Irish and Italian immigrants who built the subways. They came to America at the turn of the century looking for a better life. Working on the subways was dirty and dangerous work, but they were glad to get it. In 1917, this man settled in Brooklyn with his young wife and two small children. He was fleeing the war in Europe, so instead of digging trenches on some battlefield, he wound up digging even bigger trenches for the New York City subway. That was O.K.; his body was built for digging. Look at the size of his hands and the length of his arms. For generations men like him have been toiling on construction jobs without complaint. His ancestors probably built roads for the Romans.

So when the construction supervisor knocked on his young wife's door one day and told her that she was a widow, she took the news stoically. She was half expecting it; after all, many men were killed building the subways. His name was John Panacola. He was one of my grandfathers.

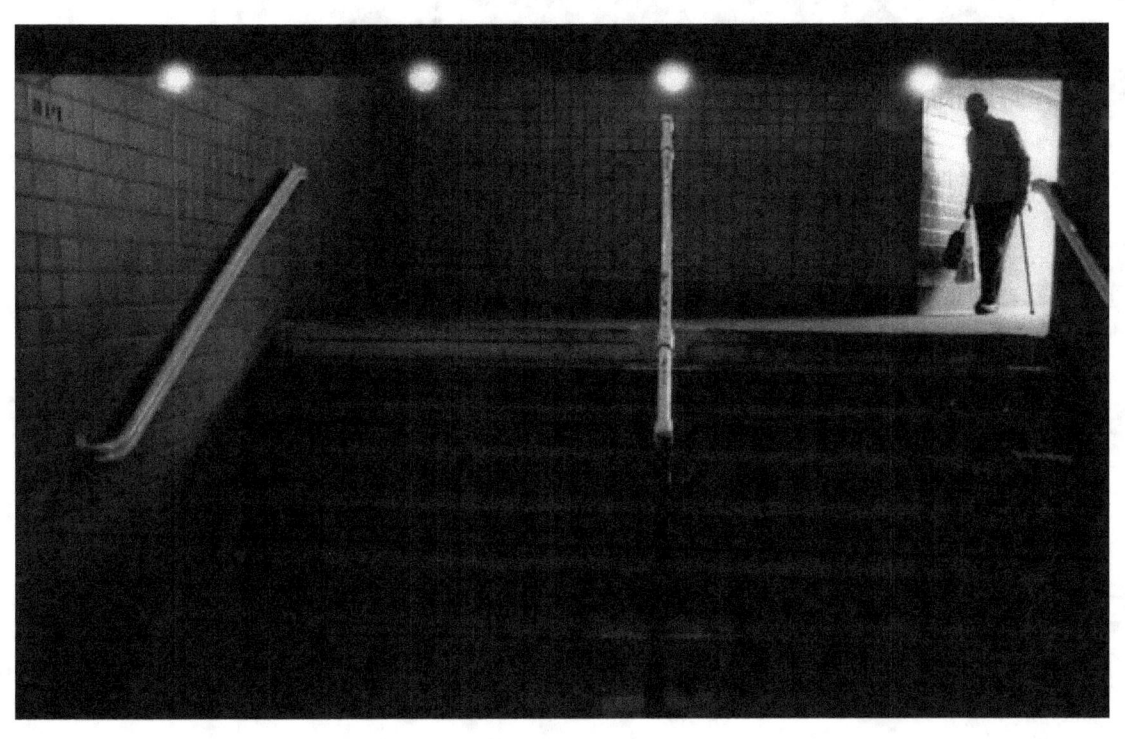

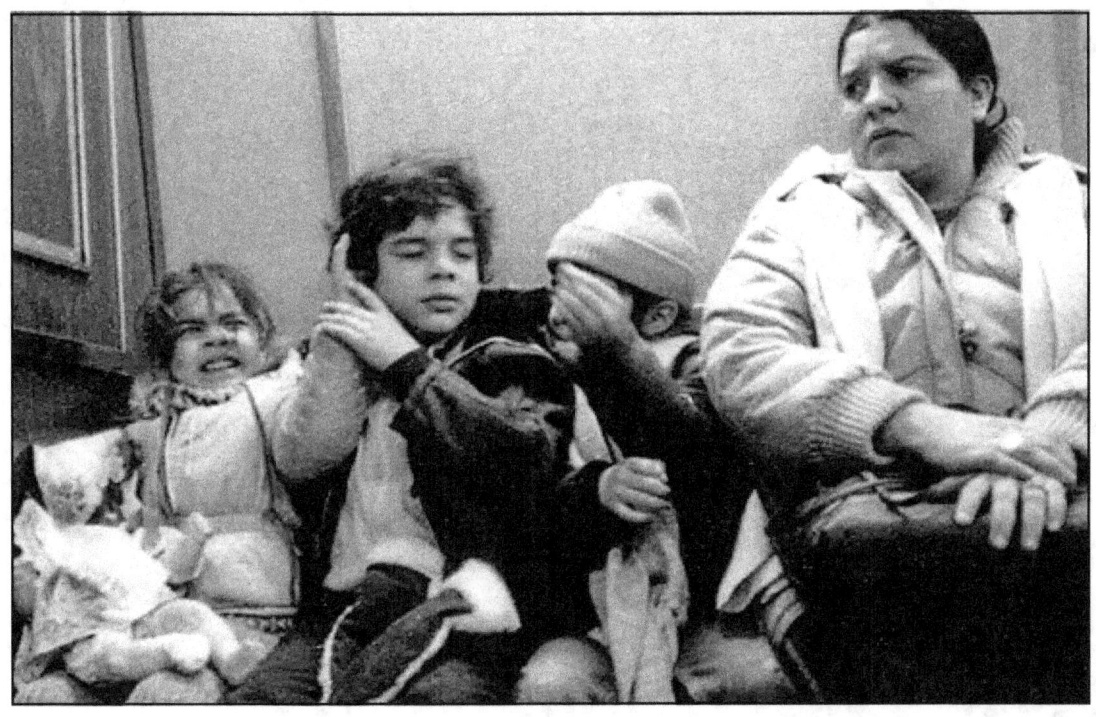

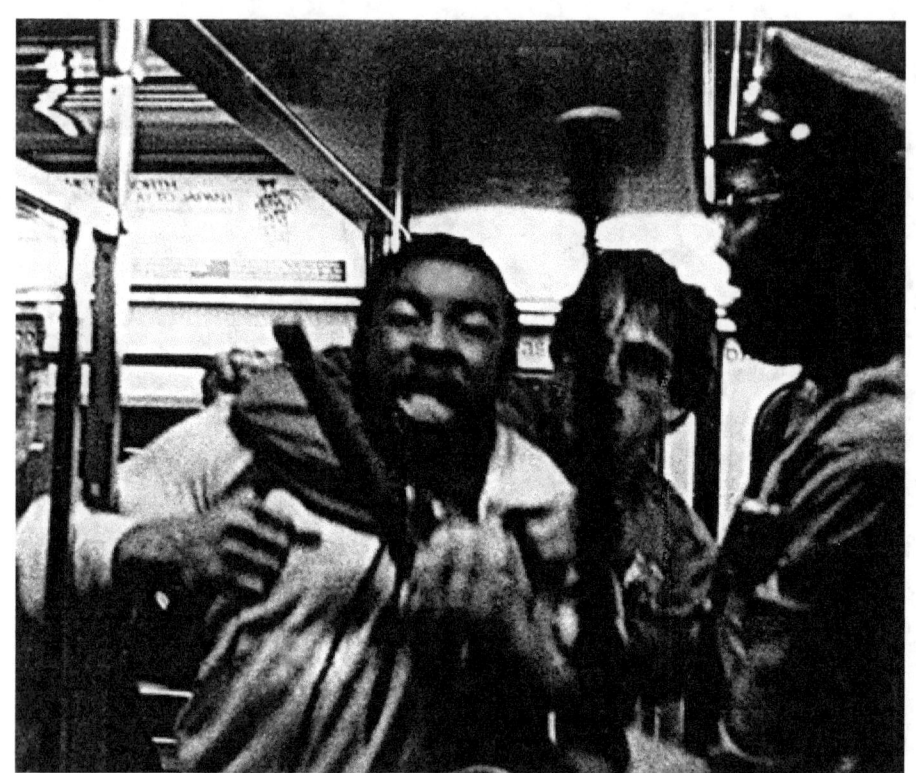

The police wanted to arrest this guy for disorderly conduct and he resisted. Then, he went berserk. It took half a dozen cops to restrain him.

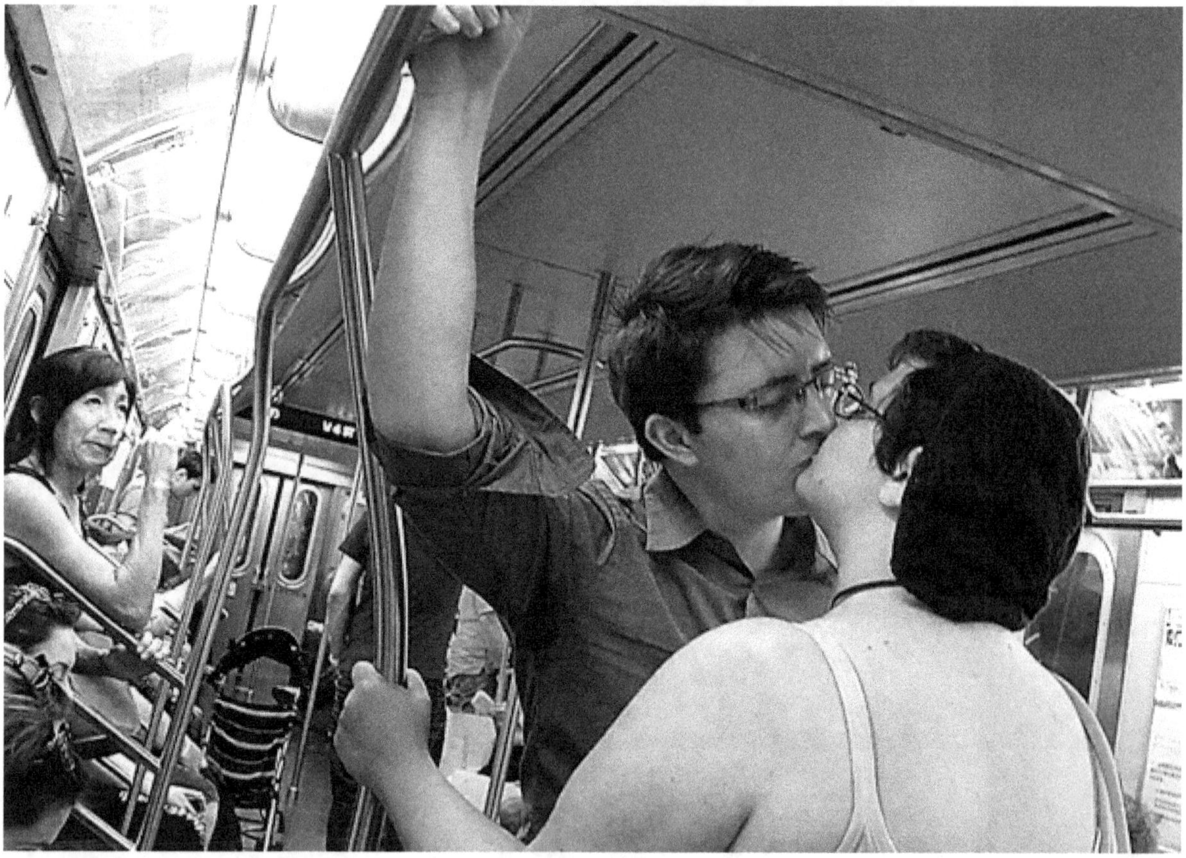

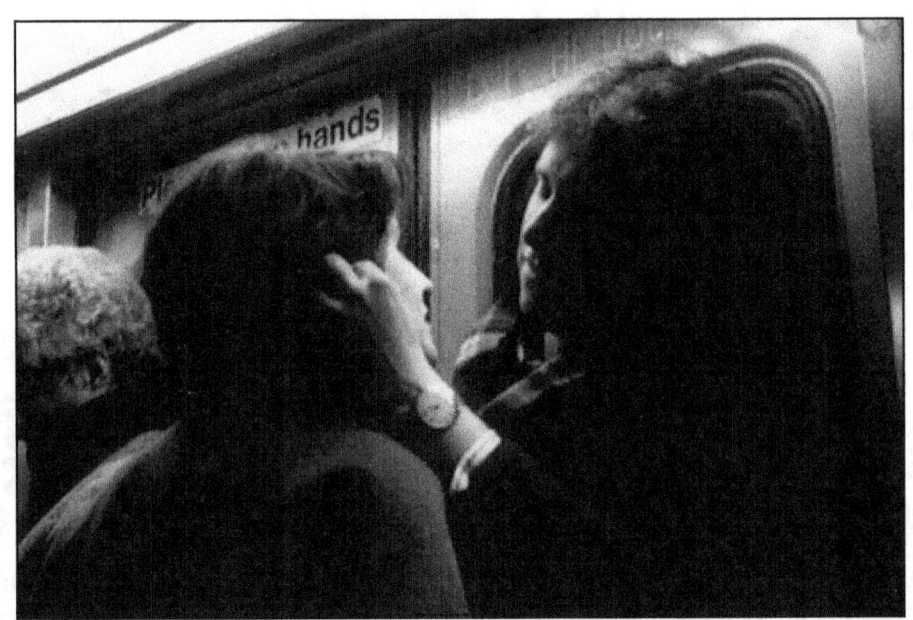

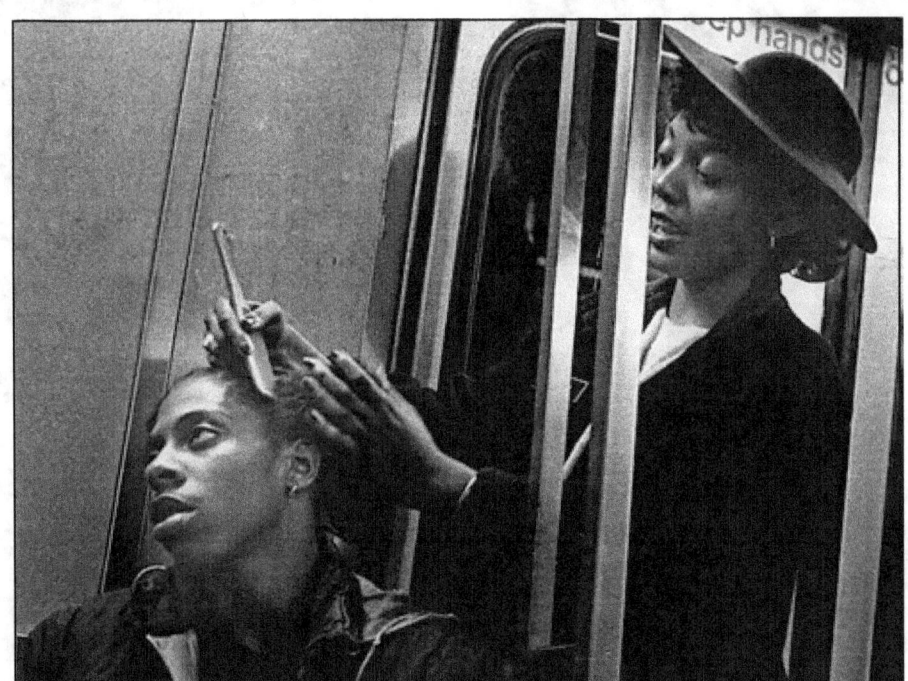

The confrontation

Being confronted by subjects is extremely rare. This was one of those occasions. I took this shot with the camera in my lap. It was a very quiet camera, so I was surprised when the woman in this picture heard it go off. She asked me if I took her picture. I said, 'No.' Don't ask me why I lied, I just did. I waited a minute or two, then I took another one. This time it was the guy who asked me if I took his picture. His voice had an undertone of menace about it. I said, 'No.' He glared at me, and I stared right back at him. I was a lot bigger than him, but guys can do stupid things when they're with their woman. He blinked first, then they looked at each other and shrugged. They knew I was lying, but they couldn't prove it.

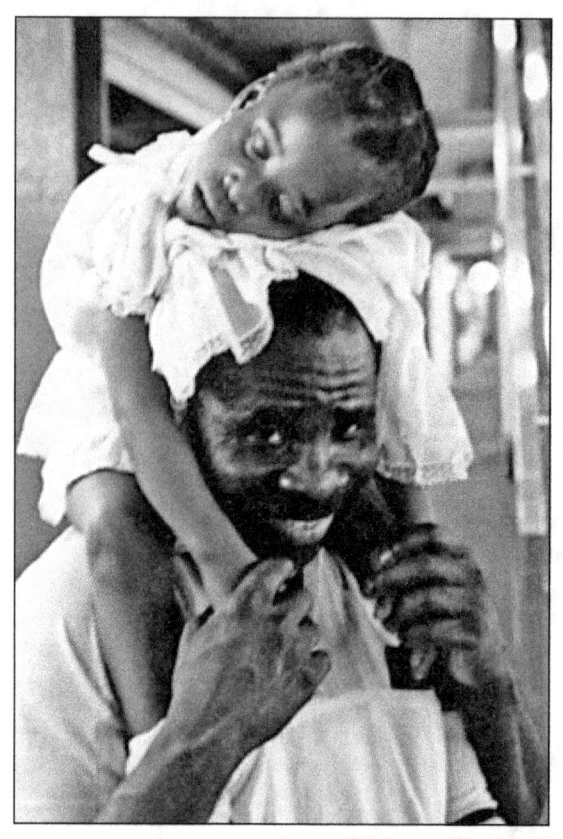

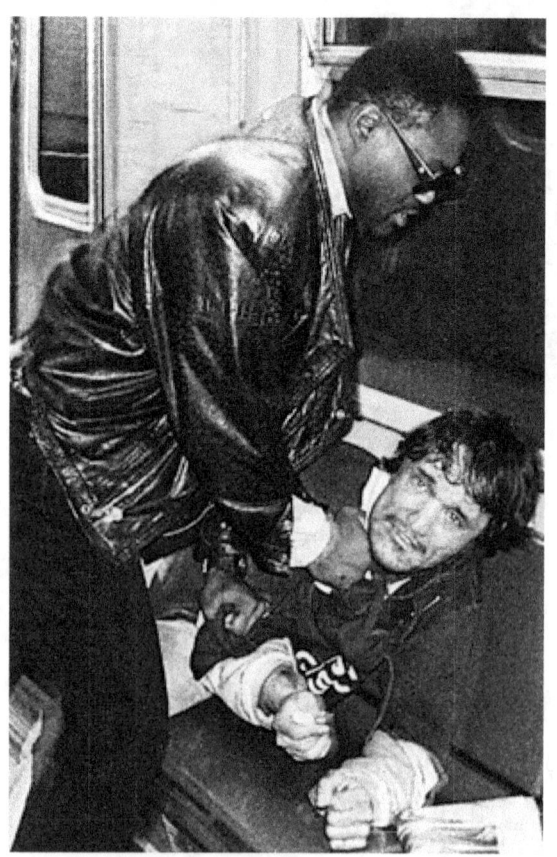

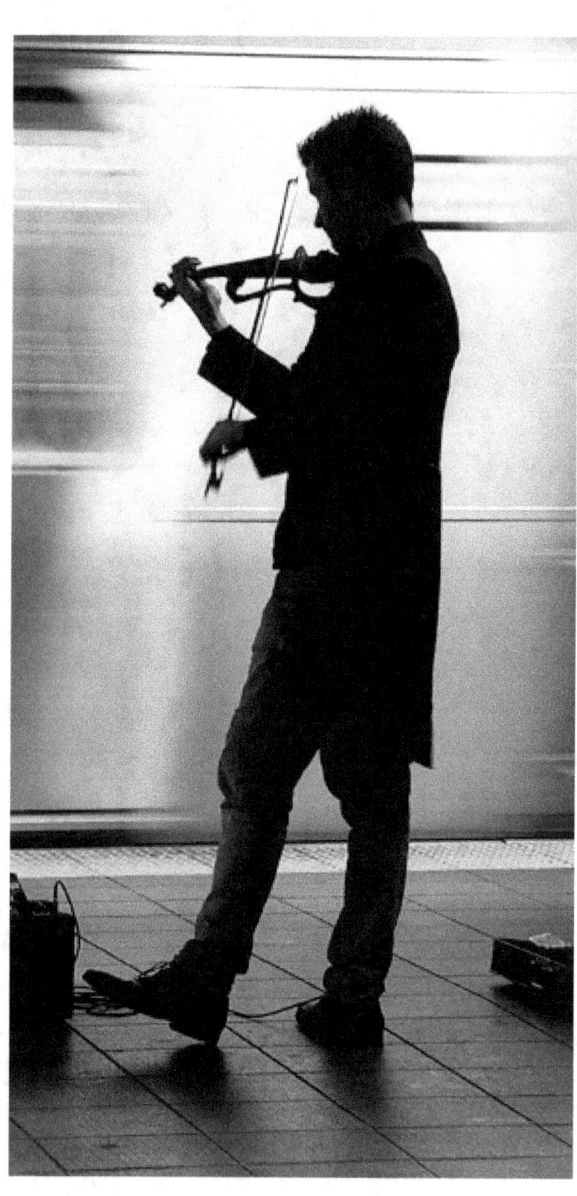

The guy standing-up found this other guy going through his pockets while he was sleeping. He's holding him until the police come.

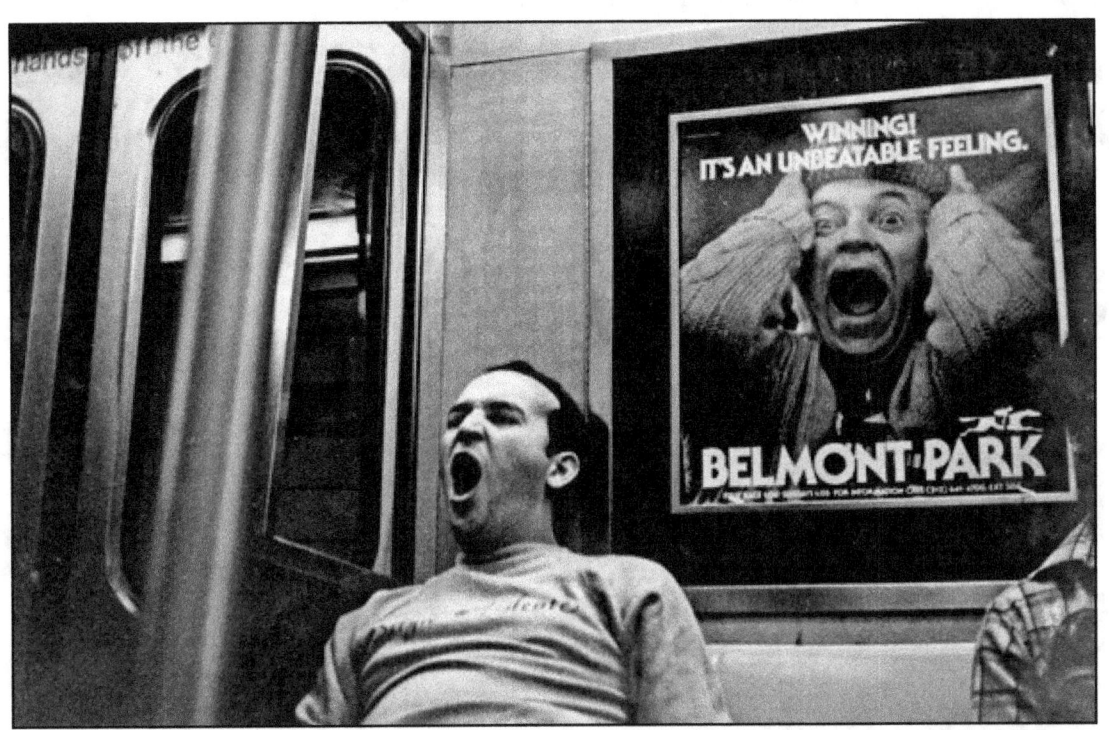

A yawn is just an angel escaping.
- Irish proverb

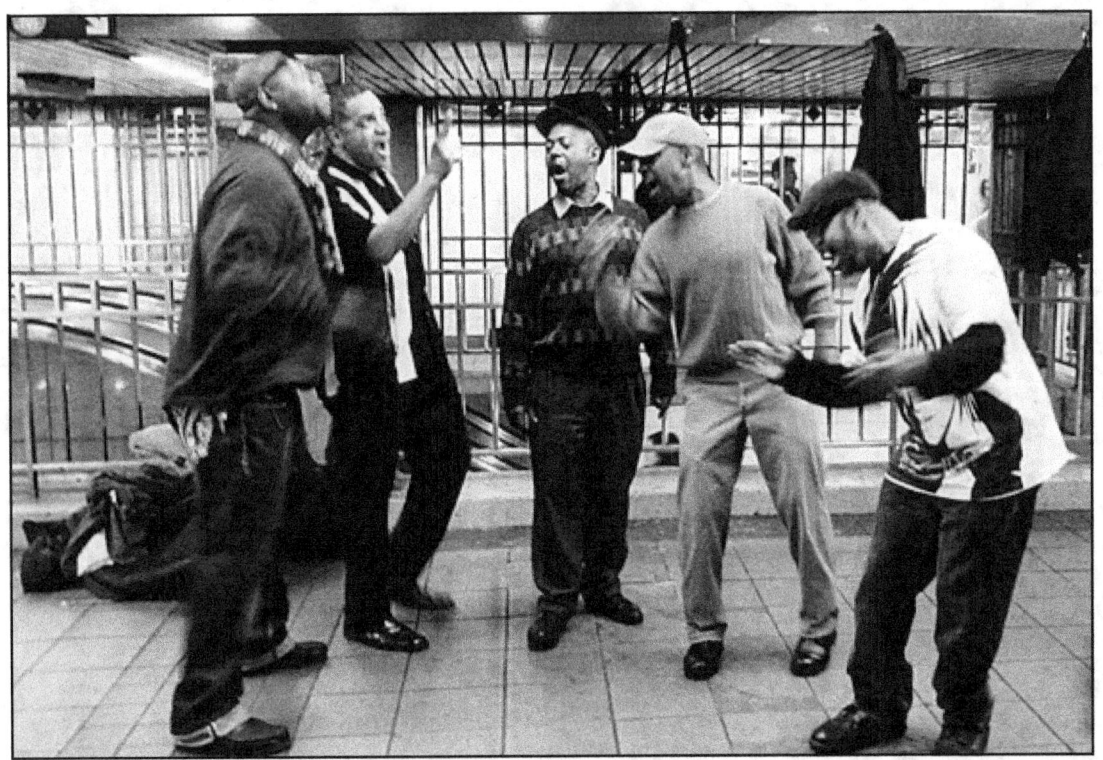

There was a time when the cops would chase guys like these out of the subway; today the city pays them to entertain harried commuters. These guys were actually quite good.

Chapter 4 — *Five Short Stories*

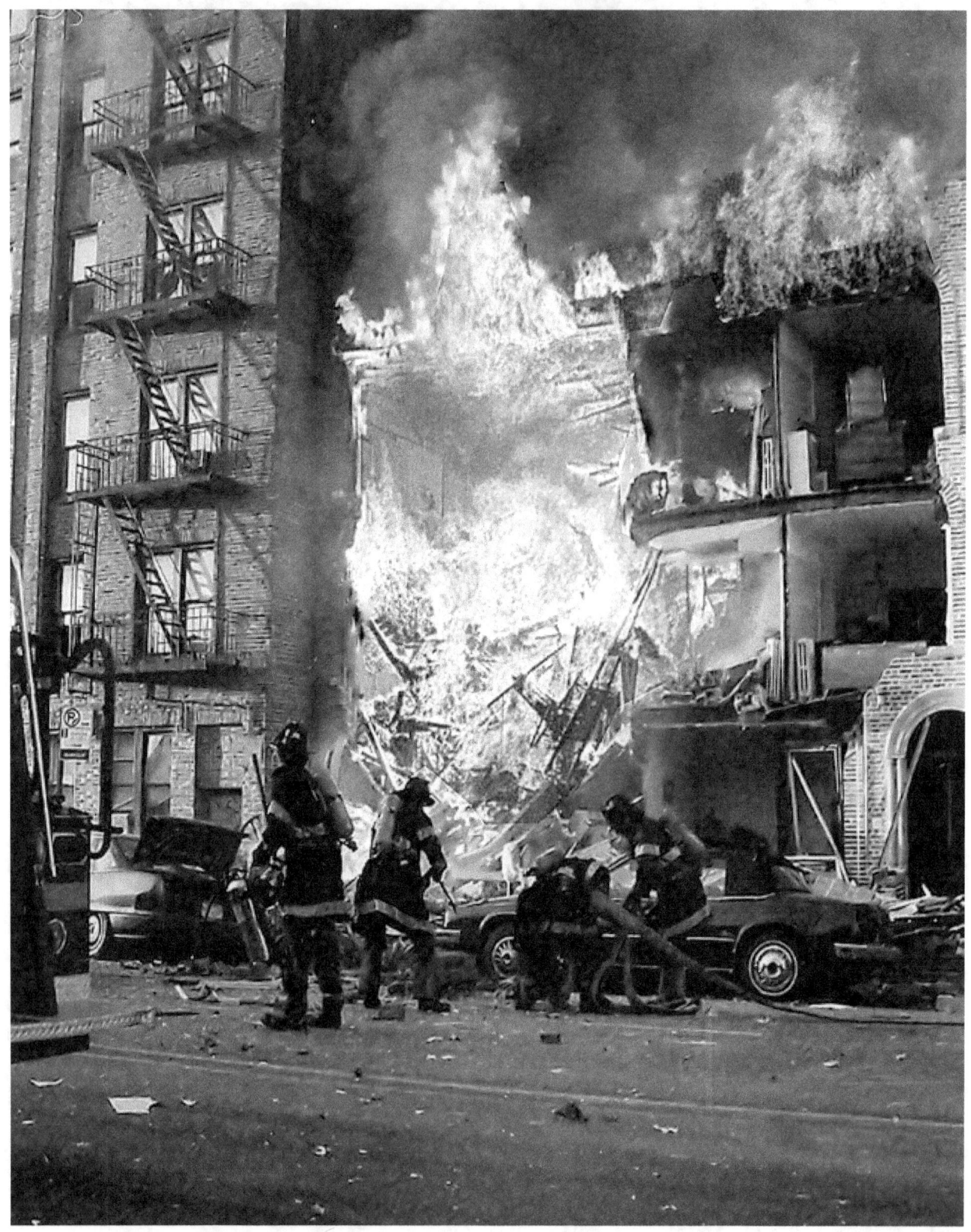

Firemen begin to tackle the blaze, which is starting to spread.

1. Sudden Death on a beautiful day

It was labor day 1992, around 7 p.m. I just got back from the city. I hit the couch, threw off my shoes, and turned on the T.V. And then KABOOM! a huge explosion shook the whole house. I ran to the window and looked out. Halfway down the street a mushroom shaped cloud of black smoke rose into the air. It looked like a miniature atom bomb. I grabbed my gear, and flew down the stairs. I was one of the first on the scene.

What I saw was both horrible and amazing at the same time. A powerful explosion had blown off the facades of two adjacent buildings, leaving the interiors completely exposed. They looked like gigantic doll houses, with all the furniture in place. Pictures were still hanging on the walls, and knick-knacks were still on their shelves. Ominously, flames began to lick at the base of the rubble, fed by the gas line that had caused the explosion in the first place. I hoped that there weren't any people inside. Unfortunately, there were. Two people died in the initial explosion, and several passerbys were injured by flying debris.

People from the neighborhood began to help the injured. In the background the wailing of fire engines could be heard. The fire grew in intensity very quickly and the entire two buildings were completely engulfed in flames.

On covering fires

You have to be very careful at fire scenes, there's plenty of ways to get hurt. First, you have to take care not to trip over the fire hoses, which snake all over the ground. If the weather is cold, the water from the fire hoses will freeze very quickly and become quite slippery. Many firemen are injured every year this way. You also have to watch out for burning debris that the firemen sometimes throw out of the windows of a burning building. If smoke gets in your eyes, it can blind you instantly, and there's nothing worse than losing your sight when you are in the middle of an emergency situation.

On top of all this, you have to remember to keep your equipment dry. Even a small amount of water will knock-out most cameras. My advice to young photographers is to stay away from fires, but I know my words fall on deaf ears. People are drawn to disasters inexorably, like moths to the flame.

On dealing with photo editors

Right after I took these pictures, I went to the Associated Press in Rockefeller Center. They already knew about the fire, but because it was a holiday weekend, they were short-handed, so they didn't have anyone covering it. I was the first one to show-up with pictures. They developed the film right there, when I saw the shots, I knew I had gold. I asked to see the person responsible for buying pictures.

'She's in a meeting right now', this guy says, 'she'll be out in about half an hour.' From experience, I knew what he was doing. He was stalling for time. He was hoping that another photographer would show-up with similar pictures, thus making mine far less valuable. I knew that there weren't any other photographers at the scene, I was sure of that, so I was dealing from a position of strength.

'Tell her she has 30 seconds to get her ass out here, or else I'm leaving,' I said. She was out in 10 seconds. She was a very attractive young lady, she offered me 500 dollars for the shots. I said, 'I want a thousand,' she said, 'you got it.' Then she asked me if they could own them. I said 'no, you have a 24 hour exclusive, but that's it.' This is the way you deal with these people. They play hard ball and you have to play hardball back, just like in any other type of business.

Short story #2

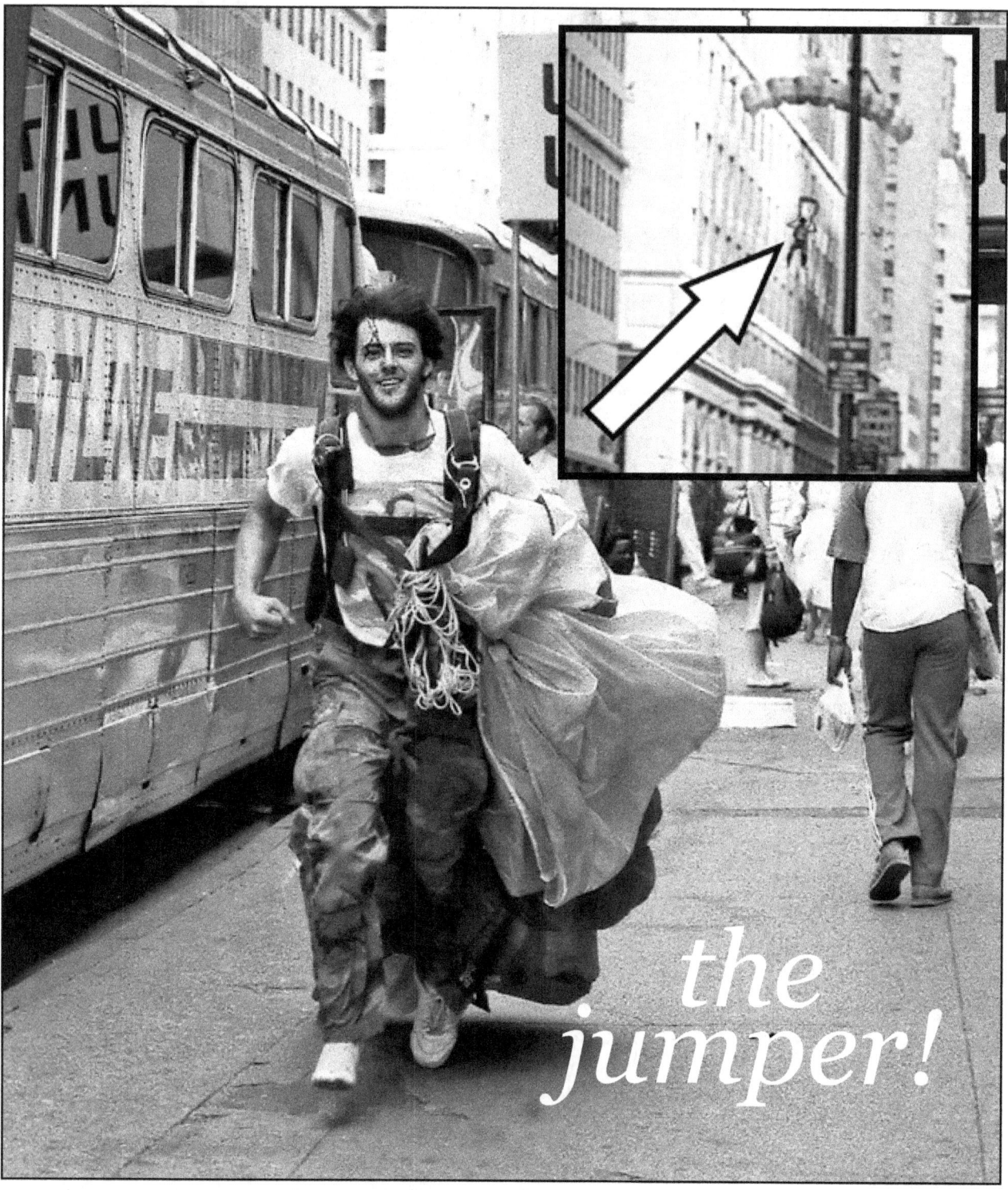

the jumper!

This is a man who has just cheated death. He is running past me, after he landed on 34th St. He escaped down the subway.

This guy from Ohio drops in

I was walking down 34th street one day, on the same block as the Empire State Building, camera at the ready, looking for shots. Suddenly, some movement in the sky got my attention. I wasn't sure what it was, until I put the camera to my eye, and zoomed in. It was a guy falling from the Empire State Building in a parachute. I took some quick grab-shots. After he landed, he began running towards me, so I waited until he got close, and took a few more shots. He had a cut on his head, and was missing a shoe, but otherwise seemed just fine. He had the look on his face of a man who had just cheated death. I should have gone to the papers with these shots, I probably could have gotten them published, but I didn't.

What I didn't realize was that two guys had jumped off that day. The other one landed on Fifth Avenue, out of my sight. I would find out about him, ten years later, when we met by chance, in a small bar in Brooklyn.

Ten years later

The Thirsty Duck was a small bar, tucked away on a side street, in Bay Ridge, Brooklyn. I lived in the neighborhood, so it was my favorite hangout. It was a Saturday night, and all the regulars were there. However, there was a new face this time. He sounded like he was from the Midwest, so we started talking. His name was John, and he was from Ohio.
- "What brings you to Brooklyn all the way from Ohio?" - I asked.
- "I got a job I have to do tomorrow. I'm going to change the light bulbs on top of the Verrazzano bridge."
- "How the hell did you get a job like that?"
- "Well, the regular maintenance men on the bridge are scared to do it themselves, so I do it. I change a lot of bulbs on the entire East coast. I go from city to city, just changing light bulbs on very high places, where no one else will go."
- "That sounds dangerous."
- "Not really, I know what I'm doing. I don't take any chances, I prepare carefully, and besides, if anything does go wrong, as a last resort, I always wear a parachute."

When he said the word parachute, I had an instant flashback, to that day on 34th street. Everyone in the bar was listening in now. You could hear the proverbial pin drop. Everyone knew about the shots I had taken ten years earlier. God knows, I probably told that story a hundred times.
- "You know, about ten years ago, I took pictures of a guy jumping off the Empire State Building in a parachute." -John looked at me for a long time, he was sizing me up.
- "Well," -he said- "about ten years ago, me and my friend Tom jumped off that building. It was the stupidest thing I ever did, almost got killed. I got down just fine, but I landed in the middle of Fifth Avenue, and almost got run over by a bus. My friend said that there was a guy there taking pictures. We looked in the newspaper the next day, we didn't see any picture, there was nothing."

I could tell that he didn't believe me. Then I said to him, "John, how did your friend lose his shoe, and how did he cut his head?" He looked at me and smiled. He knew that I had to be there, if I knew such details.
- "Show me the pictures." he said.
- I said, "Don't go away, I'll be back in two minutes."

I returned with the pictures. They were of his friend Tom.
- He looked at me and said, "We can't go on meeting like this." I gave him the pictures to keep, then he left. I never saw him again.

Short story #3

A bad day for some good samaritans

It was a beautiful summer day, and I was bike-riding around Prospect Park Lake in Brooklyn. I was listening to my walkman, so I couldn't hear the fire engine behind me. It cut right across my path, almost hitting me, it went over the grass, and the bridal path, and continued to the lake. I followed it. There was a crowd gathered there. It seems a small child had fallen into the lake and two good samaritans had jumped in trying to save her. The kid was alright, but the two would-be rescuers never came up. The lake bottom is very mucky, it's possible that their feet became stuck in the gooey mud.

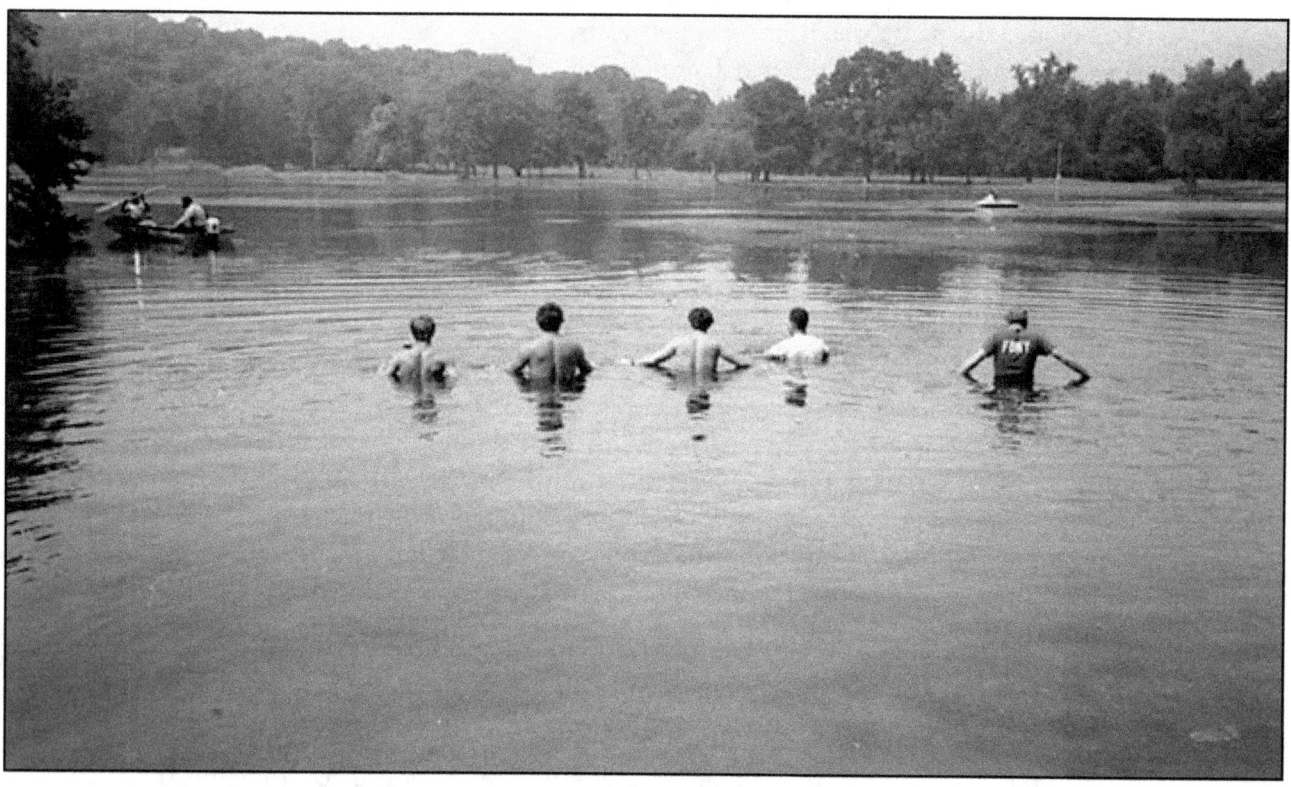

These are firemen in the lake, searching for the bodies of the two missing men. They were very methodical, forming straight lines, holding hands, and feeling for the bodies with their feet.

The shot not taken

Picture a young black boy sitting by the side of a lake. He's about eight years old. His head is bowed, tears are streaming down his cheeks. He's just witnessed the death of his two elder cousins. A huge fireman hovers over him, he's trying to console the boy, but without actually touching him. An invisible barrier separates the two, and the fireman will not breach it. I've known guys like this my whole life, big, gruff men, from the bars of Brooklyn. Their fathers never showed them physical affection, so they were hapless when trying to express it themselves. It was so painful to watch. I didn't know who to feel more sorry for, the boy or this awkward fireman. It would have made a powerful picture, but I figured they had enough to deal with. They didn't need me sticking a camera in their faces. I just went home.

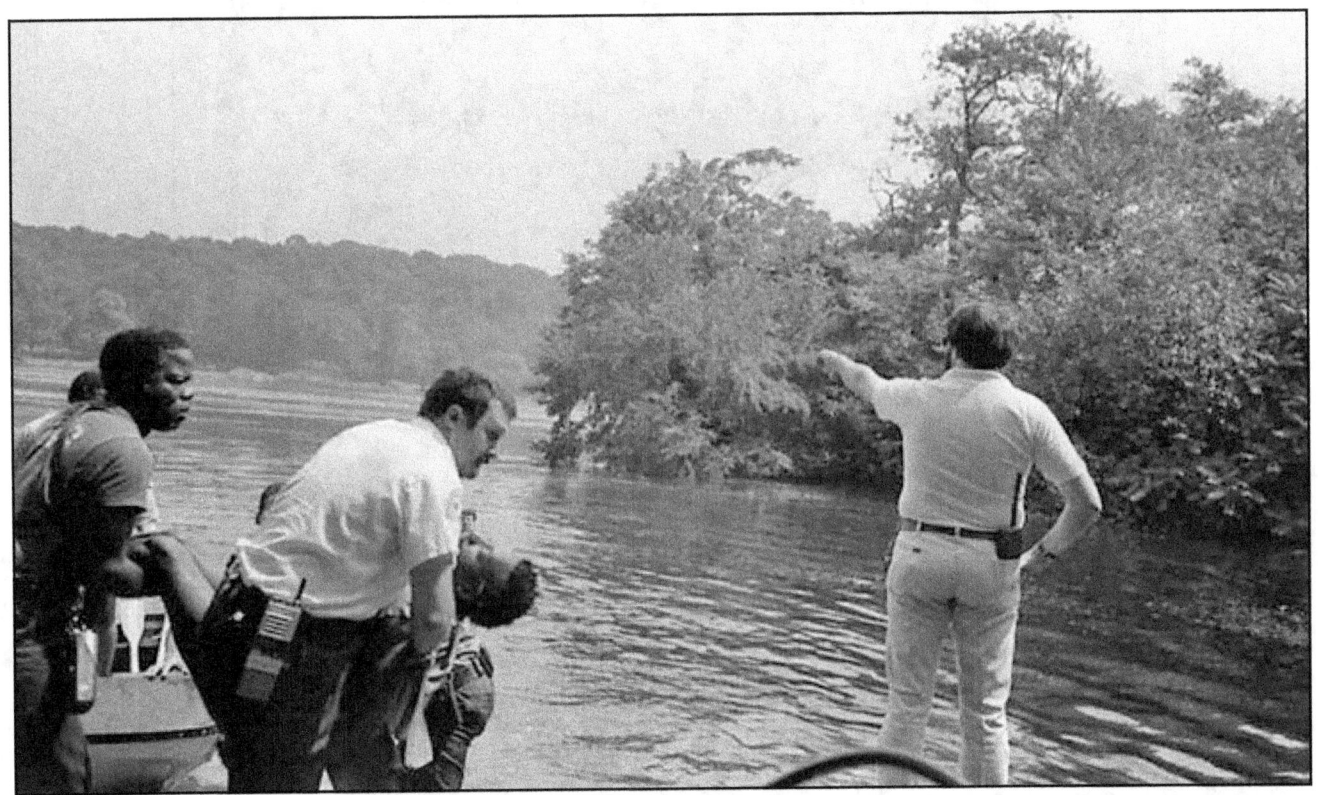

Here, one of the victims is brought to shore by some paramedics. They found the other one later. They were cousins.

Short story #4

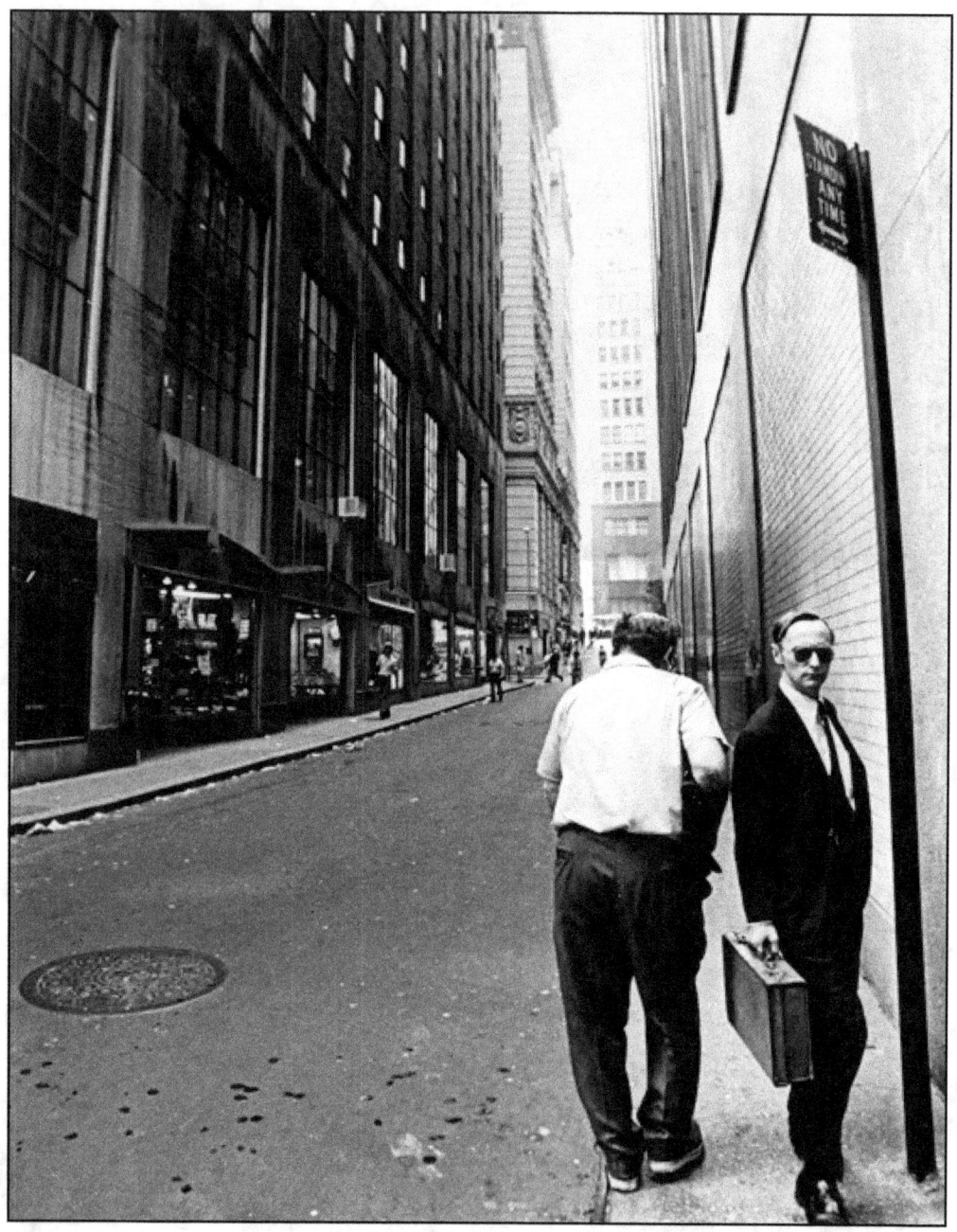

Power play on Wall Street

    Two men approach one another on a very narrow sidewalk in the Wall Street area. One is probably a messenger. He's wearing sneakers and carrying a package. Many of them are mentally challenged. On the Wall Street pecking order, they're on the bottom rung. The guy on the right is obviously a 'suit.' They are on the top rung. Now, as everyone knows, when you pass someone in such a situation you're supposed to pass to the right. However, the 'suit' will have none of that. He's pulling rank on the messenger. He has taken the inside track and thus forcing the messenger into the street. The messenger knows exactly what's going on and refuses to be shoved into the gutter. He may not be too bright, but he still has his pride.

Short story #5

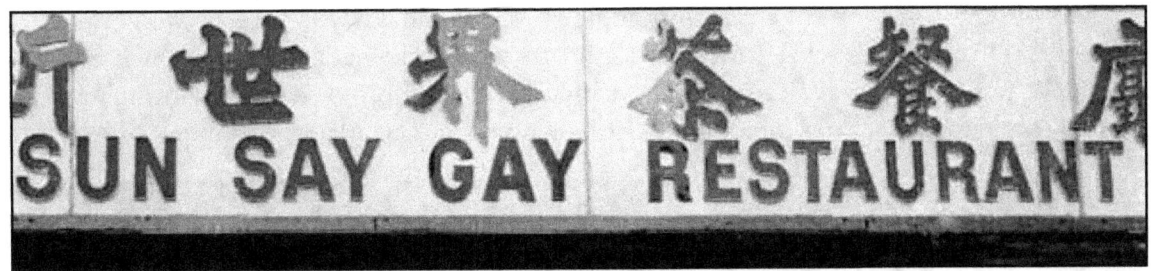

Lost in translation

I took the above picture of this Chinese restaurant sign, and made a postcard of it. It sold very well, especially in the gay sections of New York City. Legend has it, that somehow, word of this got back to the owner's son. He was supposedly mortified when he found out what the sign said phonetically in English.

Below, is the same restaurant after they changed the sign. I felt bad, because it must have cost a lot of money to do it.

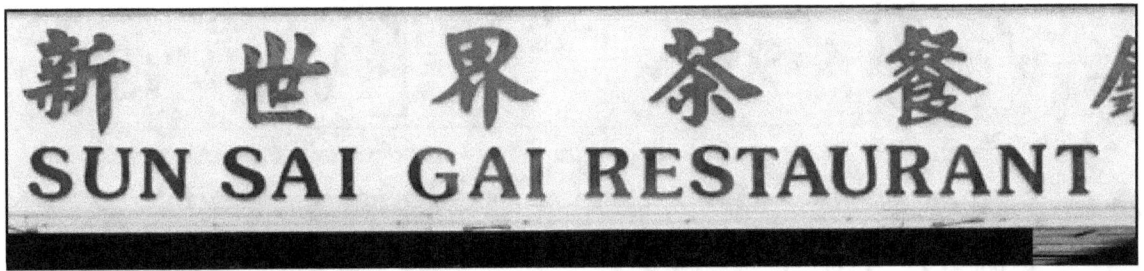

Signs of the times

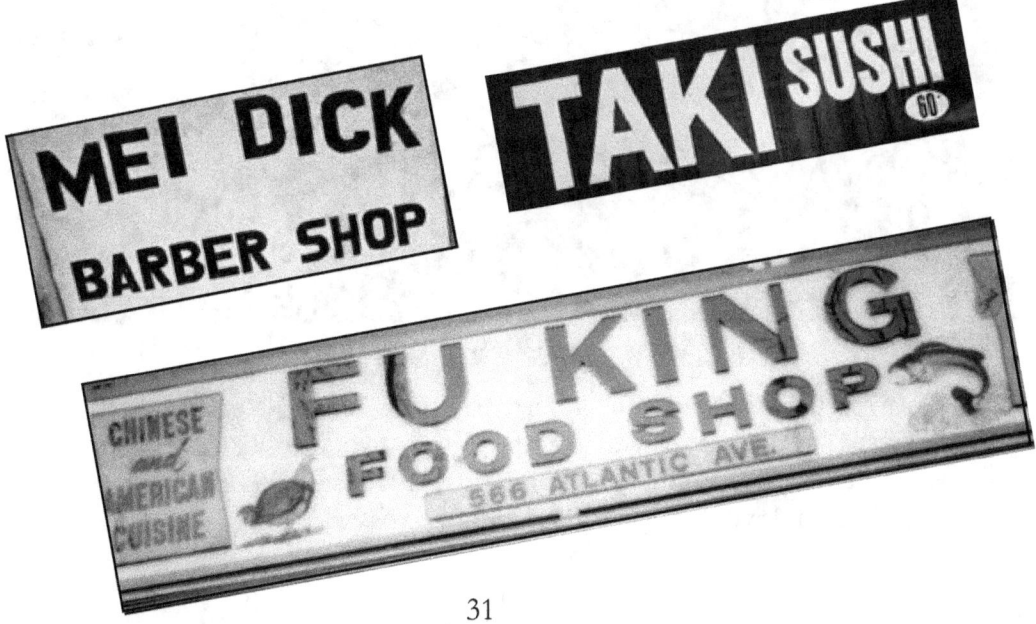

Chapter 5 — *Taking it easy*

How anyone sleeps in the middle of Manhattan is beyond me. Forget about the noise and the racket going on, just the thought of someone going through my pockets while I was asleep would give me the willies. Only God knows how many creeps there are, cruising around, just looking for targets of opportunity.

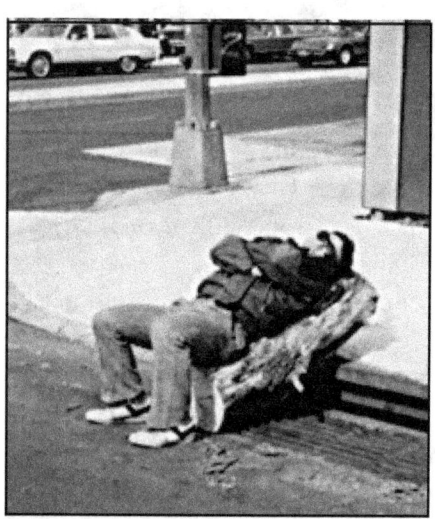

Bump on a log

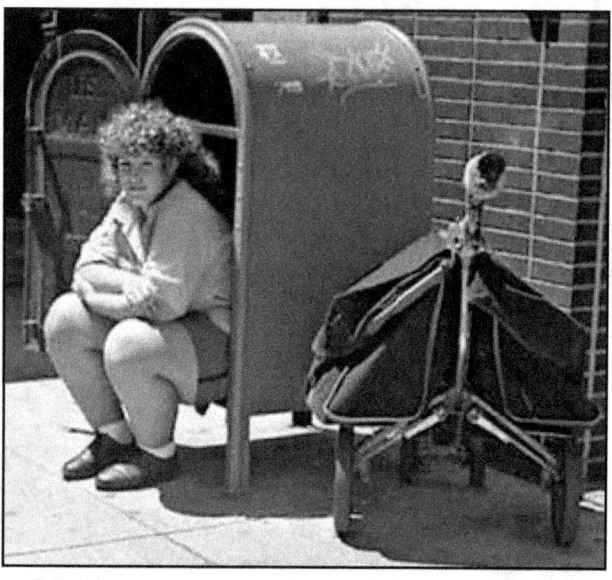

'Neither snow nor rain nor heat nor gloom...'

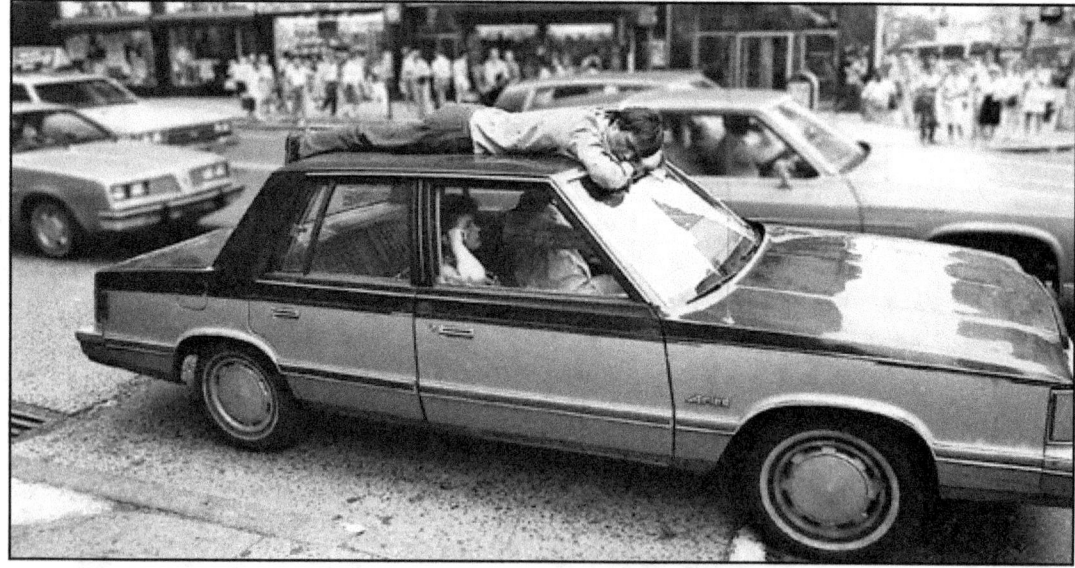

You can't make this stuff up

This guy was obviously under the influence of something. He climbed on top of the car, knocked on the windshield and said 'Take me home.' The driver gets out and says 'Get off the f--king car.' The guy says, 'Take me home.' The driver says 'You wanna go home? I'll take you home,' and then drives him to a cop standing across the street.

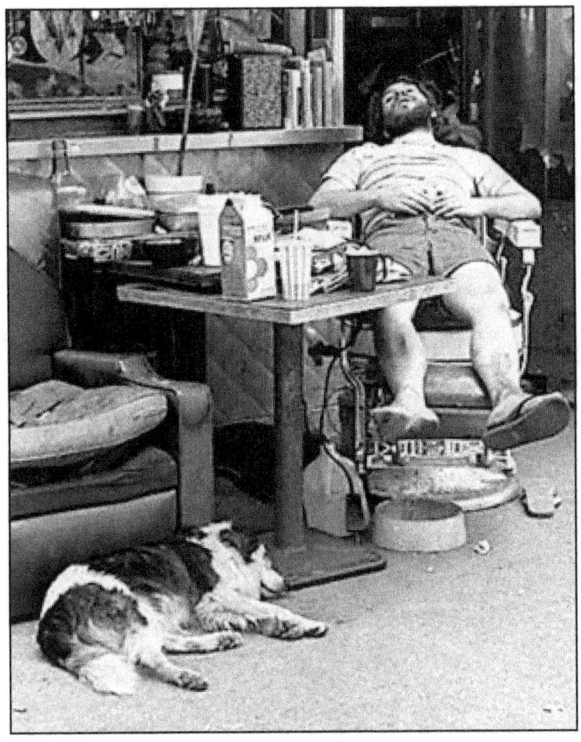

This was in Greenwich Village in the 1960s. Guaranteed, both him and the dog are stoned.

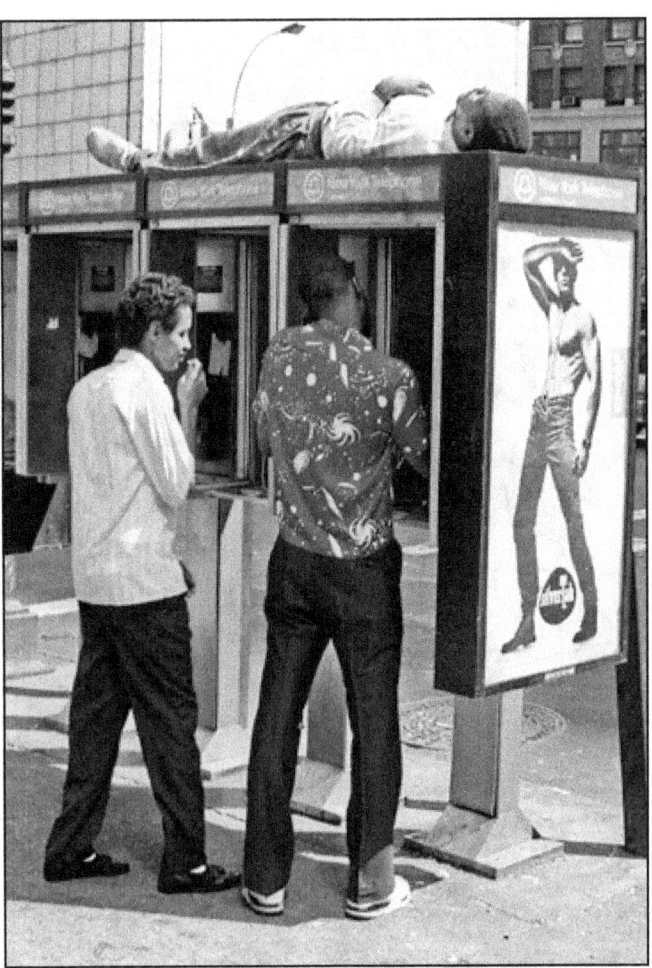

This guy's got his own private, rent-free sun-deck right in the middle of Times Square, He's high enough so kids and dogs can't bother him. Even the cops leave him alone.

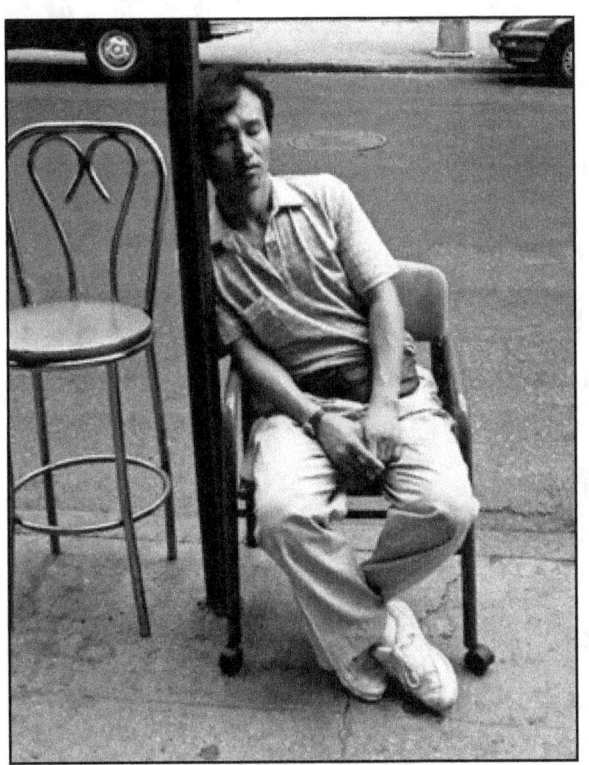

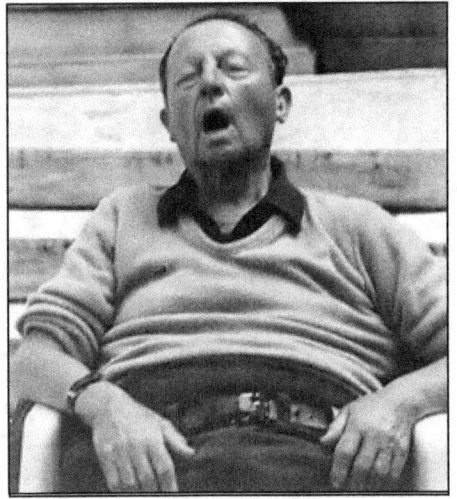

This guy is catching flies

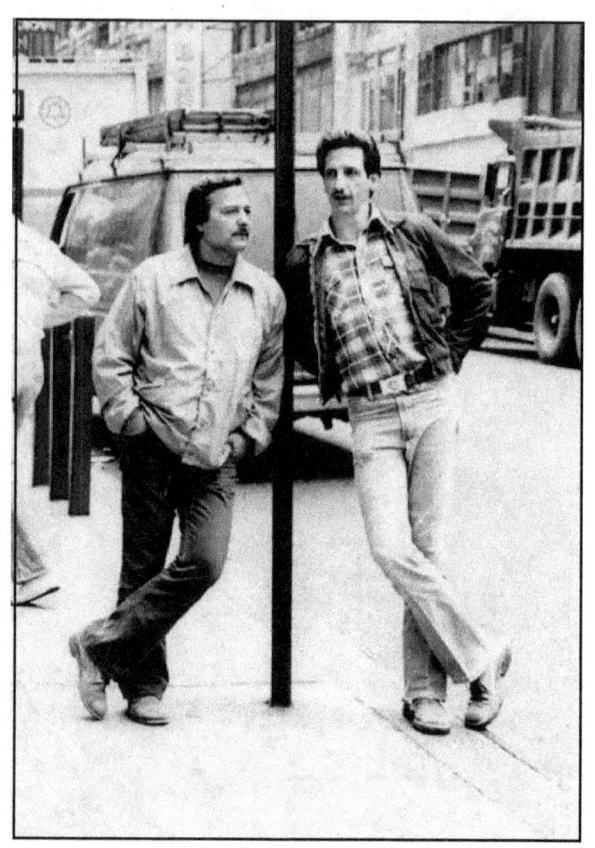
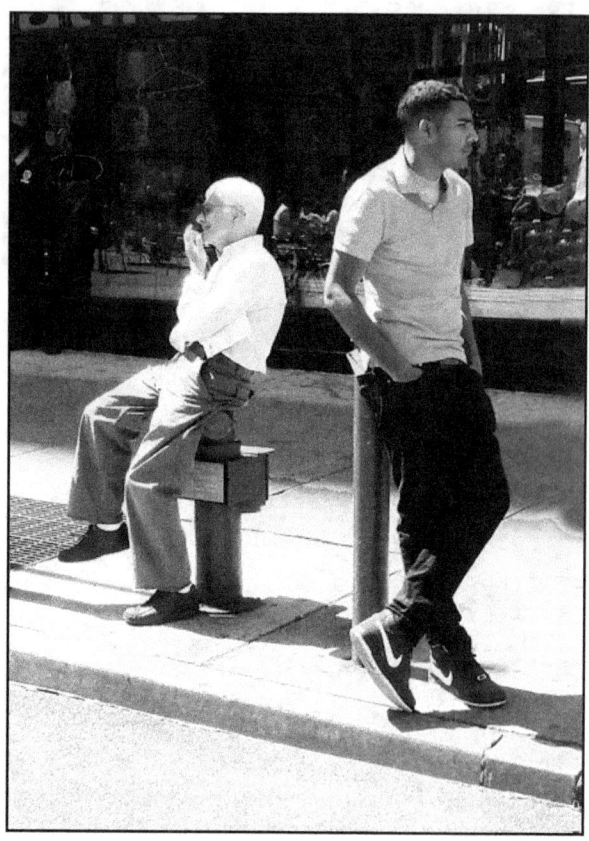
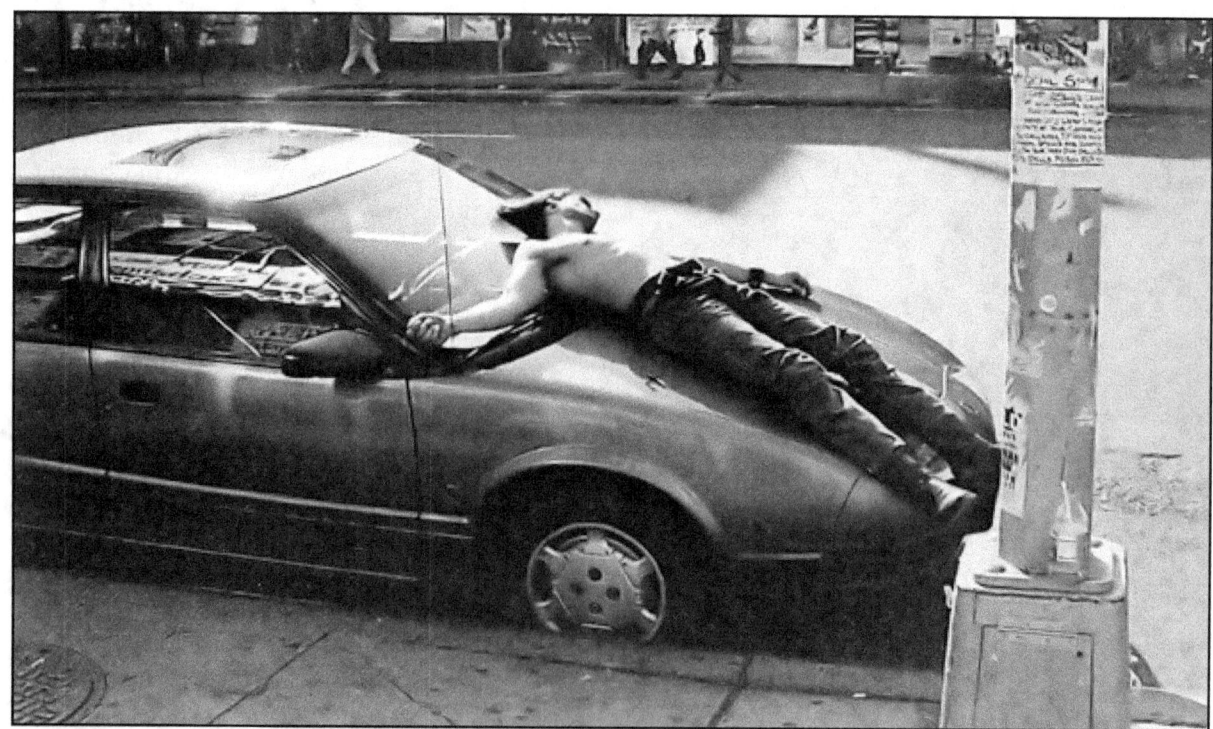

The crucifixion

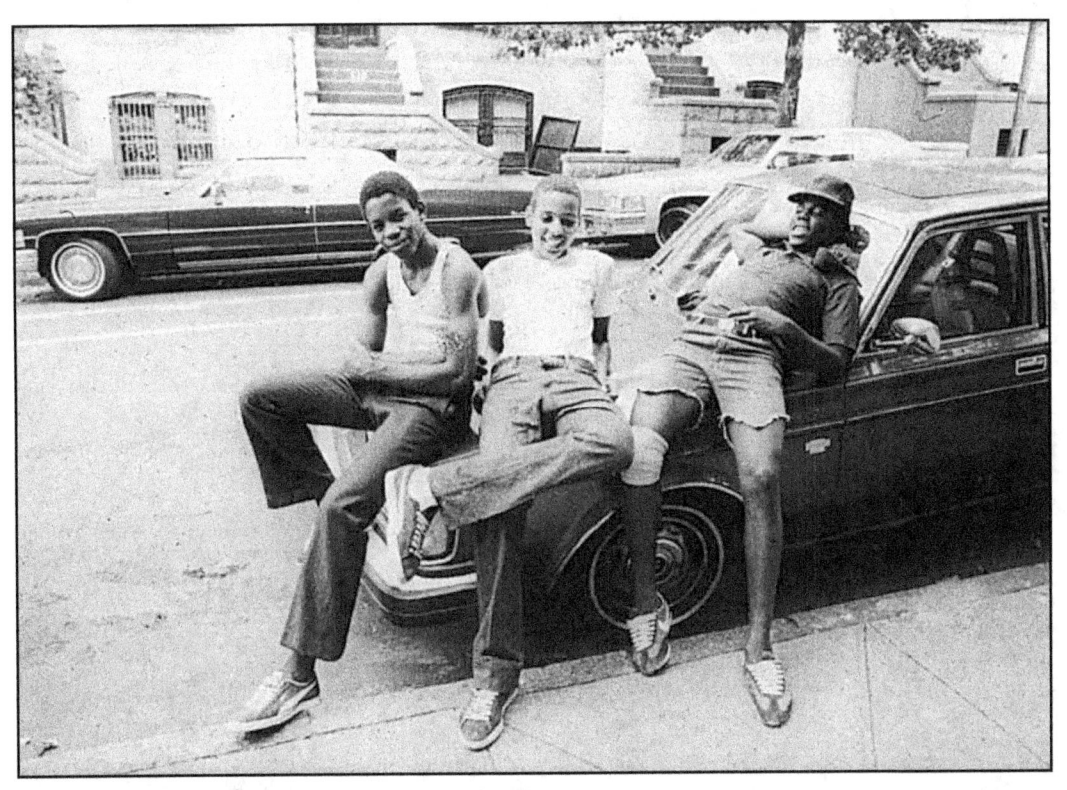

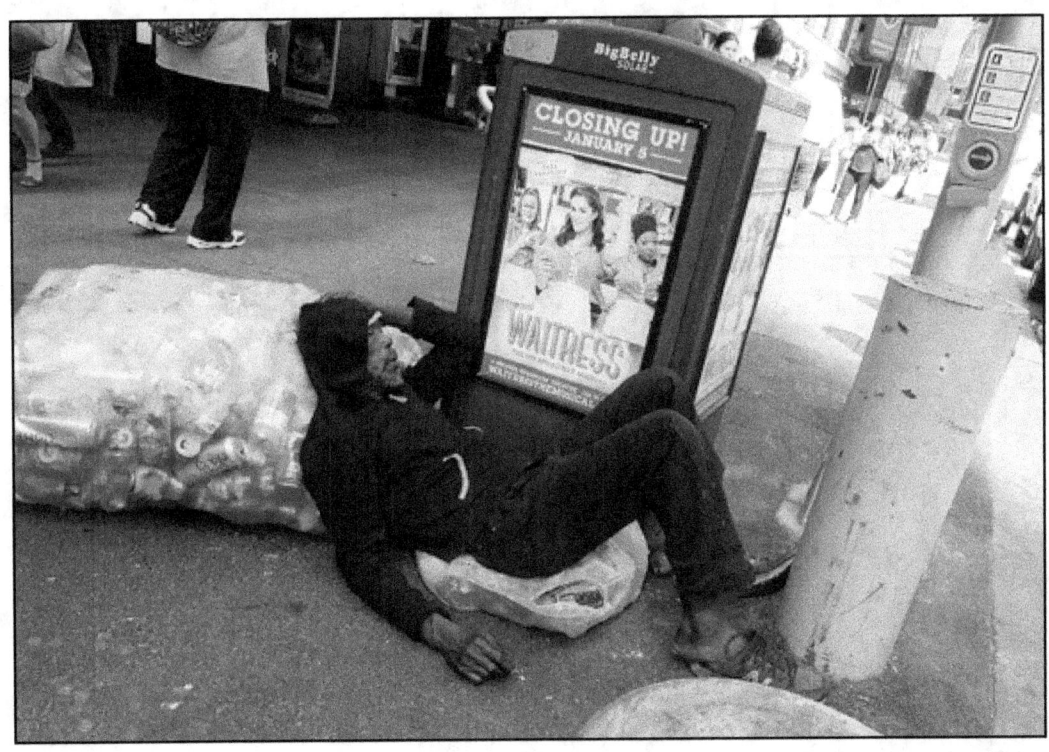

Chapter 6 — *Do you believe in angels?*

A friend of mine was going through my portfolio one day and she said, "You know Nick, you'v[e] got pictures of angels here, lots of them" I said to her "What do you mean angels?" She pointed ou[t] some of the semi-amusing juxtapositions I had taken. "Oh, those are just some silly little coincidences[,]" I said. "No" she said "there are too many of them to be coincidental, they're angels. All God's ange[ls] come to us disguised." Angels or silly little coincidences, you decide.

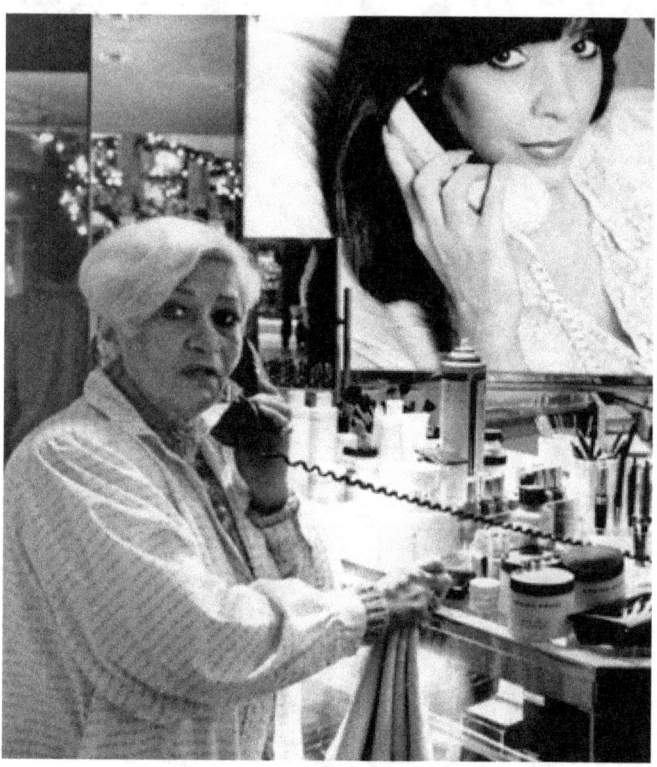

Call your angel, she will come.
- Oprah Winfrey

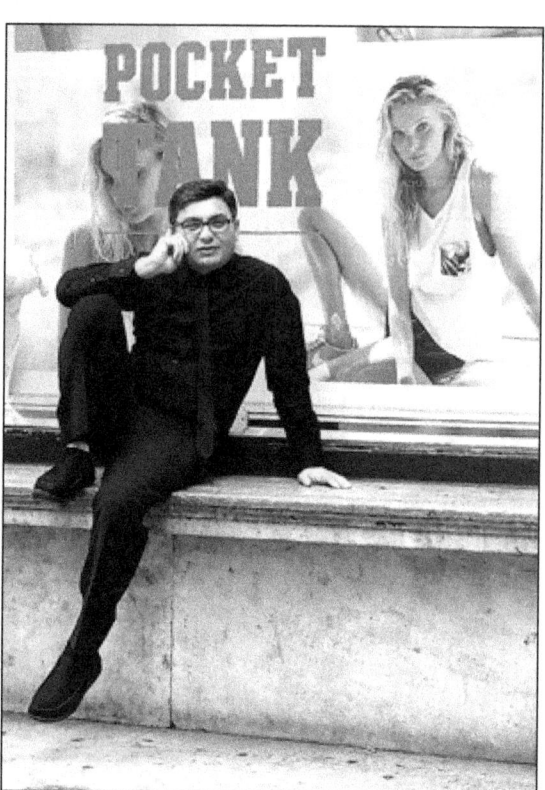

If you believe in God, your angel always be at your shoulder.
-St. Girard

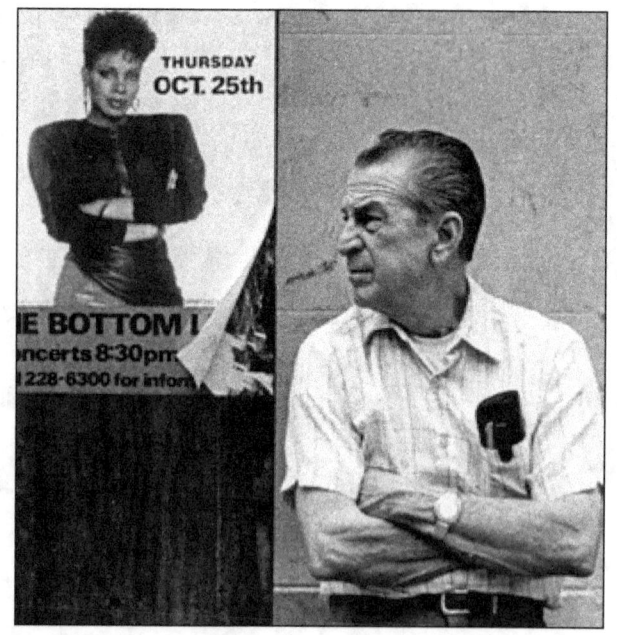

In heaven, an angel is nobody in particular.
-George Bernard Shaw

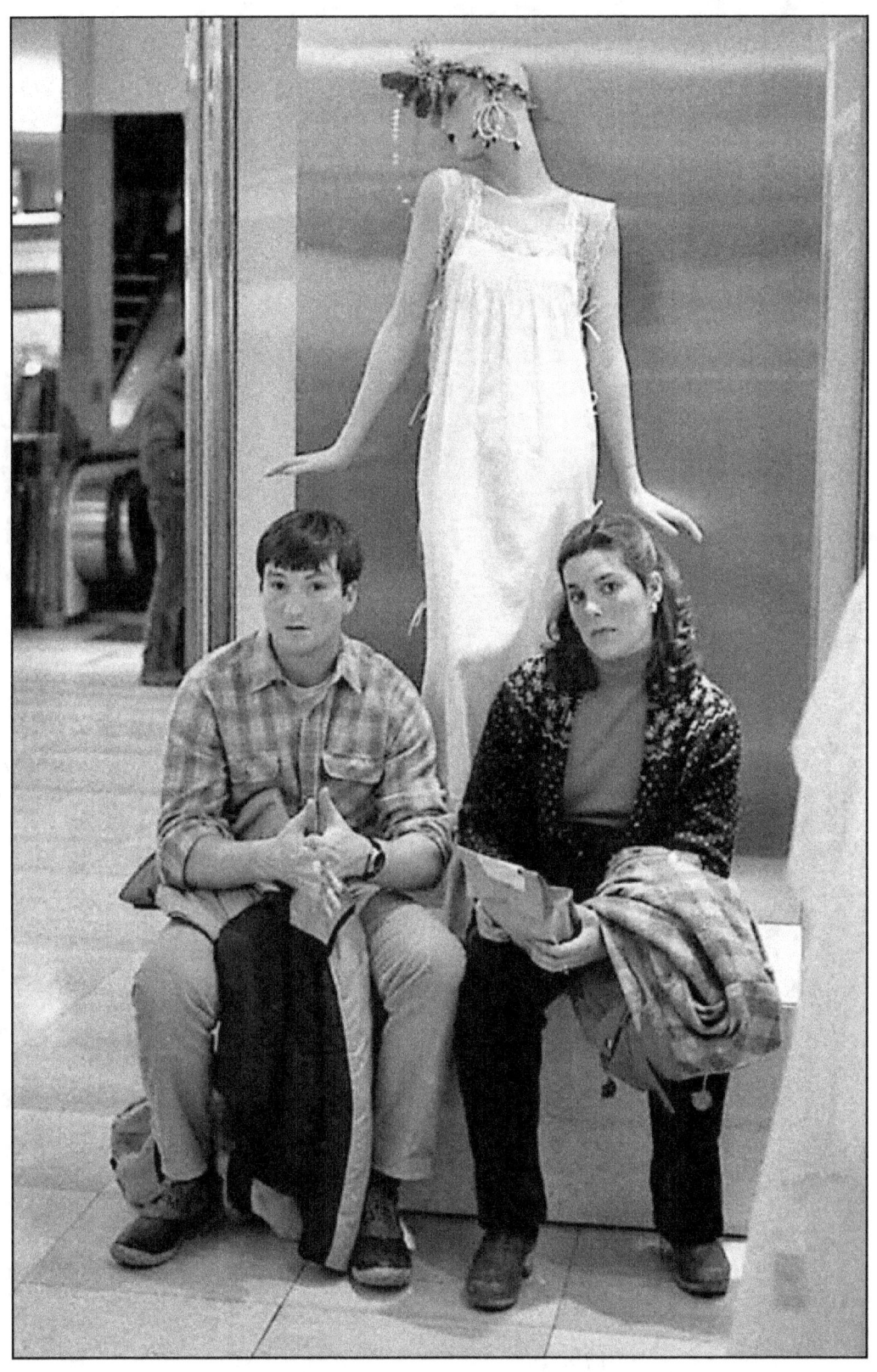

*May an angel of God, from up above,
come to Earth, to bless your love.*
                                    - St. Thomas

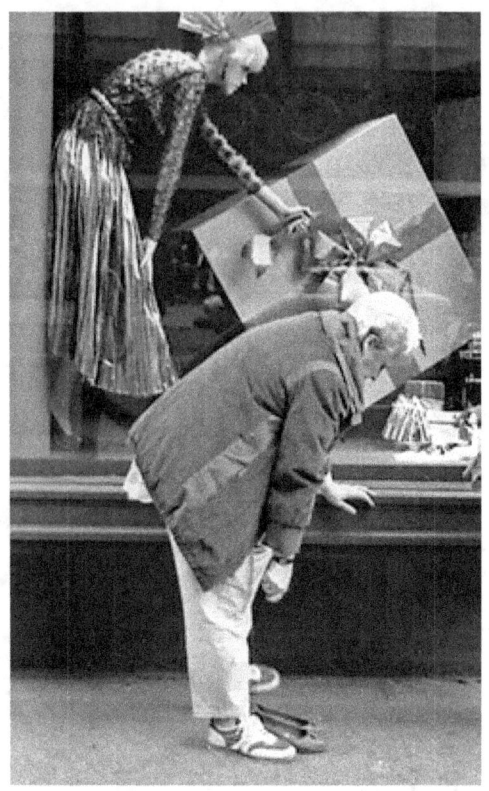

Every blade of grass has an angel that bends over it, and whispers grow, grow.   - The Talmud

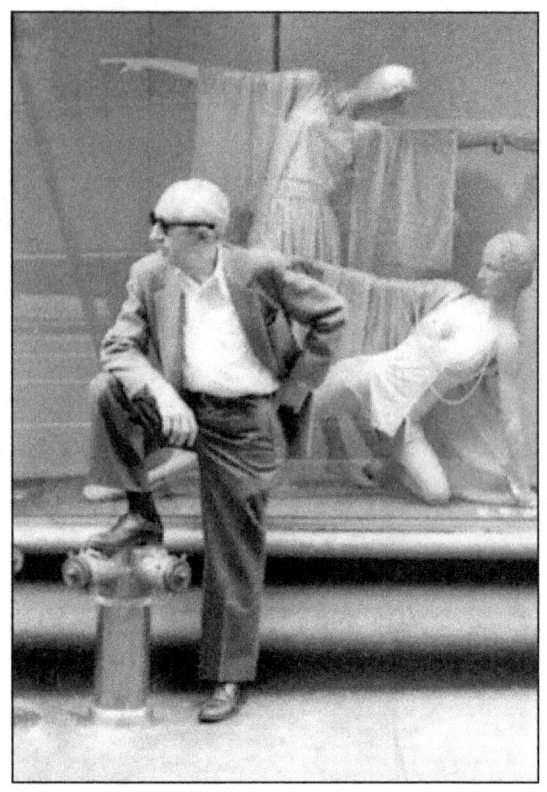

Every man hath a good and bad angel, attending on him, all his life long.
                          - Robert Burton

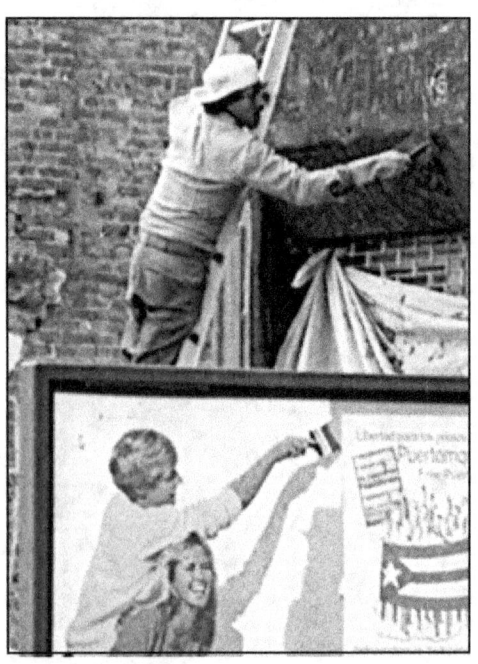

Who's to say, that the outstretched hand from a stranger, is not the act of an angel in disguise? - James Russell Lowell

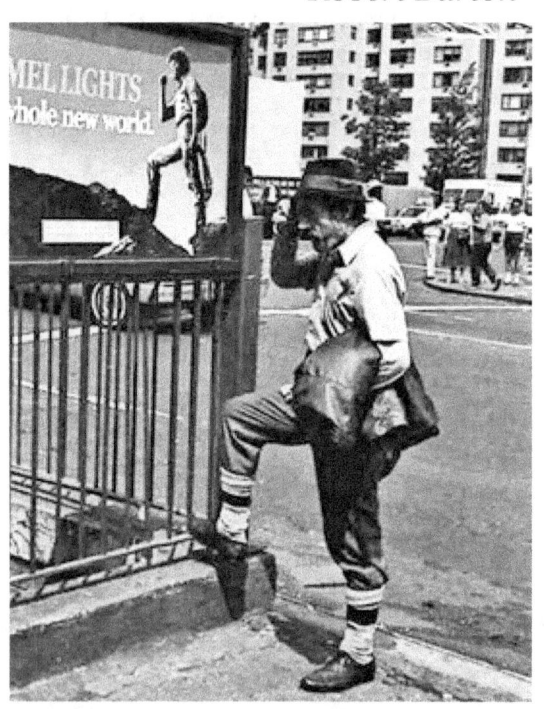

Your journey maybe long, but if you believe in angels, you will never walk alone.
                      - St. Augustine

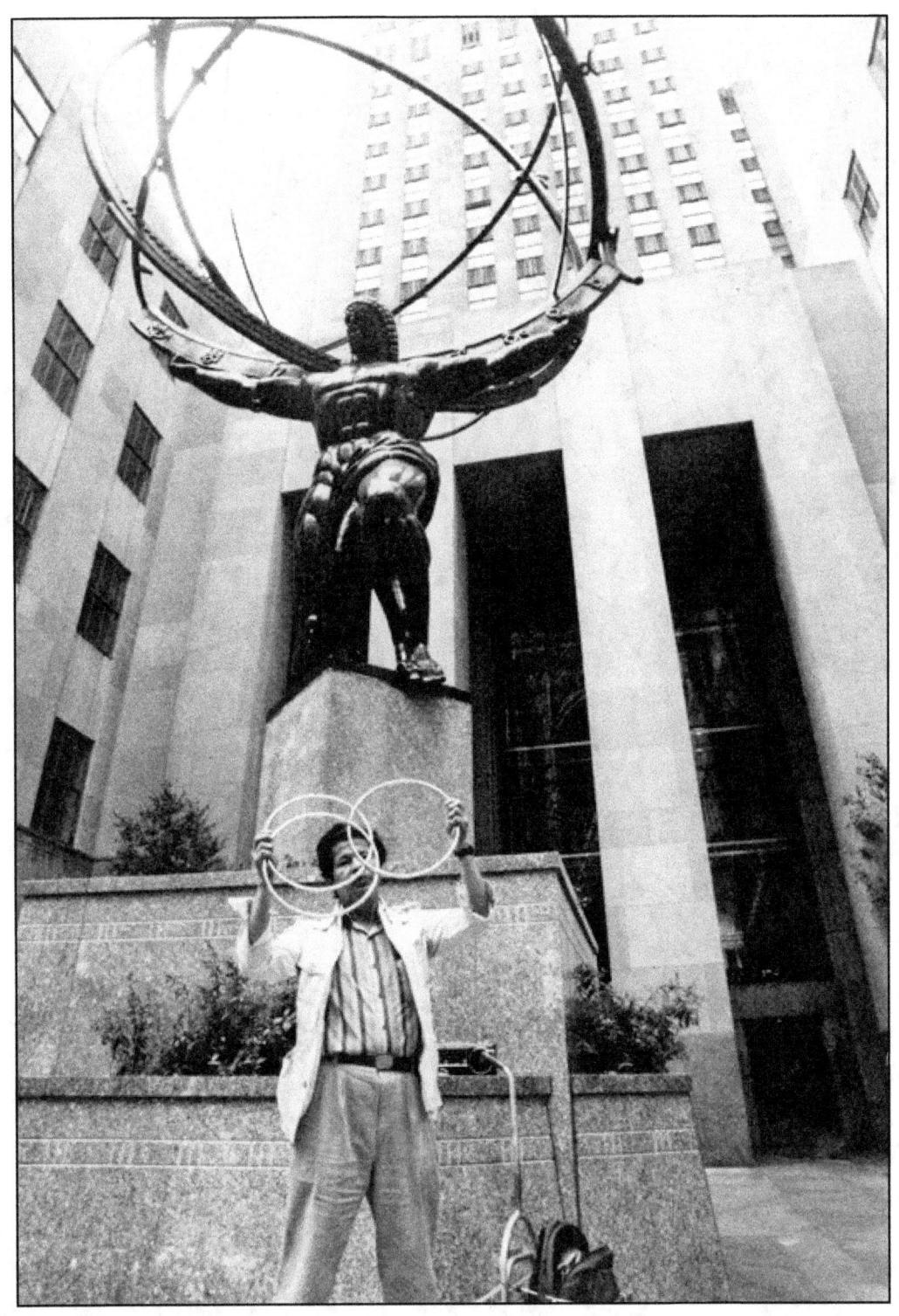

As you travel life's winding road, may an angel help, to share the load.
— Irish proverb

Chapter 7 — *Lunch time*

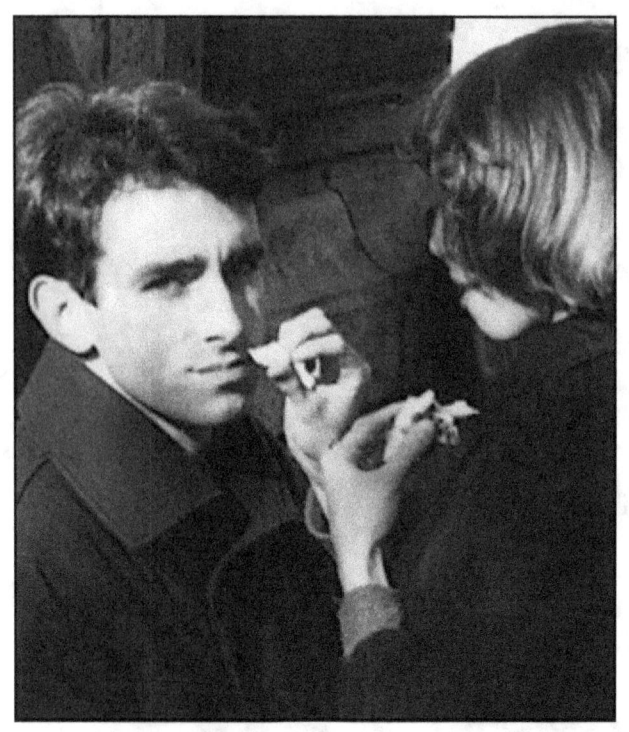
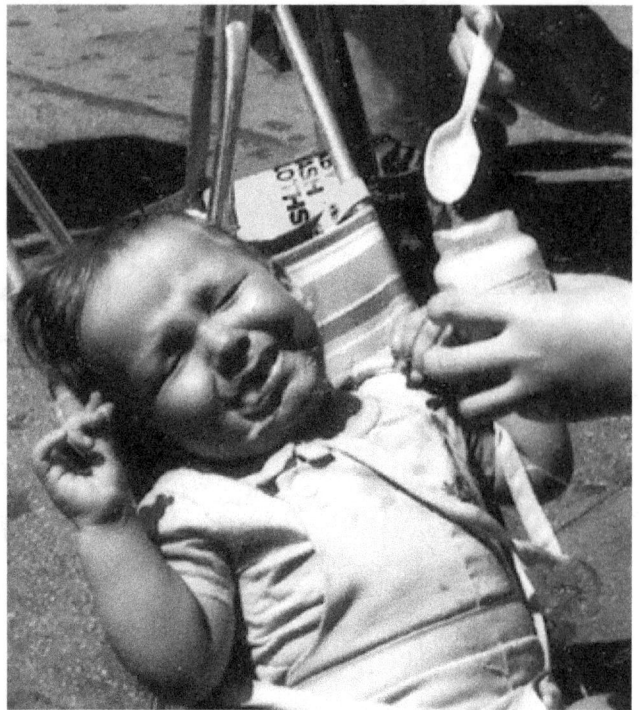
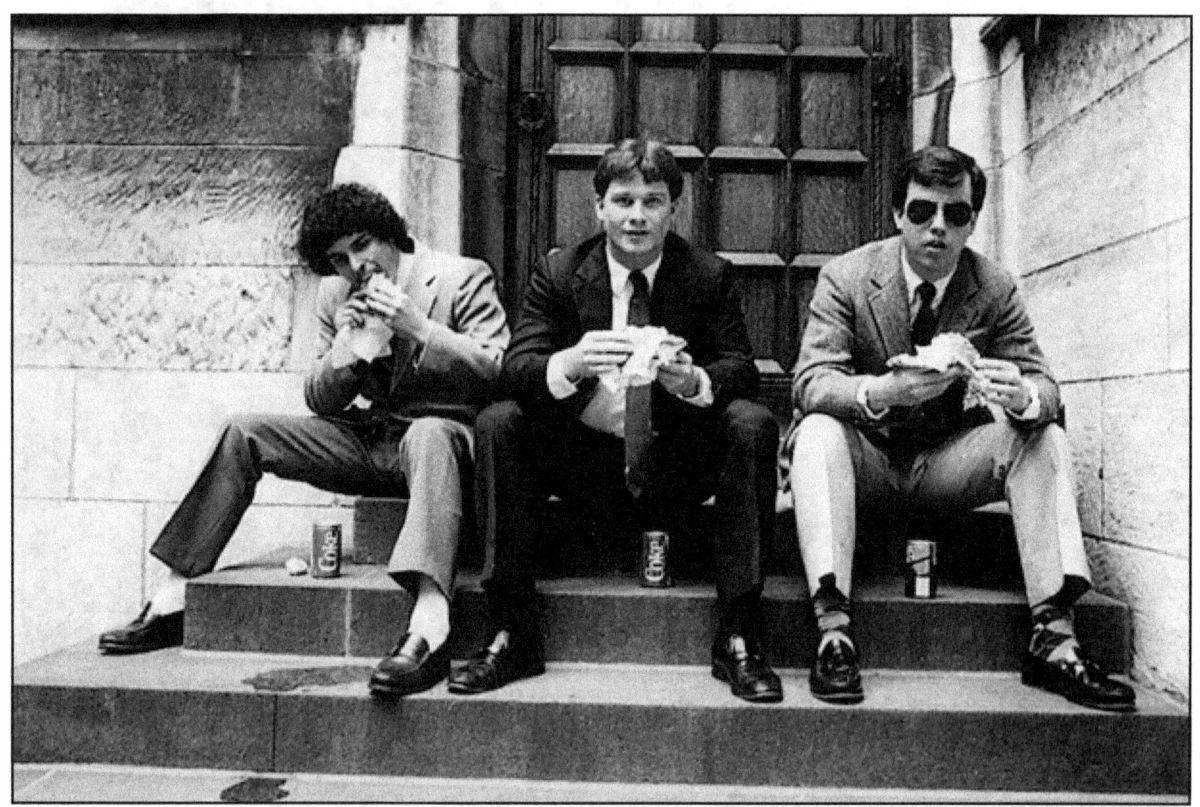

- "You know this guy?"
- "Nah, probably a tourist."

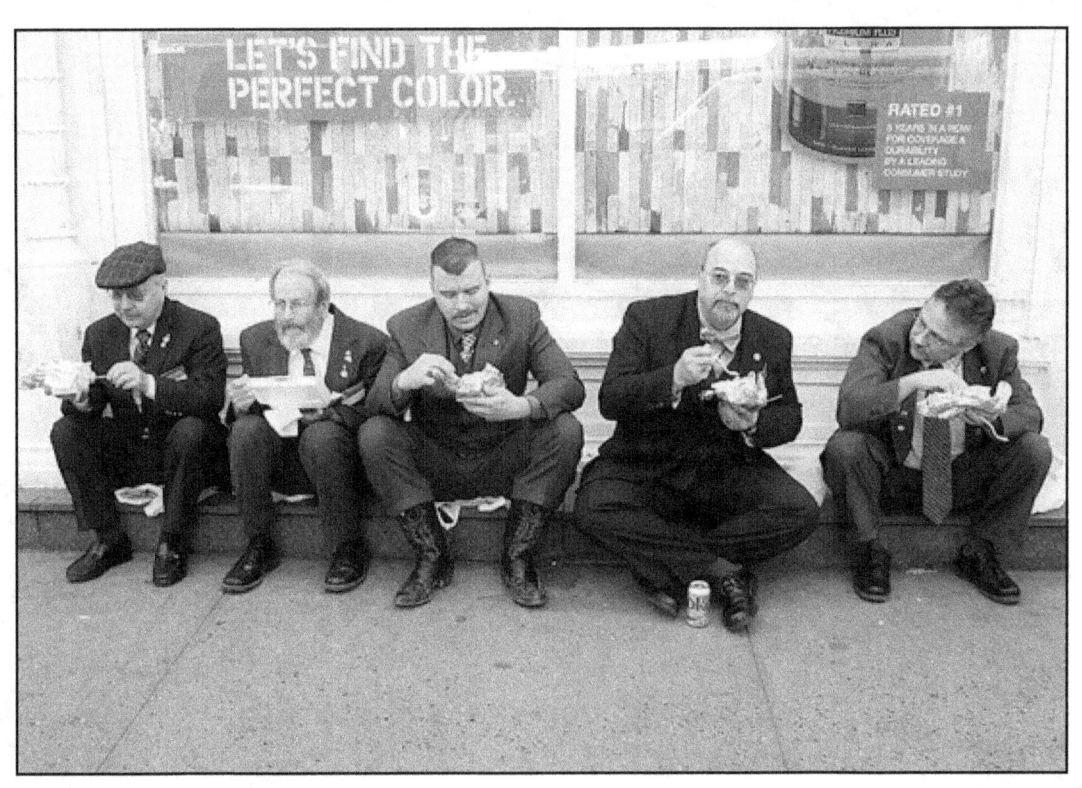
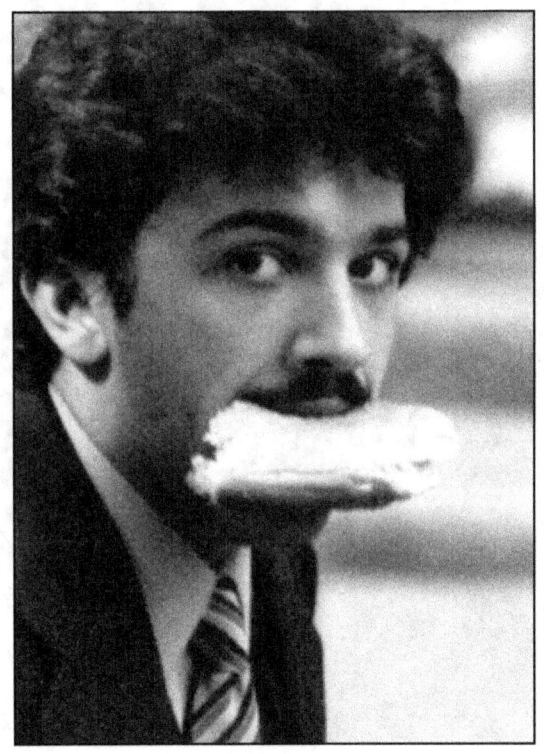
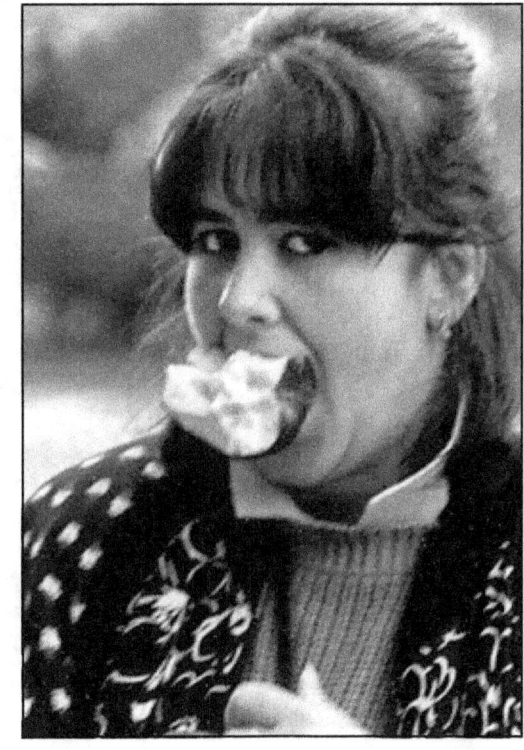

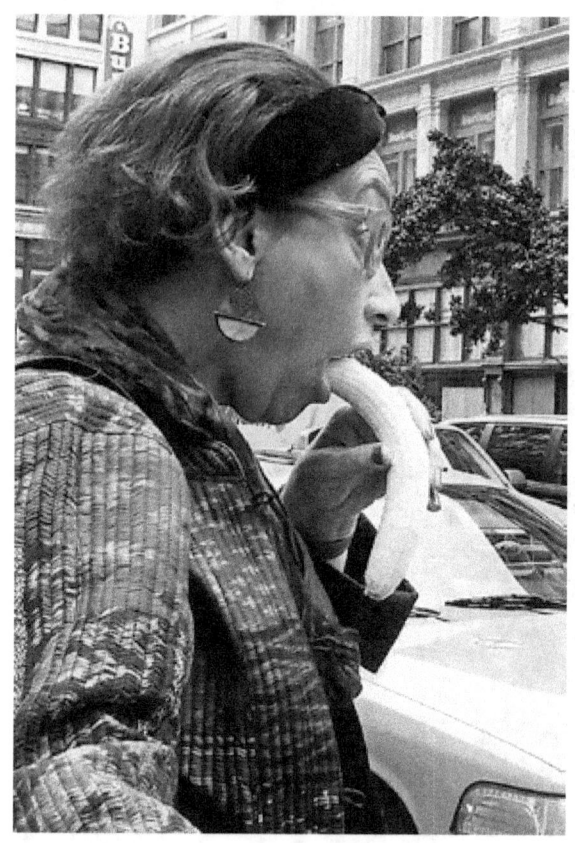
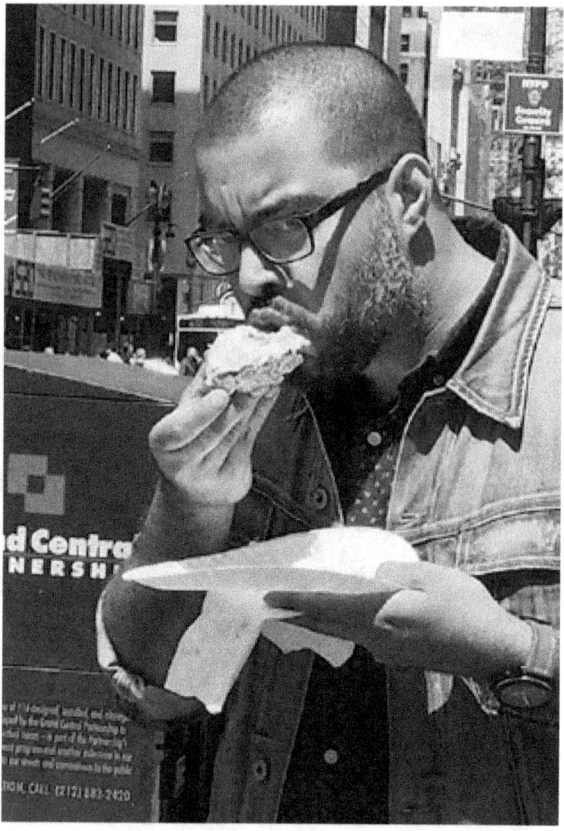
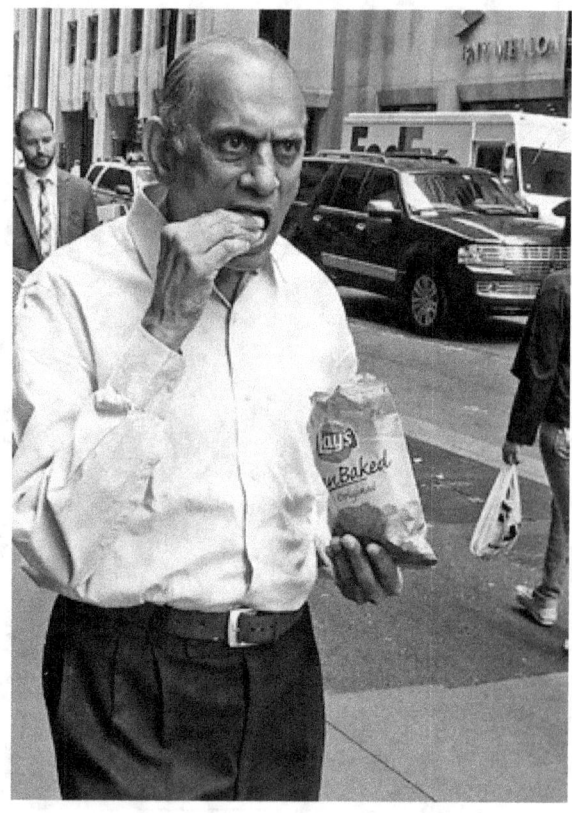
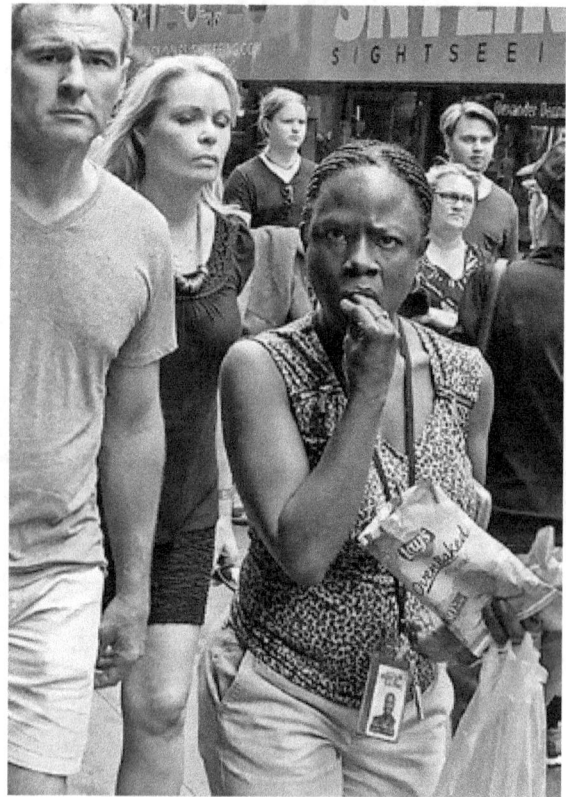

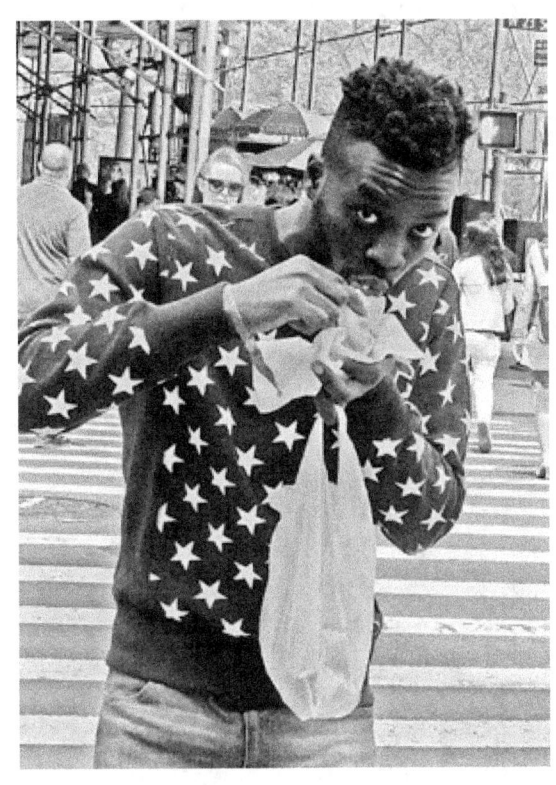
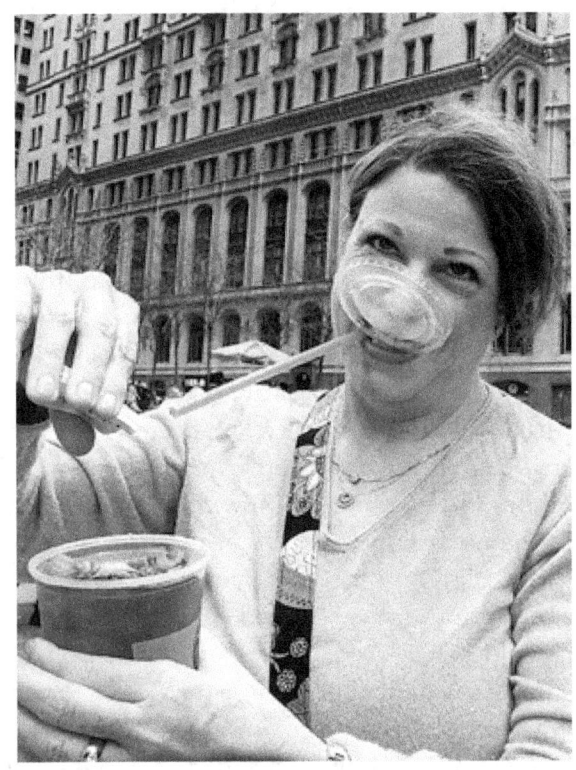
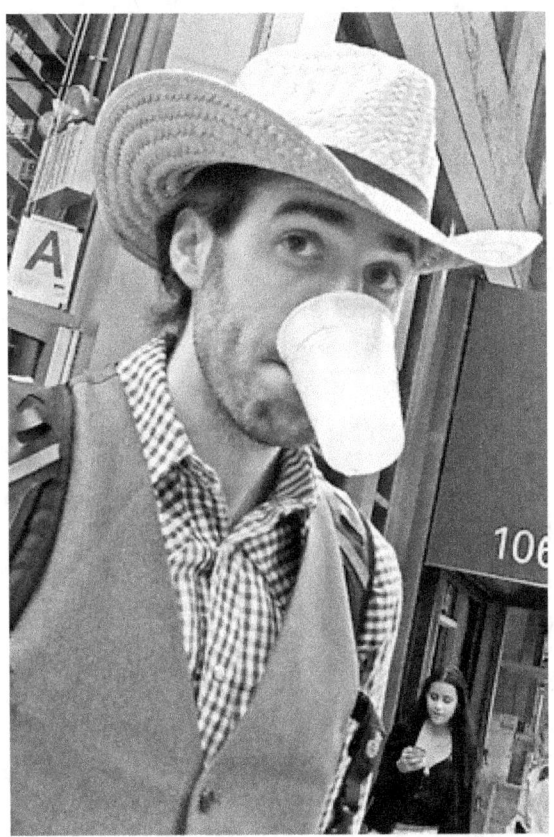
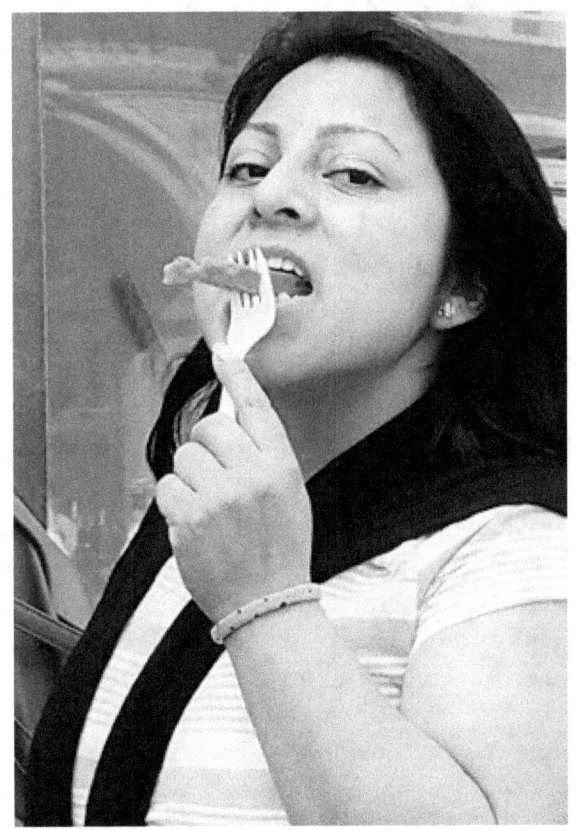

Chapter 8 — *Five more short stories*

The day they shot Big Moe

Big Moe was big. He stood about 6'4", and weighed around 300 pounds. He ran a Three-card Monte game on Broadway and 43rd, right in the heart of Times Square. When Jim Croce wrote his song "Big bad Leroy Brown" everyone was sure that Big Moe was his inspiration, a notion that Big Moe did nothing to discourage. He tried many lines of work before settling on Three-card Monte. He was a bouncer, a collector for a loan shark, he sold drugs, he was a pimp for a while, and he had an alias to go with each occupation. He was smart and well educated. He knew how to conjugate his verbs, but he could turn the street talk on and off like a faucet.

He came from the mean streets of Bed-Stuy in an era when you got what you wanted with your fists. Now things were changing, everybody and his brother were carrying guns. Being big didn't mean that much anymore when some guy half your size had an equalizer. Our lives would intersect on the violent streets of Times Square. Moe's Three-card Monte game required six people to operate: A dealer, two shills, and three lookouts. The lookouts kept an eye out for the police. Especially plain clothes officers who could sneak-up suddenly and bust the dealer. The problem was many of these lookouts would mistake me for a plain clothes cop because of the police radio which I had plugged into my ear. When I approached, they would give the alarm, throwing the whole game into disarray. This was bad for business, so Moe would point me out to the lookouts, explaining that I was just a photographer, not a cop, and that I wasn't a threat.

I used to eat lunch at Nathan's and once in a while Big Moe would come in and sit next to me and we would chat. This is how I got to know him. He would complain about how hard it was to make a living these days "I got to make a 300 dollar payroll every day before I even begin to make a profit." What really worried him though, were all these young punks carrying guns. "They got no respect for human life. Years ago, my size was an asset, now it's a liability. I'm too big to fight, so they're just gonna shoot me. I know it Nicky boy, I just know it, and it will be some kid half my size, and for some dumb-ass reason. I have nightmares about it all the time." I knew what he meant about nightmares, I would have them too. I worried that I was pushing my luck, hanging around the Deuce and Times Square all the time. I was taking too many chances, taking too many pictures of all the wrong people. I was worried that someday, I'd shoot the wrong guy and he would return the favor, but not with a camera.

The day Moe was shot was one of those hot, muggy August afternoons. I was walking up 8th Avenue in the forties, when I heard gun shots. People began screaming and running, there was much confusion. It was hard to tell what was going on. When things settled down, there was Moe, lying on his back, a pool of blood beneath his right leg. I ran toward where he was lying. He was surrounded by his crew. The guys were in shock, the women were crying. I knew better than to take a picture of him in this condition.

I looked at Moe and said to him – "You're lucky Moe, it's only in the leg, and there's an ambulance coming now." He looked at me and said – "Didn't I tell you that this was gonna happen Nicky boy. We were just talking about this last week, and for a lousy 20 bucks." The paramedics were there now. They placed him on a stretcher. They cut his right pants leg open with a pair of scissors, and then they raised his leg to put a tourniquet on it. That's when the contents of his right pocket spilled out onto the pavement. There was a bunch of keys, a wad of cash wrapped in a rubber band, and a neatly rolled joint. The paramedic picked up the keys and the cash and handed them back to Moe. He pretended not to see the joint. That was nice of him. However, the cop standing just a few feet away might not be so generous. Moe looked scared. If the cop saw the joint, it could send him back to jail because he was still on parole. The joint was just a few inches from my left foot. I covered it with my foot and slowly ground it into dust. Moe saw the whole thing, he looked relieved. As they put him into the ambulance, he looked at me and said – "I owe you one Nicky boy, I owe you one." The kid who shot Moe was found floating in the Harlem River a week later. He was beaten so badly his own mother couldn't recognize him.

I didn't see Moe for a couple of weeks; he must have been recovering from his wound. I was on 42nd Street one day just walking along, sort of daydreaming. Suddenly, an empty beer can goes flying past my head, just missing me by inches. I was the only one in the area, it was clearly meant for me. I turned around, standing just 10 feet from me, were three young Hispanic kids. They had smirks on their faces, the kind of looks that said "Do something about it white boy." I was in a bad position, running wasn't an option. I was weighed down by my camera bag. I wasn't defenseless either. I had a collapsible club in my bag. That would even things up, but they might be armed too. My mind was racing like crazy. There's no shame in backing down when you're outnumbered three to one. Everybody watching would know that, it was how you did it that mattered. I had to treat them with complete contempt, like they weren't worth my time. If I looked scared, I'd never be able to walk down that street again.

Suddenly, their cocky smirks vanished, replaced with looks of total apprehension. They weren't even looking at me anymore. They were looking past me, above me. I turned around. There was Big Moe, standing right behind me with two of his crew. He said "Hi Nicky boy, I got your back." He pointed to one of the kids and said "Get that little motherfucker on the left." His guys grabbed the kid and brought him to Moe. The other two took off, running like scared rabbits, down 42nd Street. Moe said to the kid "What you doing chuckin' cans at my friend for." The kid was terrified. He said "I didn't throw nothing" Moe looked at him and screamed "Don't lie to me motherfucker, I seen you throw it." Moe smacked the kid in the face. The noise sounded like a rifle shot. The kid screamed. I said "Moe this ain't necessary" Moe said "Leave this to me Nicky boy." He said to the kid "Where you from?" The kid said "The Bronx" "Well, from now on you gonna stay in The Bronx, you hear. I don't wanna see your rice and beans eaten Puerto Rican ass around here no more. The kid said "I'm not Puerto Rican, I'm Mexican." Moe said "Same thing, and don't get technical with me." Moe slapped him again. I said "Moe, the cop is looking this way." That got his attention. Moe didn't want any trouble with the cops. He was still on parole. He let the kid go. He looked down at me and said "We even Nicky boy, we even." He turned around and walked down 42nd Street. He was still limping a little. A few months later, Moe had another scare. Some kid pointed a gun at him and pulled the trigger but the gun misfired. That was enough for him. He quit the street life and got a legit job. The last I heard he was a night watchman at a parking garage. So much for Big Moe.

Jenny

Jenny was a 40 years old social worker who lived in Park Slope. She was one of those rabid feminist types. She would go on a date with a guy, and spend the whole night lecturing him on how evil men were for exploiting women. Then she would wonder why nobody ever asked her out for a second date. Thus, she was reduced to having affairs with married men. They were the only ones who would tolerate her lectures, in exchange, of course, for some cheap sex.

At this time, Jenny was having an affair with a married fireman. Several times a week, at lunch time, the fireman would walk the two blocks from his firehouse to her place. She lived on the top floor of a four story walk-up. The problem was, the buzzer on the front door didn't work, so she would throw the whole set of her house keys down to him from the fourth floor and he would let himself in.

One sunny afternoon, she throws the keys down to him, and he loses them in the sun. This half-pound of brass, coming from four stories up, hits him right in the middle of the forehead knocking him out cold. Jenny runs downstairs but she can't revive him. She runs the two blocks to the firehouse where he works to get help. His co-workers rush to his aid in a fire truck and take him to Methodist Hospital just three blocks away.

Right across the street from the hospital was a flower shop, and guess who worked there? -The fireman's wife of 20 years. She sees them taking her husband into the hospital on a stretcher with this strange woman beside him crying hysterically. The wife was no fool, she put two and two together and the whole truth came out. The fireman wound up losing his job, his wife and kids, and his health. Moral of story – avoid women who live in four story walk-ups.

That picture looks familiar

I just got back from the city, I spent most of the day in Macy's taking pictures of the girls putting their make-up on. I grabbed a beer from the fridge and turned on the TV – Breaking news! An entire ten story building has just collapsed on Broadway and 31st St. "Holy crap" I said to myself, I just missed it. I walked down that street just an hour ago. All night long the whole city followed the story because there was a young girl trapped in the building and she was still alive. Rescue workers were trying desperately to get her out.

I went out that night and had dinner, then I bought a late copy of the Daily News. On the front page was a picture of the trapped girl in happier times. It looked like she was dancing at some sort of party. She was a very pretty, 21 year old, who was engaged to be married. I got the feeling that I had seen her somewhere before. As a matter of fact, the picture itself seemed kind of familiar. I chalked it up to 'deja vu' and continued on to my favorite hang-out in Park Slope, a restaurant called McFeeley's.

When I walked in, the whole place was abuzz about the drama playing out in the city, and for a good reason. It was the bartender's sister who was trapped in the rubble. It seems that reporters from the Daily News had already been to his house seeking information about her. It was he who gave them the picture of his sister that appeared on the front page. It was a shot of her dancing at his wedding. And then it hit me why the picture looked so familiar. I was the photographer at his wedding. I was the one who took it. The young girl survived and got married a few months later.

The day I ran into Jacqueline Kennedy Onassis

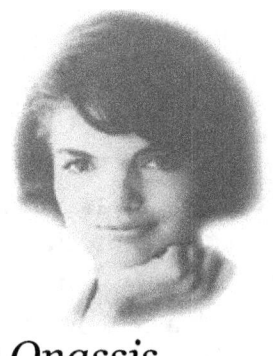

It was a perfect sunny day in September and I was on Madison Avenue looking for a birthday gift for my girlfriend. It didn't take me long to conclude that Madison Avenue was way out of my price range. So I was just window shopping when she turned the corner from 70th street onto Madison Avenue. Even from a block away, I knew who she was. So tall and slender, dressed in a gray pants suit. She seemed to glide along on a cushion of air. It was Jacqueline Kennedy Onassis.

She was alone and obviously in a good mood. She glanced over her shoulder (probably checking to see if she was being followed by the paparazzi.) She wasn't. She continued down Madison Avenue as she waved to someone across the street. She was just half a block away now, enjoying the beautiful weather, a big smile on her face – and then she saw me. Her whole countenance changed instantly. She looked like a gazelle, who has just spotted a lion, crouching in the tall grass, creeping towards her. We were no longer on Madison Avenue; it was the plains of Serengeti. She looked desperately from side to side, looking for an escape: A cab, a store, anything to avoid me. I immediately switched the camera to my left hand and held it by the lens. You can't take a picture holding a camera this way. She picked-up on this instantly, as I knew she would. After all, this was a woman who grew up surrounded by cameras. Her whole body language changed immediately. She wasn't running anywhere; she was going to face me head-on. She began walking towards me. We were just ten feet apart now, and the look on her face said everything. Please don't betray me, please don't take my picture. The camera stayed in my left hand. As she passed me, she smiled and said thank you. It was the most sincere thank you I've ever gotten, before or since.

Some of my friends said I was crazy not to take a picture; "you could have made a lot of money." I had no regrets; after all, I'm a street photographer, not a paparazzo. There's a big difference. A real street photographer has a heart once in a while. The paparazzi never do.

The day I almost killed my Principal

When I was a young boy, I went to P.S. 31 in Brooklyn. It was in one of those old, majestic buildings that said to a student "Education is a serious business." My teachers and classmates were, for the most part, easy to get along with. My father deliberately sent me to a public school, as opposed to a nearby Catholic school, because he wanted me to learn how to get along with everyone. I was six years old, and in the first grade when this unfortunate incident occurred.

Even as a young boy, I fancied myself as an artist. I loved to draw, and to paint, and to sculpt things out of clay. My parents encouraged me, by buying all kinds of art supplies for me. So when my art teacher announced that there would be an "Art contest" held at school, I was very excited. We were instructed to paint anything we liked, on a large piece of paper. The winner of the contest would have their painting hung in the main office, right above the principal's desk! The judge of this contest would be the Principal himself.

I got right to work. I said to myself, if I were the Principal, what kind of painting would I want above my desk? To me, the answer was obvious, a picture of the school itself. I worked on it for several hours and was happy with the results. It looked a little like one of those Grandma Moses paintings. It showed the school in the background, with kids playing in the schoolyard in the foreground. I covered the edges with masking tape so they wouldn't get frayed.

The next day the contest was held. When I looked at the competition, I was confident that I had a good chance of winning. The Principal, Mr. Silverman, was a tall man with grey hair and glasses. He was around sixty years old. He came into our room, and gave a little speech about how important art was Blah, Blah, Blah, and then announced that he would pick the winner of the contest. He paced back and forth, peering at the paintings over his glasses. Then he stopped in front of my painting and said "I like this one" "Who did this?" He asked. I raised my hand. The whole class gave me a round of applause, and the Principal came over to me and shook my hand. I was bursting with pride. I thought it would go on forever. Of course, I was too young to be familiar with the old Roman Proverb that said "All glory was fleeting." Little did I know that in just moments, my painting would be destroyed, my pride would turn to shame, and the Principal would almost die, all because of me.

Mr. Silverman took the painting and said "Nicholas, come with me, you're going to help me put it up." We walked to the main office where his desk was. Behind his desk was a large swiveling office chair with small wheels under the feet, so it could roll around. Mr. Silverman stood on the chair and told me to hold it steady so it wouldn't move around. Then he asked me to hand him the painting. It was right there, so I gave it to him. Then he positioned it against the wall and asked me if it was level. I said that it looked level to me. Then he asked me to hand him the roll of

Scotch tape that was on the desk. The roll of tape was slightly out of my reach, so I leaned over to get it and took my foot off the chair for just a second! That's all it took. The chair shifted, and Mr. Silverman lost his balance. He let out a scream as he fell sideways and grabbed onto the molding that ran along the wall. He screamed to me, "Nicholas, push the chair under me" I pushed with all my might, but I only weighed sixty pounds, he must have been over two hundred pounds. I couldn't get the chair to budge! He was holding on literally by his fingertips. He screamed for help again, but nobody came. He was hanging at a forty-five degree angle with his hands clutching the molding and his feet tangled up in the chairs armrest. Right below him was a cast- iron radiator, If he fell and hit his head against it, he could be killed! I was frantic, I didn't know what to do. I screamed for help again! I pushed with all my might, to try and get the chair under him, but I just wasn't strong enough. Then he said to me "Nicholas, do you see that small button on my desk? Push it and call for help. That's the button for the PA system." I pushed the button and screamed for help in the principal's office! Two seconds later, there must have been a hundred people there. They got Mr. Silverman down and laid him on his desk. He was having trouble breathing. The school nurse asked me if I was alright, and I said I was fine. And then it occurred to me that the whole school heard my frantic screams for help over the PA system. What would they think of me? And what about my painting?. Well, I could forget about that. During all the mayhem, somehow it got torn to shreds. Mr. Silverman had a minor heart attack, whatever that is, but luckily he recovered. As for me, would anyone remember me as a great artist?...No. Would anyone remember my valiant efforts to help Mr. Silverman? No. Would everyone remember me as the guy who almost killed the Principal…Yes. Such is life.

Chapter 9
Construction workers

These highly skilled workers do a job that's dirty and dangerous. Sure, they may be a little rough around the edges, but without them, the city would not exist.

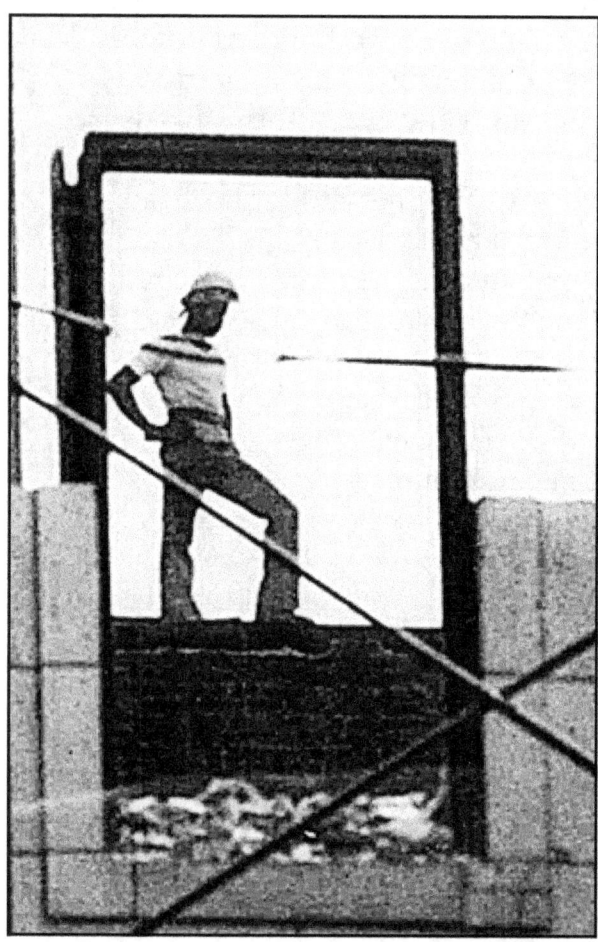

Tearing a building down is more dangerous than putting one up.

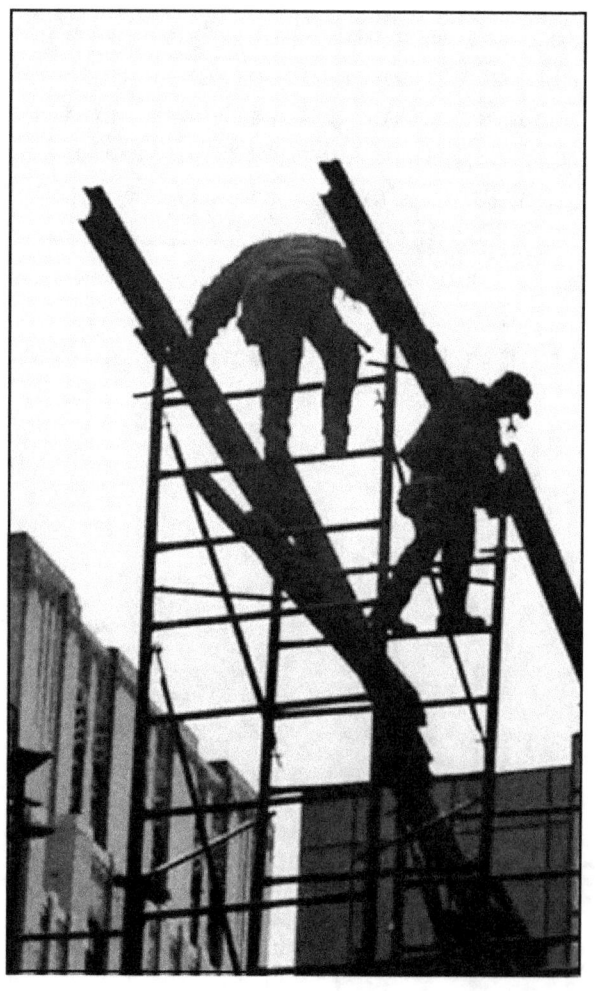

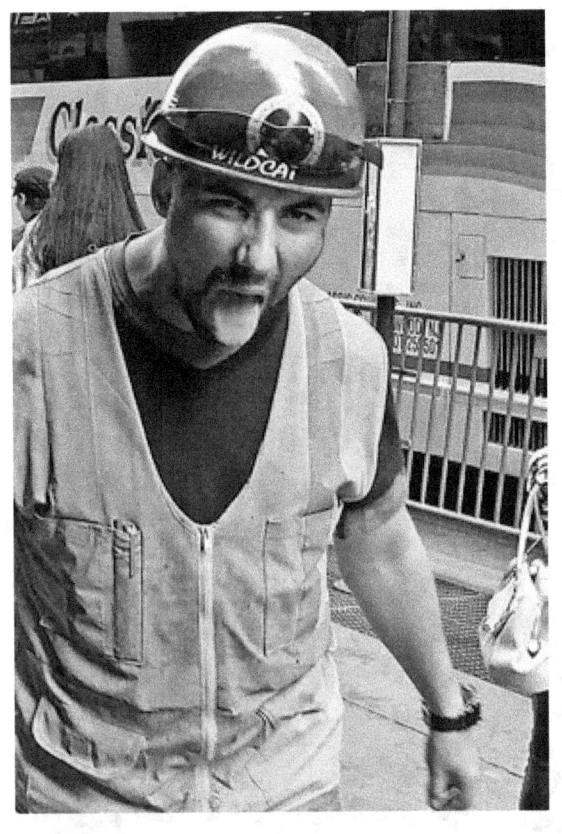
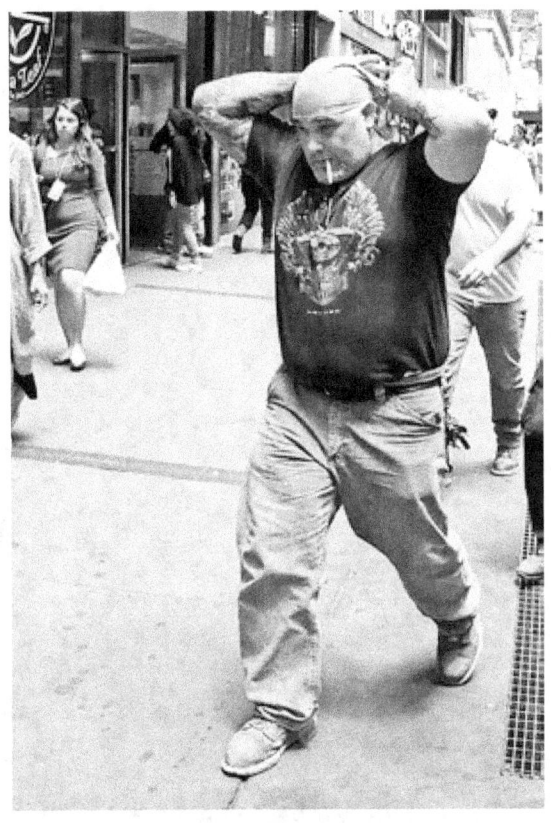
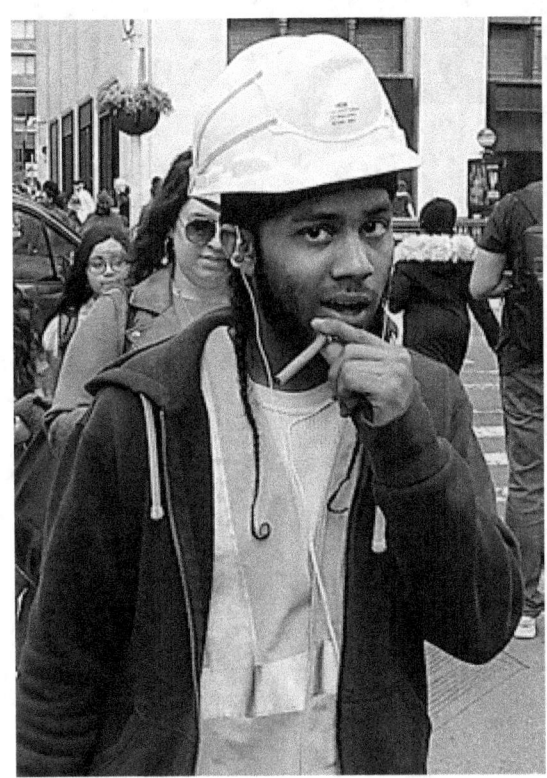
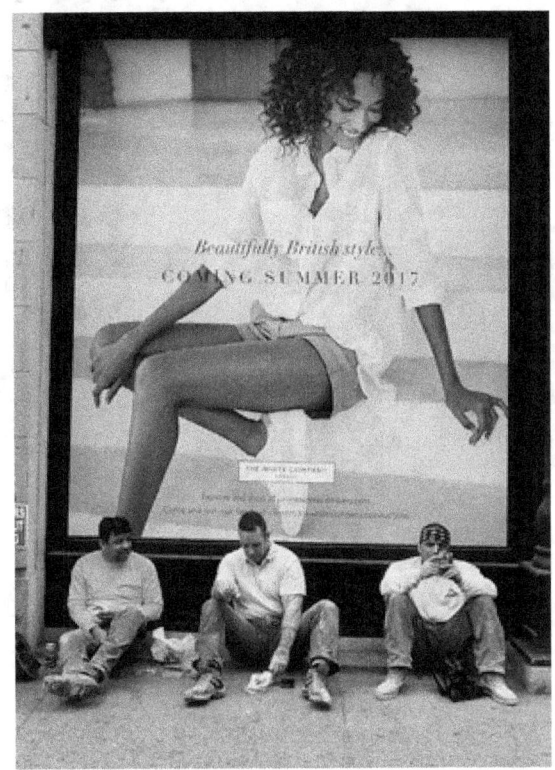

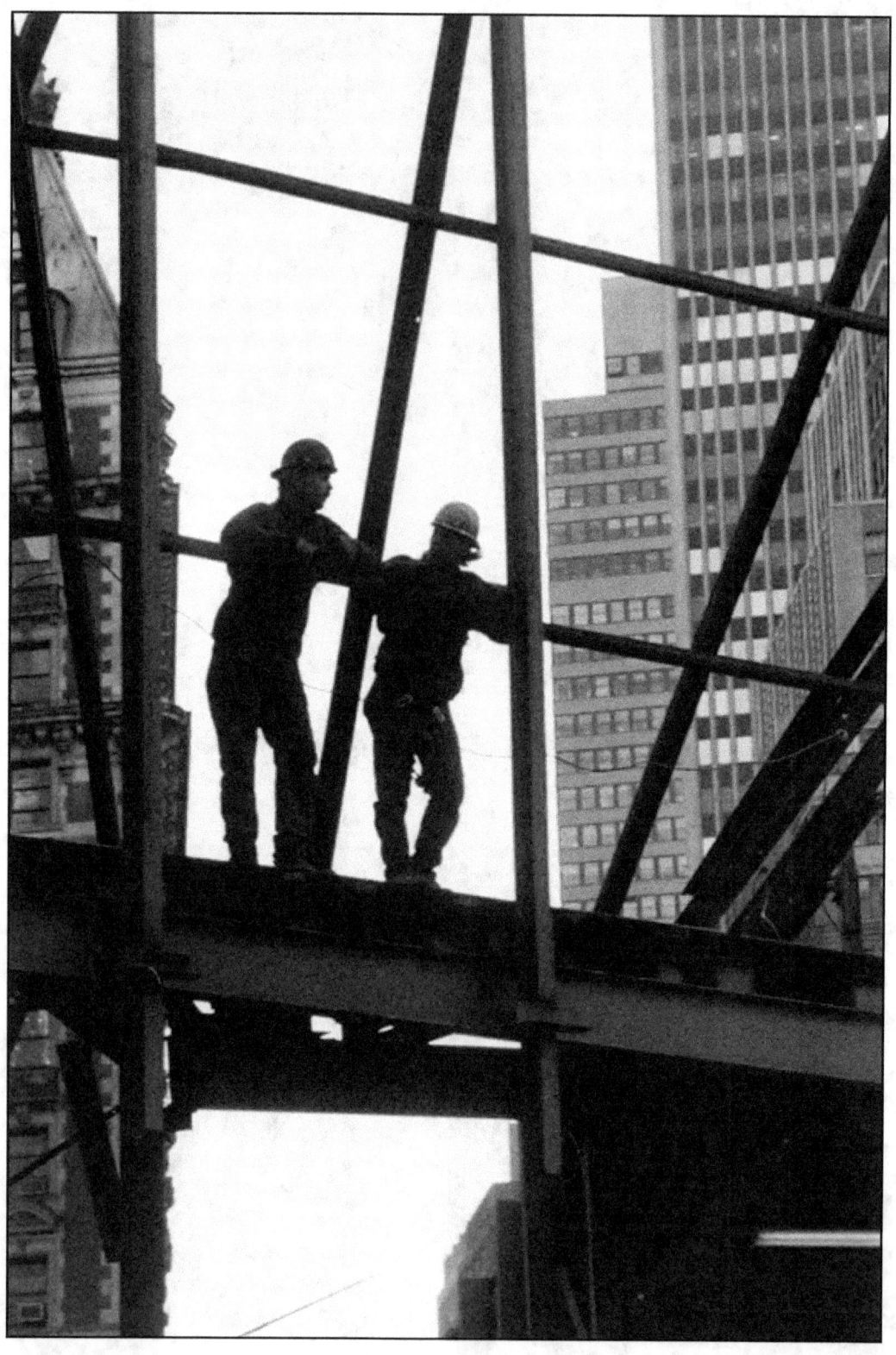

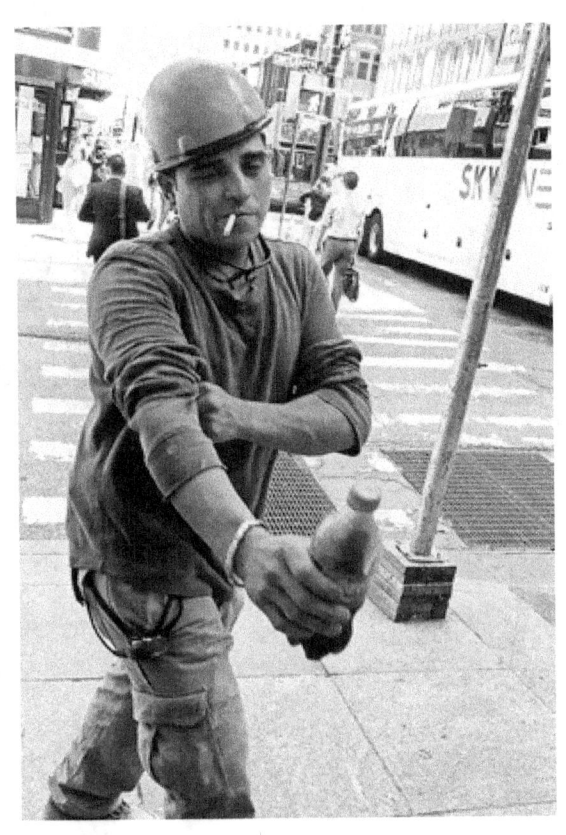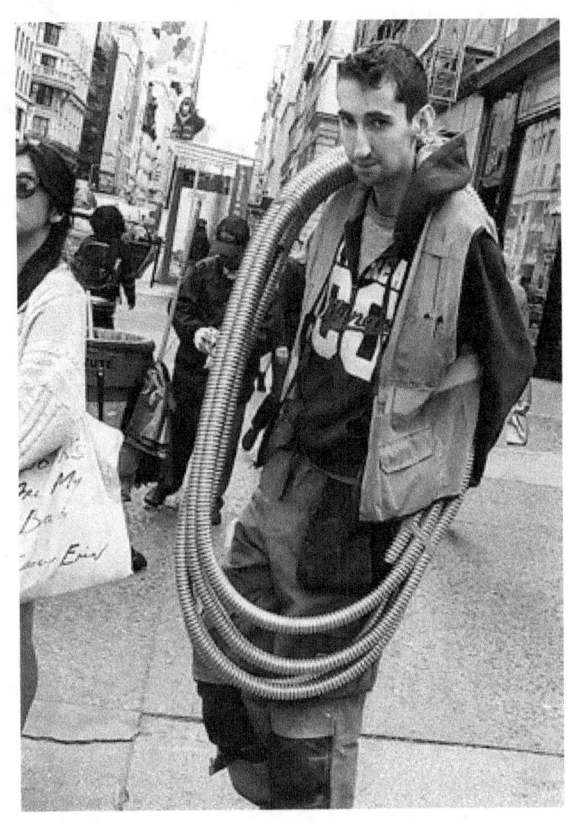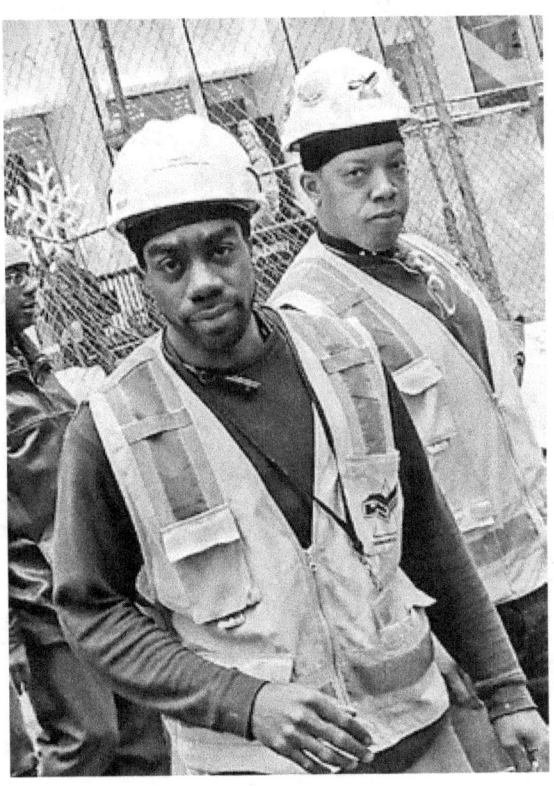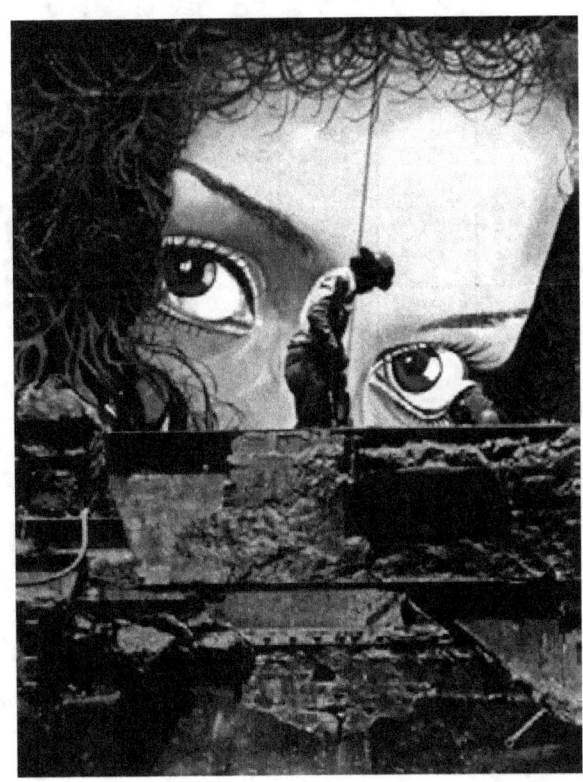

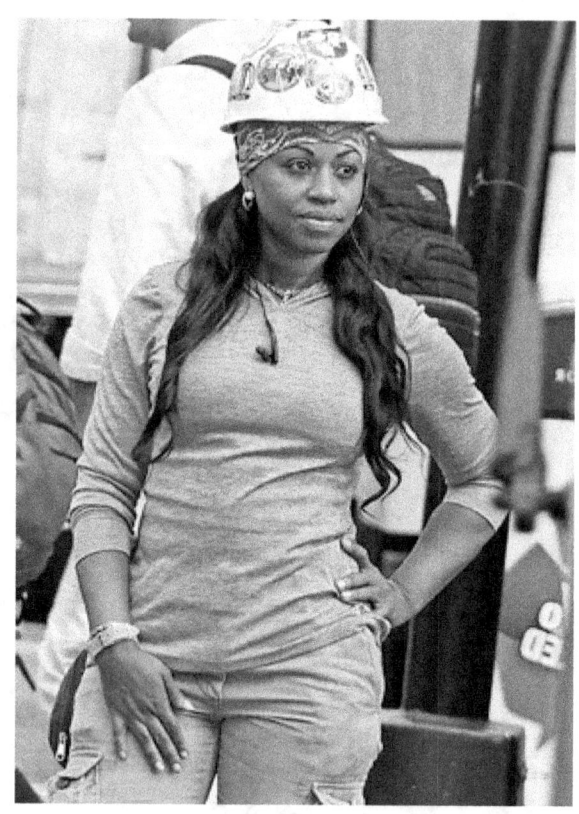 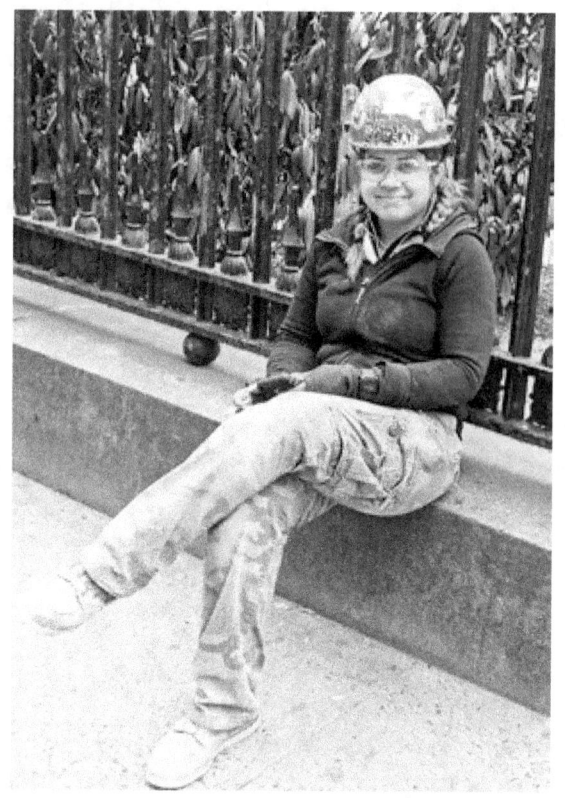 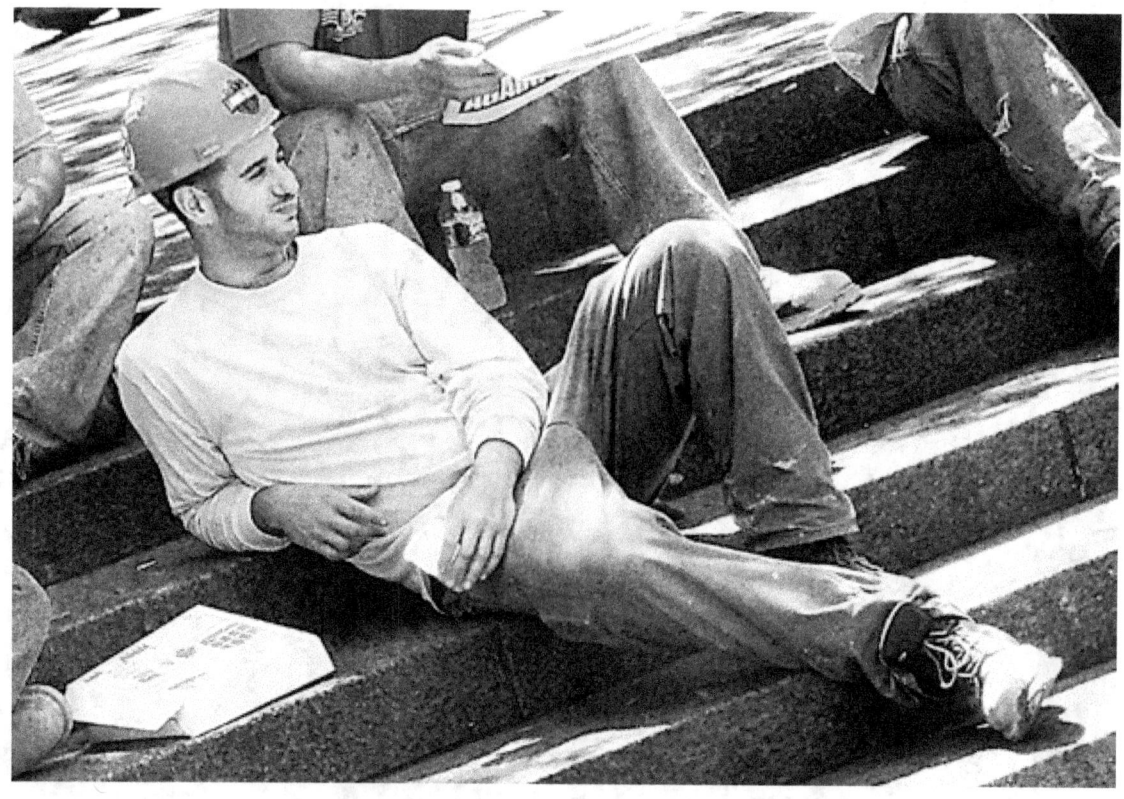

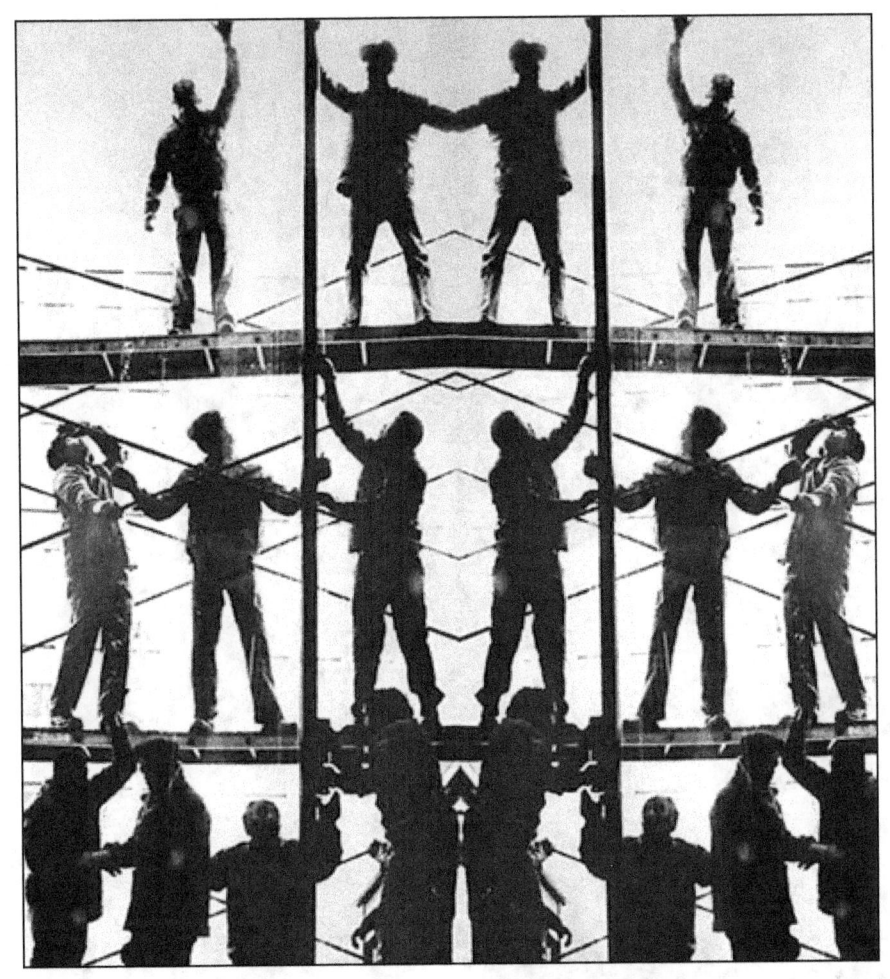
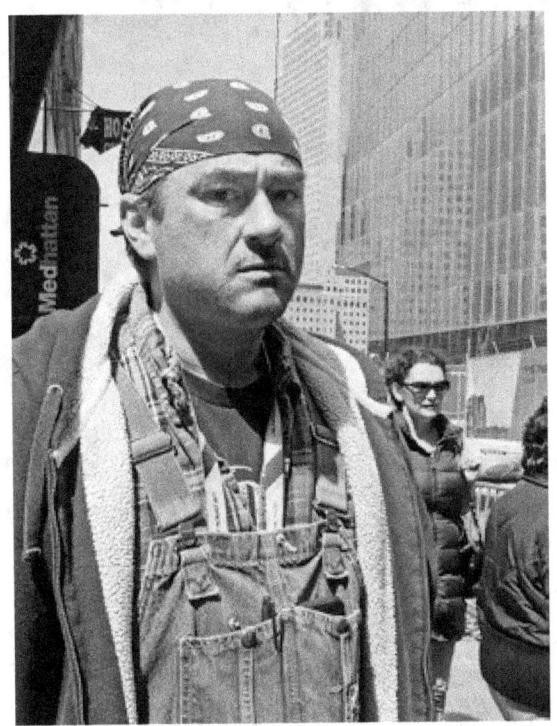
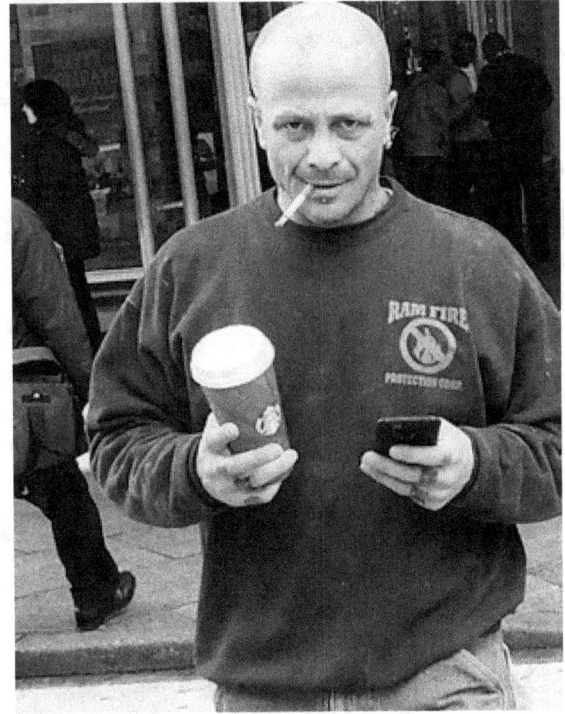

Chapter 10
When buses pull up

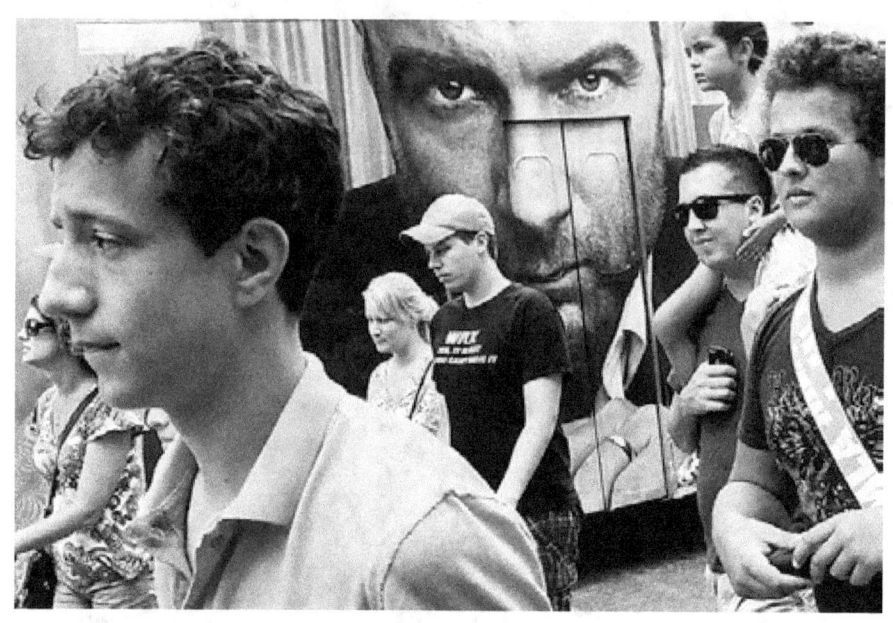

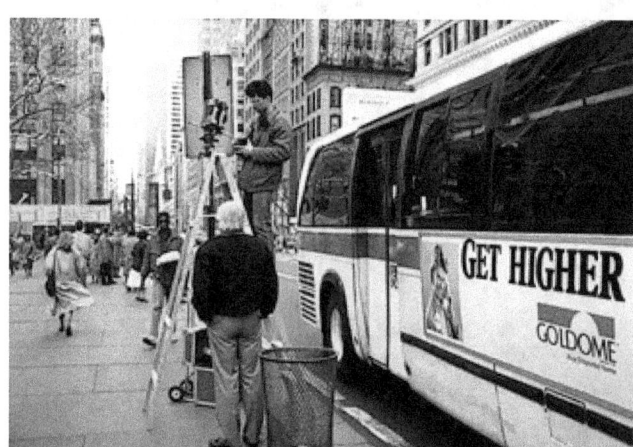

Get higher!

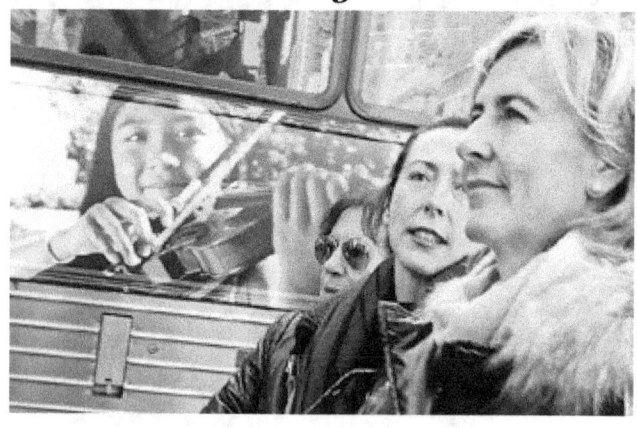

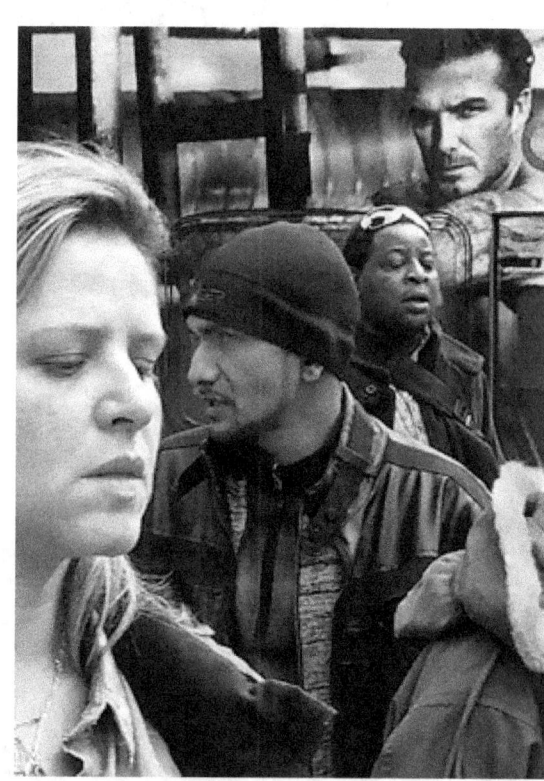

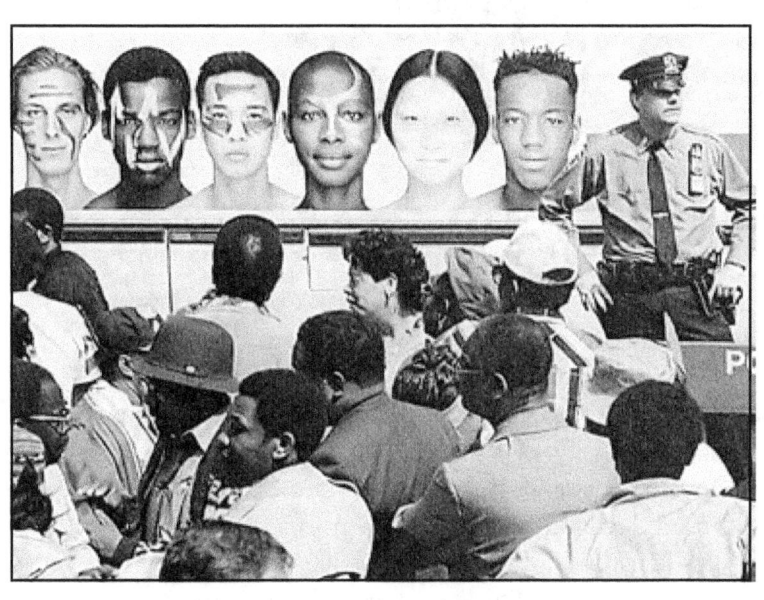

The line-up

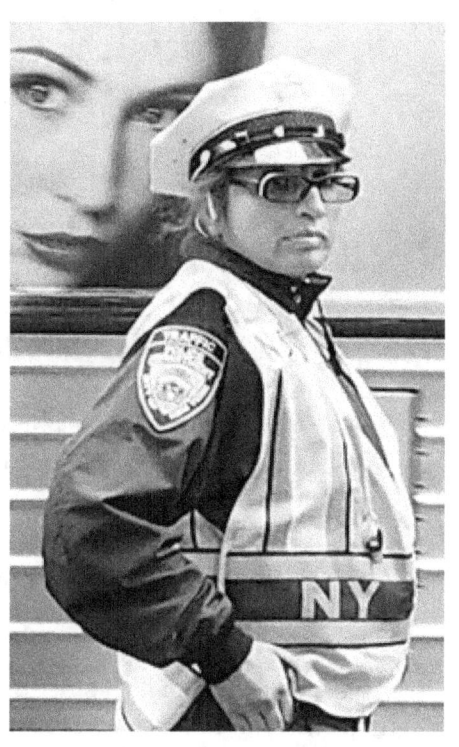

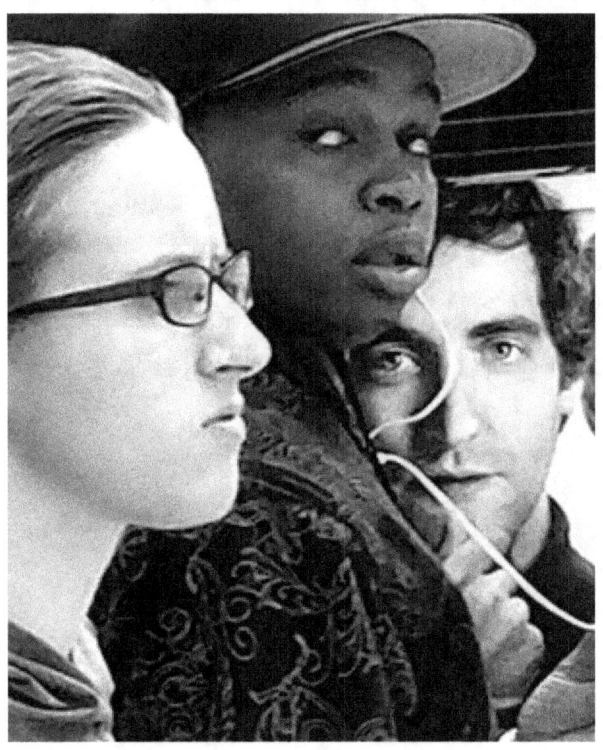

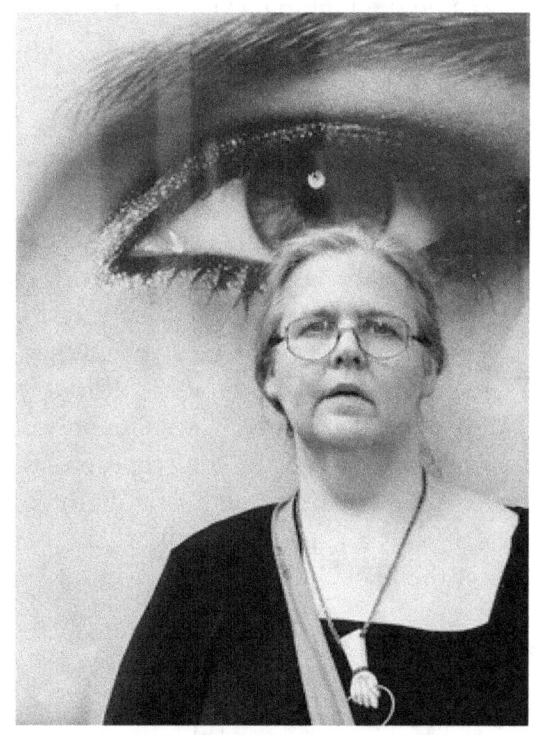

Chapter 11

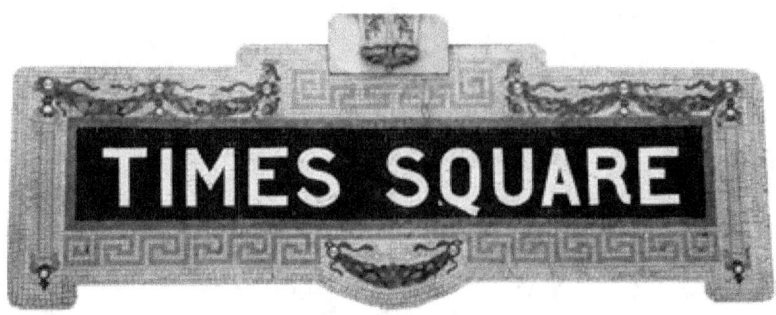

(In the bad old days)

    The year is 2011 and I'm walking around Times Square and I can't believe how much it's changed since the bad old days. There are thousands of tourists strolling about, taking in the sights, not a care in the world. The groups of young thugs that used to be, on every corner, are nowhere to be seen. There are no cops running to and fro, no sirens screaming, no cries for help.

    Thirty years ago, I would stand on the corner of 7th Ave. and 49th St. and watch 2 to 3 muggings happen every hour, in broad daylight. I would spend hours just tailing wallet snatchers, pick-pockets and muggers just waiting for them to strike, so I could get pictures of crimes as they were actually happening. These guys usually operated in groups of between 4 to 6 people and they were armed. I became very good at tailing them without being spotted.

    It was not just Times Square that was dangerous. All of midtown Manhattan became the hunting grounds for gangs from Brooklyn and upper Manhattan. Every month thousands of people were attacked in the middle of the day, on crowded streets. These thugs were almost always young black men, the victims, almost always white. Needless to say, this did nothing to improve race relations in the city.

    My friends would often ask me if what I was doing was dangerous. Yes, absolutely, that's why I was so careful not to be seen. However, there was another aspect to it. I spent so much time on the street that without realizing it, I became a street person. People saw me so often that they became acclimated to me, the way the lions in Africa become acclimated to wildlife photographers. I became part of the landscape, and they just ignored me. Today there is almost nobody to follow, most of the bad guys are in jail, where they belong. I call it the 'Pax Giuliani.'*

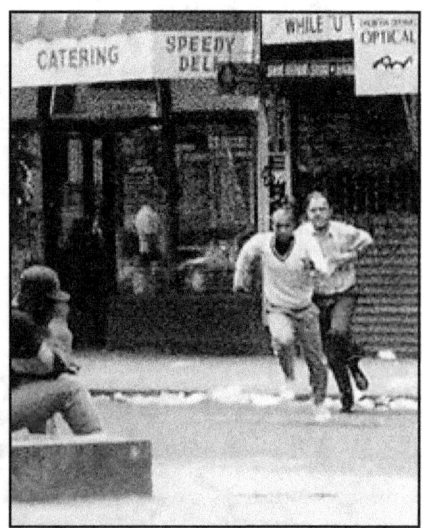

Chasing a wallet-snatcher

* Pax means peace in latin.

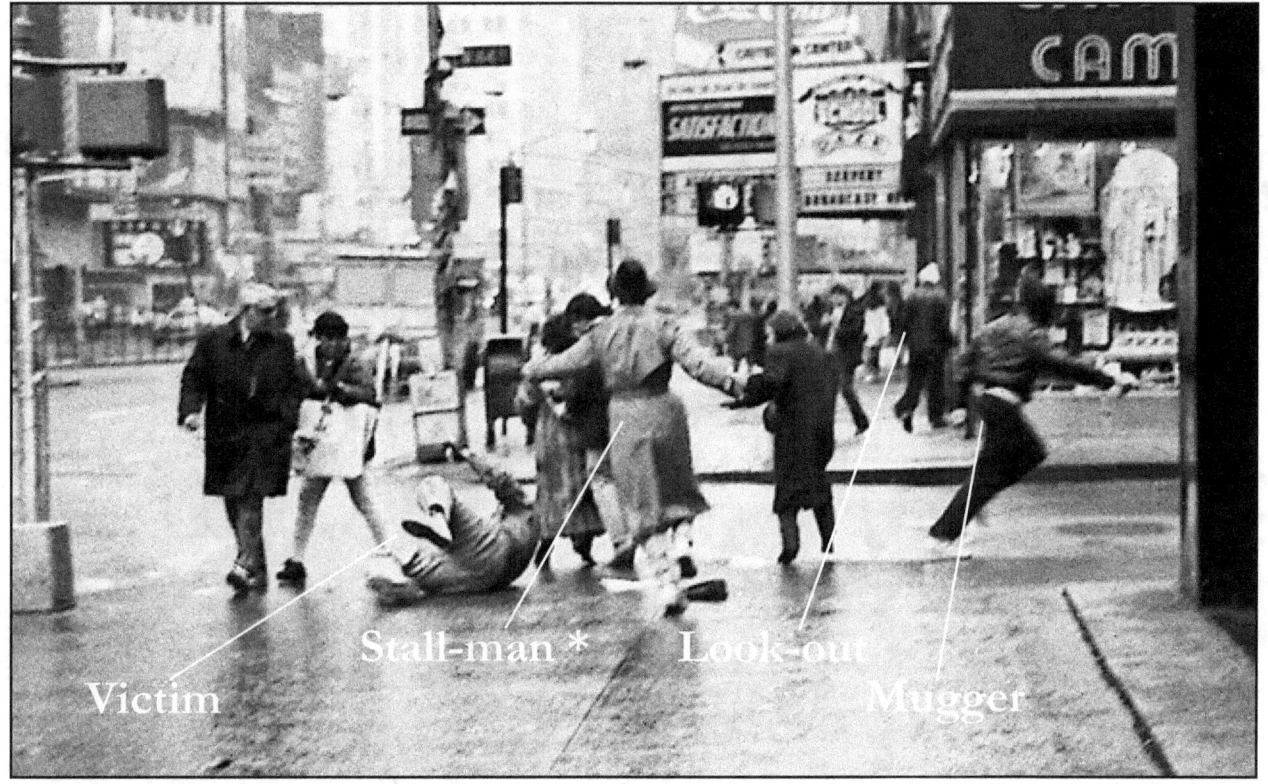

Anatomy of a mugging

    This attack took place smack-dab in the middle of Times Square, 11 a.m. on a Saturday morning. These muggers would often watch an ATM machine to see if anyone would make a large withdrawal. Then they would follow the victim and ambush him in a pre-selected spot. There would be look-outs watching for the police, and backup-man to jump in, just in case the mugger got into trouble.

    The guy lying on the ground had a big fat wallet in his back pocket. He was attacked on the corner of Broadway and 44th St. At the time, I was walking down the street, and was taken completely by surprise by what was happening. I managed to get one shot off before the mugger disappeared up the block. The whole thing was over in five seconds.

* The stall-man's job is very important. Initially, he starts out as a lookout, but after the mugger strikes, he runs over to the victim, pretending to be a concerned bystander. His job is to delay the victim from pursuing the mugger, so he can make a clear getaway.

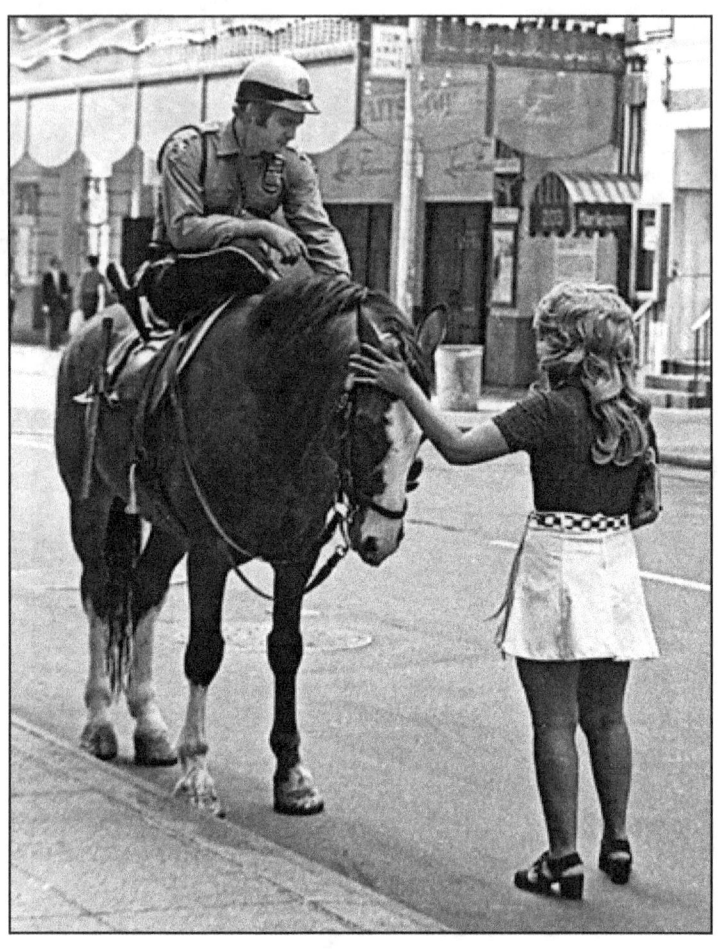

The truce

The woman in this picture is a hooker, normally the mounted cop would be shooing her off the street, but today they have something in common, their love of horses.

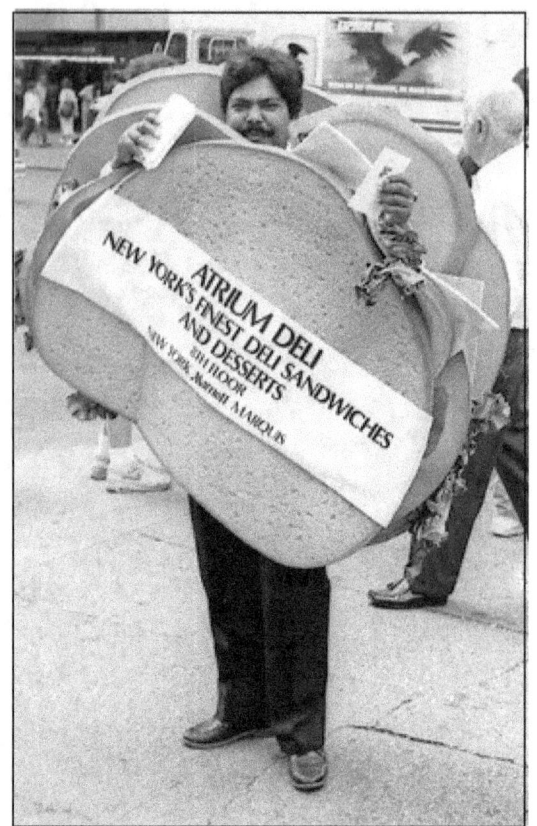

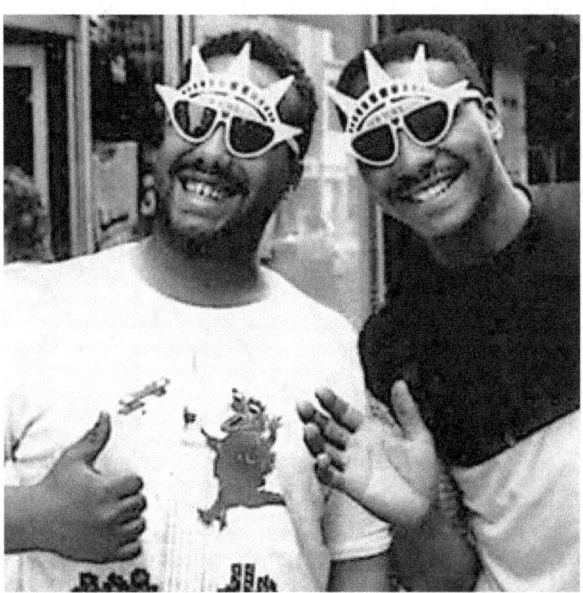

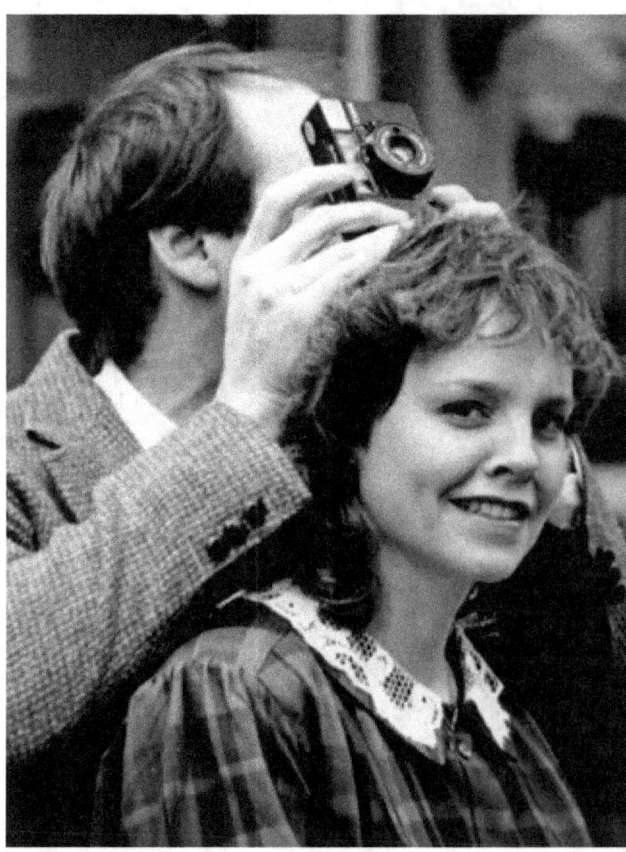

Tourists

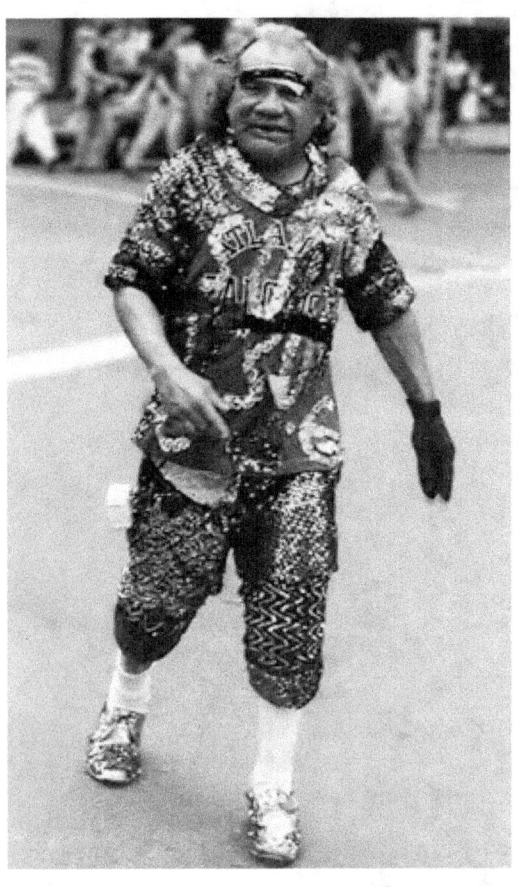

The mayor of Times Square

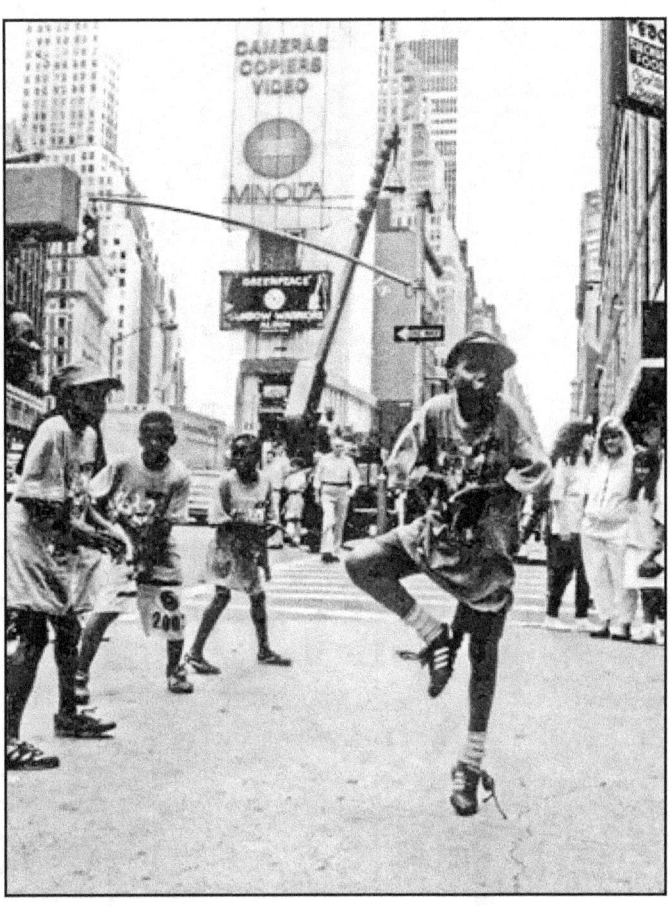

Young boys break-dancing on Broadway.

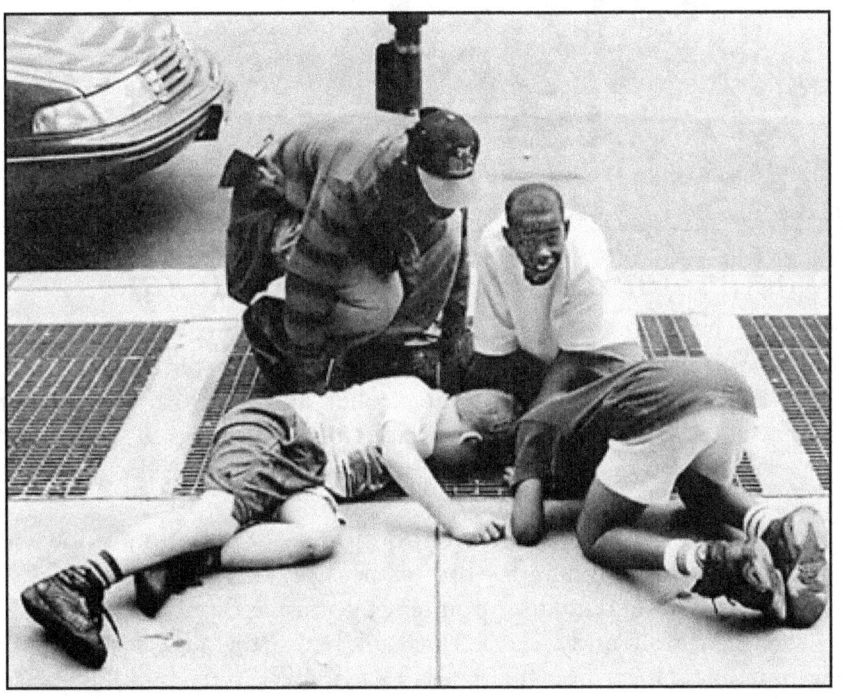

Fishing in the city

These guys are fishing for loose change that's fallen through the grating. They take a small lead weight and tie a string to it. Then they put a piece of sticky chewing gum onto the lead weight. The idea is to hit the coins with the lead weight so that they stick to the chewing gum. Then they pull the coins up through the grating.

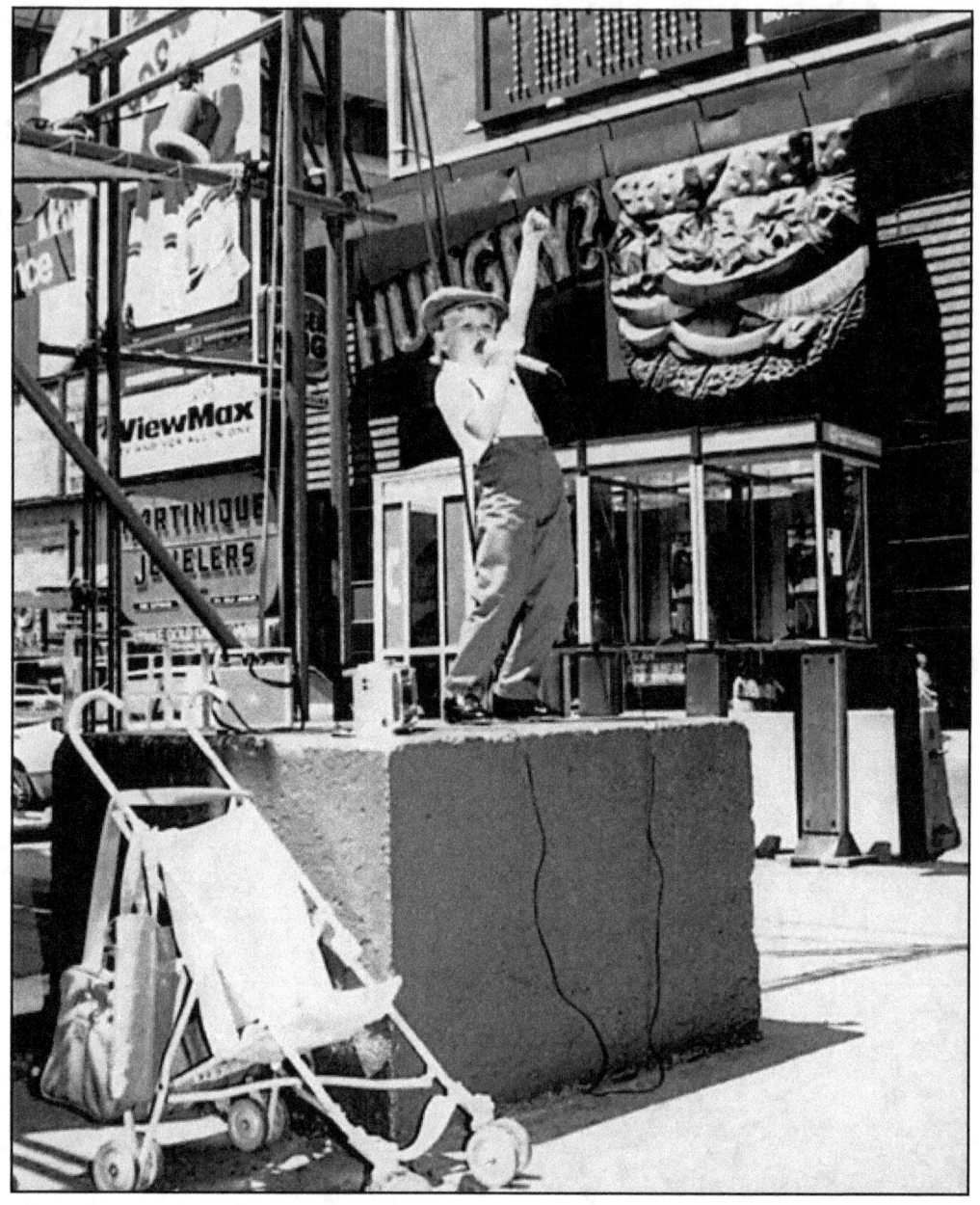

There's a broken heart for every light on Broadway

It was a beautiful Sunday morning, Times Square was empty. I was taking a break. I watched this woman with a small boy in a stroller approach me. They looked like tourists from the midwest. They stopped a few feet from me and smiled. Then the kid gets out of the stroller, and his mother places him on top of this concrete block, which he used as a stage. He has a portable microphone in his hand, and a tip can at his feet. Then this kid starts to sing and dance. I was the only one there, and to be honest, this guy was no Michael Jackson.

I listened politely, and clapped every now and then. This went on for about ten minutes, but he simply could not draw a crowd. His tiny voice was no match for the vastness of Times Square. I was still the only one there. I felt sorry for him. The kid looked so disappointed. I got up and put a dollar in his tip can. The mother said thank you. I started to walk away, I took one look back, the kid was looking in the tip can to see what I gave him. He must have forgotten that he had a live mike in his hand, because I heard him say, 'a lousy dollar, what a cheapskate.'

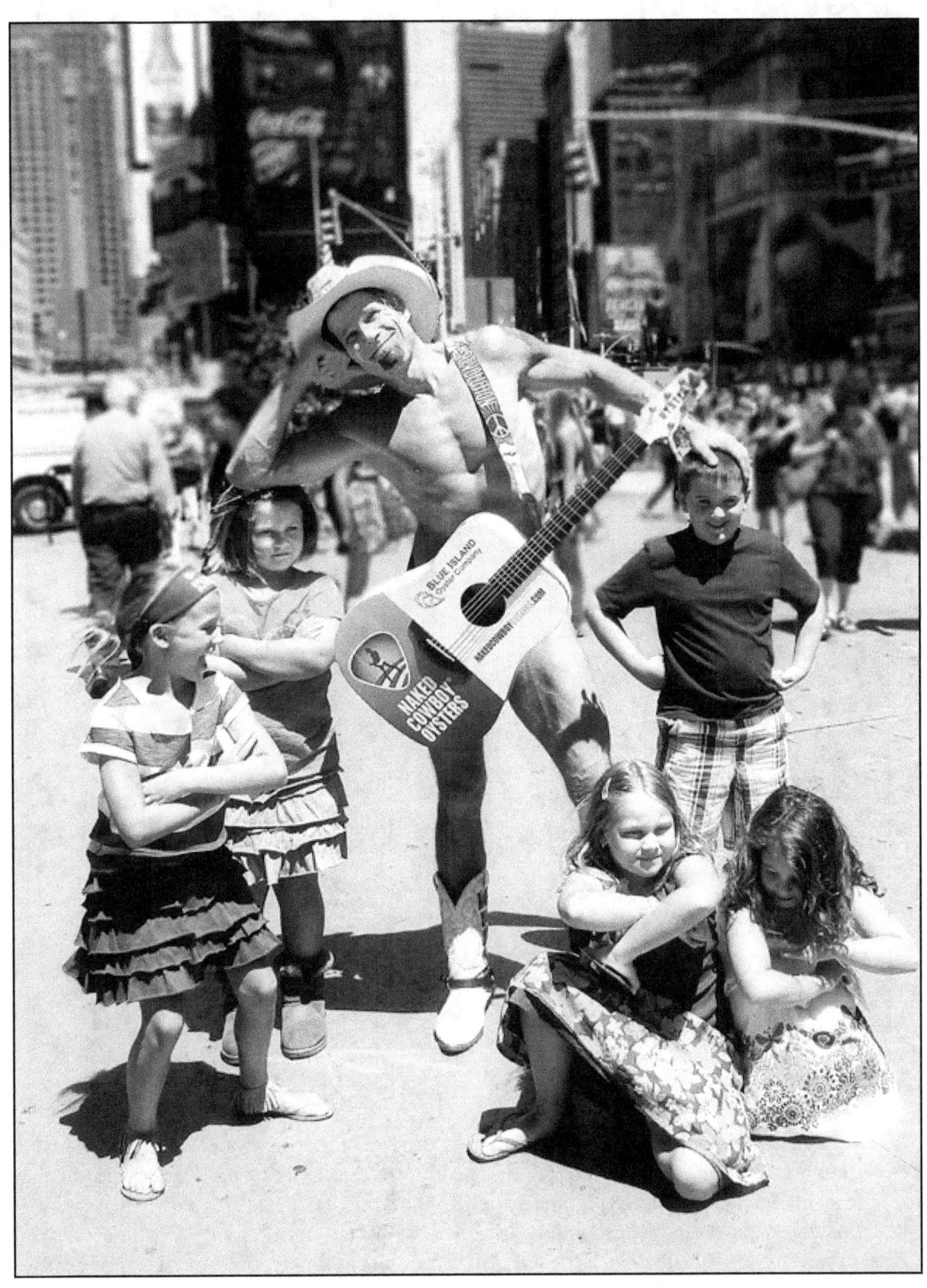
Robert John Burck, AKA The Naked Cowboy.

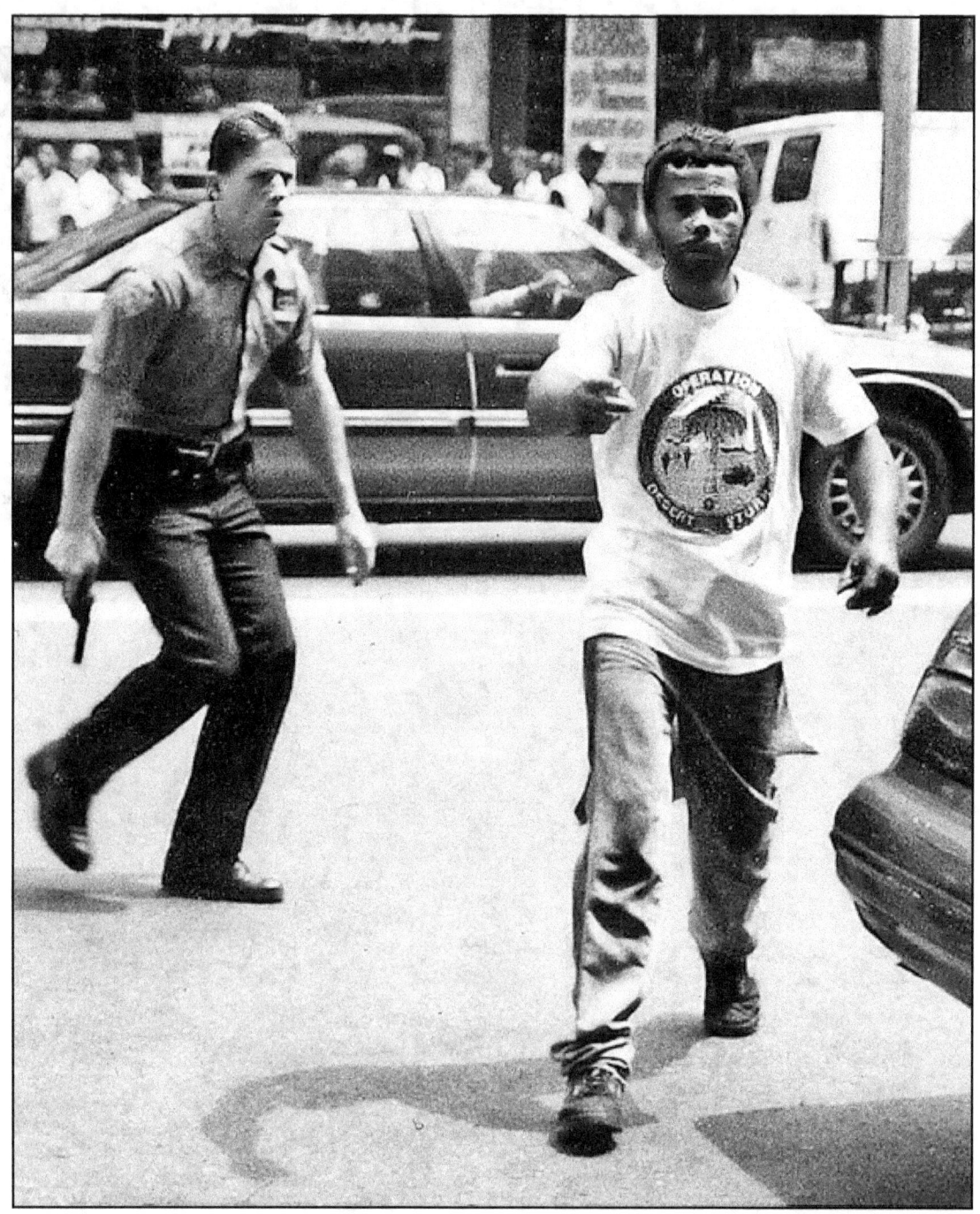

Gun-run, Times Square

This shot was taken through the window of a donut shop, looking out onto Times Square. Five minutes earlier, I had a minor disagreement with the gentleman on the right. In his over-heated imagination, he thought that I had threatened him with a gun. Now he wants the cops to arrest me. I was listening to a police scanner at the time when the call came over. I realized that they were talking about me. I got off one shot before deciding that this was not a good time to be holding a black camera in my hands. Luckily, the cop knew me, and the whole thing was defused.

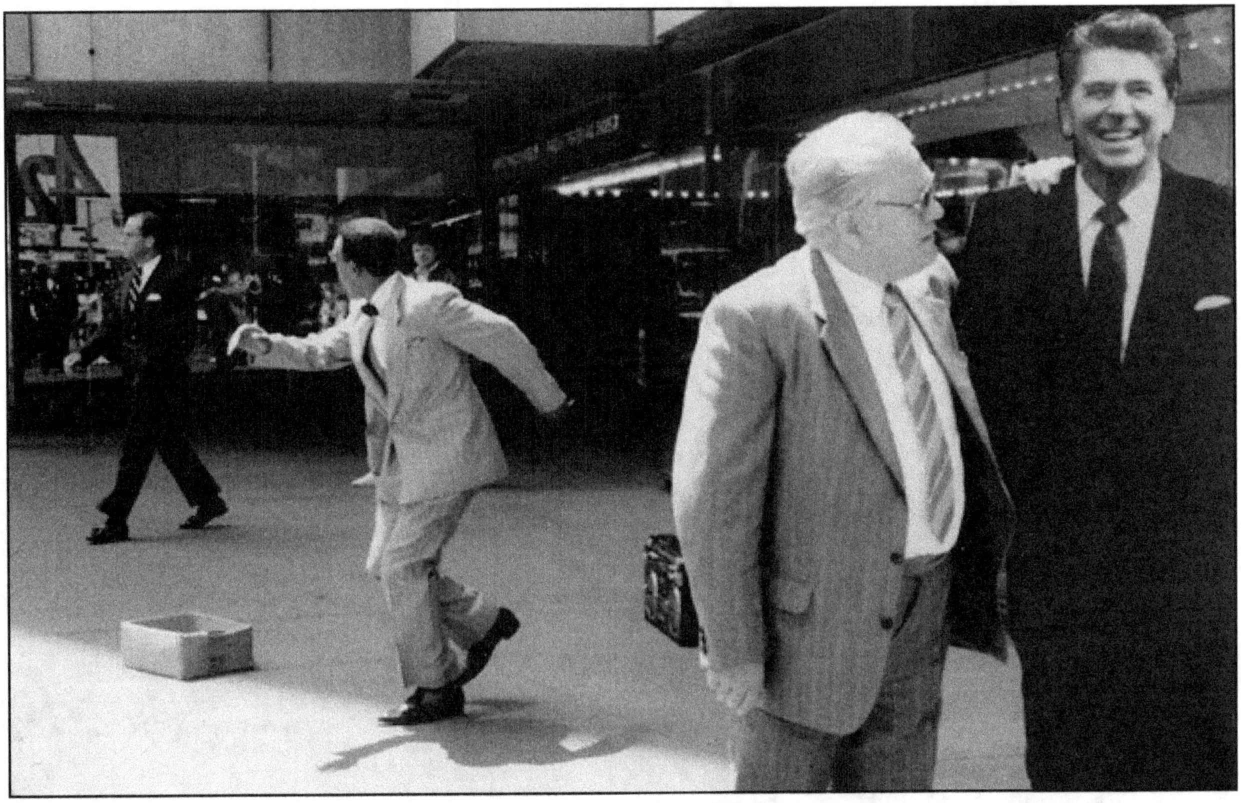

Everybody's gotta make a livin'

A photographer sets up a cutout of president Reagan outside the Marriot hotel on Broadway. Reagan was a very popular president, and this guy made a lot of money taking pictures of him posing with the tourists.

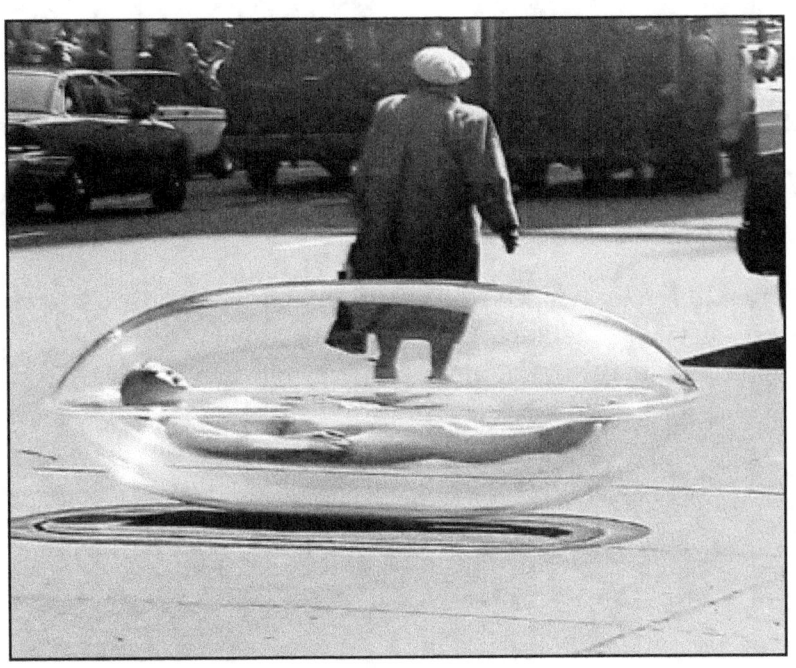

This performance artist set-up her "work of art" in the middle of Times Square. I imagine she thought that hoards of people would gather around discussing its purpose and the meaning of life. That's what performance art is supposed to do. Unfortunately, no one paid any attention to her.

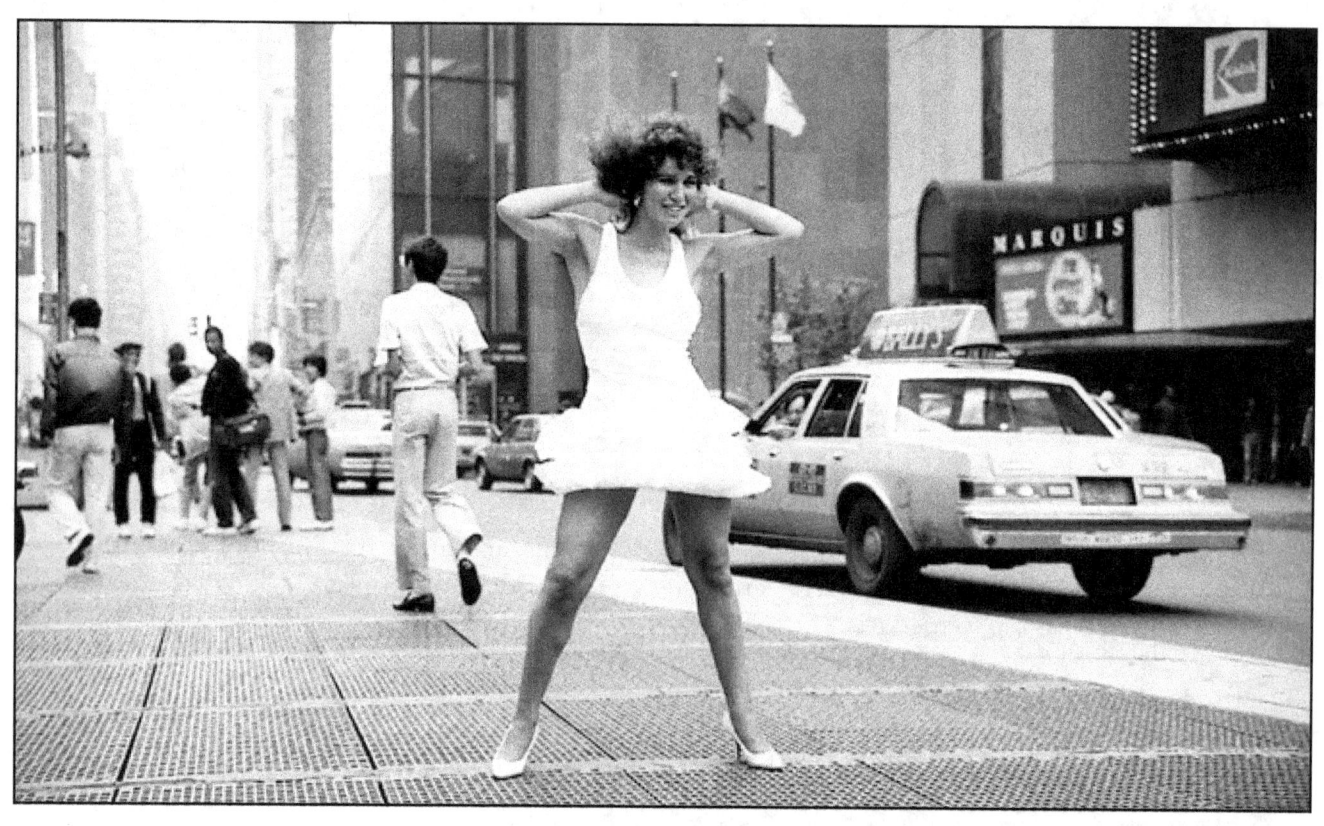

This leggy model, strikes a Marilyn Monroe type pose in the middle of Times Square

Right after I took this picture, this lady stepped backwards and both of her heels became stuck in the grating. Instead of taking a picture, I ran forward and helped her regain her balance. It was another indication that I was getting soft in my old age.

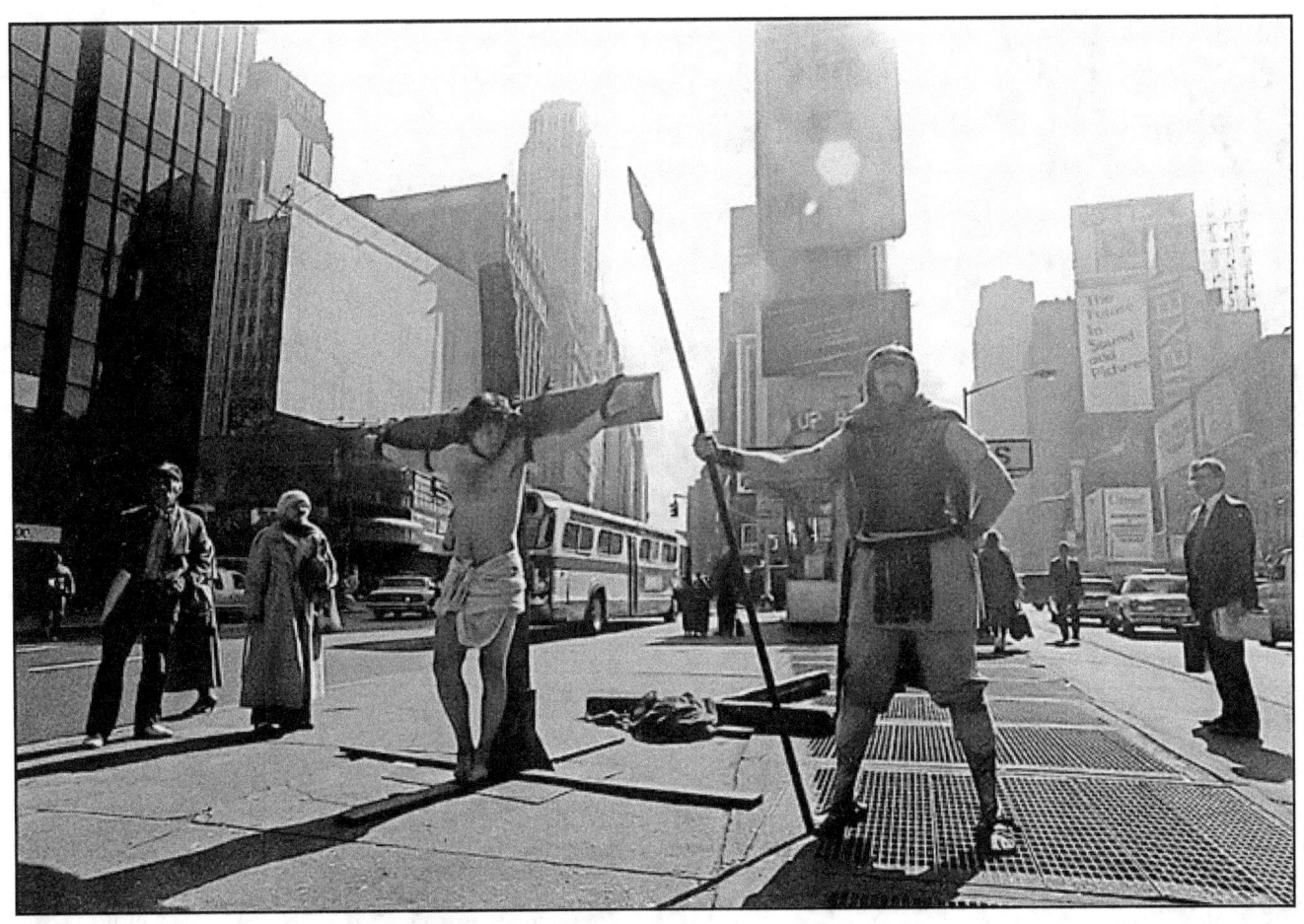

Good Friday in Times Square

Every year, this small group of devout Christians, stage a mock crucifixion in the middle of Times Square. They go to great lengths to make it look authentic, with a real cross and several actors dressed as soldiers. As you can see from this picture, very few people bother to watch. The original crucifixion probably had more spectators. I wonder what this says about the state of organized religion in this country today.

The Bible toting chain snatcher

It was in the middle of Times Square; at the TKTS booth were the tourists line-up to get cheap theater tickets. He was a young man with a bible in his hand, and he was spreading the word of the Lord. He was working the crowd like a pro, getting close to people, pressing the flesh, putting them at ease. What he was really doing was casing the crowd, looking for really good jewelry, not just the cheap knock-offs. He got close to one Japanese tourist who was standing right next to me. She was wearing an expensive gold chain. He asked her if she wanted world peace. She said, "Yes." He asked her if she would pray with him for world peace. She said, "Yes." He placed his hand on her shoulder; it was now just inches from the gold chain. He said to her, "Close your eyes and pray with me for world peace." As soon as she closed her eyes, he snatched the chain right off her neck. As he ran down the block, he opened the bible which was hollowed-out inside and threw the chain inside it. He made his escape down the subway. The whole thing was over in seconds. The young girl started crying because the chain cost her over two hundred dollars. Somebody in the line started a collection for her and she had the money back in just a few minutes.

A window washer and his guardian angel.

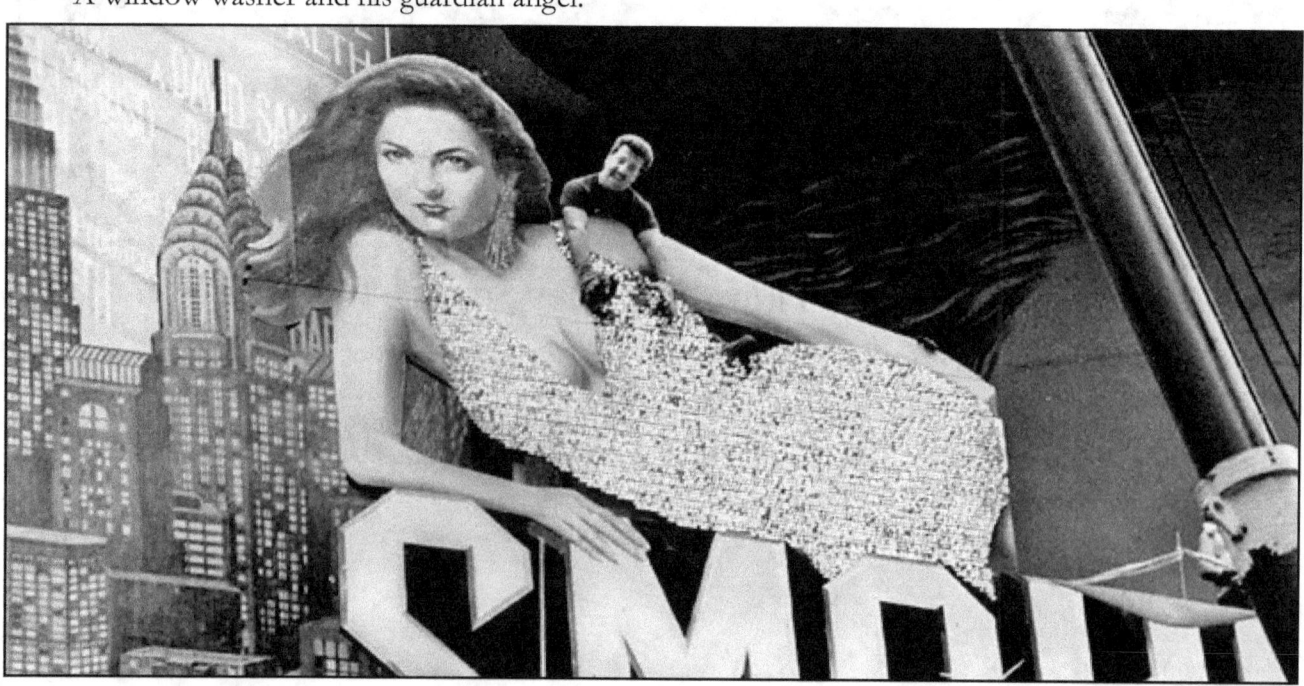

Times Square is a three dimensional space. You have to look up to fully appreciate it. The sign riggers are a bunch of show-offs. Often, they will interact with the signs at the request of the tourists.

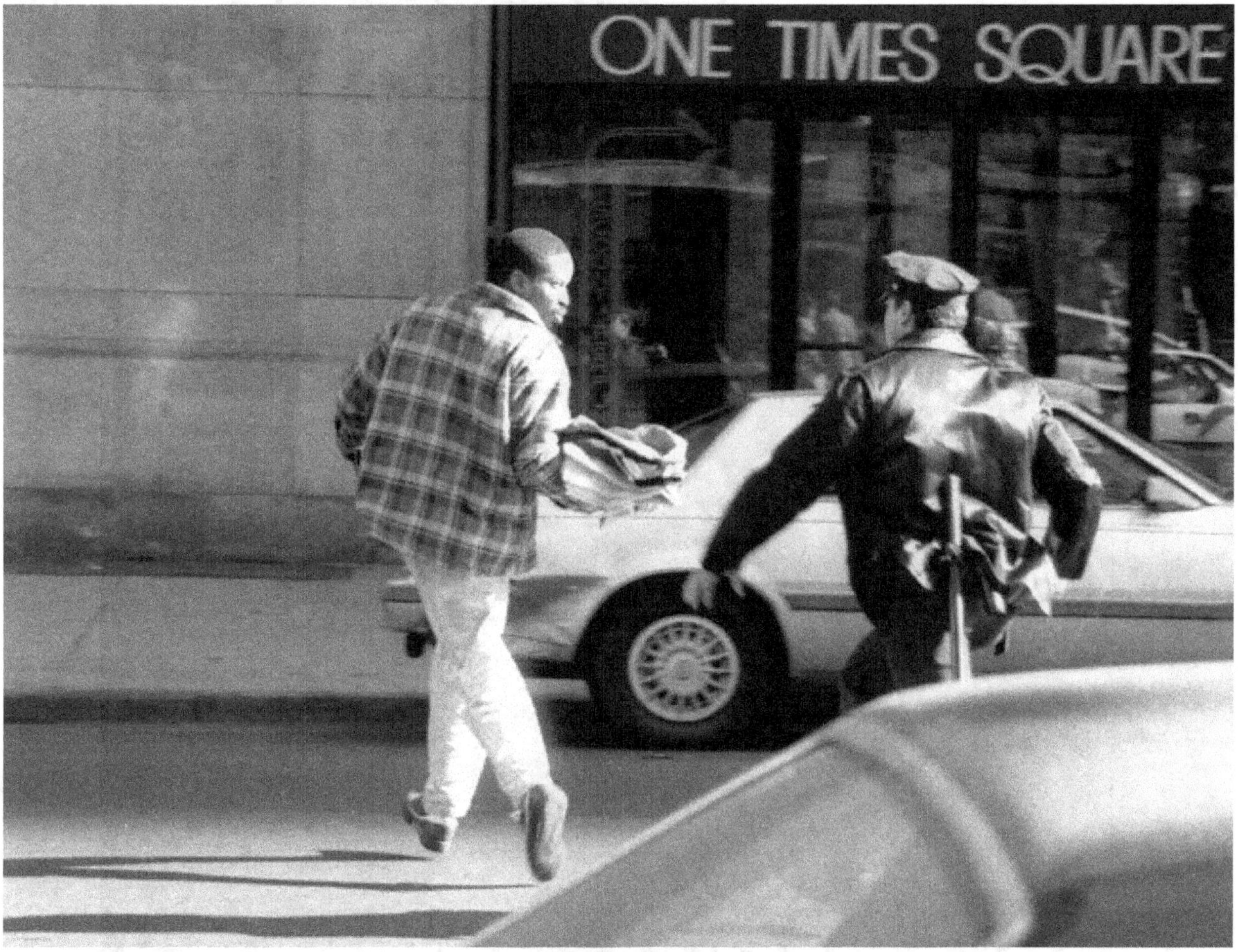

A young man is seen running from a store on 42nd St. He's holding a pile of shirts he just stole. A cop is right on his tail.

'Wilding'

In the 1990s, the word 'wilding' entered the lexicon. It was the term young people used, to describe the tactic of entering a store, all at once, and overwhelming the security guards with sheer numbers. Then they'd scoop-up piles of clothing and take off.

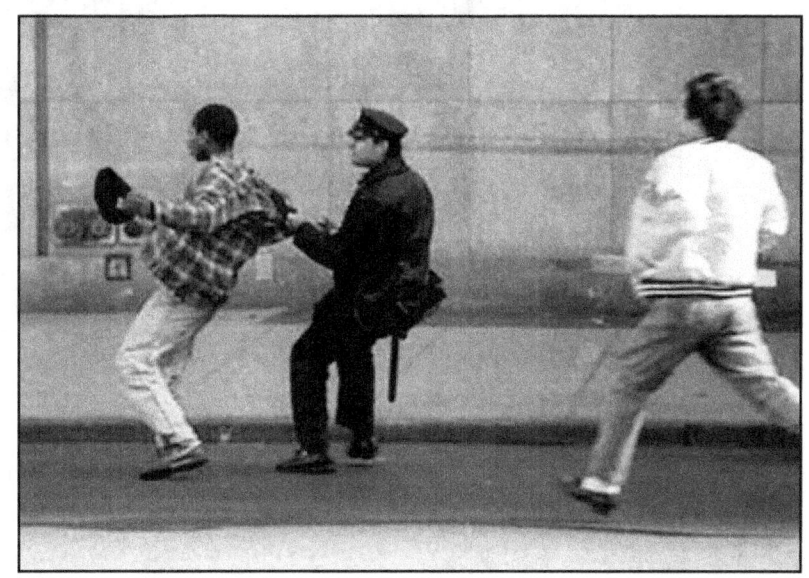

Here the cop makes the collar. The guy to the right is the store owner with a two by four in his hand.

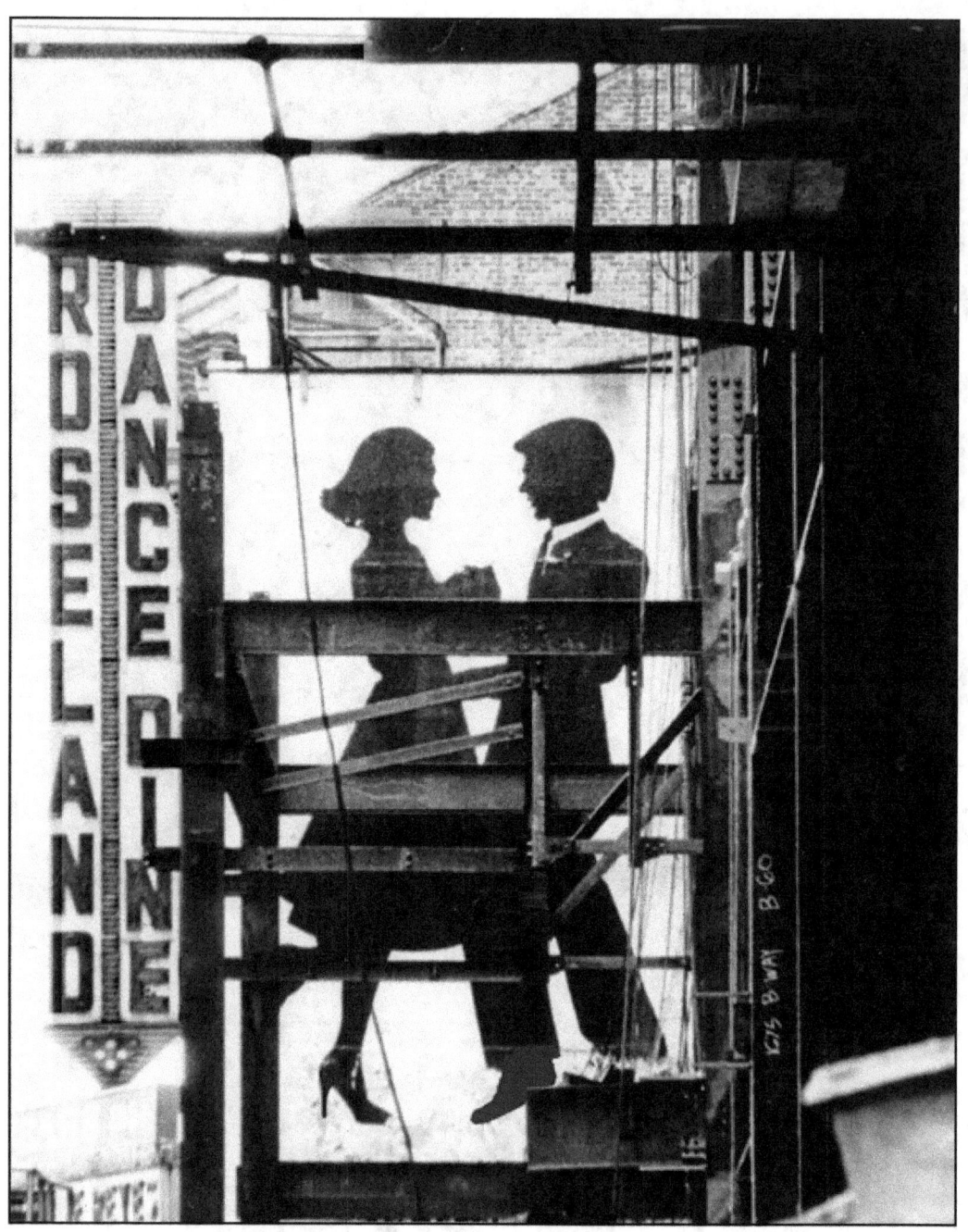

Roseland Dance Hall

The original Roseland Dance Hall opened in 1919 on 51st St. It specialized in ballroom dancing. During the Big Bands era of the 20s and 30s. Major stars played there, such as Louis Armstrong, Glenn Miller and Tommy Dorsey, to name a few. The original place was torn down in 1956, and the new Roseland opened on 52nd St. In the 80s, it started catering to the hip-hop and disco crowd. Trouble ensued, one kid was actually murdered on the dance floor. In the 90s, the building next door to it was demolished, revealing the old mural seen in the photo. It was a nostalgic reminder of the good old days when people actually touched when they danced.

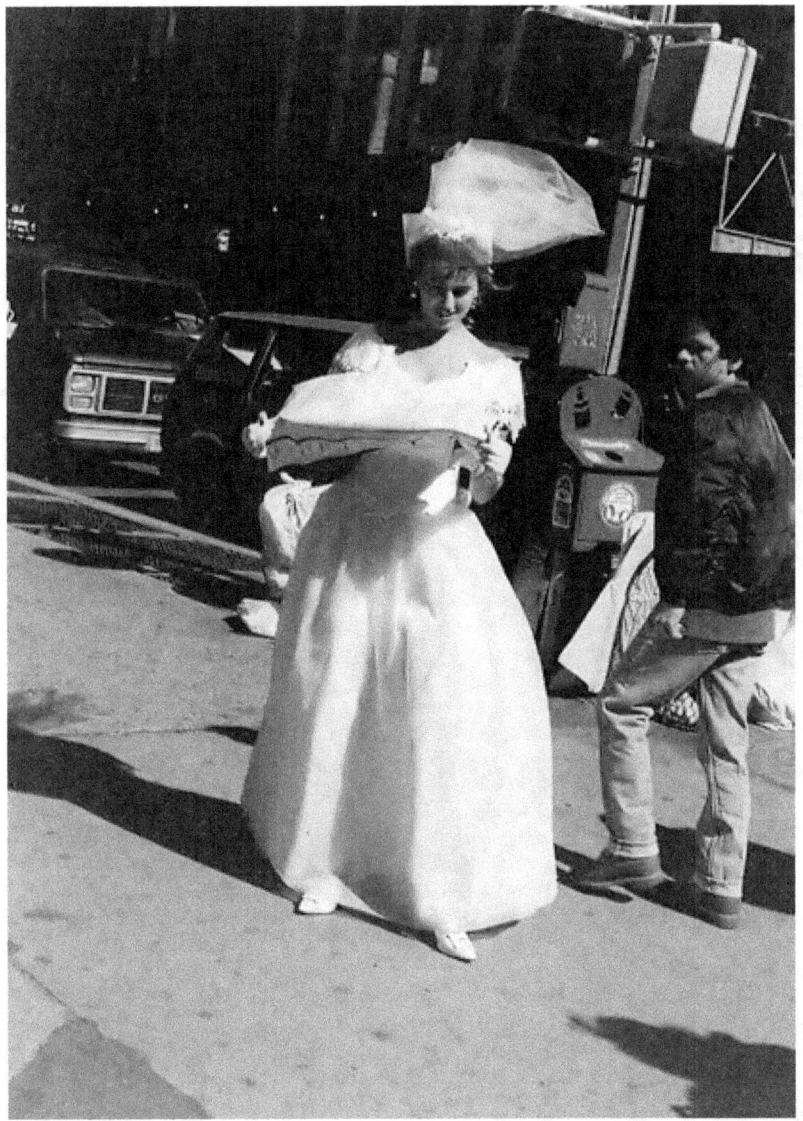

Get me to the church on time

    I was walking down Broadway one day and I see this young bride-to-be looking at a map. She seemed to be completely lost, people were asking her if she needed help. She politely declined. I thought it was funny, so I started taking pictures. Suddenly, some guy taps me on the shoulder and says to me:
- "Hey pal, you're standing right in the middle of our set."
- I said, "What do you mean 'set'?"
- "This is a photo shoot for a fashion magazine and you're standing right in the middle of everything."
- "You mean this isn't real?"
- "No, she's a model we're taking pictures of, and you're in the way."
- "Oh, I'm sorry" I said. I felt stupid and disappointed, I thought it was real.

Chapter 12 — *The tourists*

Tourism is New York City's largest industry. Over 60 million visitors come here every year. Most of them are from this country.

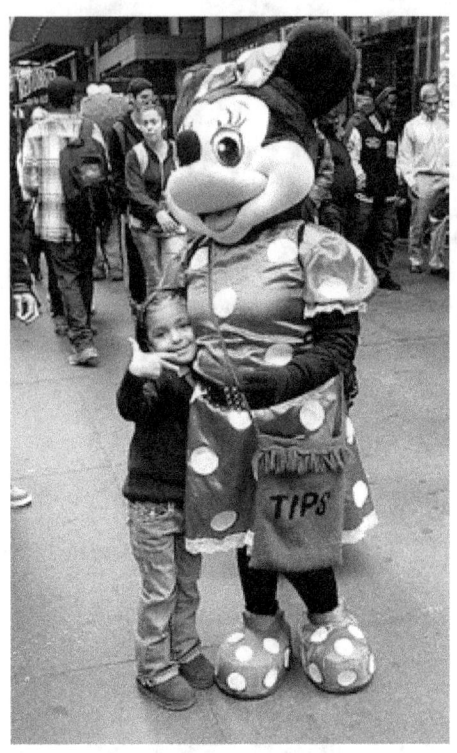

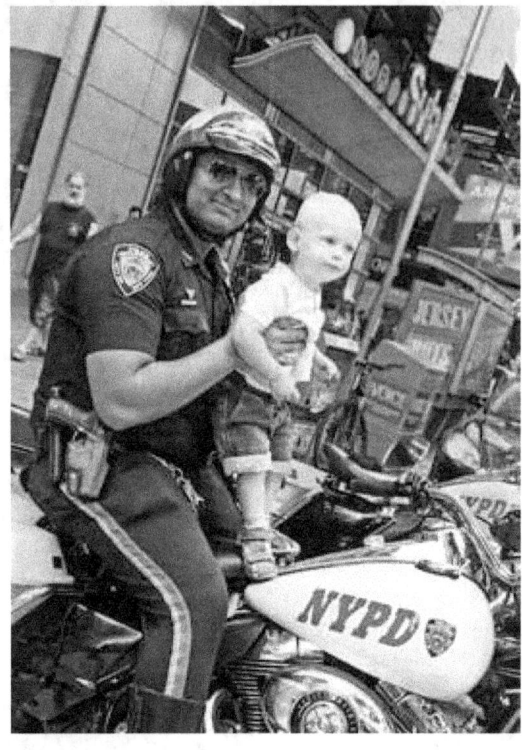

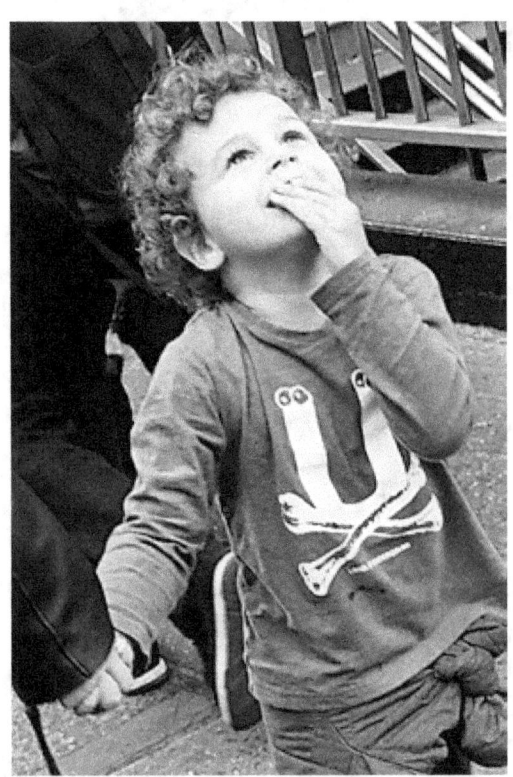

This boy is seeing the Empire State Building for the first time.

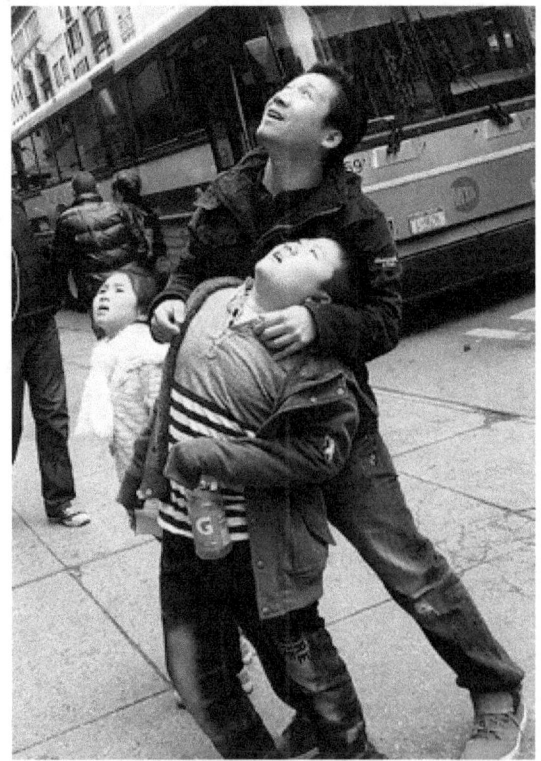

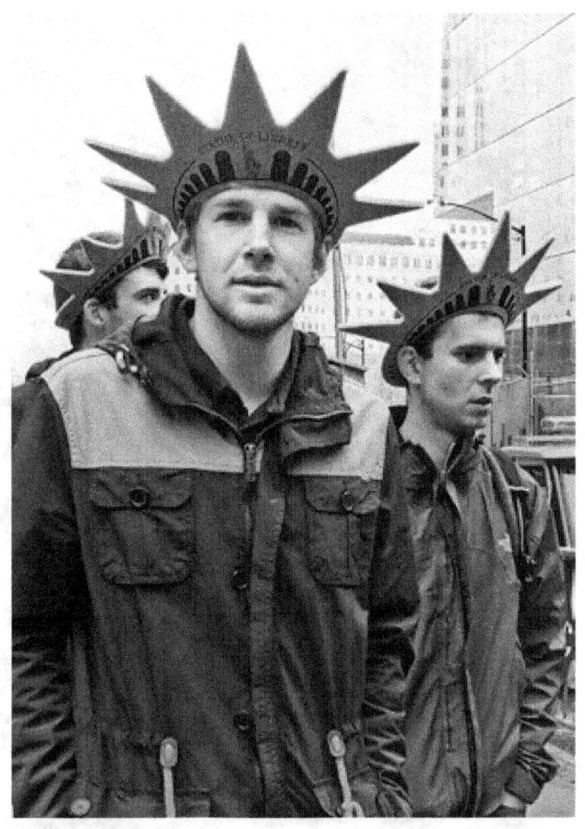
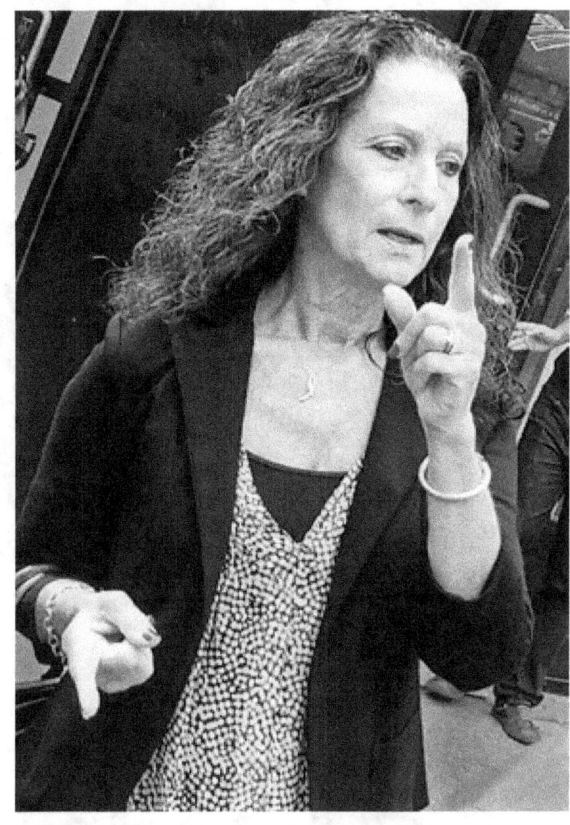
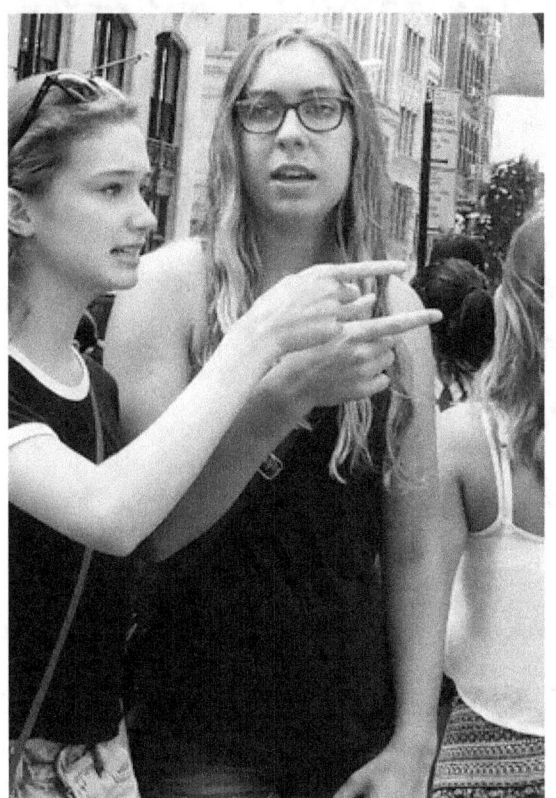
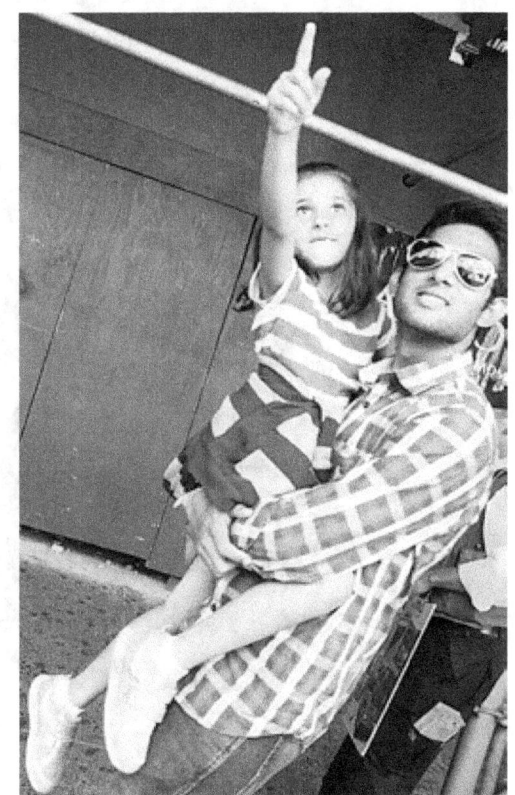

Tourists are always pointing

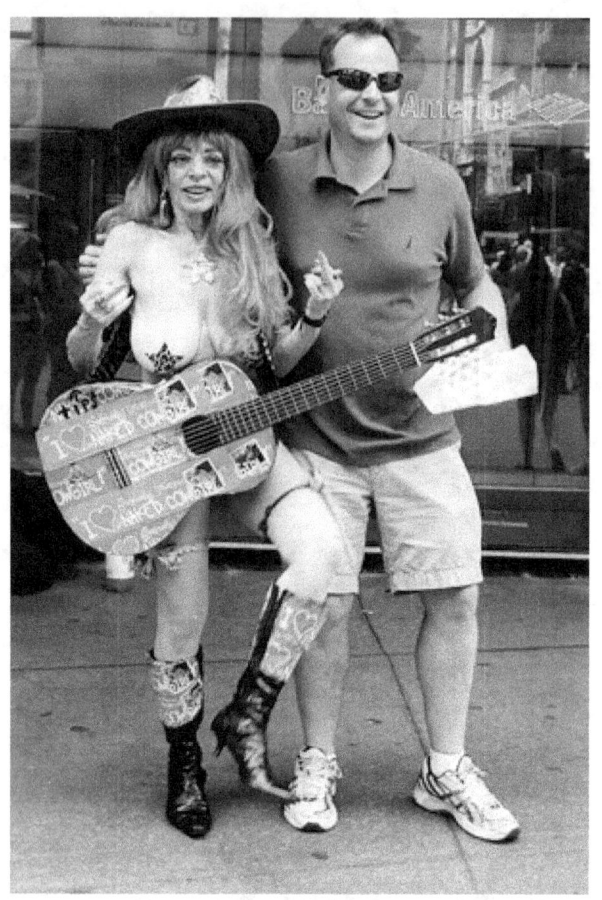
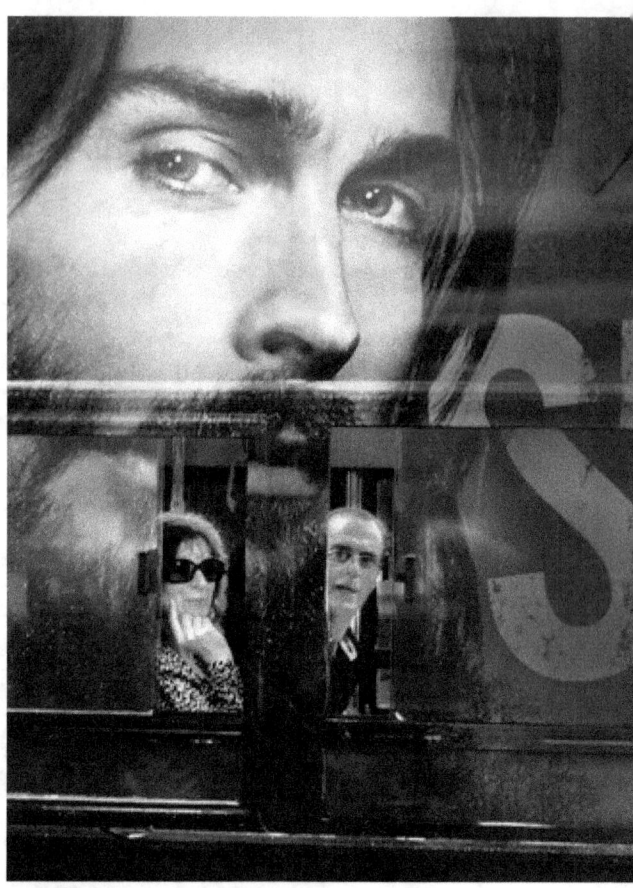

Official greeter in Times Square

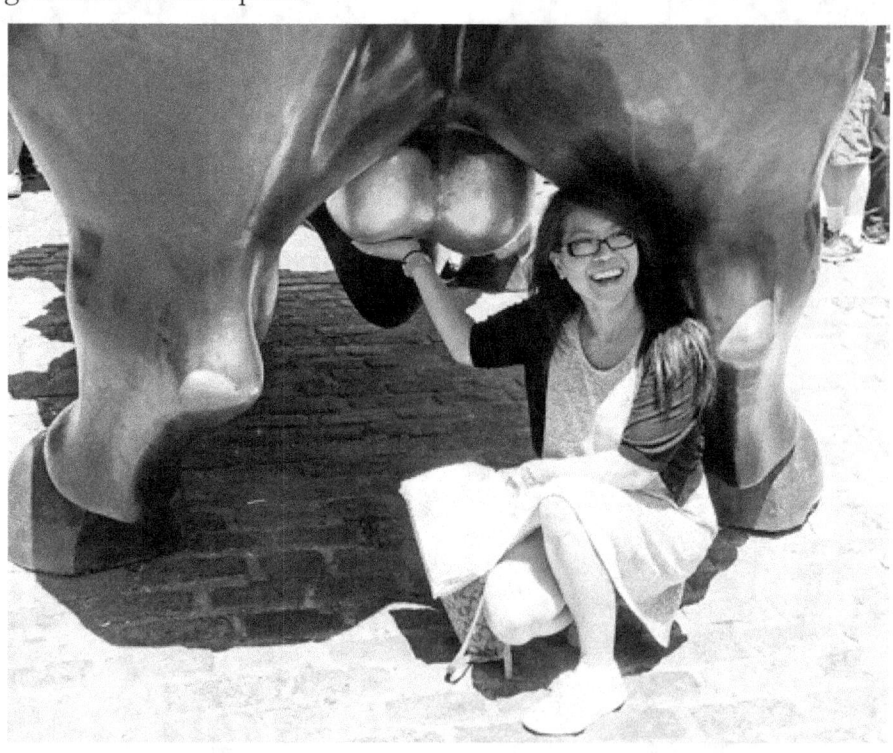

Tourist rubbing the testicles of the bull of Wall Street.

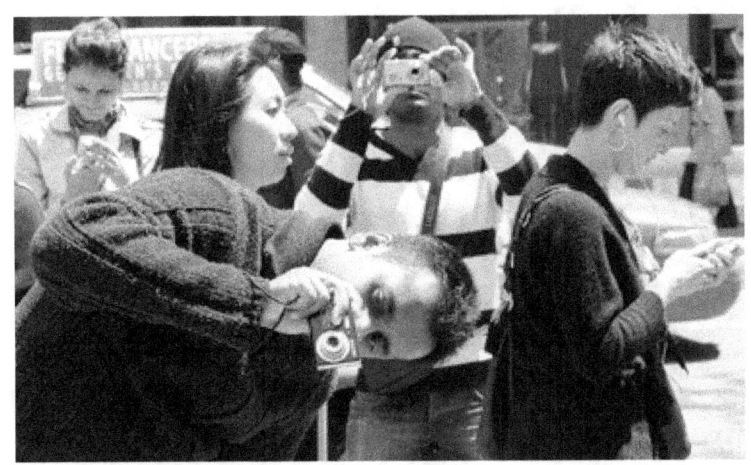
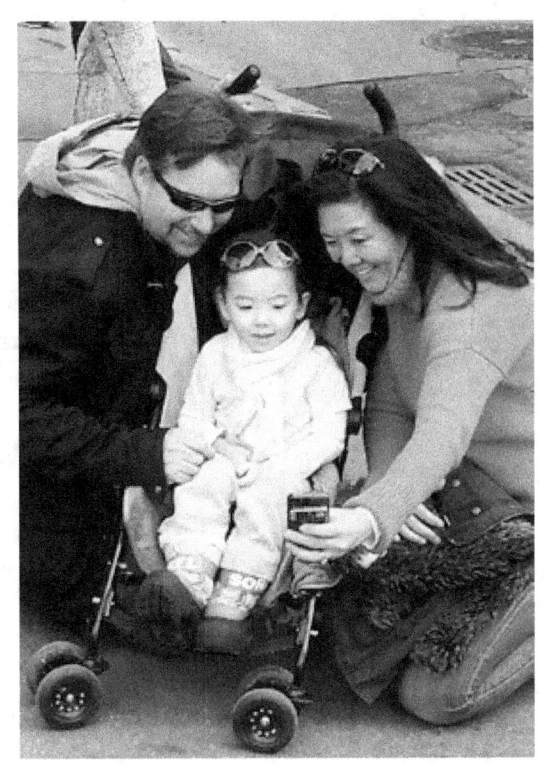
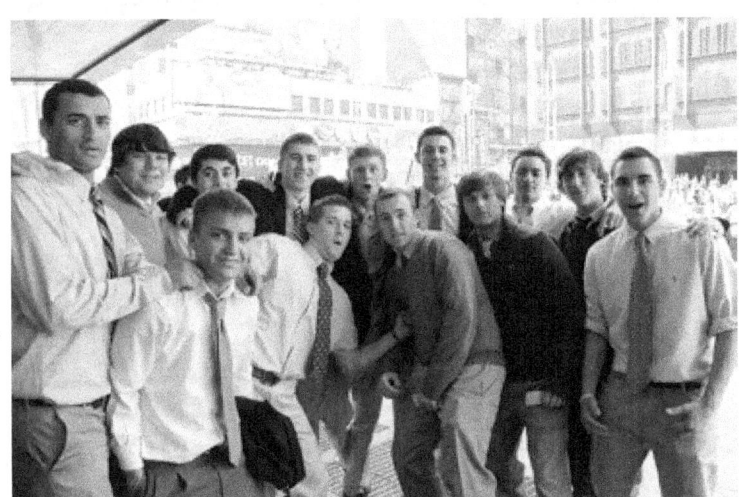
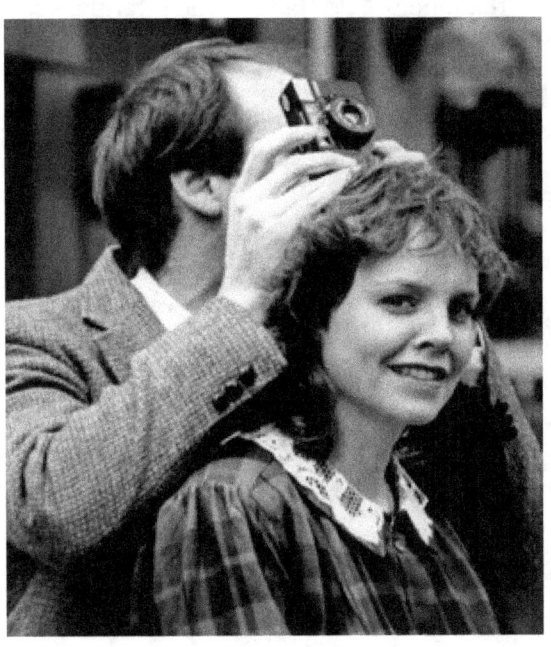
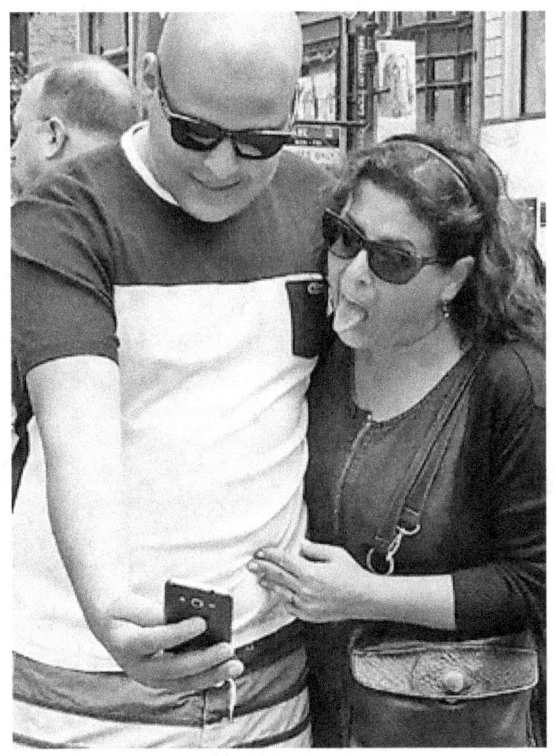

Chapter 13 — *Four more stories*

My date with a lipstick lesbian

I was sitting in a bar in Park Slope minding my own business, reading a magazine. She sat next to me. I could see from the corner of my eye that she was quite good looking, and stylish. She looked out of place, because in those days the women of Park Slope usually dressed like a bunch of bohemians left over from the Beatnik era. I didn't say anything to her; there were so many single women in the Slope that it was a buyers' market. Eventually, she started a conversation; she was new to the area and claimed to be an artist. That threw up a red flag. Most artists are nuts. So from that point on, I had my guard up. We talked for about an hour and the impression I got was that she was pretty level headed, had a good sense of humor, and most important of all, liked to cook. I asked her out to dinner for next week and she said "sure." She gave me her number and left.

A week later, I picked her up at her place. She had a small but tidy apartment. She looked great. She was dressed to kill. I asked to see some of her artwork. She said, "Not now, maybe later." That struck me as being odd. Artists are usually eager to show their work to anyone who will look. Another red flag went up. We walked to the restaurant. It was the best one in the Slope. I knew most of the staff there, so we got great seats and impeccable service. She was a good talker and a good listener. The conversation went smoothly for a first date. I was enjoying her company. Around the middle of the main course, I asked her very matter-of-factly if she was ever married. She said, "No. I'm a lesbian." Upon hearing these words I said to myself, "I don't believe this, here I am spending a small fortune on this broad and now she tells me she's a lesbian." There was a long silence then I said to her "You mean, you're bisexual" "No," she said, "I'm a lesbian." – Another long silence. I could see that she was looking at me intently; she was looking for some signs of emotion. This was the big payoff for her, to see the guy squirm, as he absorbed the awkward information presented to him. I wouldn't give her that satisfaction. I played it cool, I'm good at that, always have been. Why I didn't just summon the waiter over and ask for separate checks is beyond me. Or maybe I should have just thrown a glass of wine in her face!

After another long silence, I said to her, "So what are we doing here?" She said, "Why, we're having a good time, I enjoy your company, don't you enjoy mine?" She had a sly grin on her face; she was playing with me, the way a cat plays with a mouse just before killing it. I said to her, "We could've had a good time over a few slices of pizza too. This meal is going to set me back at least fifty bucks. "Well" she said, "You shouldn't have asked me out if you couldn't afford it." Now she was twisting the knife. She had all the answers at the ready. I realized that she probably pulled this stunt many times before. I was just her latest victim. "Whether I can afford it or not, has nothing to do with it," I said, "You clearly misrepresented yourself. When I asked you out, you had a duty to tell me about your sexual preferences. Not doing so was a lie of omission, it was unethical." "Why do men think that because a woman goes out with them, they're owed something," –she said- "I don't believe that," I said. Then I realized that by answering her I was just playing into her hands. This is what she wanted, conflict, and I wasn't going to give it to her. I paid the check and we left. The walk back to her place was long and icy. At her door, to my surprise, she invited me in to see her artwork. At this point, I had nothing to lose, so I said, "OK." Maybe I was hoping against hope that this whole thing was some sort of big joke and that she was going to yell "April fools," but no such thing happened. She made some coffee and brought out her artwork.

Up till this point I had taken her seriously. Her "artwork" changed all that. It was childish. There were six small paintings done on canvas, with acrylics. They all depicted Uncle Sam committing some unspeakable atrocity. There was Uncle Sam sitting on a woman, Uncle Sam eating the globe, Uncle Sam squeezing to death some poor third world peasants. This was clearly the work of a very angry person, angry at this country, its leaders, and probably by extension, all white men. Suddenly, I felt scared. This woman clearly had a ferocious hatred for men. I had just had some of her coffee. I wondered if she was capable of drugging me and then cutting me into little pieces the way they did in the movies. I just wanted to leave. As I was leaving, she asked me what I thought of her artwork. I said, "You need help, have a nice life."

A few weeks later I was walking down 7th Avenue and I spotted a picture of her taped to a lamppost. Under her picture, it said, "Wanted for fraud." Apparently, her latest victim decided to get back at her. These warning signs were all over the neighborhood. I removed it from the lamppost carefully and kept it as a memento. To this day when I get together with some old friends for a beer, inevitably one of the guys will say, "Nick, tell us about your date with the lezzy." I can laugh about it now, but at the time it wasn't funny, because after all was said and done, I really liked her.

The night I slept with a cat lady

It was a Tuesday night in December. It was beginning to snow. I was in a bar called Minsky's, in Park Slope. I was checking out the night life in the neighborhood because I was thinking of moving there. I was with one of my oldest and dearest friends. I don't want to embarrass him, so let's just call him George. I wanted his opinion about the women in the place. So I said, "McQuaid, what do you think of the women here?" He said that they look like a bunch of hippies and lesbians. He was right on both counts. This was in the late 70's, before Park Slope was overrun by yuppies. The entire neighborhood had the atmosphere of Greenwich Village in the 60's. That's what I liked about it, its informality.

There was a young lady sitting next to us. She was a good looking brunette with an Irish accent. Her name was Mary. I asked if she liked the neighborhood. She said she loved it because of the large selection of bars that lined 7th Avenue. We bought her a few drinks and then a few more. This lady had a hollow leg. I noticed that she had a smattering of cat hairs on her sweater, but didn't think anything of it. This oversight on my part, combined with one of George's bright ideas, would lead to the most torturous night of my life.

It was getting late and the snow was coming down really heavy. There must have been a foot on the ground by now. Mary seemed a little tipsy, so George asked her if she needed a ride home. She said, "Yes, thank you, I only live a few block away." We piled into his car and drove to her place. She lived on the third floor of a four story walkup. She got out of the car and seemed a bit unsteady on her feet. That's when George suggested that I walk her to her door. I reluctantly agreed to do it. I told George to wait for me, that I'll be right down. I helped her up to the third floor. We got to her door and she put the key into the lock, then she turns to me and says, in her lilting Irish accent, "Would you like to come in for a cup of tea?" I looked at her in the dim light of her hallway and she didn't look half bad. In a moment of weakness I said, "OK, but let me tell my friend not to wait for me." She said, "Use the window right here in the hallway, it overlooks the street." I opened the window and shouted down to George to not wait for me, that I was staying. He said, "Good luck, call me in the morning," and then drove away.

I returned to Mary and she opened the door to her apartment. It was dark inside. She turned on the light and that's when I saw them. Cats - dozens of them, all over the place, everywhere. I walked inside, there were cats on the bed, cats on the couch, cats on the chair. I was tripping over them. There were cats on the dining room table, cats under the table, cats on the kitchen counter. I tried to count them but it was hard because they kept moving around. They were on top of the refrigerator, in the kitchen sink, and on the window sills. I asked her how many cats she had. She said she didn't know. I sat down on the couch after shooing the cats off. There were cats on the coffee table, cats under the table, cats on the bookshelves. The best I could figure, she had around thirty six cats. I just stared at my feet and cursed out George under my breath for getting me into this fix. Mary asked me if I was OK, because my eyes were swelling. Then I started to sneeze like crazy. She gave me some drops for my eyes and some Dristan for the sneezing. It helped a lot. I asked to use her phone. I called a local car service. The dispatcher said, "forget it, not until the morning." There must have been two feet of snow on the ground by now. The nearest subway was ten blocks away and I wasn't wearing boots. I was stuck here for the night. Then I realized that I was freezing. I said, "Mary, don't you have any heat?" She said that it went off at ten o'clock. "Great" -I thought- "I'm gonna freeze my ass off all night."

    She made some tea and sat next to me on the couch. I noticed that the tea had cat hairs floating in it. I could see that she was a lot older than I had thought. I was in my late twenties. She must have been pushing forty. I asked her why she had so many cats. She said, "I didn't plan it this way, it just happened. I just had a few at first but they kept multiplying. But now I like having them around. I'm lonely and they keep me company. In Ireland I had plenty of friends, but here it's different. I don't have many friends. That's why I go to the bars every night and take drink." I said, "Mary, you're caught in a vicious circle. No man is going to put up with all these cats." "I don't give a shit about men;" -she screamed- "they all stink." And then she started crying. She must have cried a gallon of tears on my shoulder that night. I had to listen to all the stories of all the men who had ever done her wrong.

    Around 3 a.m., I tried to get some sleep. I got into bed with her, fully clothed, shoes and all. She called me a barbarian for wearing my shoes to bed. I told her, "I'm sorry Mary, I'm freezing." I tried to sleep but it was impossible because of the cold and the sneezing, and the itching from all the cat hairs that were stuck to every square inch of my body. I had cat hair in my ears, my eyes, and my teeth. I had cat hair between my toes, under my nails, and up my nostrils. And then she started snoring, not soft, little femenine snores, but big, honking, drunken truck driver snores. It was the worst night's sleep I've ever had, bar none.

    Mercifully, the dawn finally came. I watched the sun come up through her kitchen window. The scene outside was beautiful, the fresh fallen snow made Park Slope look like a Christmas card. I tiptoed out without waking her up. I left her to her cats. I walked the ten blocks to the subway. I was completely covered with cat hairs. When I got onto the packed subway car, people began to sneeze and everyone gave me a wide berth. I also got a lot of dirty looks. I moved to Park Slope shortly after that. I would run into Mary all the time and we became good friends. Till this day, whenever I see a cat, I think of her.

Phil and Richie hit Times Square

A friend of mine named Phil came to me one day and says, "Hey Nick, you hang out in Times Square a lot, you know where I can go for some girls." I said, "Phil, do I look like a pimp? I don't go to those places, I have a full time girlfriend. Why don't you get yourself one?" Then Phil says, "I have no time for broads. I just want something quick and easy, with girlfriends you gotta talk to them afterwards." I knew Philly for years. He was a nice kid, but he wasn't the sharpest knife in the drawer. "Fast Frankie goes to those places." I said, "I'll tell you what he told me."

"There are plenty of places on 8th Avenue in the forties, but don't go at night, and don't go alone. Plus, don't ever give money to anyone on the street, or to the girls themselves, for that matter. You only pay the guy at the door. Who are you going to bring with you?" I asked. "My cousin Richie," he said. "Oh great," I thought "another brain surgeon." This thing was going to end in disaster, I just knew it. I said, "Listen, if you're going to go through with this, make sure you have your wits about you. It's dangerous around there, even in the day time. There are con-men all over the place." "No, I'll be careful Nick. Thanks for the info."

I ran into Phil about a week later. I asked how his trip to Times Square went. "Ah…not too good, " he said. He was looking down at his feet. He was clearly embarrassed, "Me and Richie were walking up 8th Avenue, when this guy comes up to us. He was a black guy from Brooklyn named Tyrone. He had on one of those super-fly coats and lots of jewelry, like in the movies. He asked us if we were looking for girls. I said 'Yeah,' 'Well, I got 'em,' he said 'in every shape, size, and color and they're all gorgeous and clean. We run a clean operation. Our girls are right off the farm, if you know what I mean. Not like these skanky old whores peddlin' their asses on the street.' "Then I asked him if we can get BJ's" said Phil. 'Sure,' Tyrone said, 'We got one girl named Darlene, who can suck the brass off a doorknob. And today we have a special, you get a free glass of wine, a free back-rub, a free shower, and a free whirlpool, all for only twenty dollars.' 'Wow, that sounds great,' I said, 'let's do it.' 'First, let me ask you something,' Tyrone said, 'Is this the first time you've been to 8th Avenue looking for girls?' 'Yeah.' I said. 'Well,' Tyrone said, 'let me warn you, there are lots of con-men out here looking to rip you off. Don't ever give money to anyone on the street. I ain't gonna take none of your money. That's how you know I'm honest.'

"So, we go to this place on 8th Avenue and 44th Street. We can see on the top floor a big neon sign of a naked chick, you know, the one with the tits that sway back and forth. And there were go-go girls dancing in the window, they were gorgeous. So, Tyrone tells us to walk up to the fourth floor and pay the guy at the door twenty dollars." 'Oh, I forgot one thing,' Tyrone said, 'You have to leave your wrist watches with me for safe keeping. You see, you can't wear them in the whirlpool, the hot water will ruin them. If you take them off up there, the girls might try to steal them. These girls might be cute, but they ain't too honest. I'll give you a receipt for them, this way, when you come down, I'll give you your watches back.' "It sounded reasonable, so we gave him our watches and he gave us some receipts for them."

"So, me and Richie walked up to the fourth floor and when we get there, we can see in, and there are half naked women all over the place, and they were knock outs. Then the guy at the door says, gentlemen, 'it's a hundred dollars each to get in.' I said - 'A hundred dollars! The guy downstairs said twenty dollars.' 'We got no guy downstairs,' the doorman said. I said, 'Tyrone, the guy who brought us here.' 'I don't know no Tyrone,' the doorman said, 'what are you gonna do, are you coming in or not.' So, me and Richie ran downstairs and Tyrone is gone." At this point I started laughing, then I said, "So, you didn't get laid, and you lost your watches too." "No," Phil said, "I'll get my watch back." "How do you figure that?" I said. He took his wallet out and removed a small piece of paper from it. "Look," he said, "I still got the receipt." Poor Phil, he was clueless. For years after that, people would still ask him if he had his receipt.

Paulie and the cleaning lady

Paulie was a retired fireman who lived in Bay Ridge. We would hang out in the same watering holes, so eventually I got to know him. He was a cultured man who loved the opera and classical music. He would often go to Carnegie Hall and to the theater. He was stimulating to talk to because of his wide range of interests. He was in his mid-fifties. He was short and chubby, with an impish little grin. He always looked like he was guilty of something. He would constantly complain about how small his pension was compared to some of his fellow firemen. He claimed that most of them became disabled from smoking crack, and not from the smoke inhaled at fires.

Paulie was extremely fond of beer and would sit for hours downing Budweisers at one of several neighborhood bars. It was at one of these spots that he met her. She was a very attractive Russian woman in her mid-thirties. She had short blond hair and blue eyes. Her figure was ample but not fat. Her name was Svetlana. Paulie liked her at first sight. They started talking and soon discovered that they had many things in common. Both loved classical music and the opera, and they were both history buffs. Paulie noticed that she didn't drink much, a rarity for a Russian girl. Then she started delving into his personal life. He told her that he lived alone, right up the block and he didn't have a girlfriend. Svetlana then revealed that she made a living by cleaning people's apartments. "Maybe I can clean your apartment once a week. I also do laundry and cook too. I provide all kinds of services, maybe I could give you a package deal." Paulie was genuinely interested. He could use a little female companionship once in a while. And who knew what other "services" would be included in the package deal. She suggested that they go to his apartment right now, so that she could give him an estimate. They finished their drinks and left.

Paulie was having the weirdest dream. He dreamt that he was lying on his back, on the bottom of a large shoe box. The inside of the shoe box was all white and cold. His head was throbbing. He tried to sit up, but his body wouldn't obey his commands. He rolled his head to the left, then to the right. Everything was white and blurry. Slowly, little by little, he realized that he wasn't dreaming at all. He was awake, lying on his back, in the middle of his living room. His breathing was labored. This was not an ordinary hangover. He felt as if he had been drugged. He slowly sat up and looked around. His entire apartment was empty. His couch and the coffee table were gone. His TV and computer were gone. His dining room furniture was gone. He was sitting on the bare floor. They even took his rug. He staggered into the kitchen. The microwave, the toaster oven, and the coffee maker, were all gone. He worked his way to the bathroom. At least they left him his toothbrush. He looked for the phone, but that was gone too.

He knocked on his neighbor's door and asked for help. The detectives showed up and they immediately knew what happened. They told Paulie that he was the latest victim of a group of Russian criminals who drugged people and then cleared out their entire apartments. The blond with the blue eyes was part of the group. "Svetlana was in on this?" Paulie asked, "Yeah," The detective said, "she's the ringleader. She's the one who drugged you. "I can't believe it," Paulie said, "she knew all about Stravinsky and Tchaikovsky and Strauss and she's a criminal?" "I'm afraid so," the detective said. Paulie was shocked. He didn't care about the missing furniture. It was Svetlana's betrayal that really got to him.

So what does this broken, devastated, shell of a man do? He goes out and tells the whole world about it. He goes from bar to bar, recounting the whole sordid mess, blow by blow, to anyone who would listen. People were in stitches, everyone laughing at his expense, but he didn't mind. He knew it was a funny story and Paulie liked to make people laugh. They could take his couch, his TV, even the rug right off the floor, but there was one thing they couldn't take, and that was Paulie's sense of humor.

Chapter 14

Welcome to 'The Deuce'

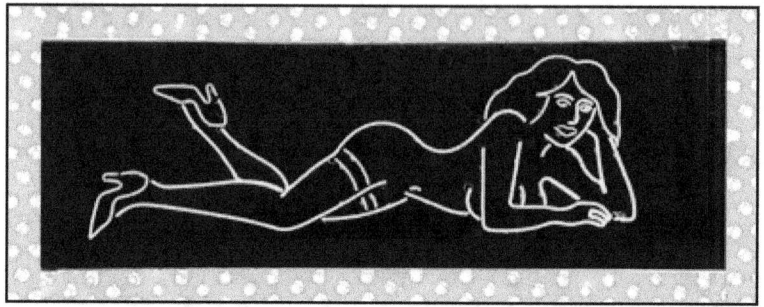

No one who hangs out on 42nd St. calls it that, they call it 'The Deuce.'

Drug dealers, drug addicts, hookers, pimps, and Johns. Con artists, chain snatchers, and every kind of pervert you could imagine. All jammed together on one block. It was by any measure, the absolute sleaziest street in the whole city, -and I loved it. If you couldn't get good shots here, hang it up, do something else with your time, like collecting stamps or something. However, if you wanted to survive, you had to obey the unwritten rules:
1. Don't stop walking. 2. Don't talk to anyone. 3. Don't make eye contact with anyone.

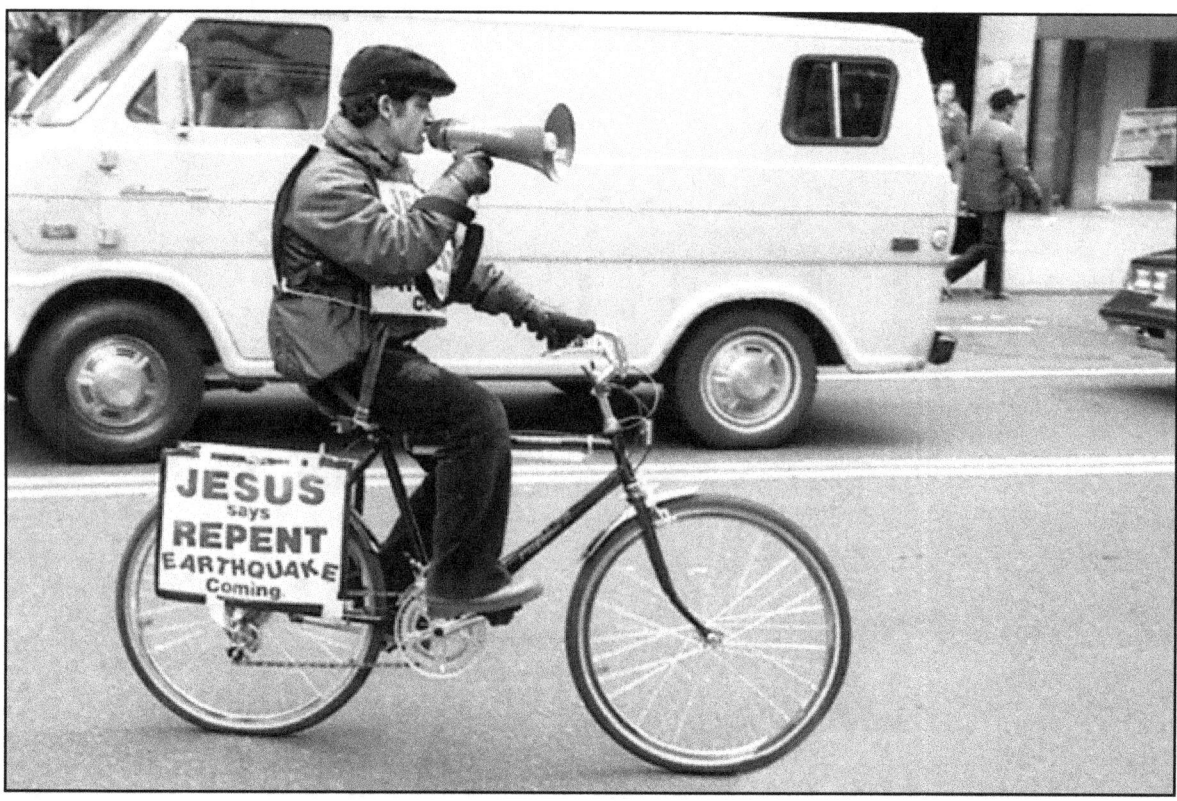

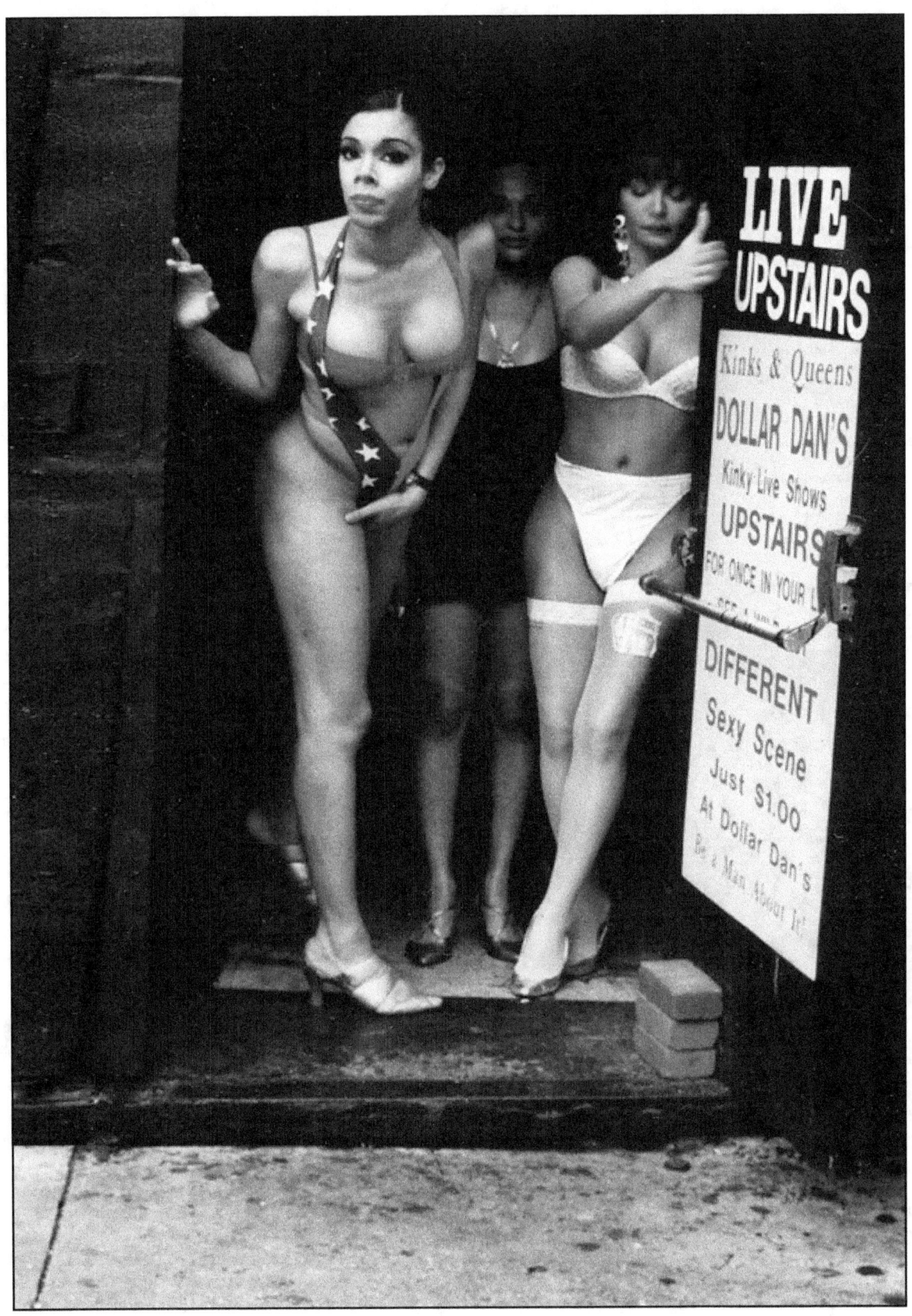

Peep show girls

Jesus vs. the Mafia

Back in the 60s and 70s, the porn industry in Times Square was run by the Mafia. Periodically, religious and civic organizations would parade up and down 42nd St., demanding that the street be cleaned up. Some of these 'Jesus freaks', as they were called, could be very pushy. One guy walked into a porno store and started throwing handfuls of girly magazines onto the street while screaming 'It's tempation, it's tempation.' Then he throws a whole magazine rack out the door. Then the store owner throws him out the door. The owner, who is really big, and really mad, hits him over the head with the magazine rack. Now this guy is rolling on the ground, amongst all these girly magazines and screaming for Jesus to help him. The owner says, 'Ain't that just like Jesus, he's never around when you need him,' then he hits him over the head again with the magazine rack. At this point, I raised my camera to take a picture, and the owner says to me, 'You take a picture, and I'll shove that camera down your throat.' I lowered the camera. The cops finally came and broke it up.

I scored it: Mafia 1 - Jesus 0.

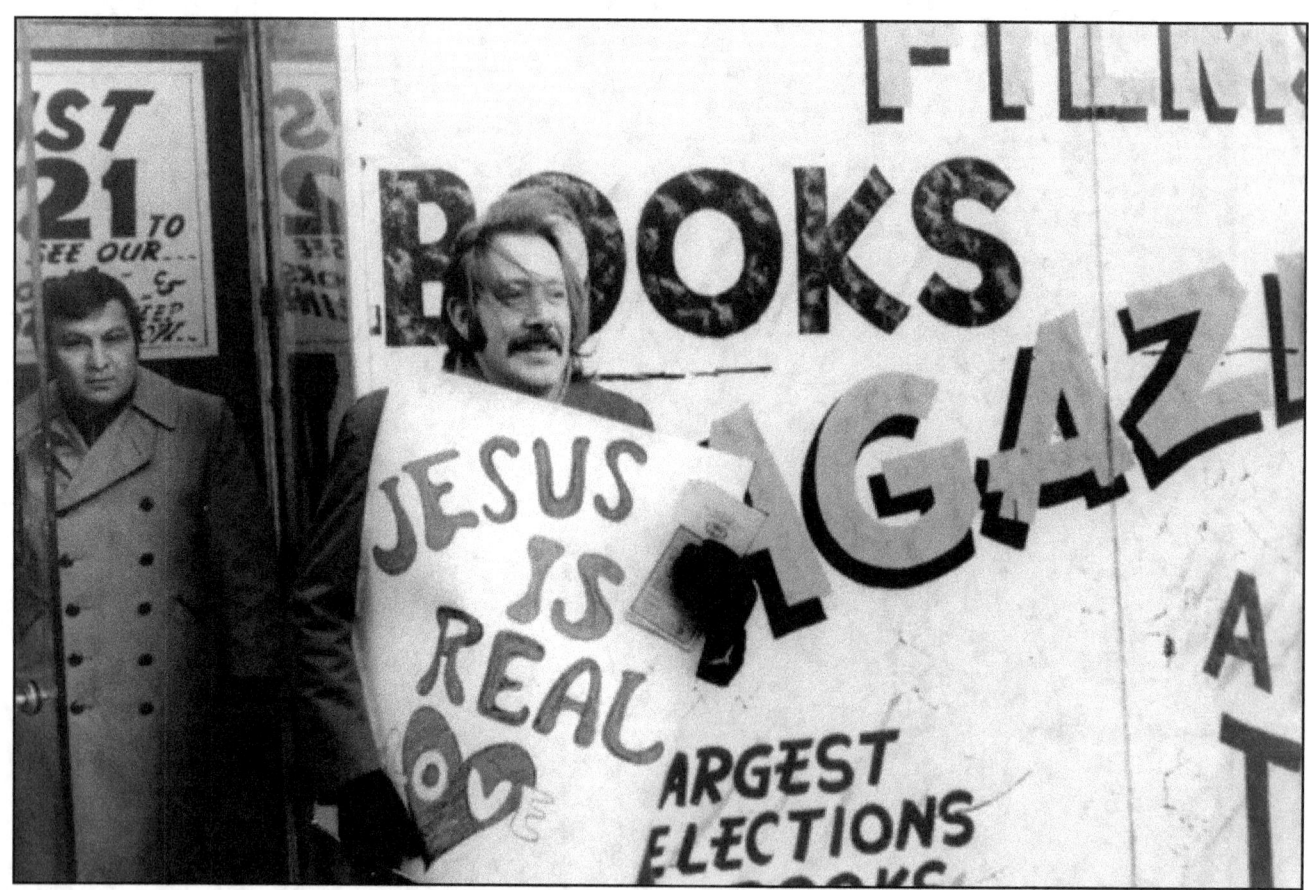

A Jesus freak demonstrates in front of a porno store.

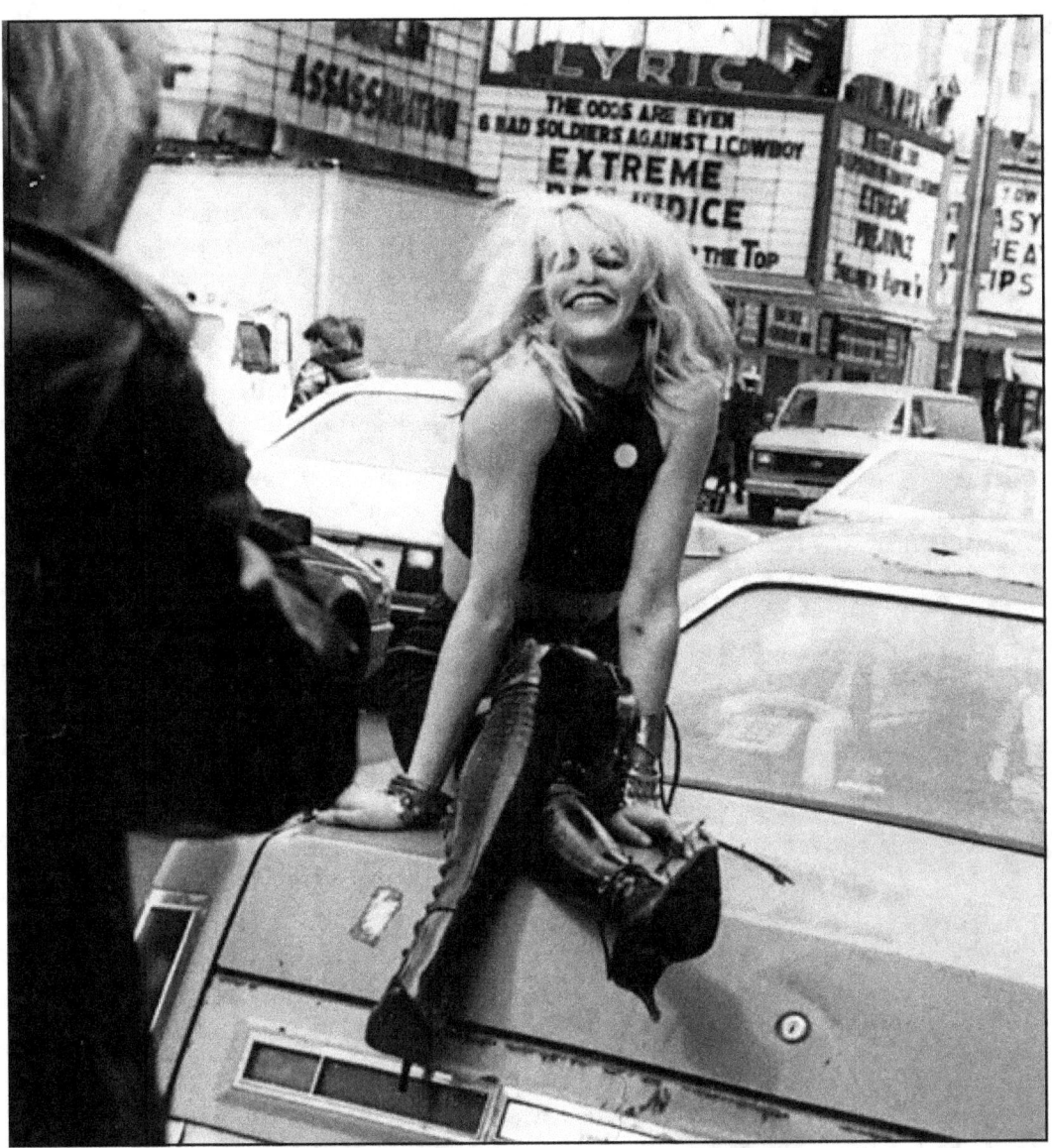

A New Starlet Comes to Town

    Every year, thousands of runaways and young people from the rest of the country come to New York seeking their fortunes. Some of these young people, out of desperation, resort to working in the sex industry, in the Times Square area. At the Port Authority Bus Terminal, teams of professional recruiters are constantly on the look-out for desperate kids to take advantage of.

    This young lady just hit town, and her 'agent' is taking pictures of her on 42nd St. She already has suspicious looking bruises on her left forearm, a tell-tale sign of intravenous drug use. Someone asked her what her stage name was. It was so filthy, I wouldn't repeat it here.

Drug bust on the Deuce

These are the first pictures I ever had published. I went to the Times first, since they were just a block away. I couldn't even get past the doorman (more on that later.) So I went to the Post, they were very receptive. They developed the film as I waited. When I saw the prints, I knew I had something. I signed some forms giving them permission to use the pictures. They wouldn't tell me anything else. 'Call us tomorrow' they said. On the way out one of the staff photographers pulled me aside and said, "they liked your shots, guaranteed they're going to use them."

I couldn't sleep that night. I felt like a kid on Christmas Eve. I got up early the next morning and headed to the corner candy store. There it was, my picture, on the front page of the Post. The store owner who knew me said, 'Nick, are those your pictures in the Post?' I said, 'Yeah!' He handed me a copy of the paper and a pen. 'Sign it,' he said. It was the beginning of a very strange day.

"Everybody should be famous for 15 minutes"

-Andy Warhol

I went back to the Post that day to pick up my negatives. They were very nice to me, people were congratulating me and I signed more papers. It was still early so I headed uptown. I stopped at a newstand on the Deuce to get some gum. The owner said, 'Camera-man' sign me a paper. Those were good shots you got yesterday. I saw the whole thing. I said, 'Thank you' then I asked 'What did you call me?', 'Camera-man', he said. 'Everyone on the Deuce calls you that. That's your handle, don't you know that?' 'No, I didn't.' I felt stupid. I had a nickname and didn't even know about it. As the day wore on more and more people would stop me and congratulate me. People who were total strangers. I was shocked. I thought I was anonymous. It's so crowded in midtown. I thought I did a good job of blending into the background, apparently not. It seemed as if half of Time Square knew exactly who I was.

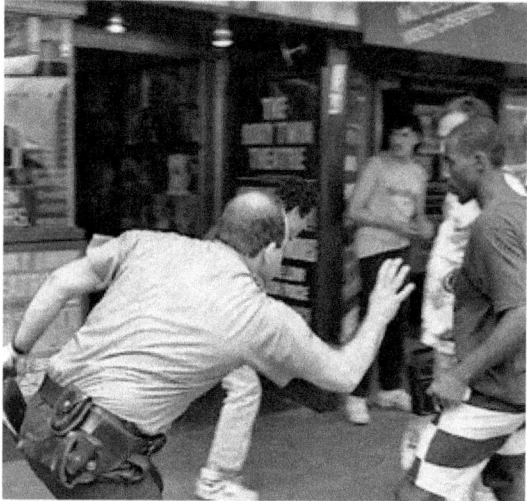

Officer Pierno frisks a suspected drug dealer on 42nd street near 7th avenue.

The suspect breaks away and bolts down the street.

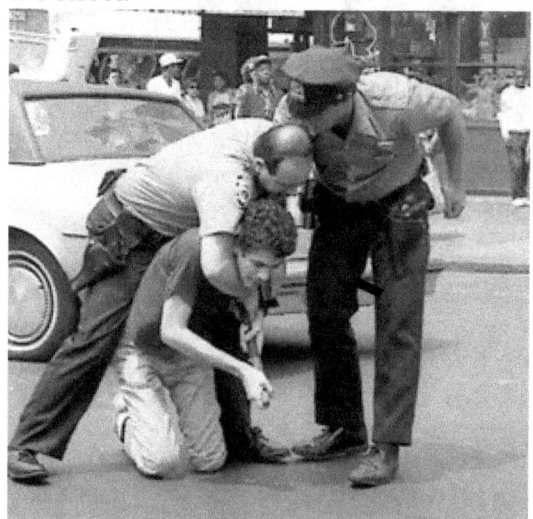

Officer Lowney intercepts him at the corner of 8th avenue and 42nd street.

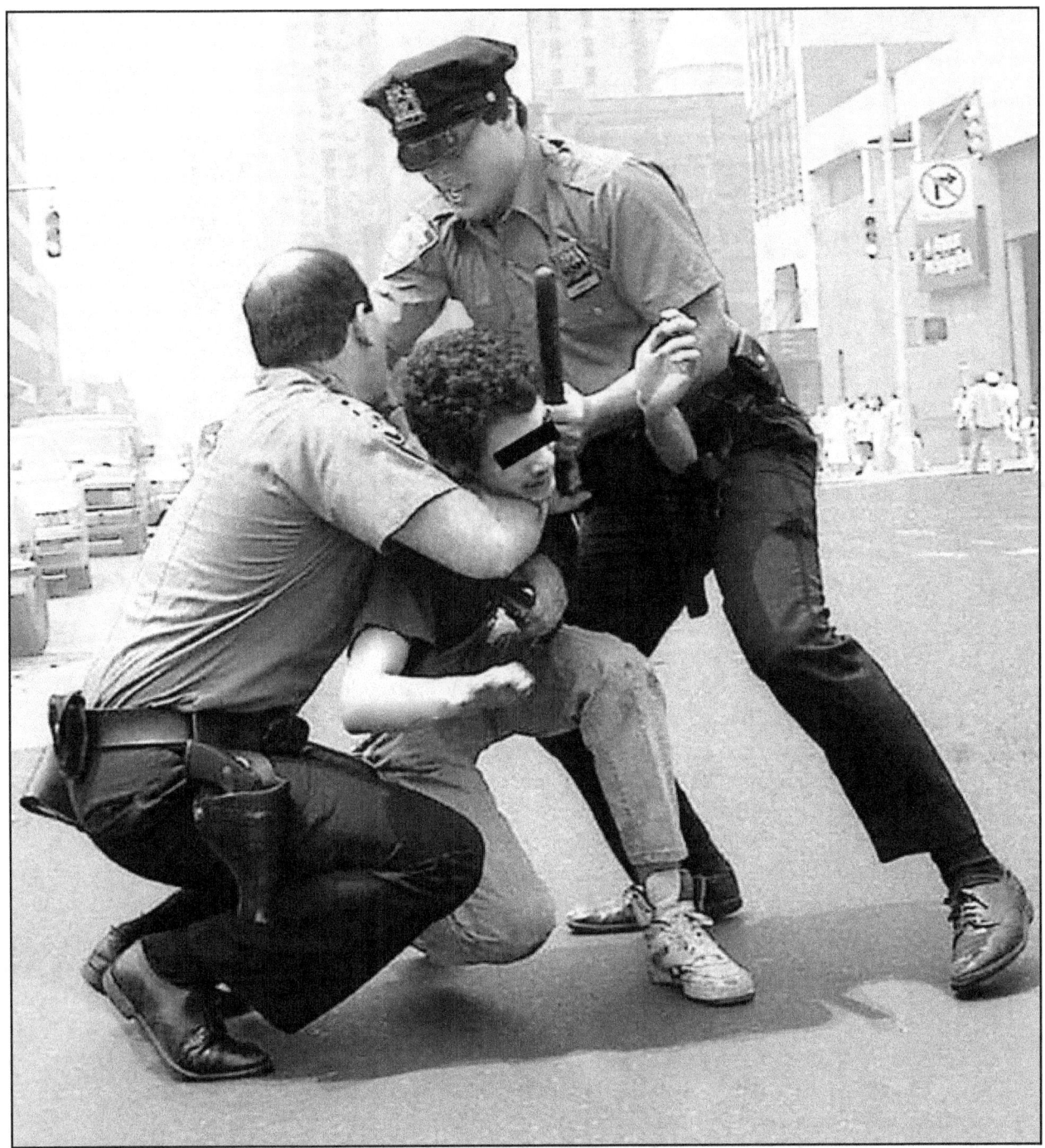
The Post put this picture on the front page. The New York Times wouldn't even look at it.

I went back to Brooklyn and I stopped at my favorite watering hole. When I walked in, the whole bar gave me an standing ovation. It was weird. I signed some more papers and got very drunk.

The next day was completely different, all the fuss ended as quickly as it had started. Nobody called, nobody asked for my signature, nobody congratulated me. I went back to being a nobody. Just another schnook walking around. My fifteen minutes was up.

(sic transit gloria)

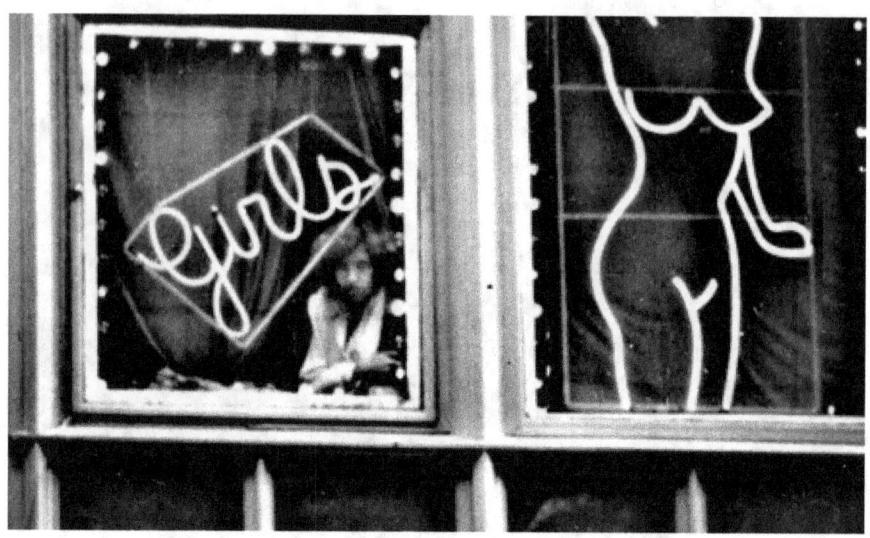

It's a small world

When I was in my early twenties, I would hang out in a small bar in my Brooklyn neighborhood. I was friendly with the bartender, and it was an open secret that he was having problems with his wife. It seems that she had become addicted to heroin, and this was causing lots of trouble. He was afraid to even leave his wallet lying around. Eventually he threw her out, but he was still in love with her. He started drinking heavily, never a good thing for a bartender. I knew his wife, a very attractive young lady. I wondered how she would support herself, not to mention a heroin habit. She didn't seem to have any sort of career.

I was walking along 8th Ave. one day, in an area that was lined with small, store-front massage parlors. About a half block away, I could see a group of people leaning against a parked car. It looked like a very scantily clad girl surrounded by several men. Their hands were all over her, she was obviously enjoying the attention. Anywhere else this kind of behavior would have been scandalous, but on 8th Ave., it was par for the course.

As I got closer, I realized that it was the bartender's wife. I couldn't believe it, I never imagined her sinking this low. I turned my head as I walked by. I didn't want her to see me. One of the men she was with said to her 'back to work honey' and she scampered into a nearby massage parlor. I felt awful, for her and her husband. Many of his customers worked in the area. It was only a matter of time before he found out. Heroin, it's a terrible drug, people will do almost anything to get it.

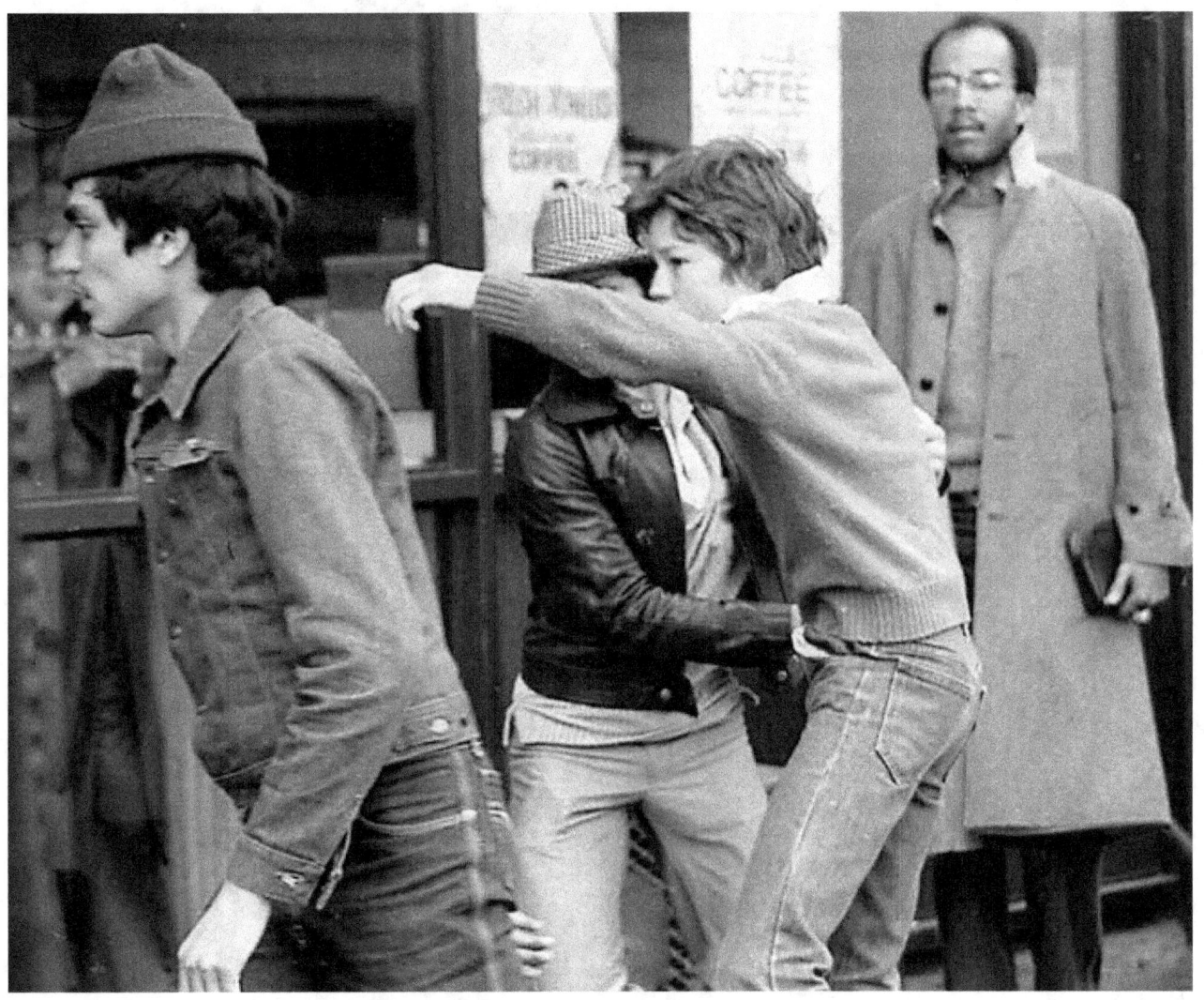

A 'chicken' gets his wings clipped

The young boy with his arm raised is a male prostitute, probably a runaway. On the Deuce, they are referred to as 'chickens.' He made the mistake of telling the guy in the black leather jacket, that he just got paid by a 'chicken hawk.' A 'chicken hawk' is an older gay man, who buys the favors of young boys. The guy in the black leather jacket is now relieving him of his recent earnings.

It was very foolish of me to have taken this picture. At the time I was no older than the kid being robbed. This corner of 42nd St. was teeming with young thugs, many of them armed. I was lucky I didn't get myself killed. Needless to say, I never showed this picture to my father.

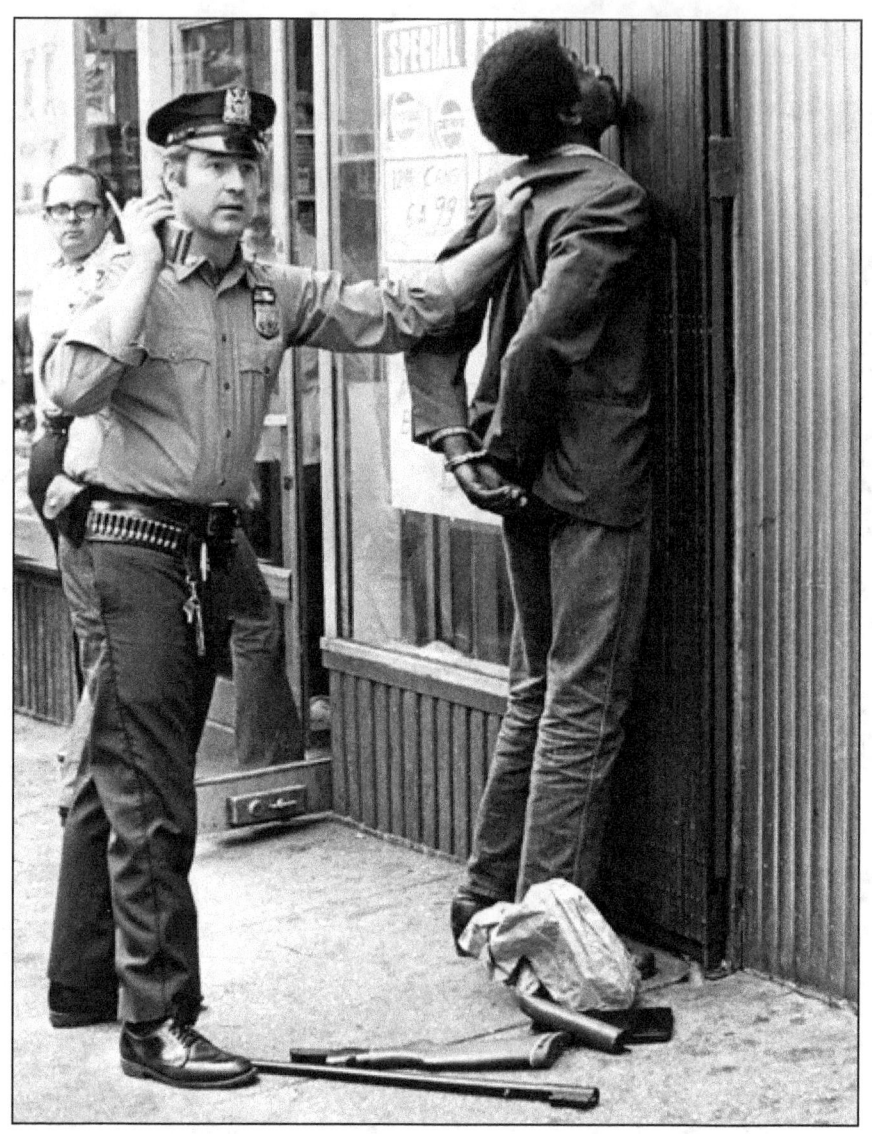

An armed robber gets nabbed on the Deuce

    I just got a slice of pizza and the afternoon paper. It was nice out so I decided to eat outdoors. As I left the pizzeria I looked right and saw this scene. I put my newspaper on the hood of a parked car, and placed the slice of pizza on top of the paper. I turned around and took this shot, (total elapsed time: 10 seconds, tops.) When I turned around my pizza was gone, my paper was gone, my happiness was gone. That's the way it was on the Deuce. If you yawned, they'd steal the gold out of your teeth.

    Notice the anxious look on the cop's face. That's because a crowd was beginning to form. And in those days, in the 1960s, sometimes an angry crowd would try to free a prisoner if they thought they could get away with it. He can hear an approaching squad car bringing reenforcements, but they can't get there soon enough.

    I was probably around 18 when I took this picture. About 25 years later, I marketed this shot (along with many others) as a postcard. They were moving very well, however, all the store owners who were selling the cards reported the same thing. All the cards of this particular picture were being bought by the same little old man. I was curious as to who this guy was, buying the same card over and over again. One of the store owners asked him, and I finally found out. It was the policeman in the picture.

The men with the empty shopping bags

It was my friend Danny who told me about them first. I thought he was just kidding because he was like that, always telling tall tales. He said that at the Port Authority Bus Terminal, the "homos" –that was what gay men were called in those days- would gather in the men's room on the ground floor. In the back would be a group of men just loitering, and they would all carry empty shopping bags. I asked Danny, "What are the empty shopping bags for?" He said, "I'm getting to that. They would hook up with one of the other men in the bathroom and then the two of them, would go into a toilet stall to have sex. The empty shopping bag was for one of them to stand in, so in case a cop came along, he would only see one set of feet in the stall." I said to Danny, "You must be kidding." He said, "No, it's true, check it out." I did, it was true.

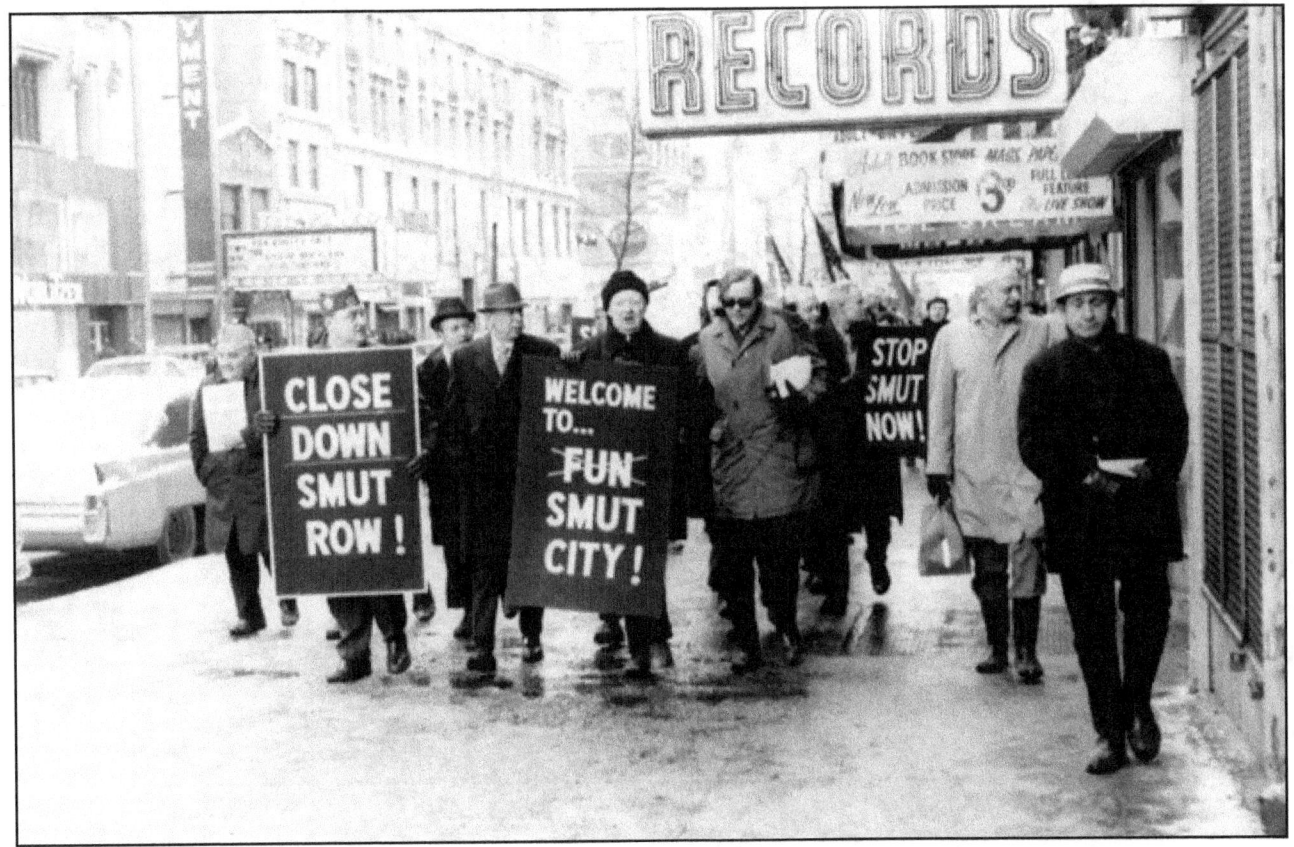

People have been trying to clean up 42nd St. for decades. These marchers above were from the Lindsey era.

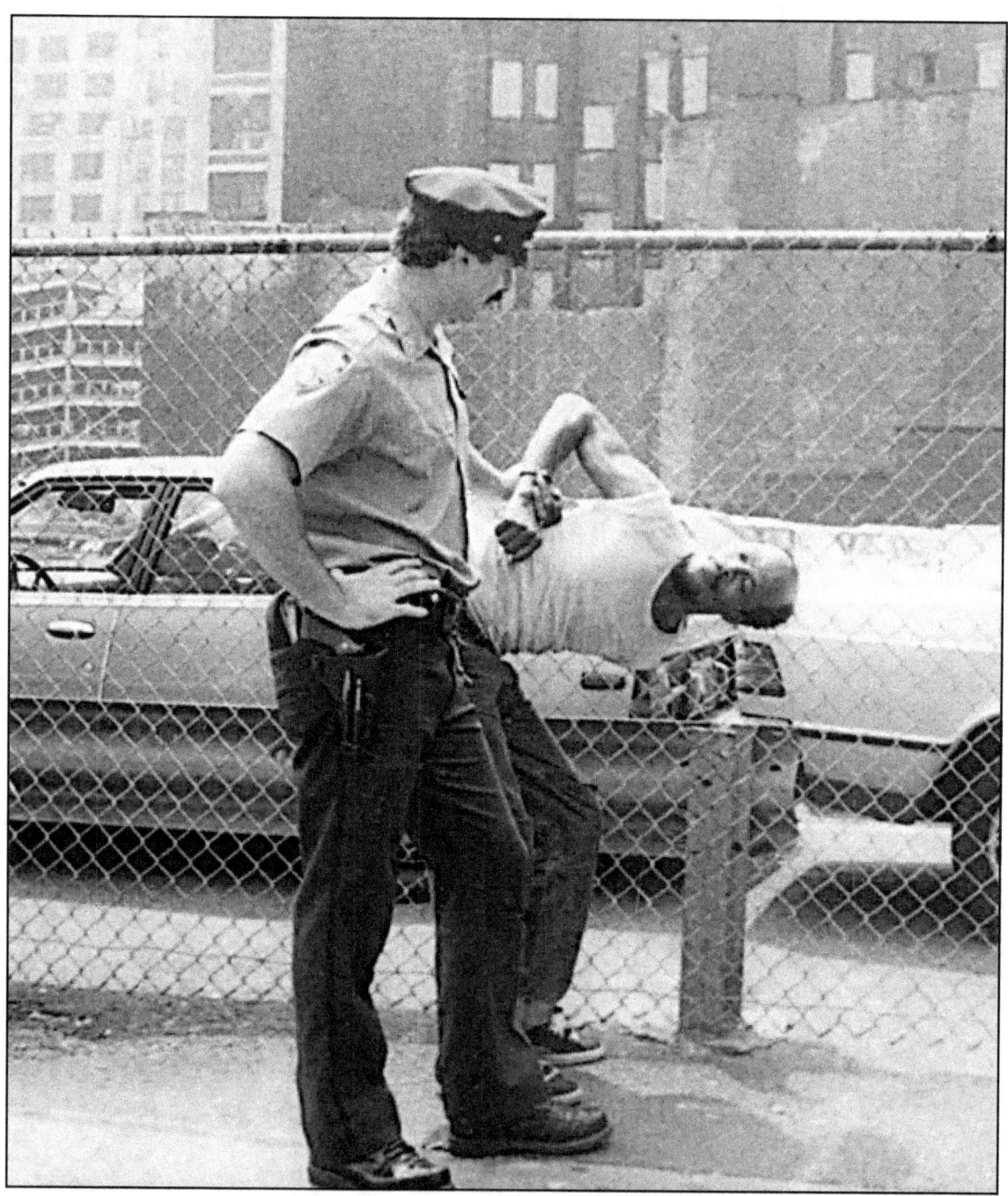

Taking back the street

    This cop told the guy to 'move on, no loitering.' Instead of moving, he gave the cop some lip. Big mistake. No cop patrolling the Deuce at that time could afford to be seen as a wimp by the bad guys. They would have eaten him alive. Corporal street justice was often the order of the day. Here, the cop is showing this guy the error of his ways. The message he was sending to everybody watching was clear. You don't own this street anymore. We do.

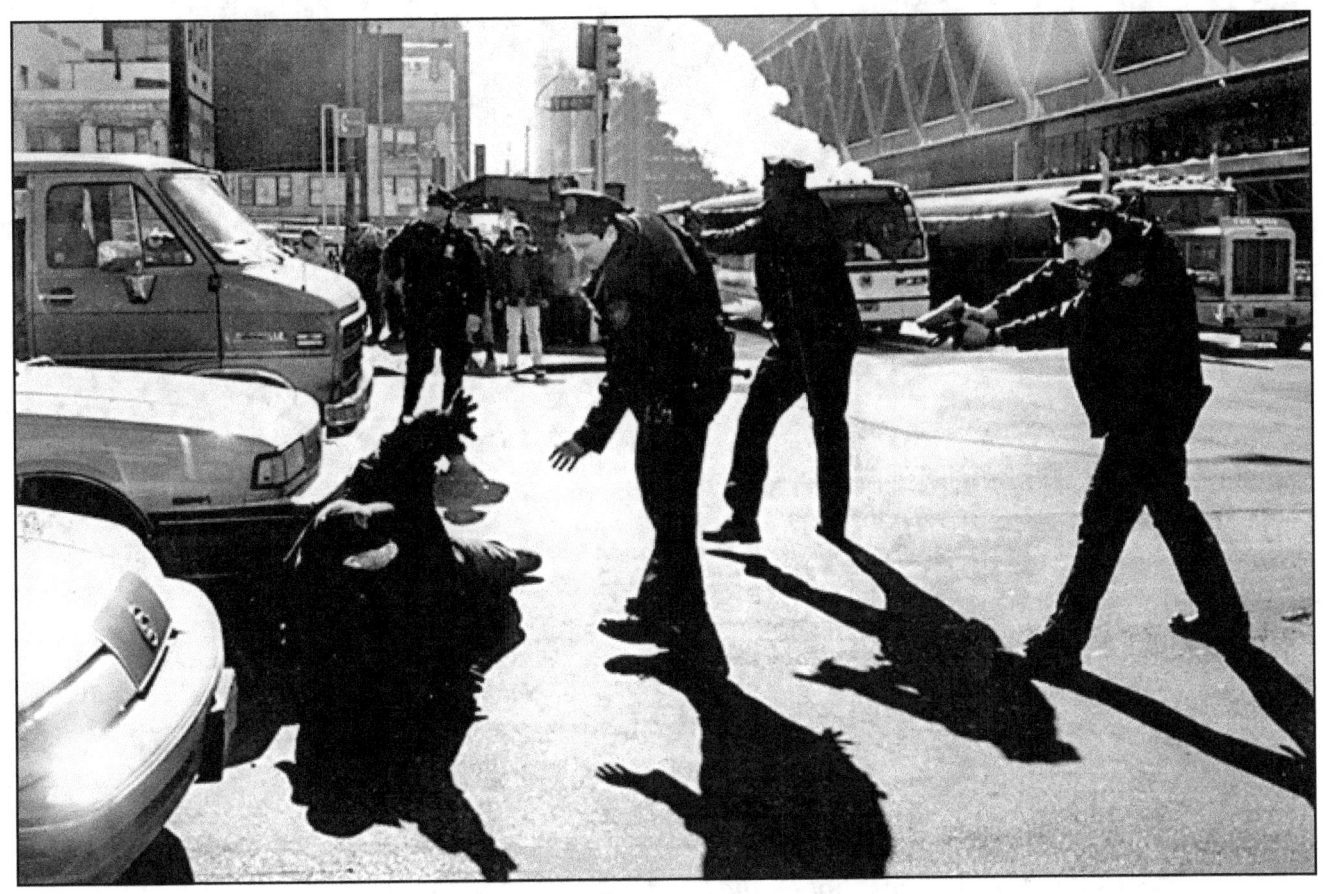

Gang bangers shoot up the Deuce

It was a bright, crisp, February afternoon. I was in a store on the Deuce browsing through some magazines. Suddenly, 'Pow, pow, pow' gunshots, right up the block. I looked out the door and 'Pow, pow, pow' more shots. The whole block was in pandemonium. People were running in all directions, people screaming, people ducking. Traffic had come to a halt. Two groups of men seemed to be battling with clubs and bricks. 'Pow, pow, pow' more shots. I could smell gun powder in the air. Three stores down from me, the window of a shop gets shot out. The whole window falls to the ground with a tremendous crash. This thing is getting very scary, my hands are trembling, then more shots. It's hard to tell where they come from, because of the echoes. A group of men start running towards me. One of them has a silver gun in his hand. When he hits the spot where the broken glass is, he slips and lands on his face, and drops the gun.

He gets up, and tries to pick up the gun on the run. He misses, and accidentally kicks the gun instead. It goes skittering down the street, right passed me. I prayed that it didn't go off. As he runs by me, I made sure not to make eye contact with him. He finally scoops up the gun, and puts it in his pocket. Then he runs to the corner of 42nd and 8th Avenue. There was a green van there. He gets into it. One by one, this whole group of men pile into the green van.

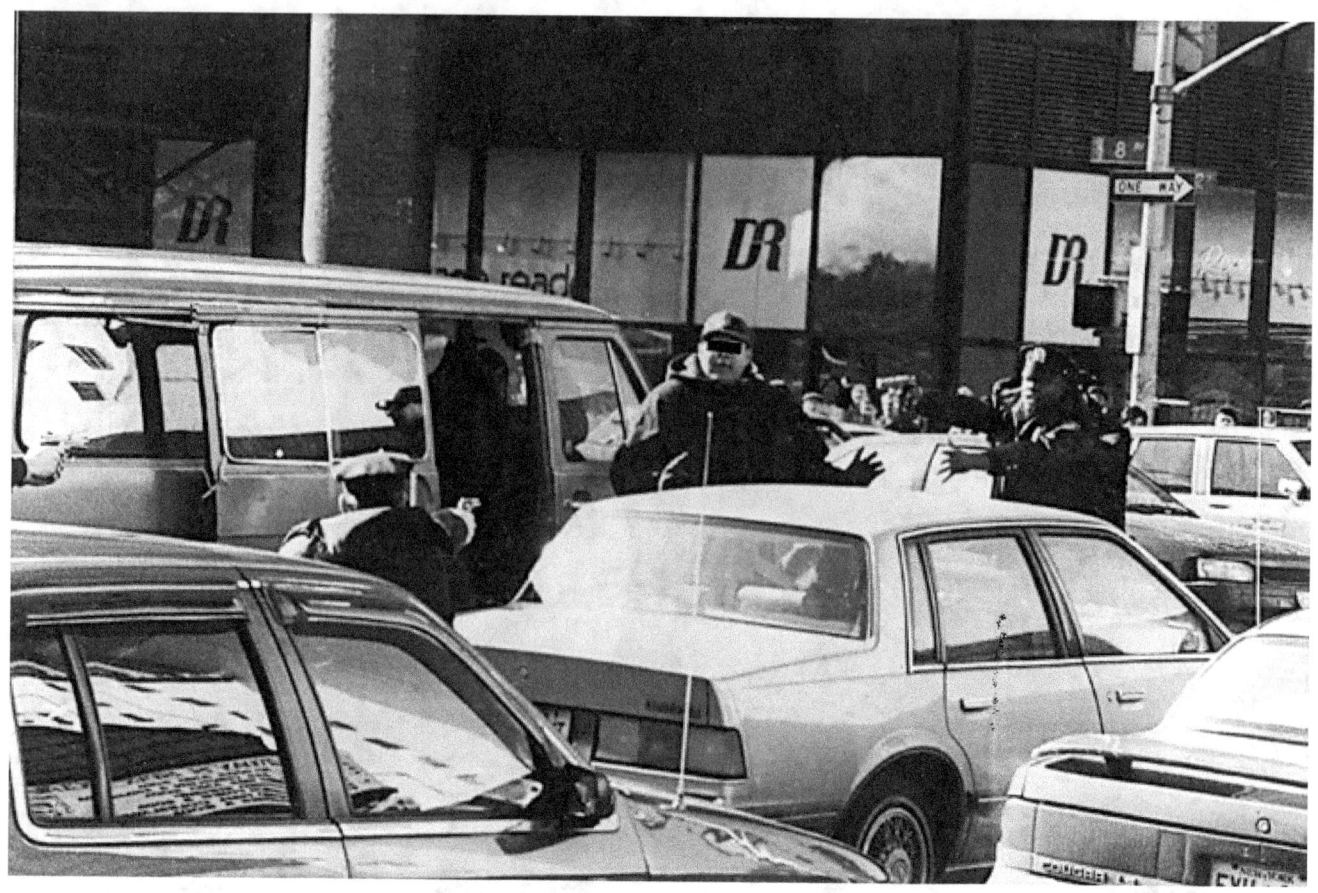

The Daily News put this shot on the front page, the New York Times wouldn't even look at it.

It's a big mistake, because this van isn't going anywhere. It's stuck in traffic. Police sirens are screaming in the distance, getting closer. Cops on foot are converging on this van from all directions. I run to the corner, and I screamed to one of the cops 'There's a gun in that van.' He says to me, 'are you sure?' 'Positive' I said. He yells to his partner 'Gun in the van.' His partner passes it on. All around the van, cops are warning each other about the gun. Being around so many cops with their guns out makes me nervous. I'm carrying a black camera, and at first glance, an anxious cop can easily mistake it for a gun.

    One by one, the gang members began to emerge from the van with their hands up. They looked scared. The cops ordered them to lay on the ground. These are the moments that street photographers live for. I'm shooting like crazy. I know that I'm going to get a lot of good shots out of this. Even the lighting was dramatic.

    Then, out of nowhere 'Bam!' something slams into me from behind. As I go down, I instinctively raise my right arm to protect the camera. As I hit the ground I see a cop sailing over me, as he lands he looks back at me and smiles. This bastard knocked me down on purpose, probably trying to break the camera. It happens sometimes. Cops don't like to be photographed in situations like this, and sometimes they can get nasty. I don't take it personal. It's part of the job.

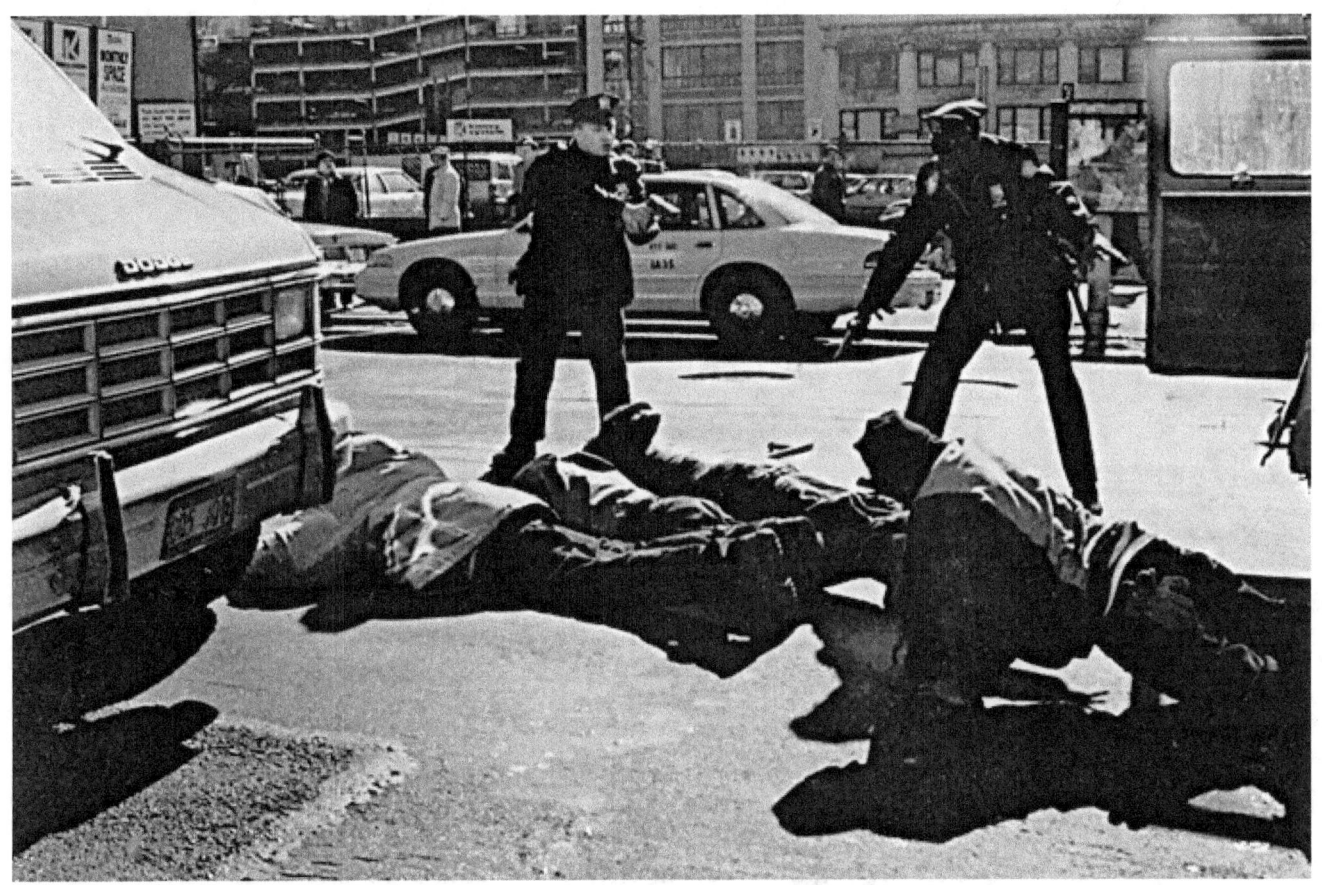

Right after I took this shot, a cop knocked me down, and I landed right here, in the foreground of this picture.

There I am, lying among all these gang bangers. The cops who just came on the scene assume that I'm one of the bad guys. I yelled to them that I'm not one of them. A cop kicks me in the leg and tells me to shut up. Now I can taste blood in my mouth, I probably cut my lip on my way down. Then I catch another wiff of gun powder in the wind. I sneak a look around. People are lying all over the place, cops waving their guns around. The Deuce looks, smells, and tastes like a battlefield. Now, I look to my right, the guy that I'm lying next to smiles at me, and I thought, 'What the hell is he smiling about?' then he asks me something in Spanish, I don't speak Spanish, so I just said to him 'no comprende.' Suddenly, a cop screams at us, 'Shut-up, no talking.' I glance up and I'm looking down the barrel of this cop's service revolver. When someone sticks a loaded gun in your face, it's the scariest feeling imaginable. There's a news camera there now, taking pictures of the scene. 'Great' I thought. 'I'm going to be on the five o'clock news and my mother is going to see me lying amongst all these mooks, looking like I'm one of them. I don't know how long I lay there, it was probably just a few minutes, but it seemed like forever.

Suddenly, someone is helping me to my feet. It's a police sargent. 'You aren't with them, are you?' he said. I said 'No. One of your guys knocked me down.' 'Do you wanna file a complaint?' he asked, 'No' I said 'I just wanna go.' 'Ok' he said, 'get lost.' I took his advice.

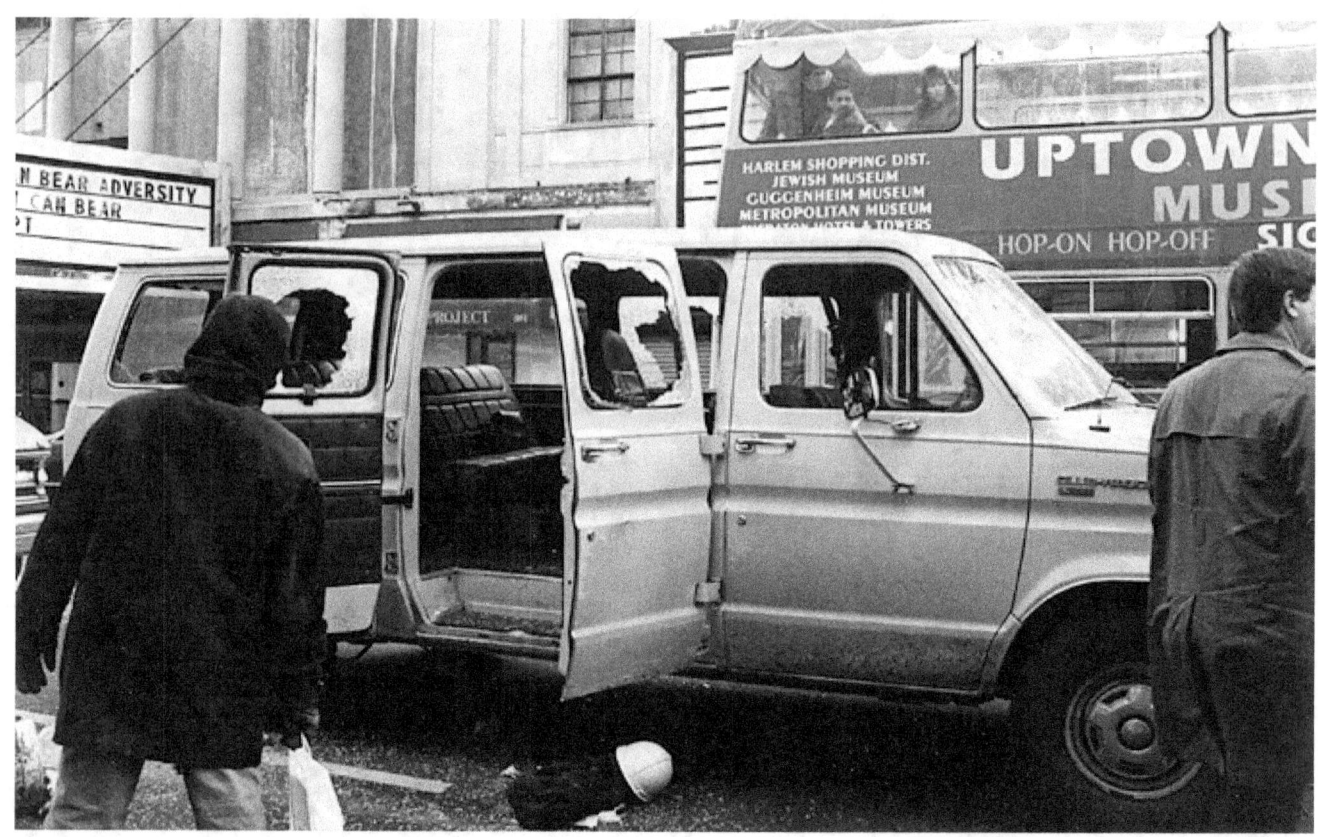

Two people were shot, and several others injured, in the wild gun battle on 42nd St. This is one of the vehicles caught in the crossfire.

    This whole episode took place one block from the world headquarters of the New York Times. I was determined to make one last effort to get something published there. This time I changed my strategy, I had the pictures developed before I went there, so I could show them to the doorman first. Maybe I could get him on my side. It almost worked, he called the photo editor and described the pictures in great detail. Then, he handed me the phone. The photo editor said to me, "I'm sure your pictures are great, but we have our own guys down there, covering this thing." I pleaded with him to just look at them. He said, "No, thanks" and hung up.

    The pictures that the Times published the next day showed two cops looking for spent shellcasings on the street (Yawn!). They might just as well have been looking for lost contact lenses. So if you've ever wondered why the photos in the New York Times are so relentlessly dull, this is why. The photo editors are some of the most closed minded people imaginable.

    So I went to the Daily News instead, and they welcomed me with open arms. They put one shot on the front page and a couple of others on the inside. It was then that I realized that about seven years earlier, I had a picture published on the frontpage of the Post that took place on the exact same spot. To this day, I consider 8th Ave. and 42nd St. to be my lucky corner.

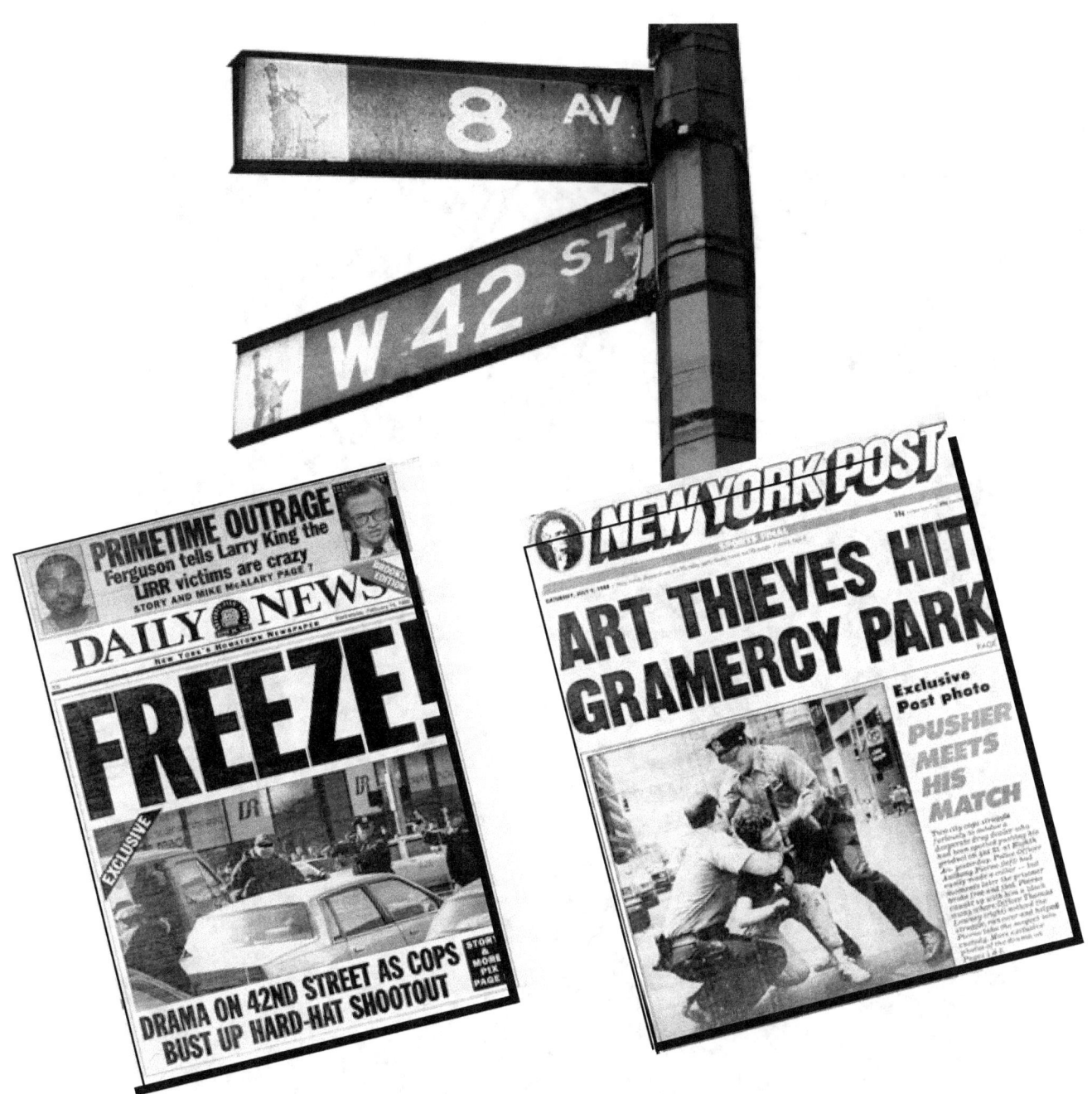

Lighting strikes twice!

These two shots were taken on the exact same spot - but seven years apart.

Chapter 15
Some interesting characters

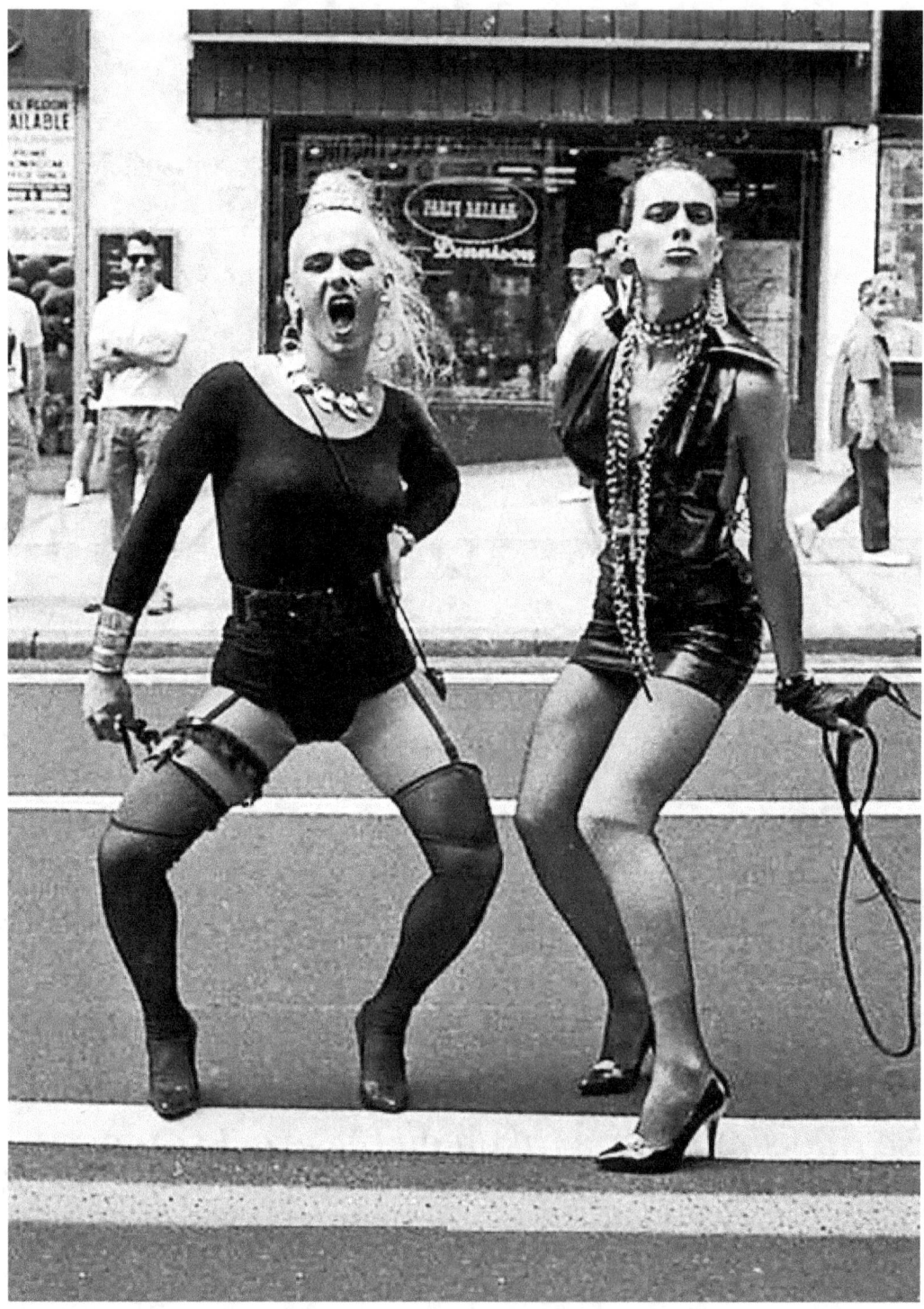

Transvestites on Fifth Avenue

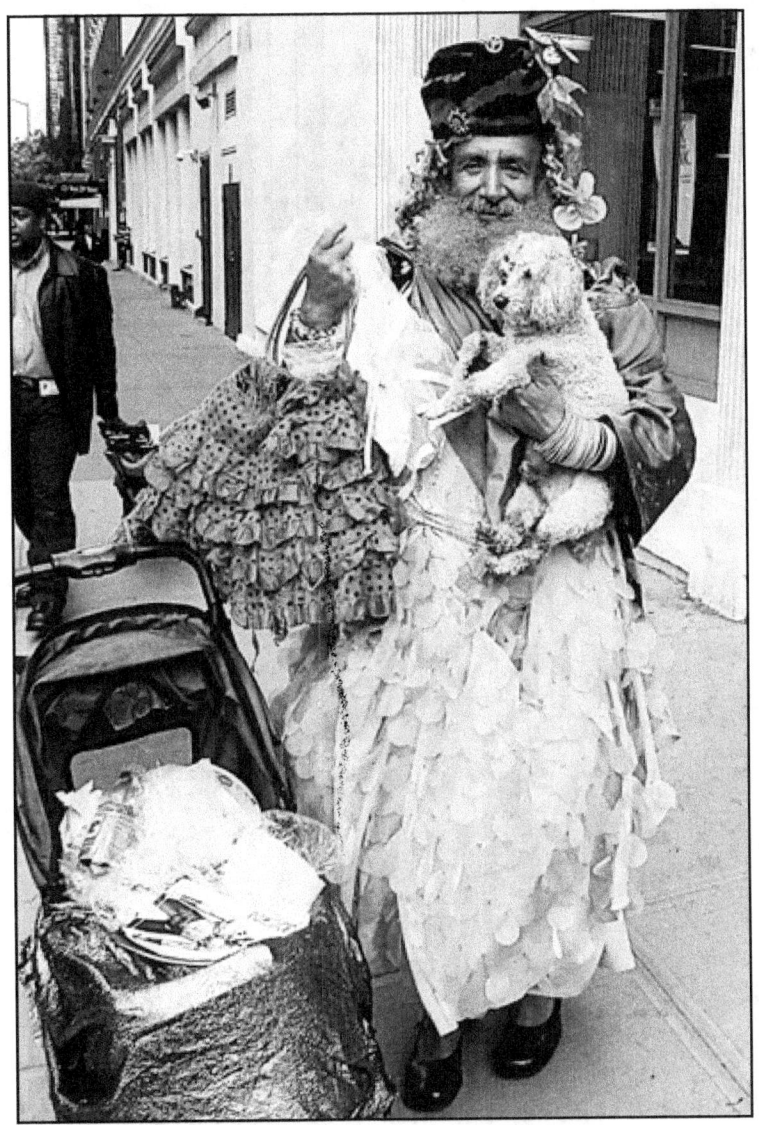

This guy has been around for years. His beard is yellow and red, his handbag is red, and his dress is yellow. His dog's ears are yellow. He has women's shoes on and strolls his dog around in a baby carriage. Maybe people didn't pay enough attention to him when he was young. I also understand that he's starting a website about how to accessorize.

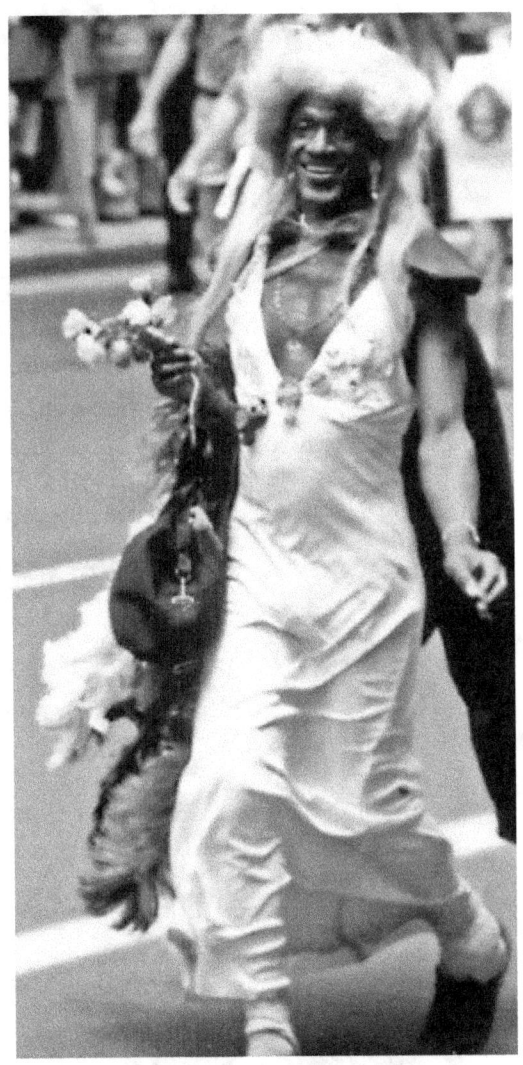

If you're going to parade down Fifth Avenue dressed like Marilyn Monroe, the least you could do is tuck-in your package.

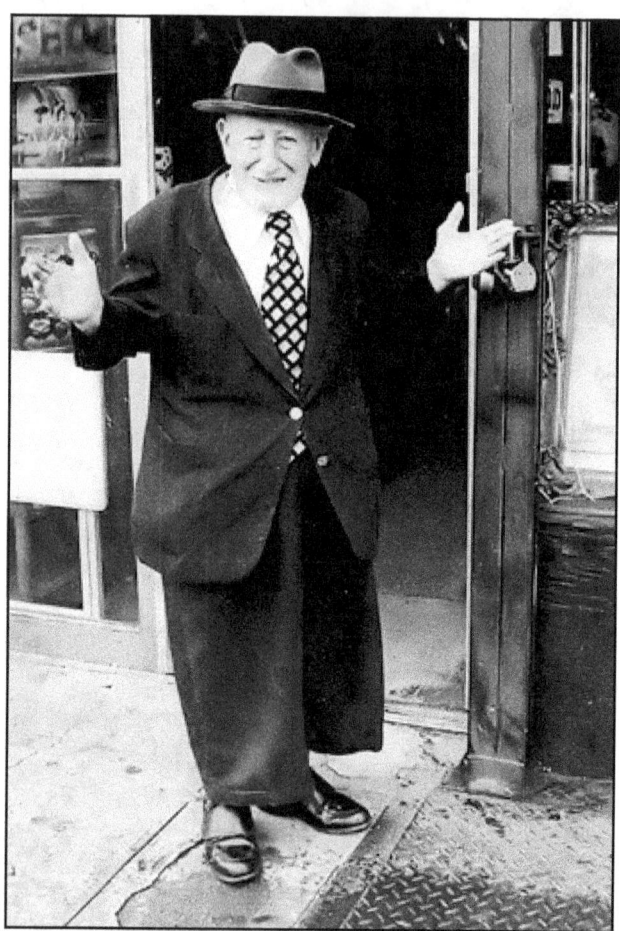

Little Louie from Brooklyn.

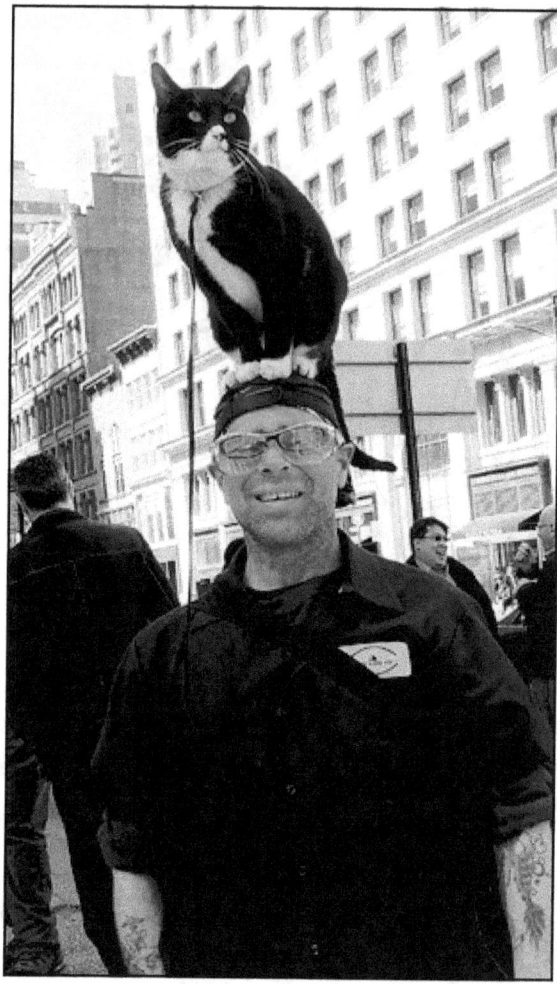

This guy stands on Broadway with a cat on his head and he makes money by charging the tourists to take a picture. I went to him and said "How much for a shot?" and he said, "Well, for you, gimme a dollar." As I was lining up the shot, he said, "Steady Nicholas." So, I lowered my camera and asked him, "How did you know my name?" (He didn't look familiar.) Then he said, "No, I'm talking to the cat."

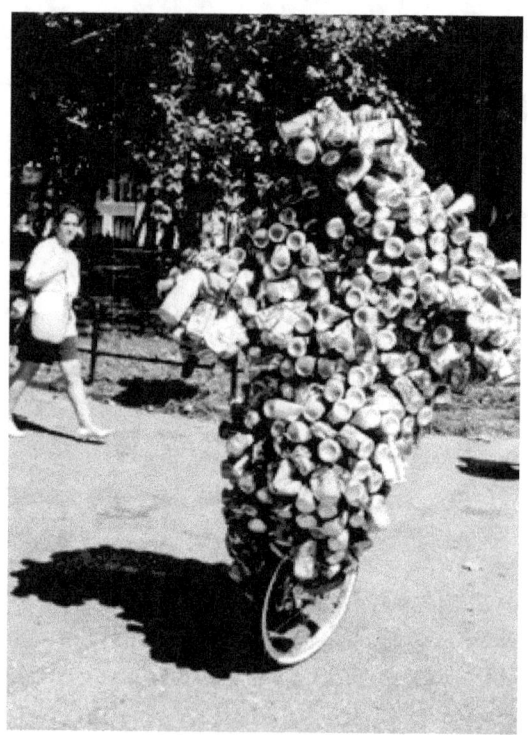

← This guy is one of the original environmentalits. He took a jump-suit and attached hundreds of tin cans to it and then rides around town on a unicycle. He's trying to remind people to recycle tin cans.

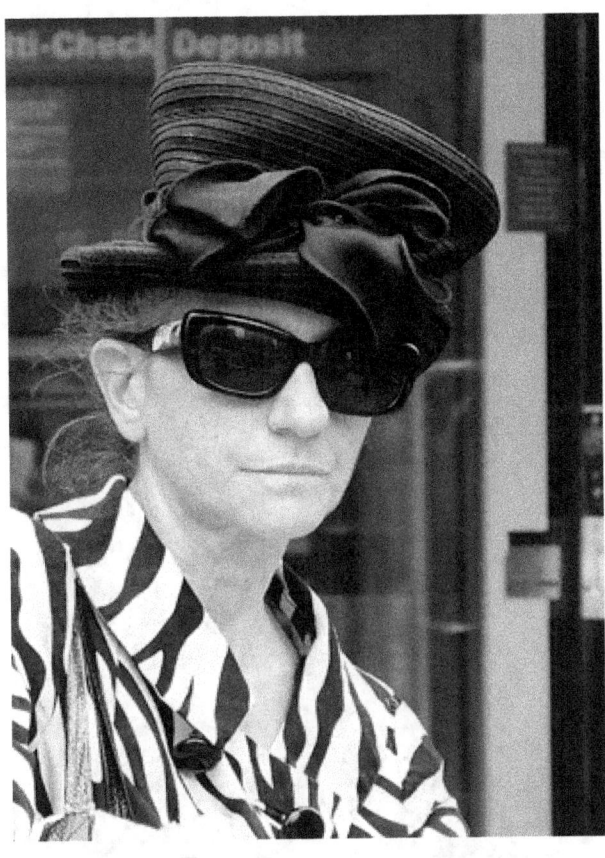

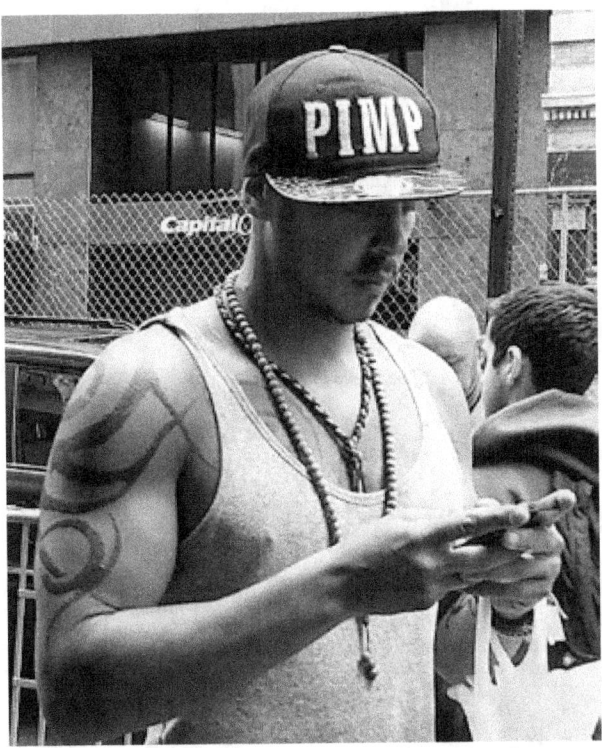

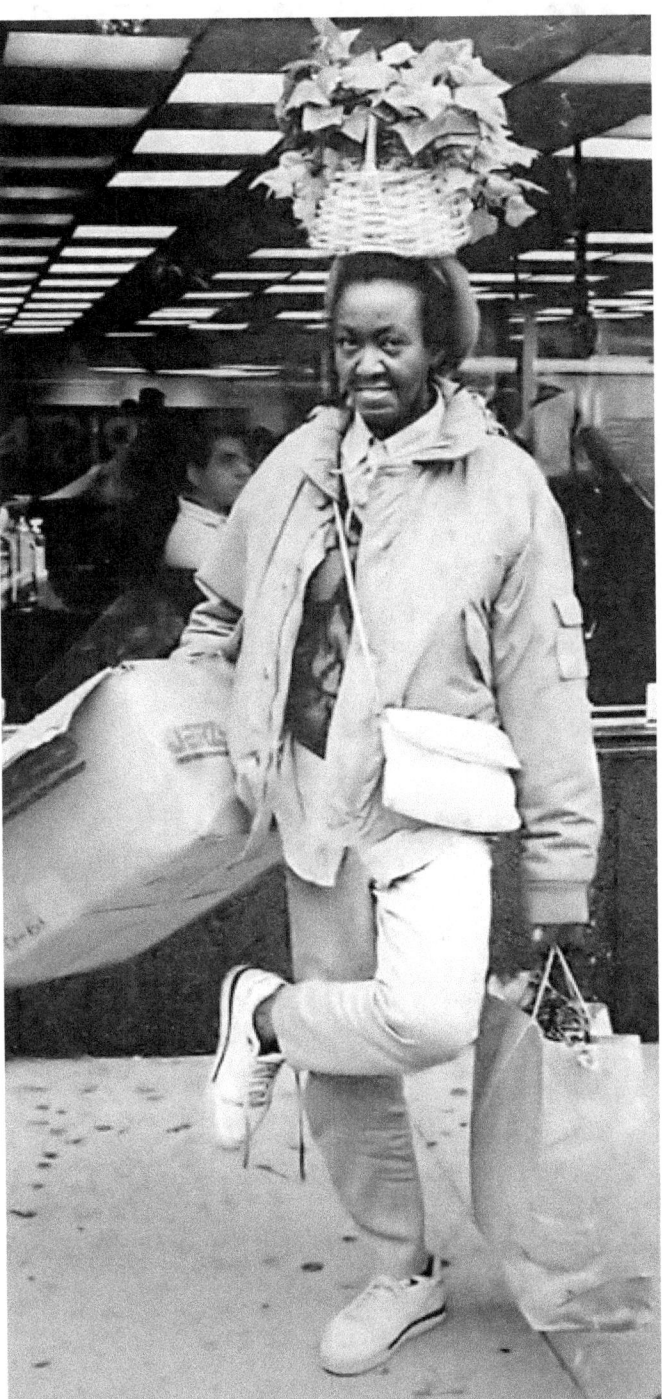

This lady is from Africa. I would run into her all over town. She carries things on her head the way they do in Africa. She was such a showoff.

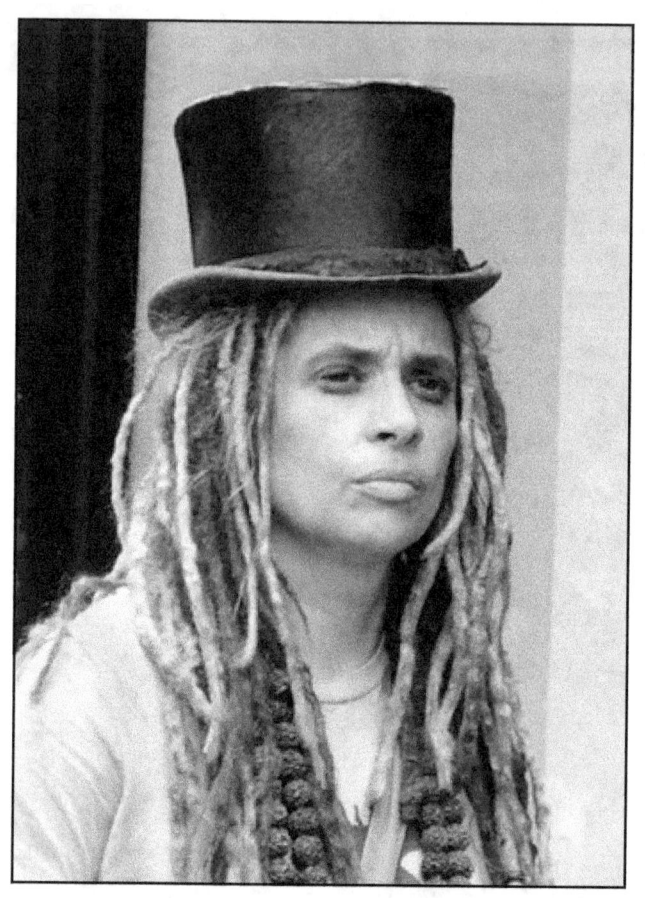
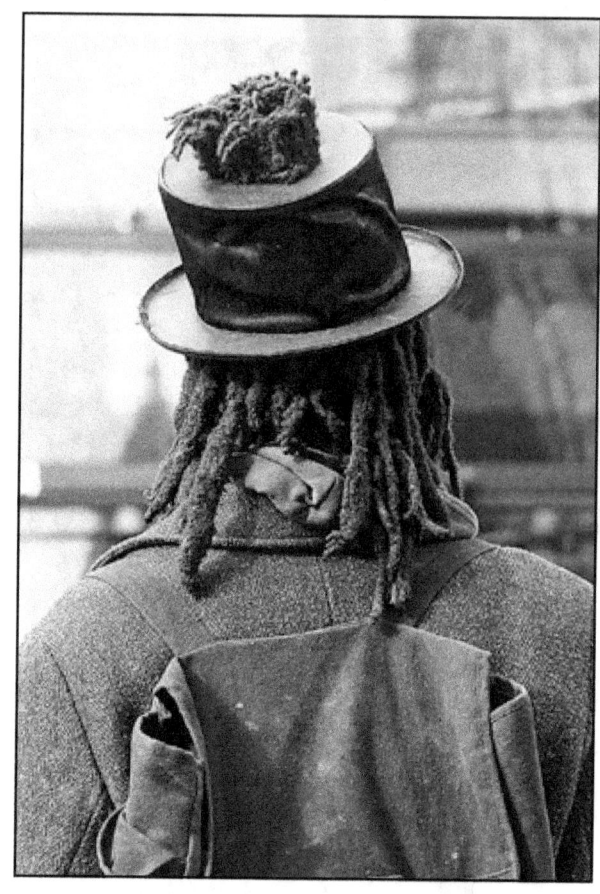
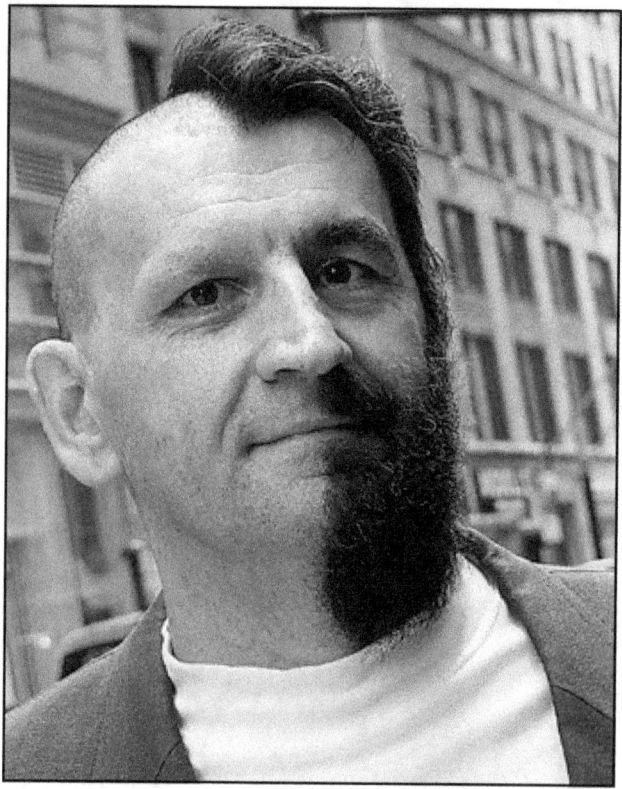
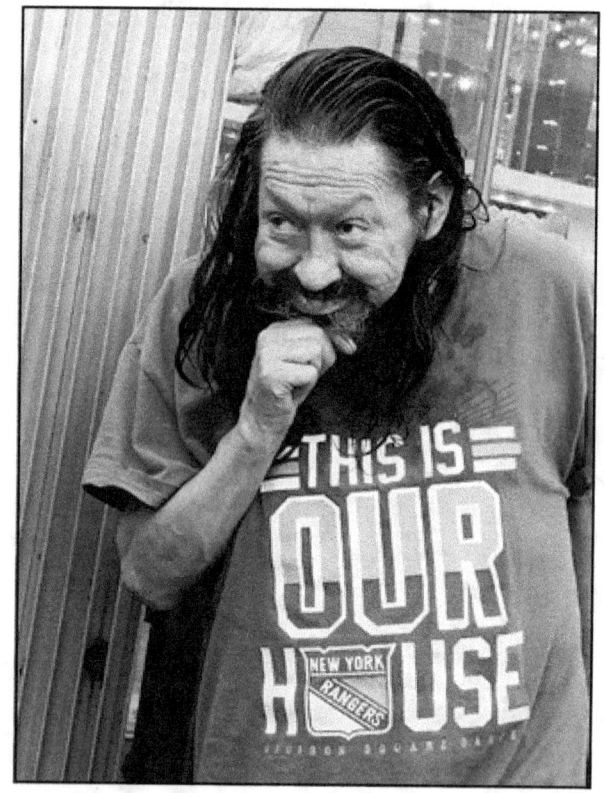

A typical hockey fan

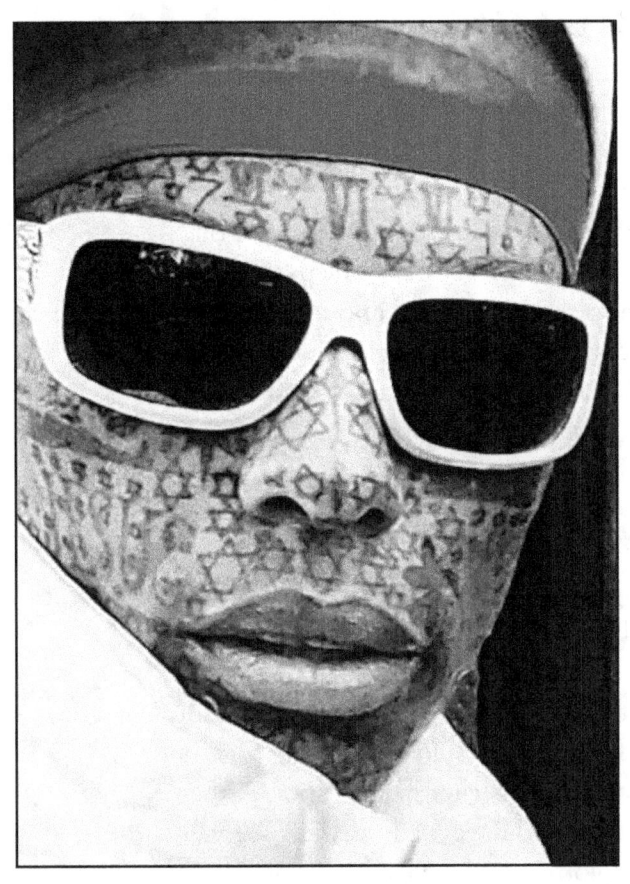

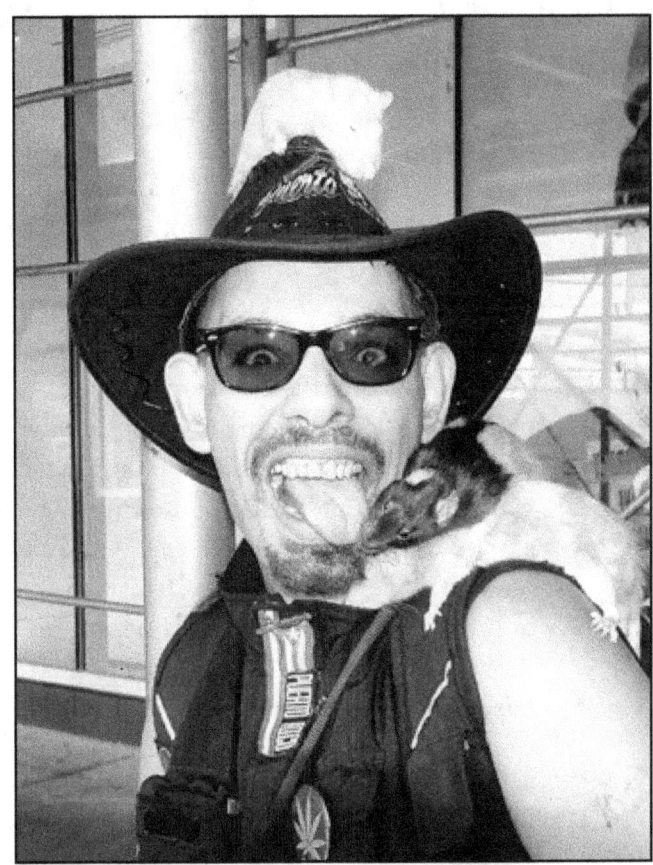

The rat man of Times Square

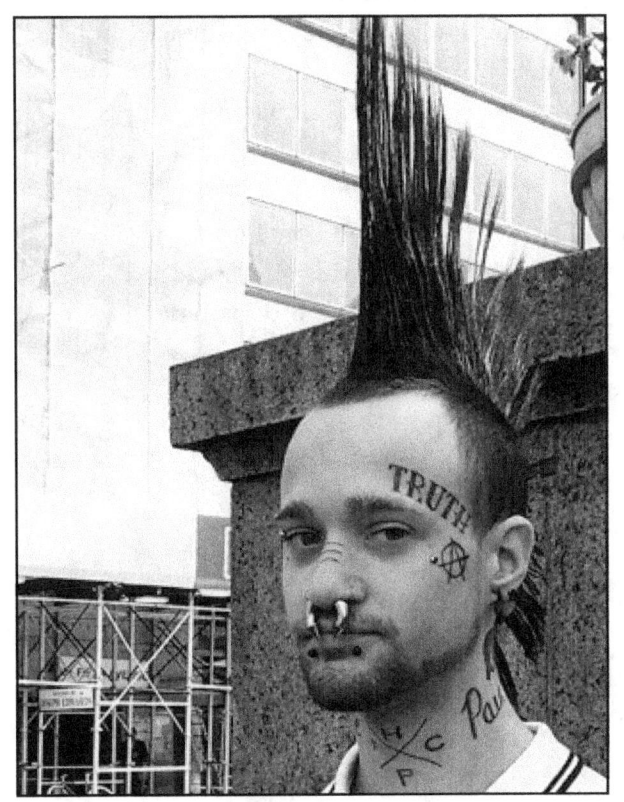

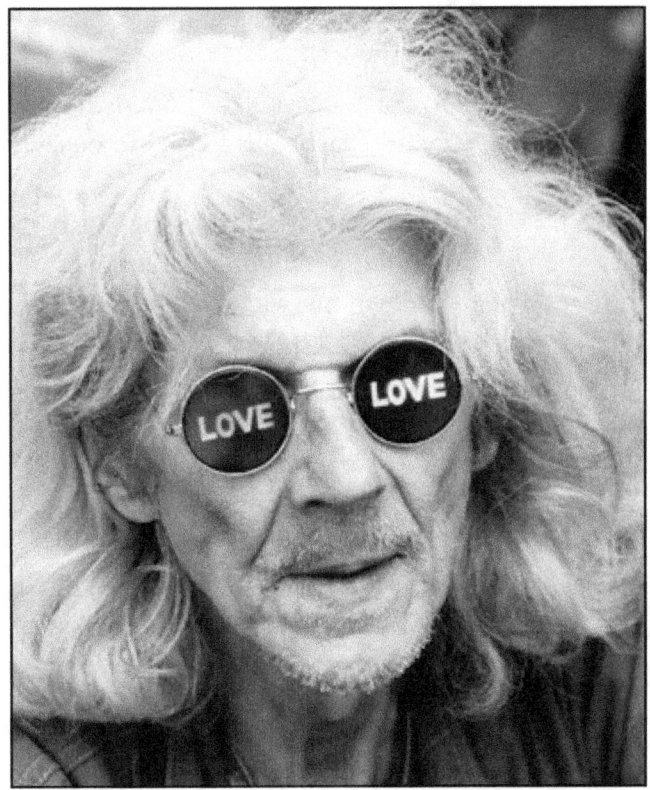

Chapter 16

Two more stories

My friend the Hitman

When I was 16 years old, my father decided that the whole family should escape the summer heat by renting a bungalow in the Catskills. Several families on my block got together and did the same thing. We stayed at a resort called "Happy Acres", naturally, the kids took to calling it "Crappy Acres." It had about a dozen small bungalows, a lake, a small golf course, and some wooded areas. To my dismay, I discovered that there was only one other guy there my age. He was 17, and a body builder. He actually came in second in the New York State body building contest. He was handsome, with dark eyes and wavy black hair. Luckily, he was easy to get along with, so we spent most of the summer hanging-out together. His name was Louie, and he wanted to become a cop as soon as he was old enough.

Louie was polite to a fault. He showed great respect to his elders. He would only address them by their last names, and he always stood up when an adult entered the room. He also had a very strict sense of right and wrong. It was as if he was raised by some sort of "code." He was constantly lecturing me about what was ethical, and what was not. He owned a couple of rifles, so we would go hunting together in the wooded areas, mostly for small game. He would instruct me to "spook" the animals first, before I shot at them, so at last they would have a fair chance. We were almost the same age, but he seemed much more worldly and mature than me. I was clearly the junior partner. There was one thing about Louie that puzzled me however. And that was his speech patterns. They were inconsistent. He was, for the most part, quite articulate. However, once in a while he would miss-pronounce a common word, or fail to conjugate a verb properly. These lapses didn't happen often, but when they did, they were jarring. It led me to believe that there were deficiencies in his education.

My father would stay in the city working, during the week, and come up to visit us on the weekends. One day he came to me and asked "who is this guy Louie you're hanging-out with ?" "He's a nice guy, he wants to be a cop." "What do you do with him?" "We go hunting for rabbits, or fishing, what else is there to do around here?" My father seemed very worried, so I asked him, "What is the matter?" He said, "I don't want you hanging-out with him." "Why not?" I said, "He's the only one here who's my age." Then my mother said "He's a very nice boy, he's very well-bred, what's the problem?" My father was very troubled about something. Then he said "We're going back to Brooklyn tomorrow." My mother and I both said "What" at the same time. Then my mother said "Nicky, what is going on, I have a right to know." "We still have a month left on this place." My father said "I know something about Louie that you don't." "Like what?" I said, and then braced myself for the worst. My father stood there for a moment and then said "His father belongs to the Mafia."

My mother and I stood there, in shocked silence. Then mom said "are you sure, how do you know?" "I know for sure" he said. "But he wants to become a cop "I said. "Sure, he's young and idealistic, he'll start off with good intentions, but they'll get to him, they'll work on him, they'll corrupt him slowly, over time, that's how these people work." "Having one of their own inside the police force is a very valuable asset. He'll be able to feed them information." "Mark my word, they'll get to him. Blood is thicker than water." My father's words would prove to be prophetic.

I said goodbye to Louie the next day. I thanked him for all he had taught me about hunting and fishing. Then I asked him if it was true that his father was "connected." He said "Yeah, it's true, but I'm not going down that path, I'm going to be a cop, and a good one too." It would be 25 years before I saw his face again.

25 years later

In 1990 I went to see the movie "Goodfellas." It was a story about the New York mob, starring Robert DeNiro and Joe Pesci. One scene showed Ray Liotta entering a nightclub filled with gangsters and greeting them one by one. To my amazement, one of those gangsters was none other- than, my old friend Louie! He was much heavier, and of course much older, but when he opened his mouth, and I heard his voice, I was sure it was him. What was he doing playing a gangster in the movies? I thought he was going to be a "straight as an arrow" cop. So I started inquiring about him. I had a lot of friends who were cops, and they said he was forced to retire from the force in 1989. He was suspected of being an associate of an organized crime family. Shortly after that, he appeared in "Goodfellas", as well as several other movies. In 1992 he wrote a book entitled "Mafia Cop." In it he told of his struggle to live in two different worlds at the same time. He even appeared on the Oprah Winfrey show to promote the book. In 1999 he was openly accused by the Daily News of committing several murders for the mob! Finally, in 2005 he was arrested in Las Vegas and convicted of murder. He is now sitting in a jail cell for the rest of his life. I always liked Louie, he was always a gentleman to me. I wonder where he went wrong. He started out so gung-ho to become a cop. He actually became the eleventh most decorated cop in the New York City police departments' history! I guess my father was right after all, blood is thicker than water.

The curse of the Donnelly family

I spent most of my early years in a middle-class section of Brooklyn called Kensington. My parents' house was on a pleasant tree lined block, filled with scores of happy kids playing in the street. The detached, three story homes were all well-kept and the lawns well-manicured…except for one. Directly across the street from us was a dilapidated house with peeling paint, and an un-mowed lawn. The kids called it The Haunted House. It was owned by a little old lady who lived somewhere else, and she was not very fussy about who she rented it to. Over the years a whole series of characters lived there who didn't fit well into the neighborhood. The house had been empty for some time, and it was with great apprehension that the whole block awaited its new occupants.

I was playing stickball in the street one day with the guys, when this old jalopy of a station wagon slowly made its way up the street. It stopped in front of The Haunted House and its occupants began to get out, and get out, and get out. It was like the clown car in the circus. Fifteen people packed into one station wagon. The parents were well dressed, but the kids were a fright to behold. They looked like refugees from some third world country. They weren't just poor, they were desperately poor. Their ill-fitting clothes were full of holes, and their toes poked thru the tops of their sneakers. None of them owned a belt, their pants and skirts were held up with pieces of rope. We just stared at them in disbelief. How could this degree of poverty still exist, in this day and age? And what made it even sadder was how pretty the girls were. There were nine of them, all with dirty-blond hair, pulled back into pony tails. The four boys were scruffy, but handsome, and you could tell that they were tough. The Donnellys had arrived. The Old station wagon pulled away and returned later. It had one mattress on the roof, and was filled with cardboard boxes. The four boys unloaded it in five minutes and that was it. All the belongings of a family of fifteen people fit into one station wagon.

The speculation and rumors started immediately. Why only one mattress? Where did they sleep, on the floor? Why were their clothes so tattered? Didn't the parents work? Was there something wrong with them? Nothing made sense, nothing added-up. The parents, Tom and Dorothy, both had good paying jobs, Tom worked for the Transit Authority and Dorothy was a school teacher. Even with thirteen kids, they should have been able to make ends meet. Something wasn't right, and the reason for their negligence soon became very apparent. Tom and Dorothy Donnelly were both rip-roaring alcoholics. Every night they made the rounds of the local neighborhood taverns and played the role of the big-shots. Buy this guy a drink, buy that guy a drink, and buy the whole bar! They pissed away their money like drunken sailors while their kids were in rags. My dad hated them, especially the father, "What kind of man is letting his kids walk around dressed like that?" My father was a doer, so he did something about it. He would drive to the lower east side and buy boxes of children's clothing wholesale. Then late at night he would leave them on the Donnelly's porch. He knew they would be too proud to accept them face to face. My father would make these trips to the lower east side about once a week. One day my mother asked him how much money he was spending on "those kids." My father got very angry with her. He said, "Don't ever ask me that again. You have a roof over your head. You and the kids are well dressed. You have a swimming pool in the yard. You spend the summers in the country. Those poor girls have nothing! Don't ever, ever ask me that again." My father was growing attached to those girls.

The Donnellys had no curtains on their ground floor windows, so I could see into their living-room from my third floor bed room. Their living-room had no rug. It had no couch or easy chairs. It had no coffee table or television. There were no pictures on the walls. There was just a small card table in the middle of the floor with four folding chairs. Their bedroom windows were covered with newspapers. So my father left a box of curtains on their porch one night so at least they could hide their poverty from prying eyes. The next day the box was gone, but the curtains weren't put up. My father was looking out the window and wondering out loud why they hadn't hung the curtains up yet. Suddenly their front door opened up and half a dozen of the Donnelly girls came out to go to school. Each one of them was wearing a new, freshly pressed skirt. They were made from the curtains my father had left the night before.

Slowly, we got to know the Donnelly kids. They were all pretty smart and well educated. I became friendly with two of the boys, Vincent and Dennis, who were about my age. One thing I noticed was that they were a lot closer to one another than say, my brothers and I. They had to be, because they knew that they couldn't rely on their parents, so they had to rely on each other. I was talking to Dennis one day, after we both had had a few drinks, and he asked me why I didn't hang out with my brothers. I explained to him that we just had different sets of friends and different interests, that's just the way it was. Then I asked him why his father seemed to be so estranged from his own children. He looked at me and said "If I tell you something, you promise not to tell anyone?" "Of course" I said. "My father isn't sure if all of the kids are his." That would explain a lot, I thought, the negligence, the drinking, the remoteness from his kids. With this one revelation, suddenly everything about the Donnellys made sense. I liked Dennis, and invited him to dinner one Sunday. He showed up in a freshly pressed white shirt with French cuffs that were held in place with paperclips. So I gave him a pair of gold cufflinks that I hardly used and he was thrilled. However, when he found out how much they were worth, he hocked them in a nearby pawn shop.

My brothers also became friendly with them. One day at dinner, my younger brother Marty said that he wanted to ask one of the Donnelly girls out. My father slammed his fist on the table and said "No, I forbid it, don't even think about it, I don't want anything to do with that family. God forbid if you got serious with one of them. Then we would have to associate with them forever, no, no way!" He ranted on about the drunken parents and threatened to throw my brother out of the house if he disobeyed his orders. Then he pointed to me and my other brother and said "The same goes for you two also." This decree by my father would lead to a serious rift with my brother that would only widen over time. This same scene was played out in all the houses on the block. None of the young neighborhood boys were ever involved with the Donnelly girls, even though they were all quite attractive.

There was one person on the block however who became very close to several of the Donnelly girls, and that was, ironically, my father. He was movie star good looking, and a few of the younger girls fell madly in love with him. They were constantly flocking around him as he did yard work, begging for kisses and just wanting to be hugged .It was sad in a way, they were so starved for male affection. My father had to constantly remind them that only one kiss a day was permissible. Somehow the Donnelly girls discovered that it was my father who was leaving those gifts for them at night. So one day, as he was mowing the lawn, one of the older girls came across the street and handed him a bright pink envelope. They had a short conversation, then she gave him a peck on the cheek and scampered off. My father opened the envelope and read the card inside. I could see that it touched him deeply. Tears were welling in his eyes. I asked him about it, and he said it was just a thankyou card. He folded it, and put it in his pocket. I often wondered what was in that note that made him so emotional. It would be fifty years before I would find out.

The oldest of the Donnelly boys, Brian, was twenty-two. Every day he would hang out on his porch and wait for his friends to come by. They would drive up in a pink Cadillac convertible, just like the one Elvis Presley had. Rumor had it that they were a bunch of young, up and coming gangsters. They would return later with all kinds of stuff that "fell off the truck," clothes, food, toys, all of it obviously stolen. His younger siblings idolized him because he was providing all kinds of material goods that should have been coming from the parents. The pink Cadillac was a regular visitor to the neighborhood, stopping at all the local bars to sell their swag out of the Cadillac's huge trunk. So when the news broke that a local gas station had been robbed at gun-point in Brooklyn, it normally would have been no big deal, but what made this story " go national" was the fact that the bandits made their getaway in a pink Cadillac convertible. The press dubbed it "The Conspicuous Chariot." The stupidity of it all brought ridicule to the borough of Brooklyn, and Johnny Carson even joked about it on the Tonight Show. As it turned out there was only one car registered in all of Brooklyn that matched that description. The "Pink Cadillac Gang" was soon rounded –up. Brian Donnelly was arrested at home, his young sisters crying as he was led away in handcuffs. Brian made bail and was out of jail the next day, his friends however stayed locked- up longer. This led to speculation that Brian had somehow cooperated with the police, a charge that he and his brothers vehemently denied.

A few weeks went by then one day Vincent Donnelly knocked on my door and asked me for a favor. "you have a darkroom in your attic, don't you Nick?' "Sure I said, why do you ask?" "Would you make me about a hundred copies of this?" He showed me a photo of his brother Brian. "What's this all about" I asked. "Brian is missing," he said. "I want to make some posters up and hang them around the neighborhood." I tried to be up-beat, but deep inside, I had a feeling of dread. "Maybe he went somewhere with his friends" I said. "No, I asked them, and they said that they didn't know where he was. But I don't believe them, they were evasive, they wouldn't even look me in the eye." "My parents are worried sick, they're drinking more than ever." A week later, Brian was still missing.

It was a warm summer night and I was sleeping with the windows open. Around 8 a.m. I could hear some sort of commotion coming from across the street. I looked outside to see a police car parked in front of the Donnelly's place. From inside their house came anguished shrieks and cries, horrible sounds, the sounds of a dozen souls in agony, the sounds of little girls crying. The police were there to tell the Donnellys that they had found Brian. His body was discovered floating face down in Prospect Park Lake, hidden amongst the tall weeds. His hands were tied behind his back, and someone had put a bullet thru his head. He was just twenty-two years old. The curse of the Donnelly family had begun!

Brian Donnelly's murder was never solved. The police were not about to devote resources to what they called, "house-cleaning" by some local gang. This incident left a palatable impact on the neighborhood. This was a safe block, people didn't even lock their doors in the daytime. That began to change, and resentment against the Donnelly's began to set in. Many people felt that their very presence was lowering property values, and everyone was aware that as soon as they moved in, things began to disappear from the block. A bicycle here, a lawn mower there, even laundry drying in the backyards. Everyone suspected that it was the "poor kids" but nobody could prove it. Then one morning two of the Donnelly girls were seen on their hands and knees scrubbing some graffiti off the sidewalk in front of their home. During the night someone had scrawled "Shanty Irish go home!" on the sidewalk. I felt so bad for them, they didn't deserve this, but their older brother Vincent, was about to do something about it. He recognized the handwriting as belonging to one of his old school mates. So he confronted him right in the middle of a stickball game, in front of dozens of witnesses. He gave him a vicious beating with a broom stick handle that left him scarred for life. Vincent was sending a message to the whole block, "You don't have to love us, but don't fuck with us!"

I liked Vincent and considered him a good friend. We were both twenty- one, and spent a lot of time together. So when he quit his part –time job, and started hanging out with a bunch of rough-necks, our friendship cooled. He asked me about this, why I was avoiding him, and I told him honestly that I didn't like his new friends. I reminded him of what happened to his brother when he got involved with some questionable characters. He lit into me angrily, "Don't be so quick to judge me" he said, "You have no idea how my family lives, my poor sisters sleep on air mattresses, I do what I have to do to survive. Do you think I can help my family with a part –time job? Get lost he said, go take a dip in your pool." Vincent and I stopped talking after that. A few months later he was out partying with his friends, they were all drunk, when their car skidded off the road and hit a tree. Vincent was seriously injured. His friends dragged him from the wreck, but he was bleeding profusely. The ambulance was late getting to the scene, so his friends tried to help him as best they could. It was no use, Vincent bled to death by the side of the road. He was just twenty-two years old.

Everyone began to suspect that there was some kind of curse on the Donnelly family, having lost two sons in a row, both at the age of twenty-two. Especially Dennis Donnelly, He was the next oldest of the Donnelly boys, and he was firmly convinced that he too was fated for an early grave. I tried to convince him that it was just bad luck, and that he shouldn't be so superstitious. He ignored me and everyone else. He began to drink heavily and behave recklessly. He was arrested for drunk driving and petty larceny. It was plain to see where this was going. When I warned him, at this rate, he wasn't going to make it past 21, He said "No, I'll get past 21, it's 22 where I get off." Dennis Donnelly's prediction became a self-fulfilling prophecy. He failed to awaken one morning, and was rushed to the hospital in a deep coma. The liquor and barbiturates had finally taken their toll. He died in the middle of his twenty-second year on this Earth, and once again the sounds of mourning came from the Donnelly's house. This time it was more subdued, they were getting used to death.

The curse of the Donnelly family had been confirmed. Three sons dead in three years, all at the age of twenty-two. There was a big article about it on the second page of the Daily News. Reporters from all the newspapers were on the block asking the residents for information about the story. When one reporter knocked on the Donnelly's front door, he was met by a very drunk Thomas Donnelly, who punched him in the face and sent him tumbling down the stairs.

Joseph Donnelly, the last surviving son was surprisingly calm about the whole thing. Everyone expected him to fall apart, but he didn't. He put a brave face on it for a time, but then, little by little, he became depressed. He wouldn't leave the house for days at a time. His sister said he was afraid that he would get hit by a car if he went out. About a month after Dennis' death the Donnellys decided to move. They claimed that it was the house itself that was cursed. The house brought all the bad luck. But everyone on the block knew that that was just a cover story. The real reason they were moving was because none of the neighborhood bars would serve them anymore. Nobody wanted to be around them, no matter how much money they spent. They brought gloom with them wherever they went. So they stole away, like thieves in the night. Once again the old station wagon pulled up and took them away, to only God knows where.

A few years passed and the block began to change. The old lady who owned the Haunted House died, and her sons fixed it up and sold it to a newly-wed couple. I moved out of my parents' house and got an apartment a few blocks away. I would see my parents once a week however, for a good home cooked meal. It was a beautiful Sunday and my mother asked me to get her a pack of cigarettes. So I went to the corner candy store. It was owned by a little old Jewish man named Irving. When I walked in he gave me a big hello and asked where I've been. I told him that I moved a few blocks away. Then he asked me "Do you remember the Donnellys?" "Of course", I said, "Why?" -"Look at the Daily News"- he said. I walked over to where the newspapers were. The front page headlines of the Daily News read "The Curse Is Broken" Underneath was a picture of Joseph Donnelly at his twenty-third birthday party. He was surrounded by his family. His sisters had blossomed into beautiful young women. Even the parents looked healthier, they must have stopped drinking. The article described in detail the bad luck the Donnellys had had over the years with their sons, and how Joseph was the only son to reach twenty-three. The curse of the Donnelly family had been broken. I brought the paper home and showed it to my parents, when they saw it, they both started crying.

Many years later, when my father passed away, I was going thru his personal papers when I came across a bright pink envelope with a handmade card inside. On it was a poem that read:

You come at night, when we're asleep,
You tip-toe up, without a peep,
You leave your gifts, for us to find,
You are so sweet, you are so kind,
But in a way, you make us sad,
'Cause you're the Dad, we wish we had.

Love, the Donnelly Sisters.

Chapter 17

The homeless

In the mid-1960's, a friend of mine went to France on vacation. When he came back we were discussing his trip and he mentioned something that I found hard to believe. He said that in Paris, there were whole families that lived on the streets, thousands of them. I couldn't comprehend this, how could this be? And then it started here.

It seemed that almost overnight a perfect storm of negative forces hit the most vulnerable among us and cast them onto the streets. They became an inextricable part of daily life in New York. Here are some of them.

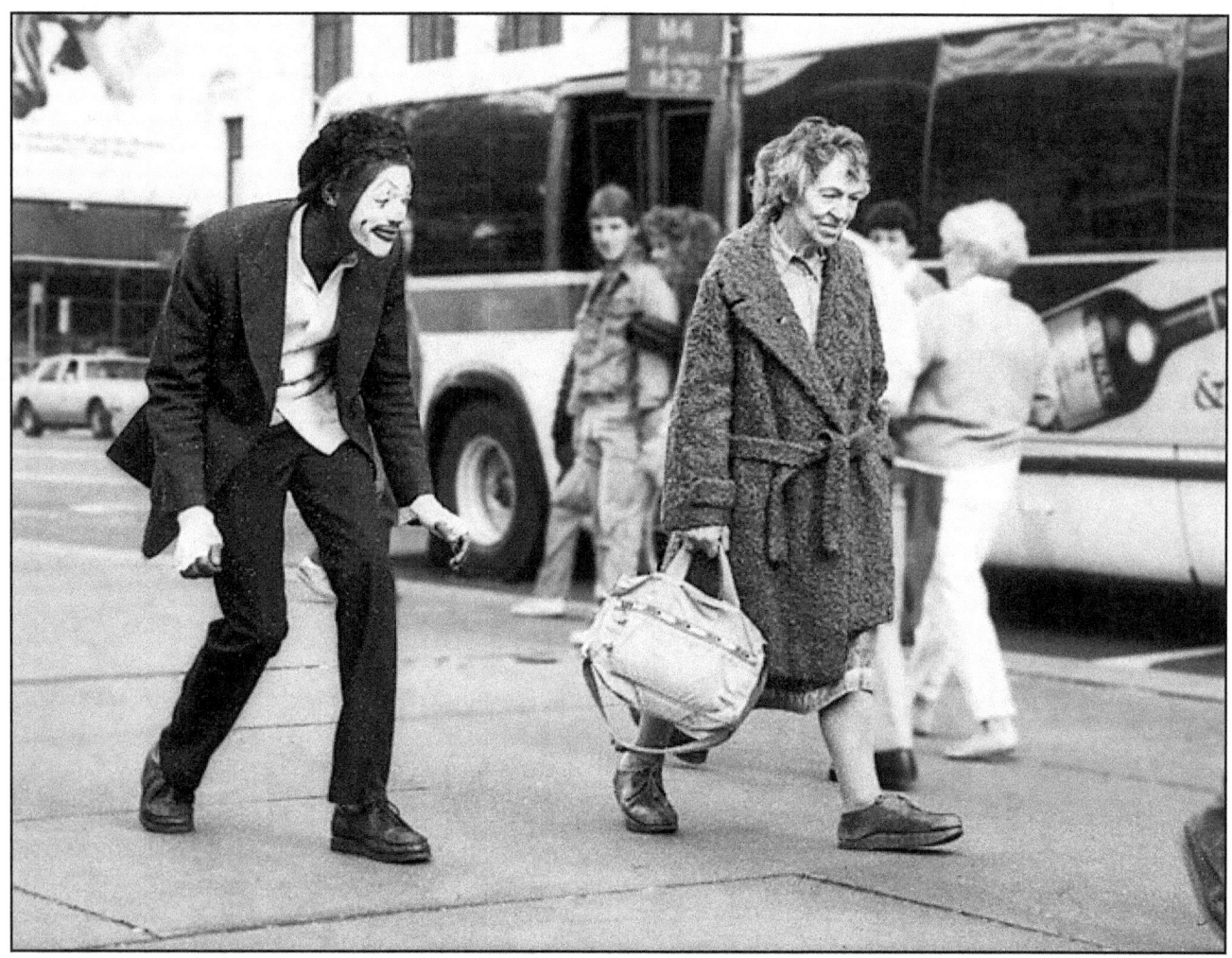

Town without pity

This poor lady looks like she just strolled out of a woman's shelter. Just because she's homeless doesn't mean the mime is going to cut her any slack. If she wanders into his territory, she's fair game.

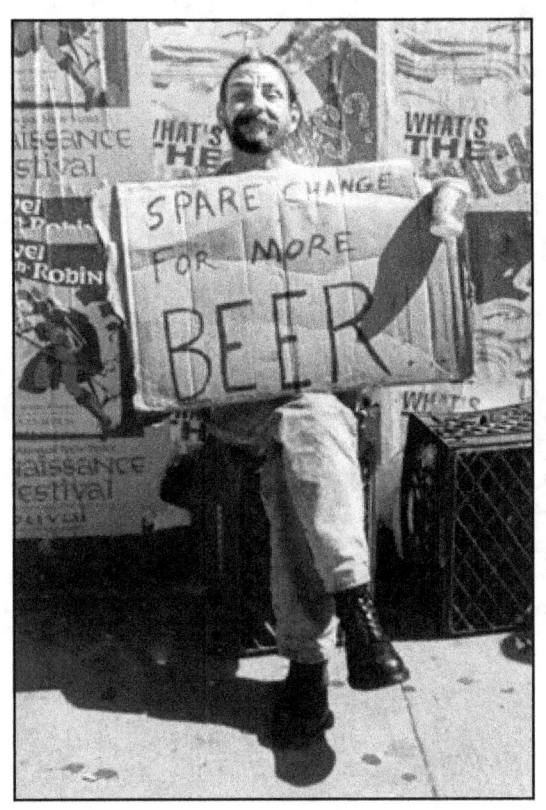
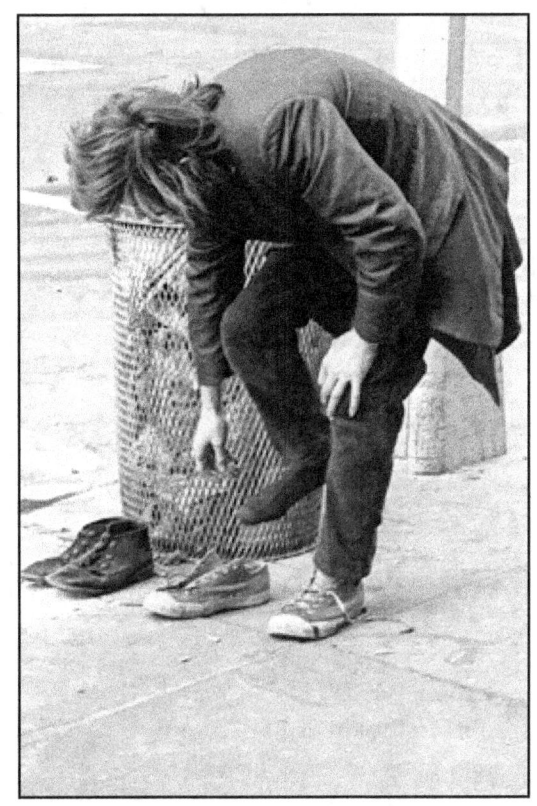

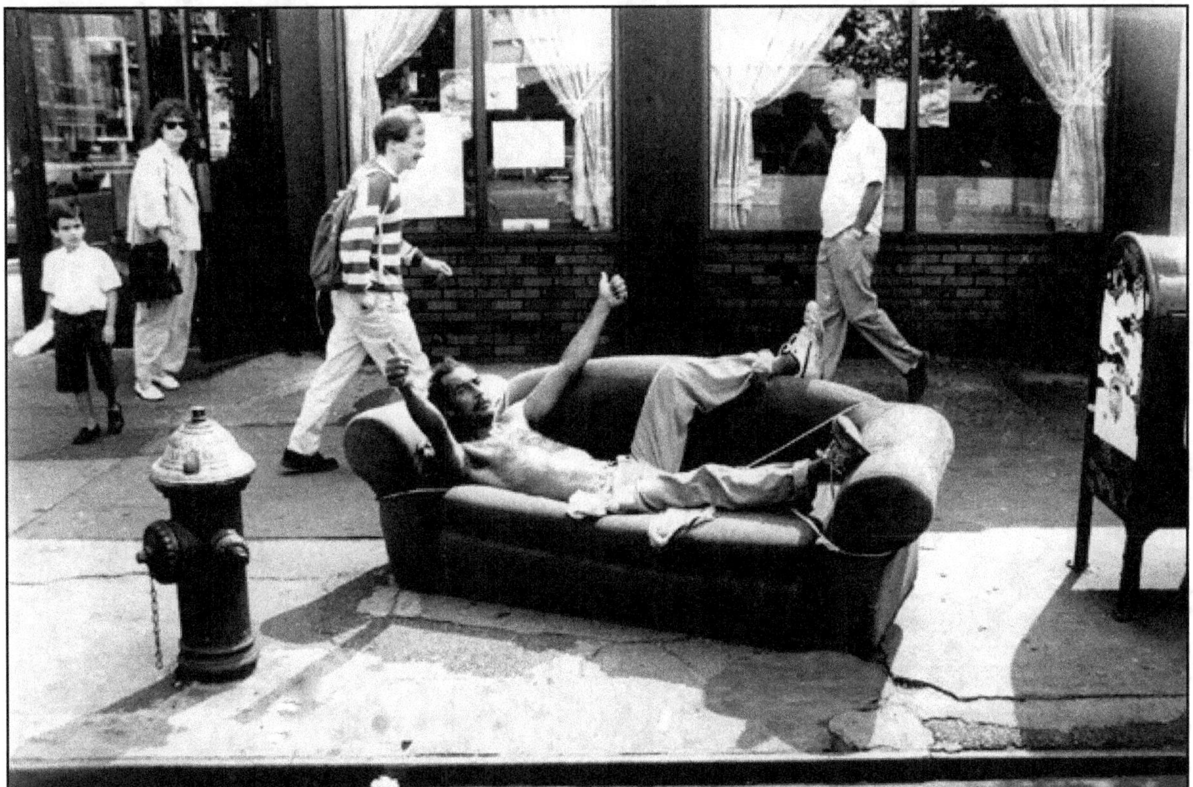

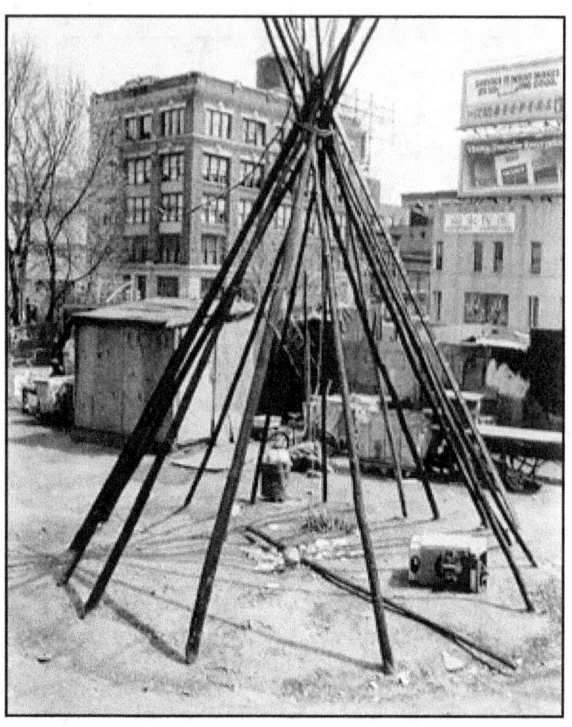
Right beside the Manhattan Bridge someone is building a teepee.

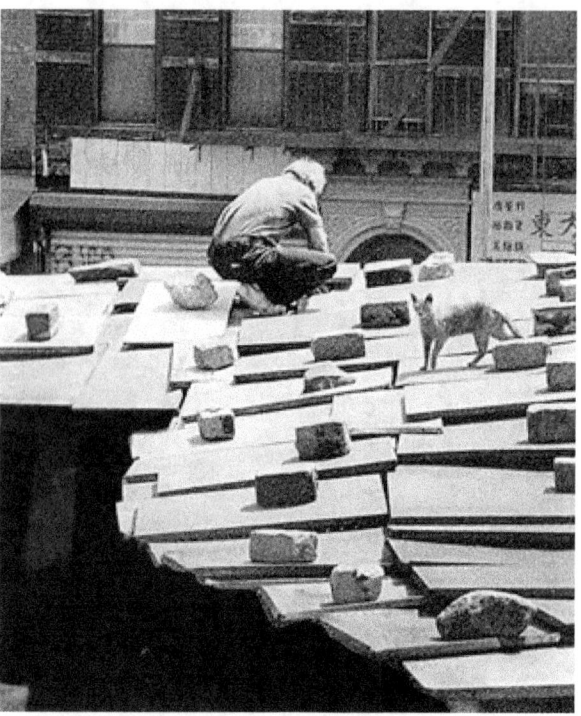
At the same site, this guy built a shelter for himself. He borrowed material from a nearby construction site.

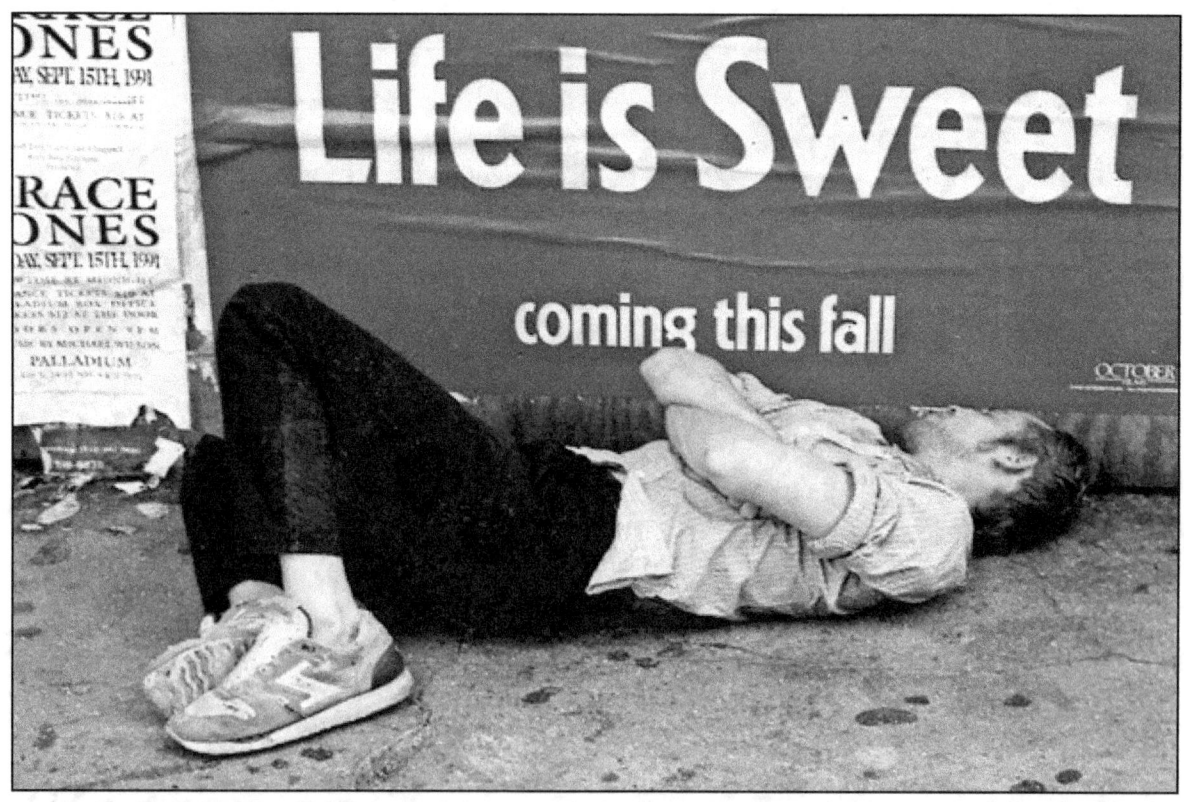
This was right in the middle of Times Square,
"The crossroads of the world"

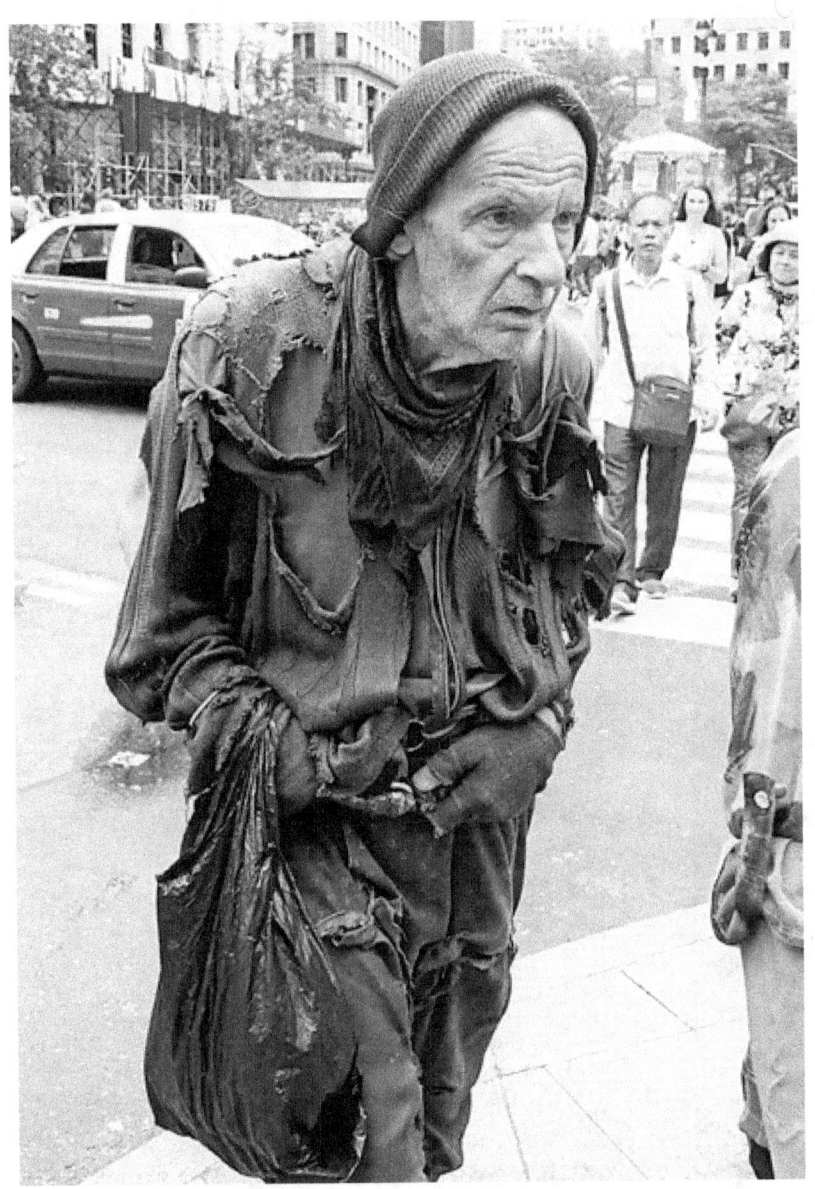
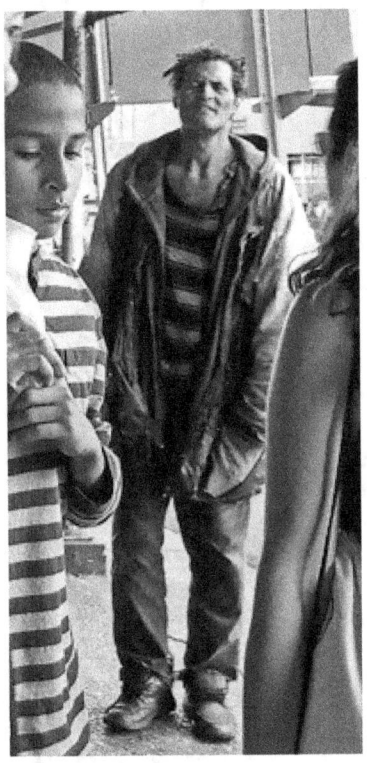
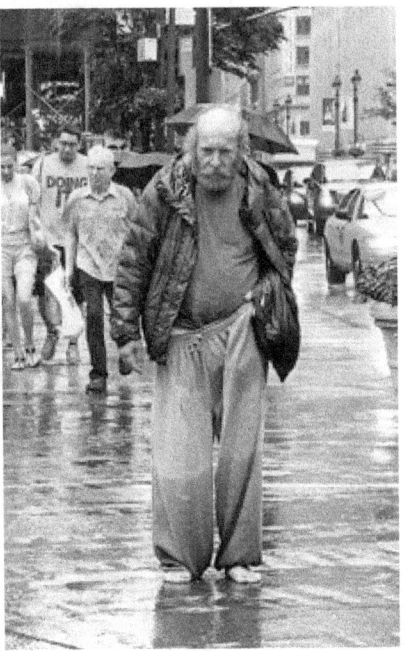

How come nobody is helping these guys?

You see them all over, people who are incapable of caring for themselves. They've fallen through the cracks and there doesn't seem to be anyone helping them. It's a disgrace.

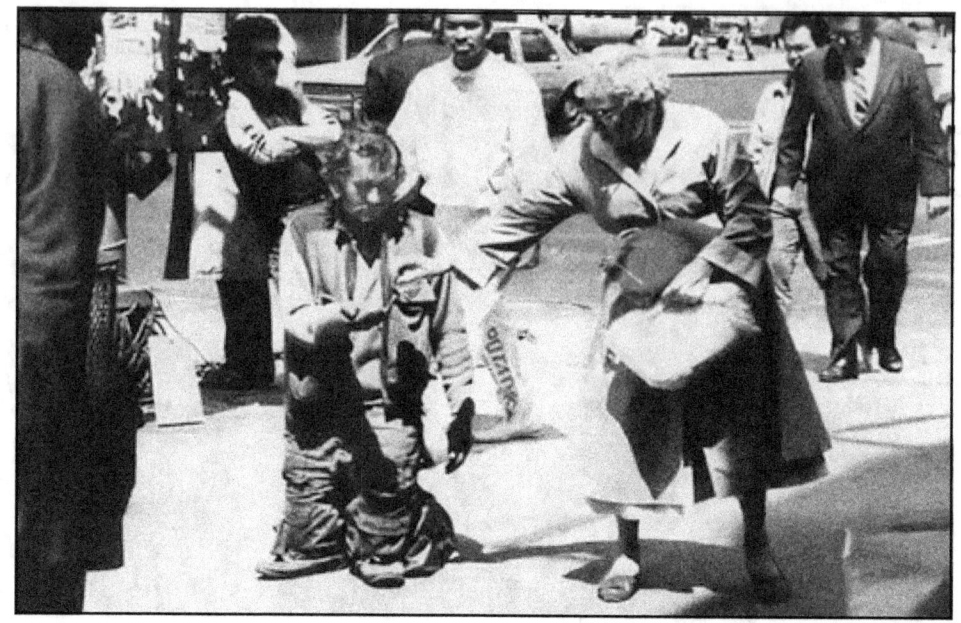

This guy is a little short on cash

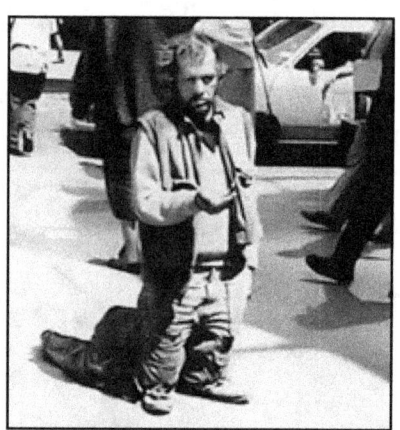

1. At first glance it looks like he has no lower legs, but this guy is actually a con-artist.

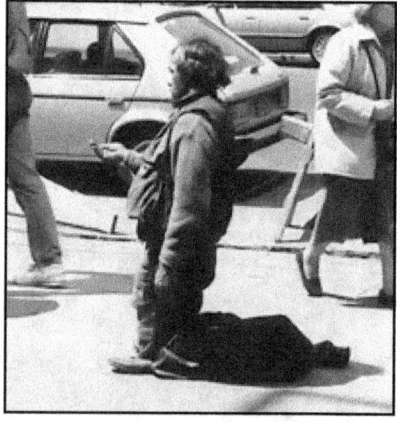

2. What he's really doing is kneeling on his shoes and covering up his lower legs with his jacket.

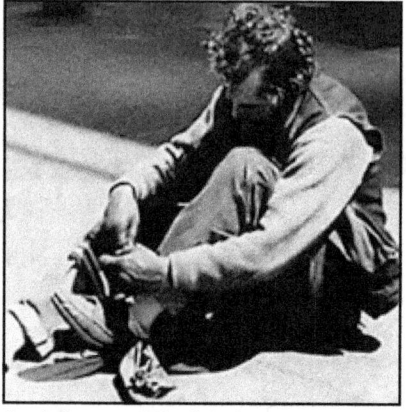

3. After awhile his legs start aching, so he has to get up.

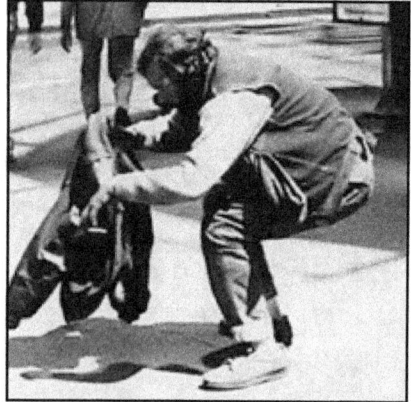

4. Then he puts on his shoes and jacket and relocates.

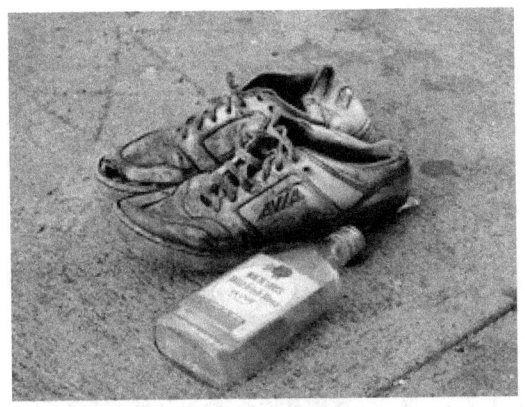

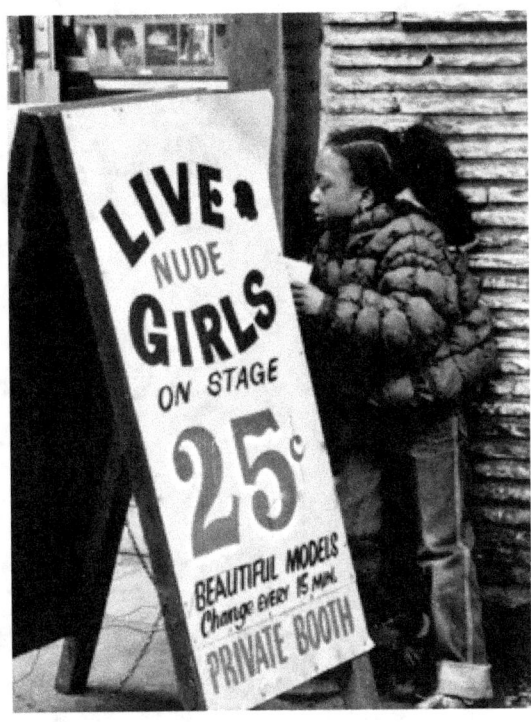

An experiment goes awry

In the 70s and 80s, the homeless problem in the city became acute. Many of these people were single women with children. As a stop-gap measure, city officials began putting these families into seedy hotels, many of them in the Times Square area. The sight of young children playing around the porno stores on 42nd St. became a public relations disaster for the city. This misguided policy was soon abandoned.

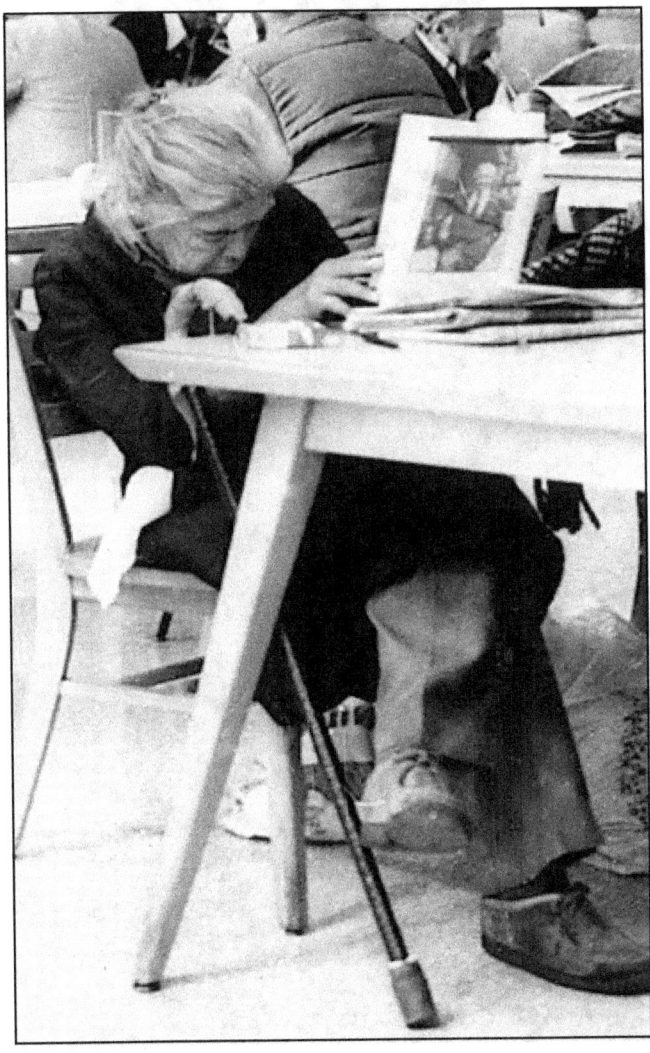

This poor old lady, would come to the library every day and sit in the same seat, and pretend to read a book, while she took a nap. She reminded me of my grandmother.

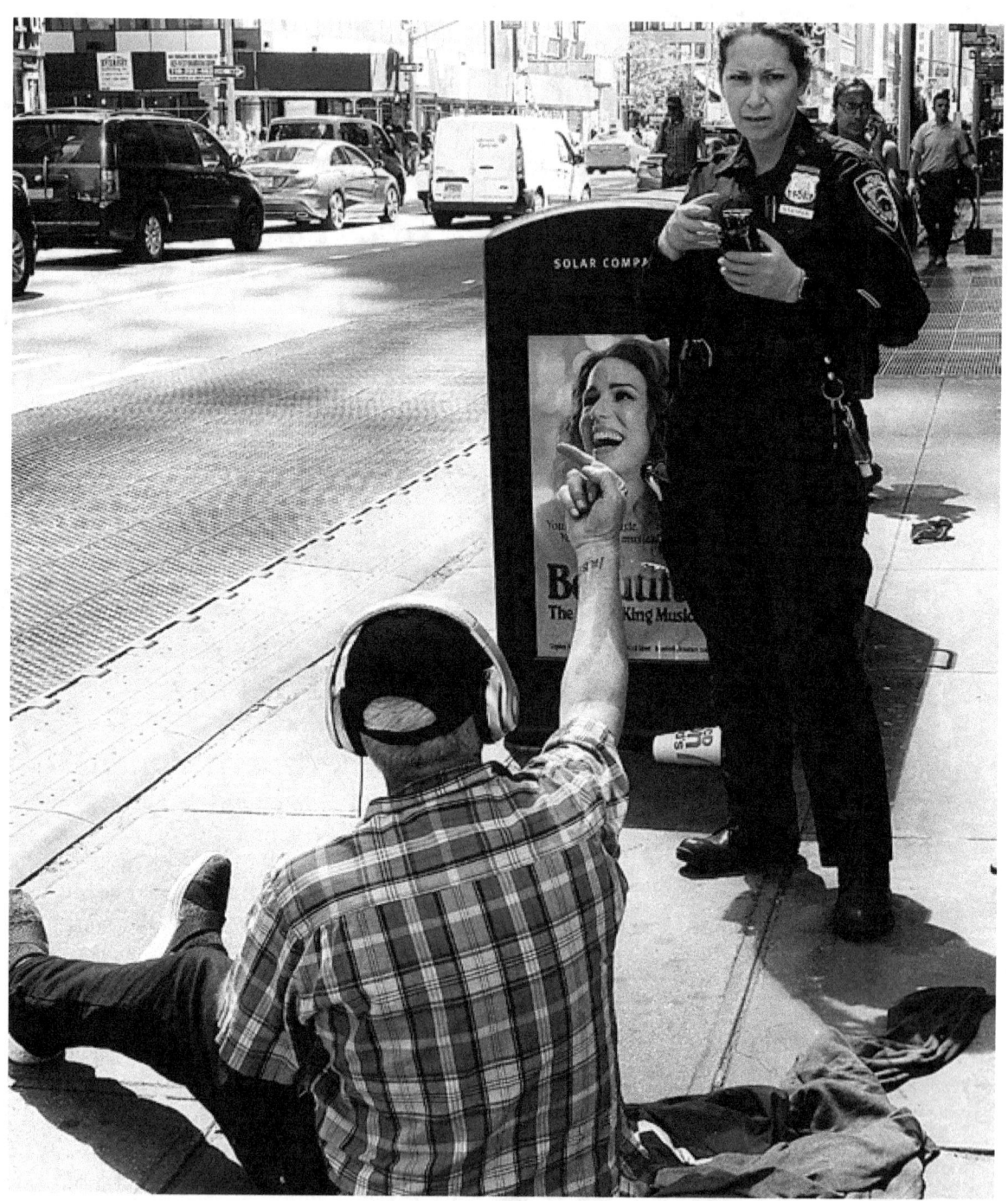

This cop just told this homeless guy that he had to move. He is now telling her what he thinks of her orders.

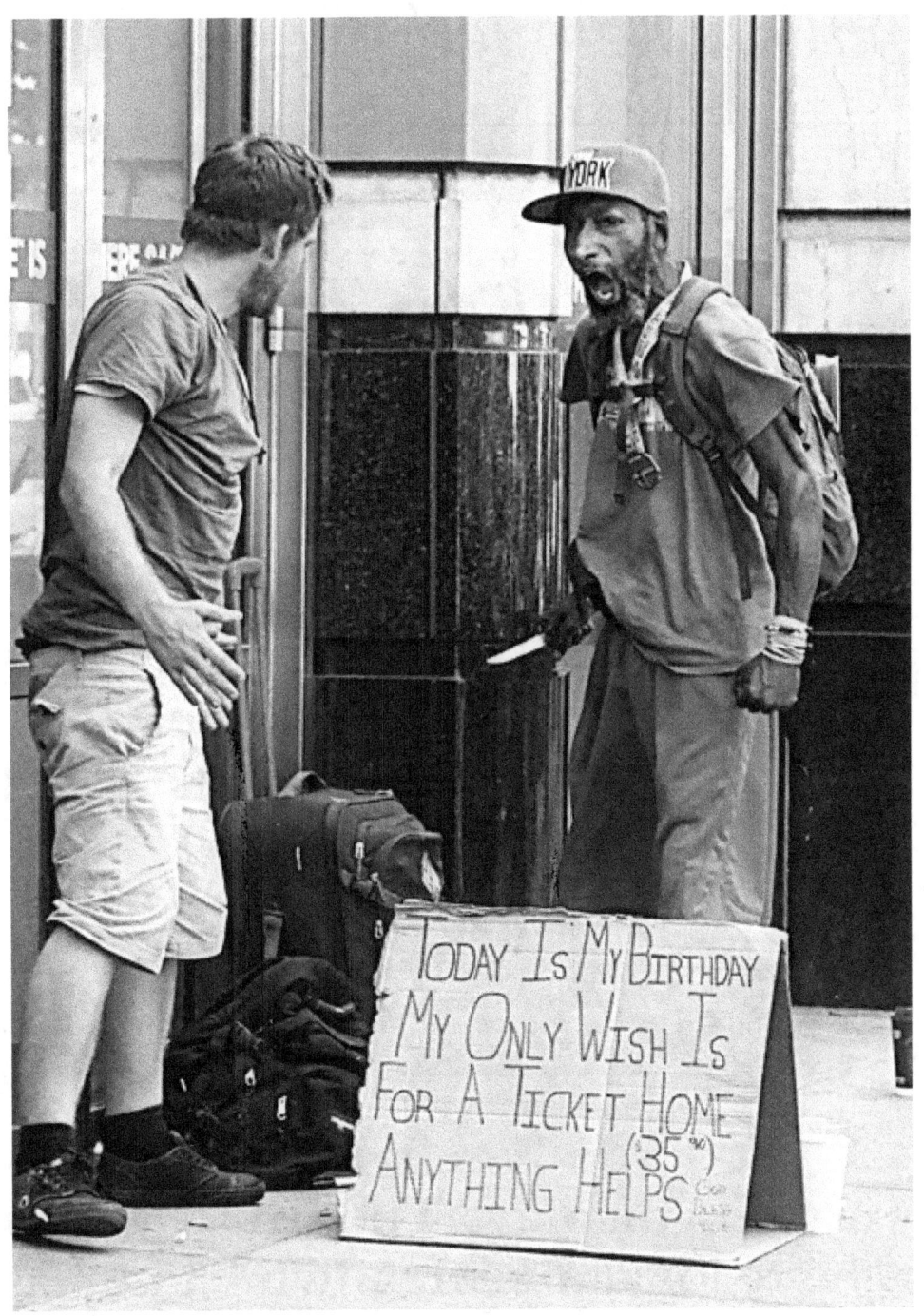

Being homeless can be dangerous
These two guys are quarreling over a prime spot from which to panhandle from. Incidents like this are quite common and can easily lead to violence.

Our beloved president

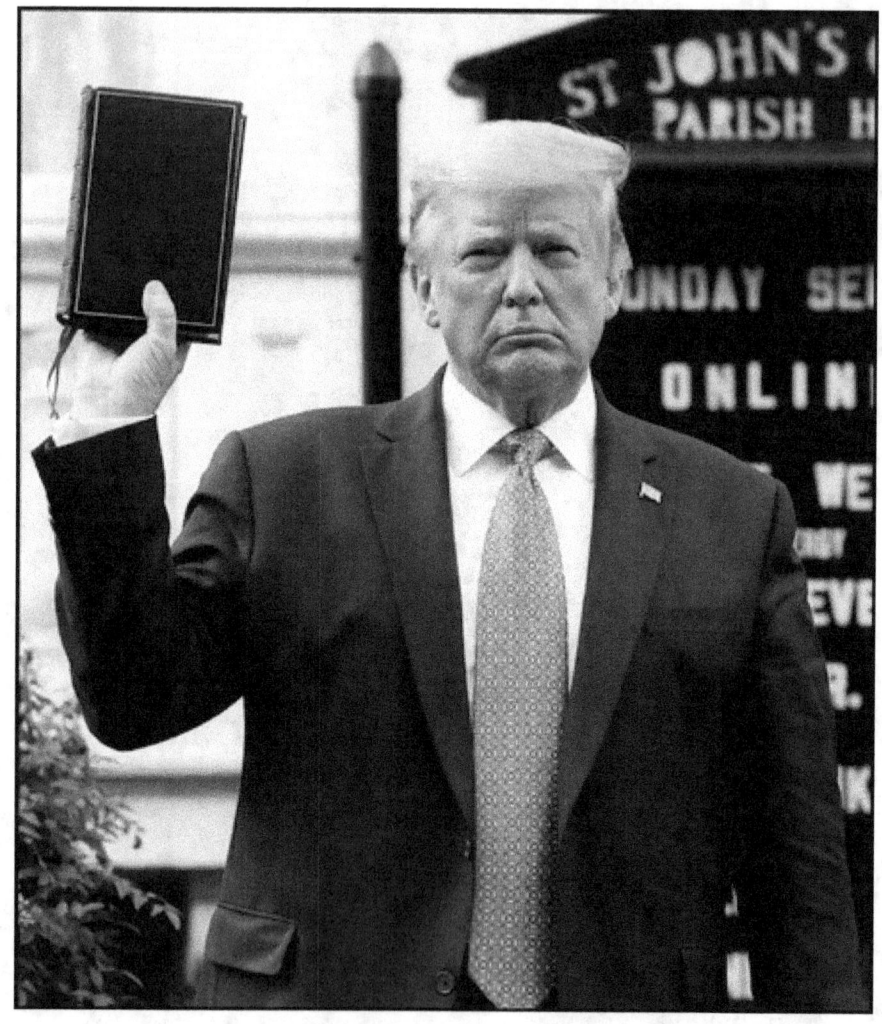

A devoutly religious Donald Trump displays The Bible, which he reads daily. Meanwhile, he has poor people tossed into the gutter on a regular basis. Nice.

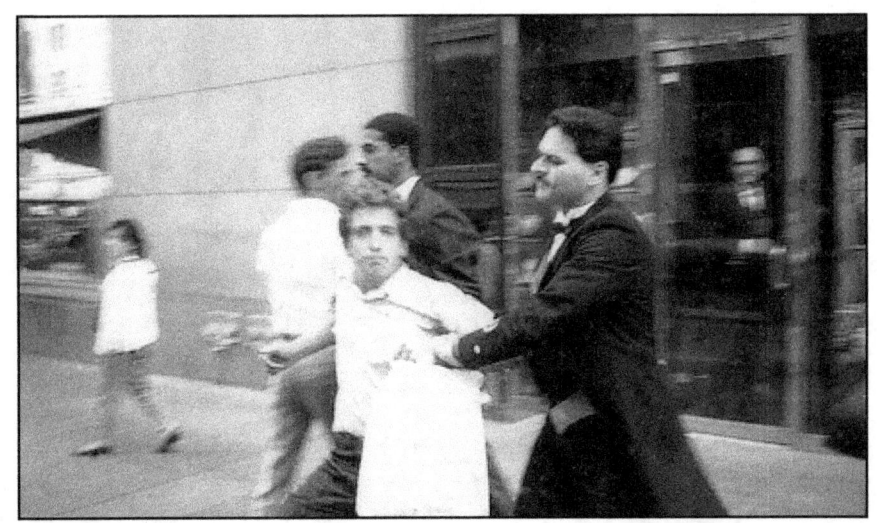

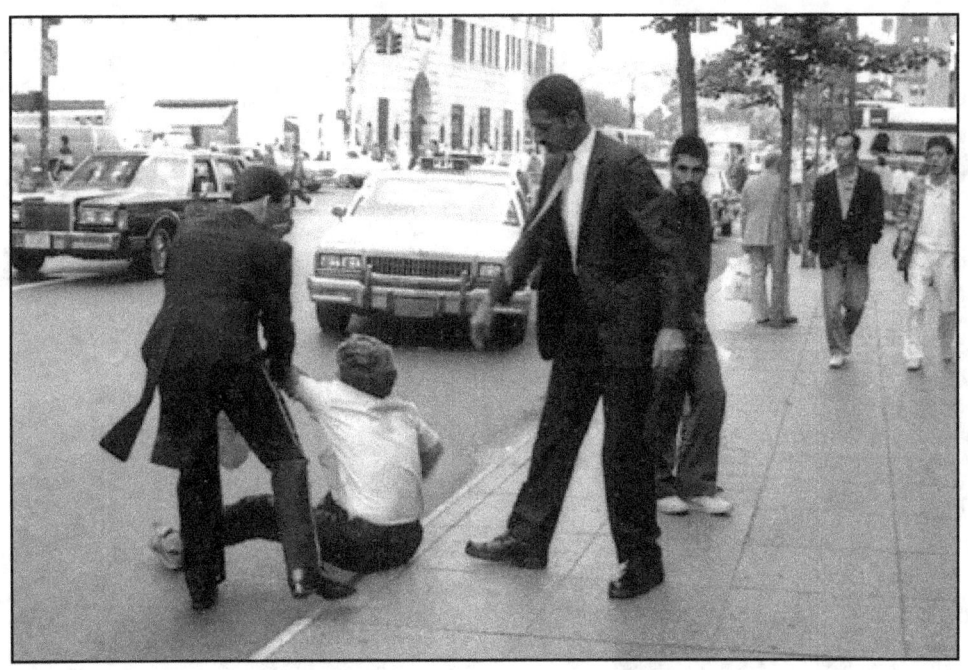

These pictures show Trump's doormen tossing a homeless man into the gutter like a sack of garbage. I confronted several of his doormen and asked them why they were treating these people so shabbily. Their answer was always the same, "It was Trump's orders." He didn't want homeless people anywhere near his building, "it didn't look good." he said, and "If they didn't move fast enough, throw them in the gutter, because these people are garbage anyway."

Chapter 18

Stacks
Stacks
Stacks
Stacks
Stacks
Stacks
Stacks
Stacks

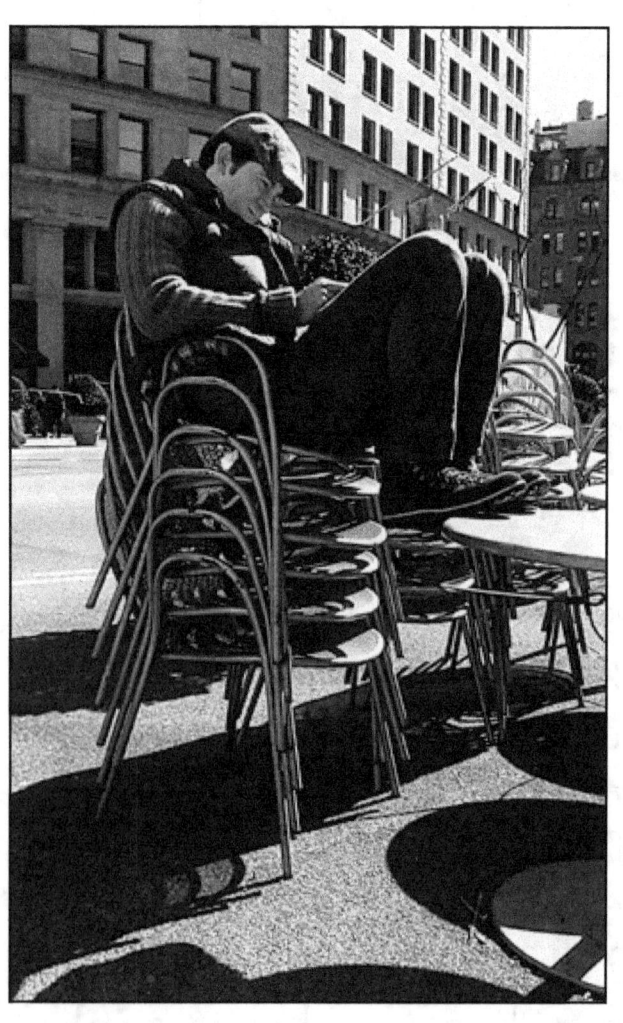
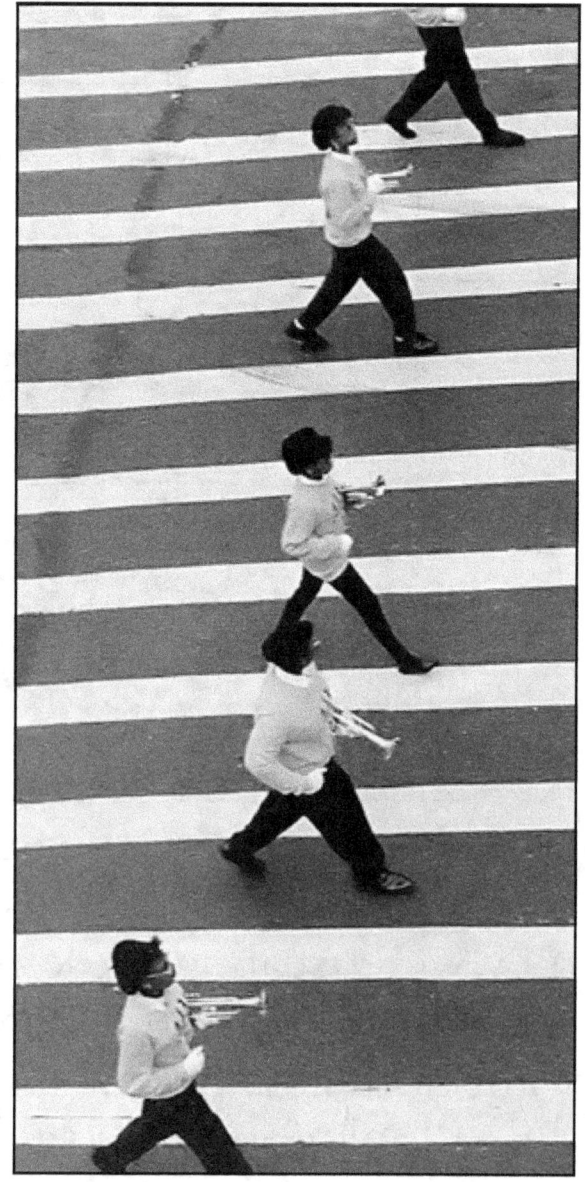

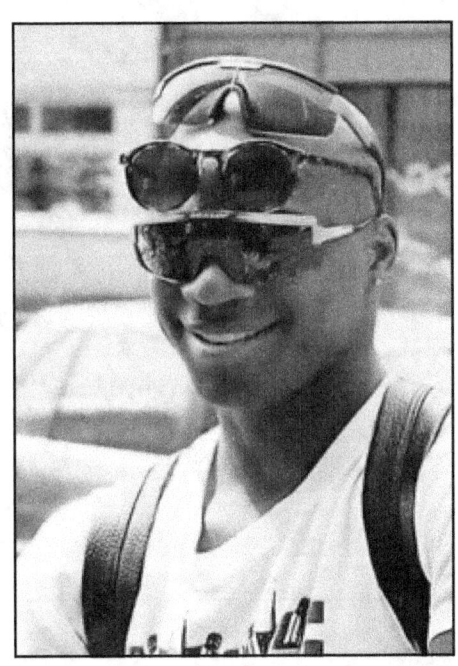

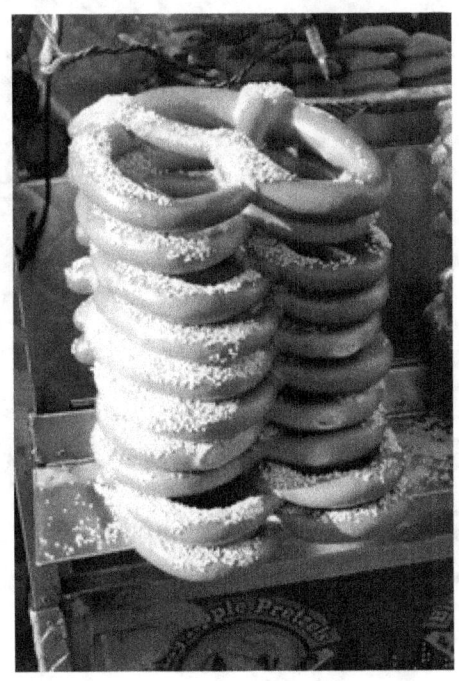

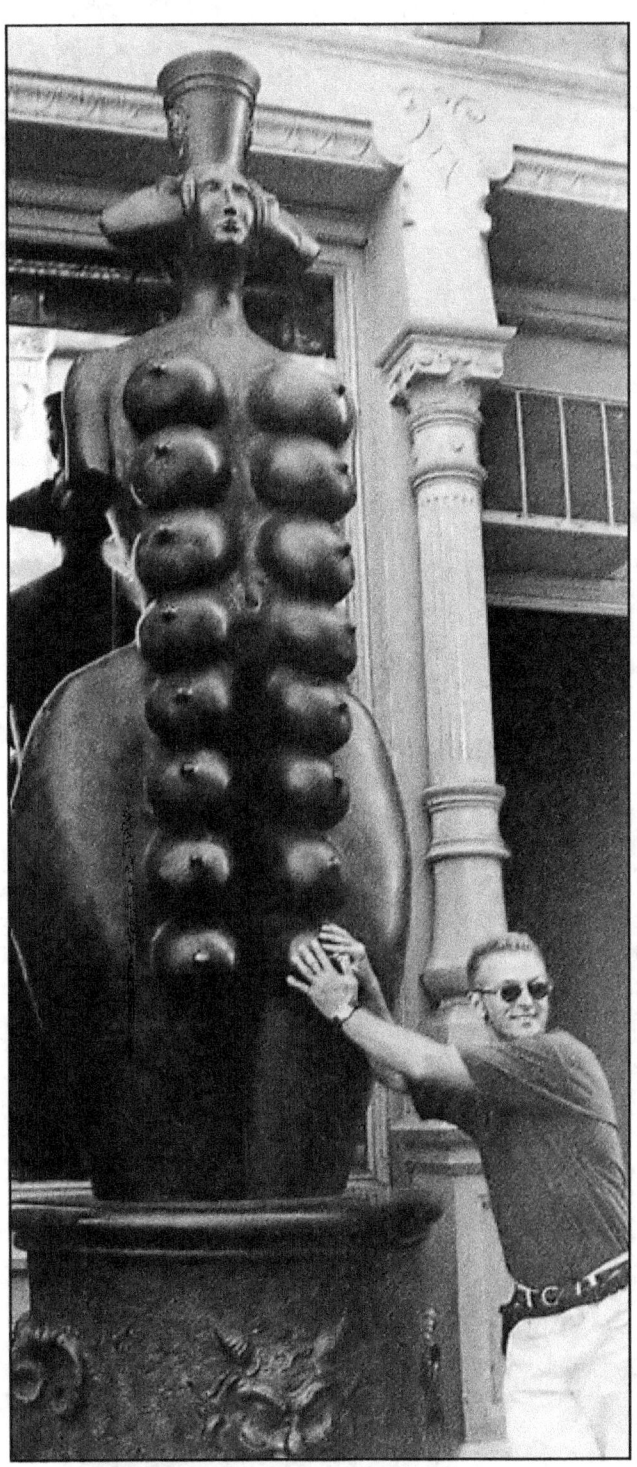

This statue was down in Soho.

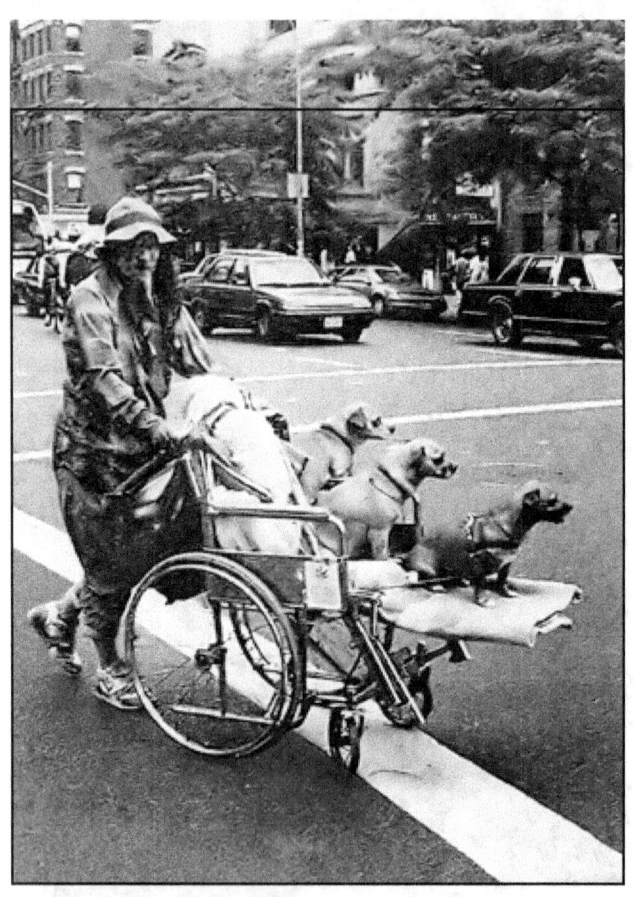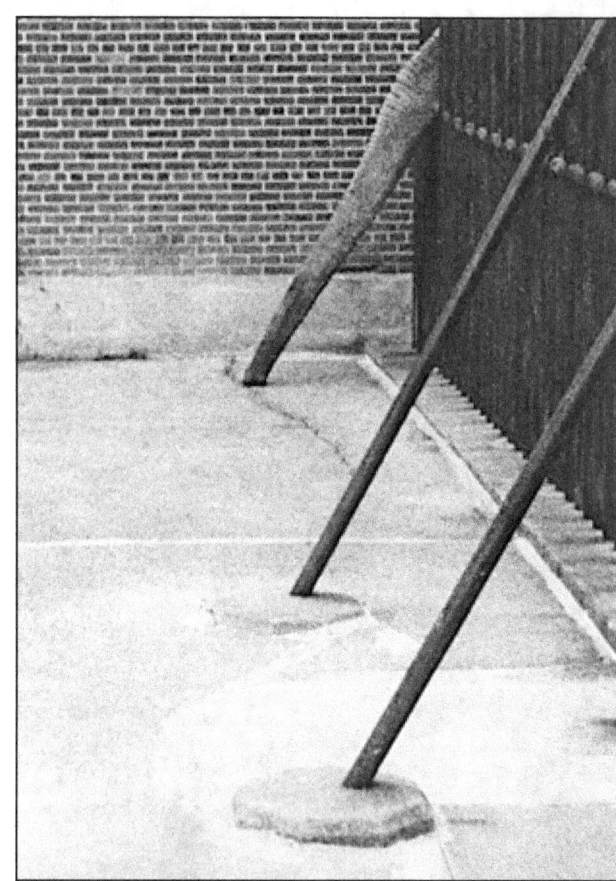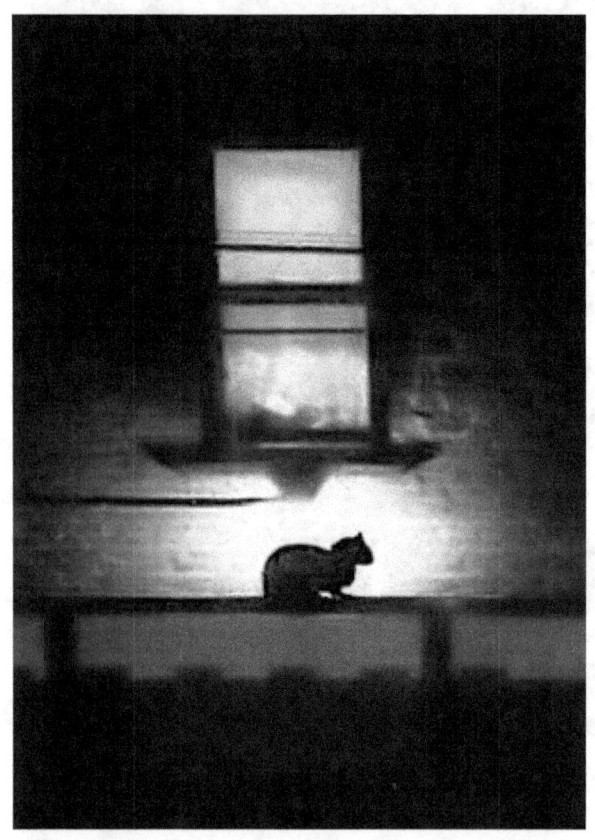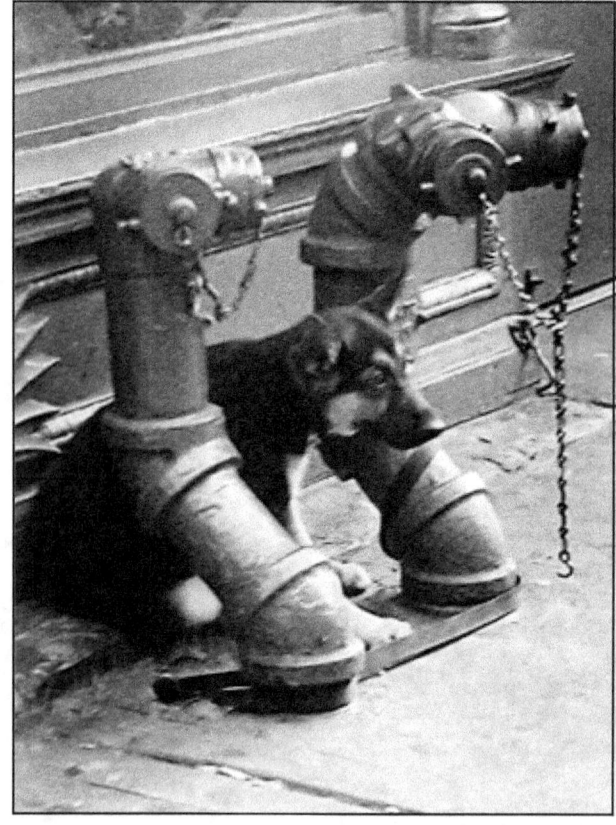

Chapter 19

City critters

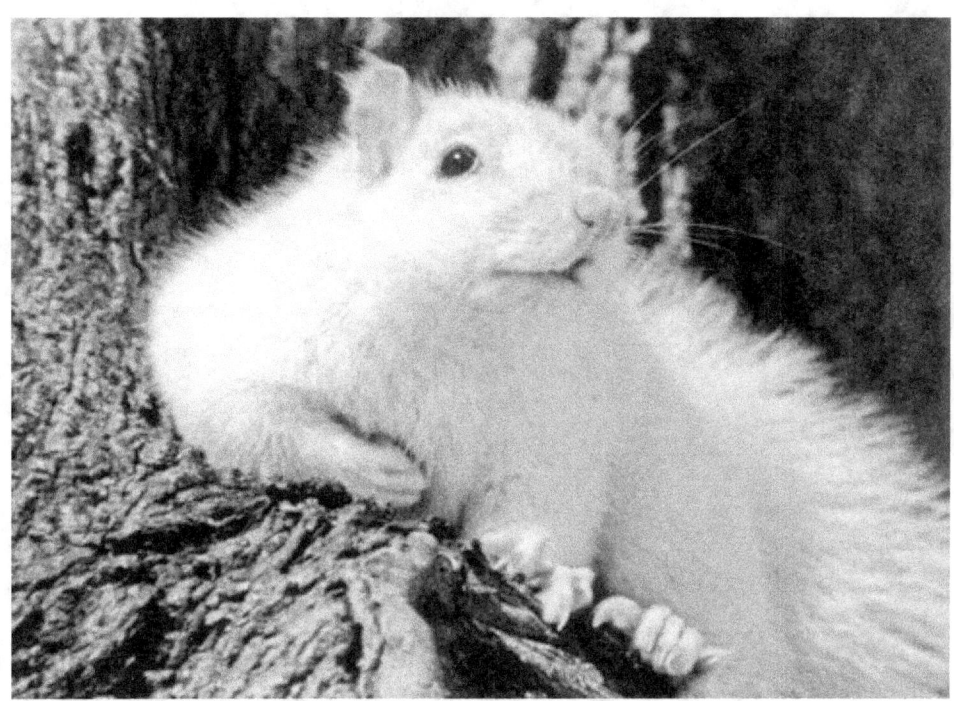

Snowflake

This is Snowflake, a completely white squirrel, who hangs out in Union Square Park. There are also completely black squirrels in the same park. How they survive is a mystery, because New York is full of birds of prey, and they must stand out like sore thumbs.

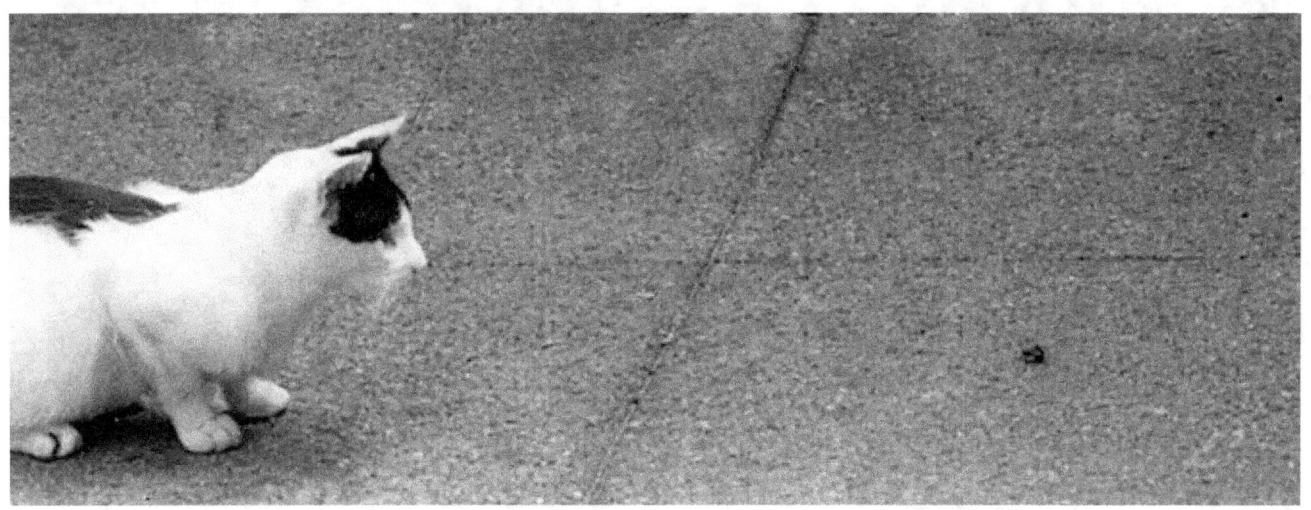

This is my cat staring at something in my backyard. I put a close-up lens on my camera and took a picture of it.

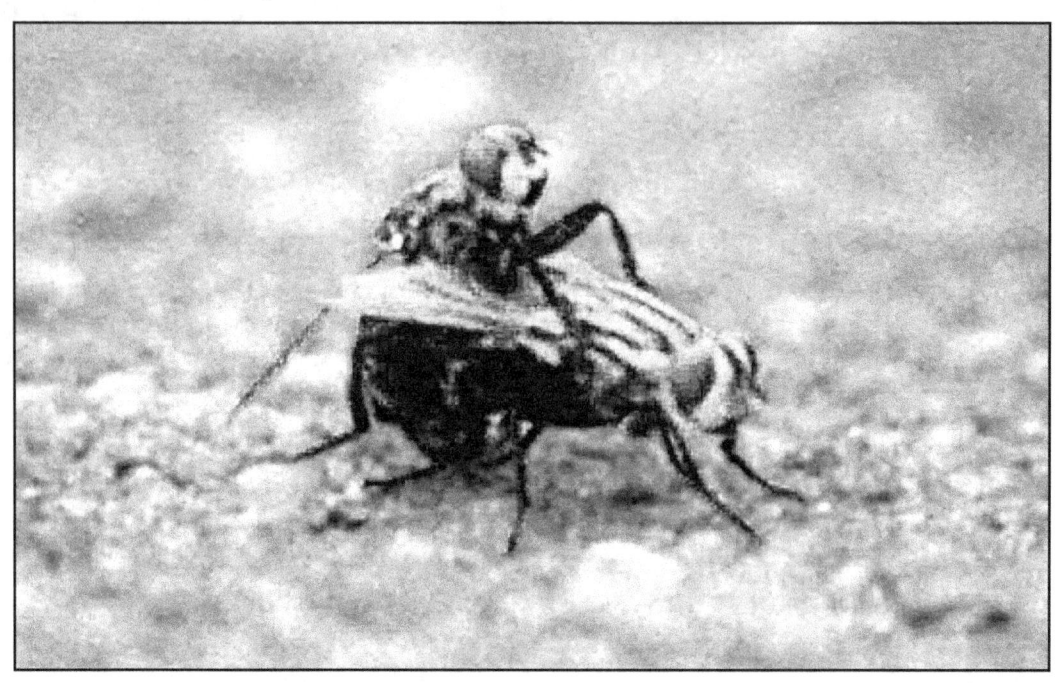

Sex and the City

I hope these two flies had a good time because this was their last act on this earth. Right after this picture, my cat ate them.

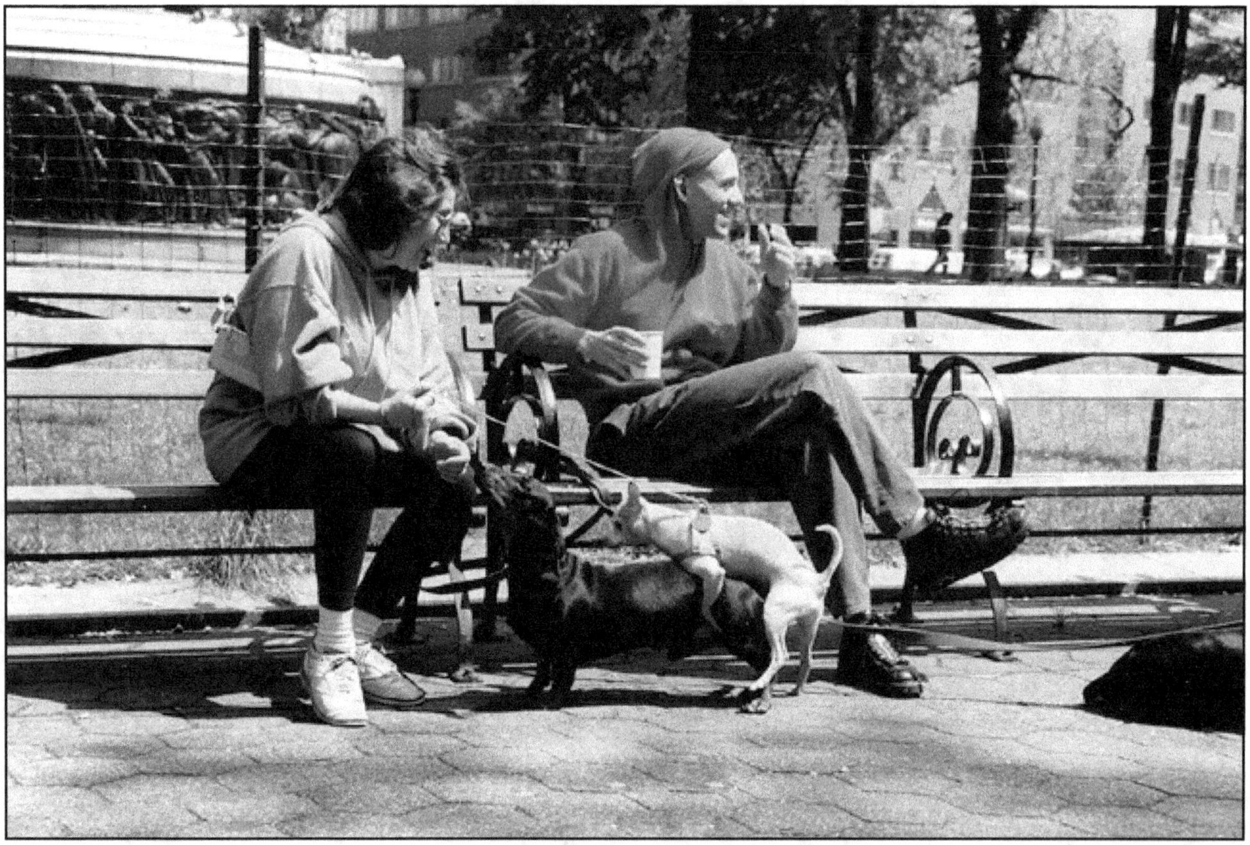

more Sex and the City

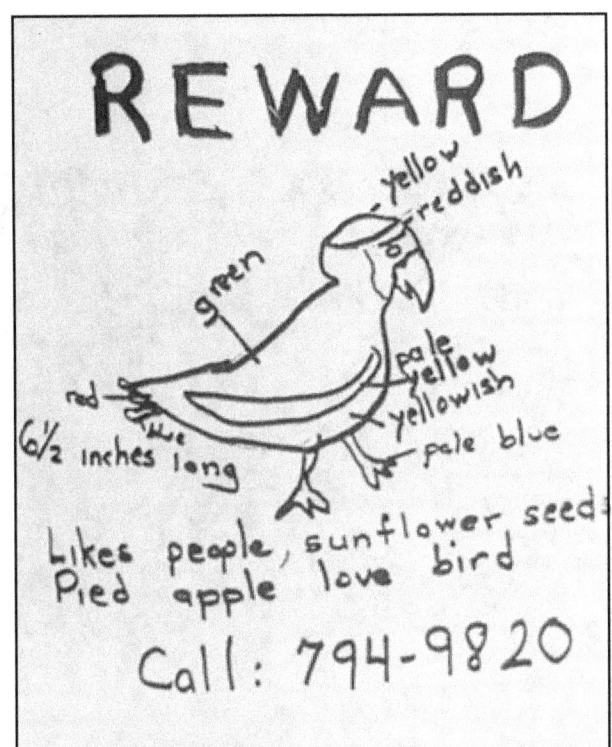
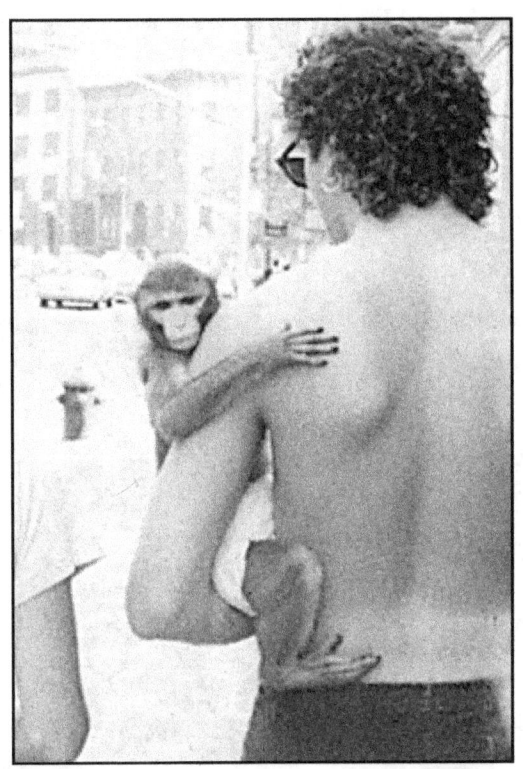

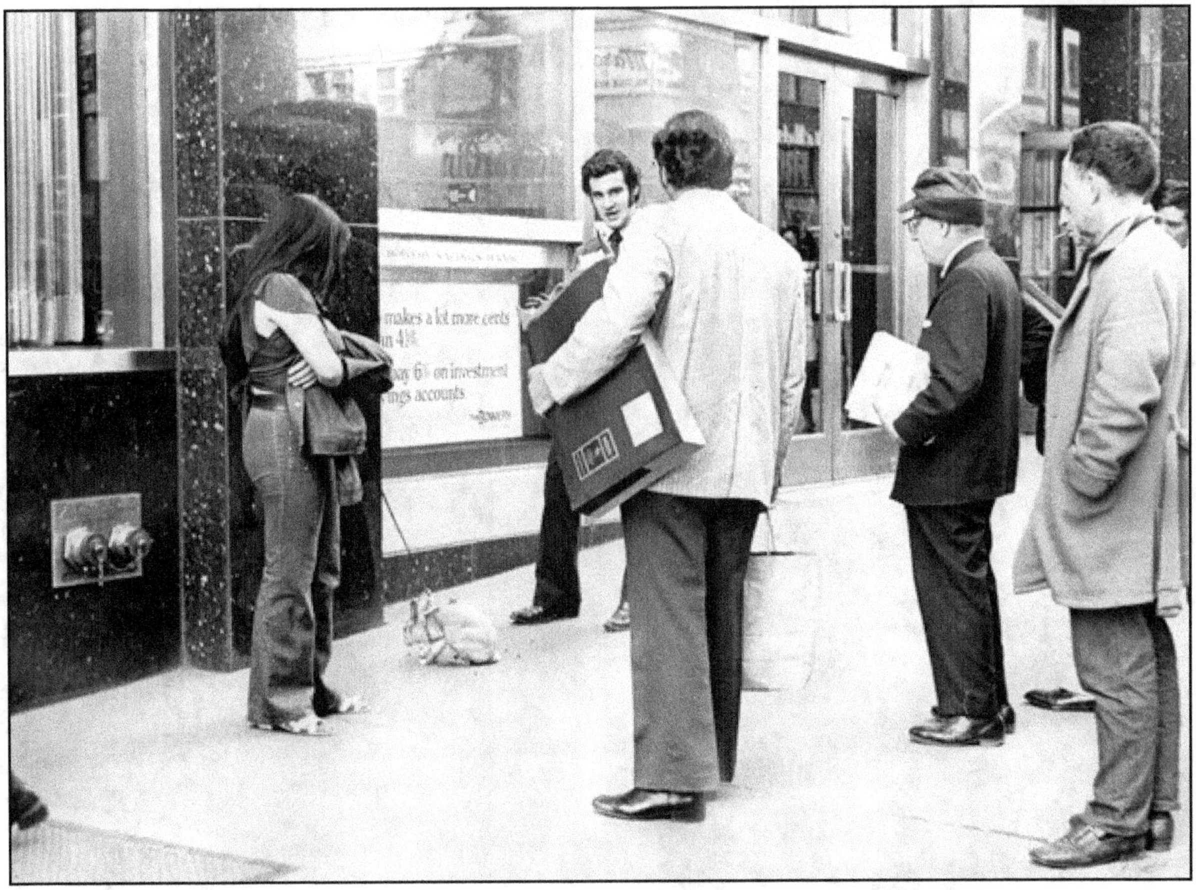

Look at these guys, you'd think they never saw a rabbit before.

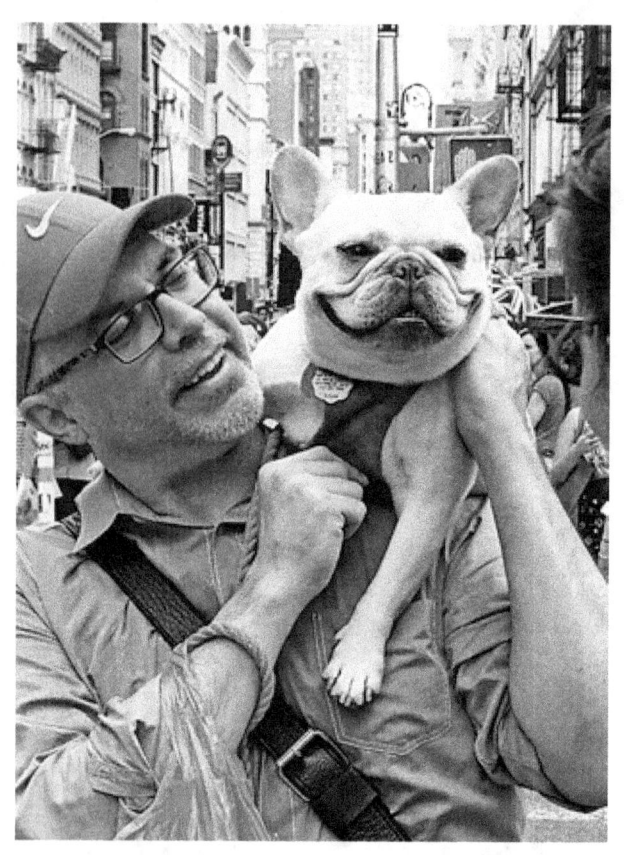
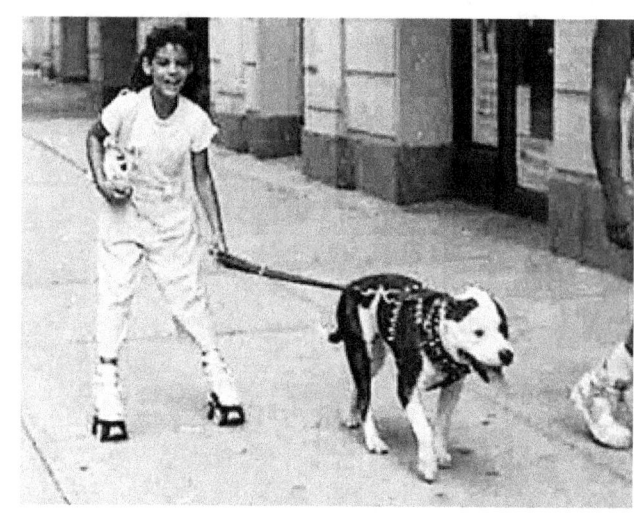
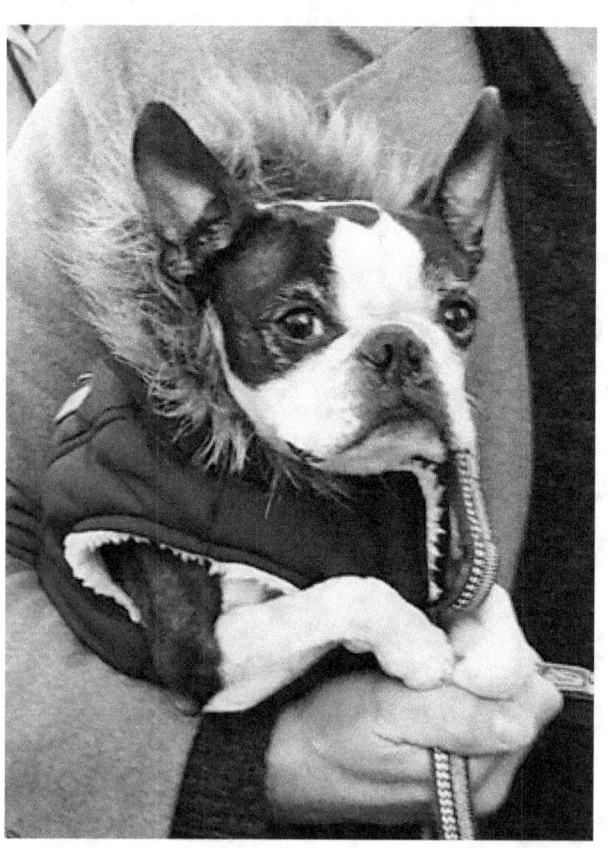
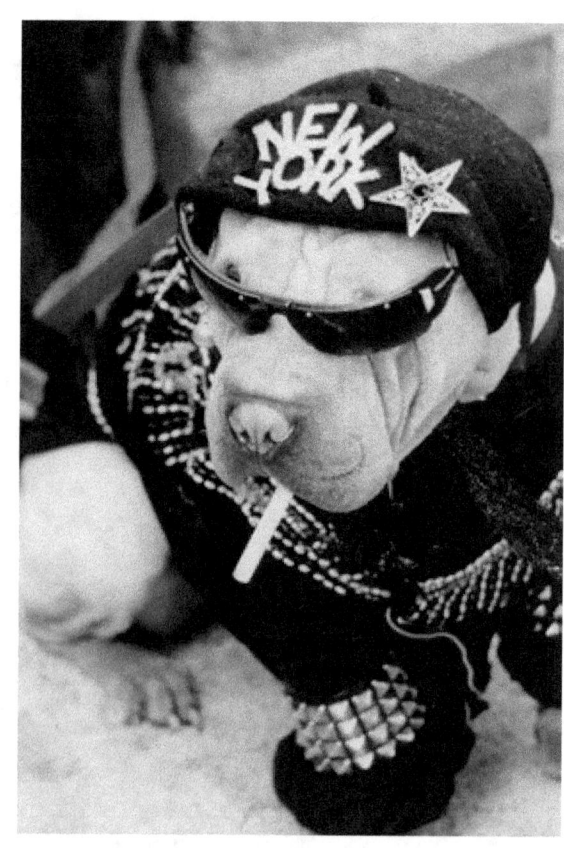

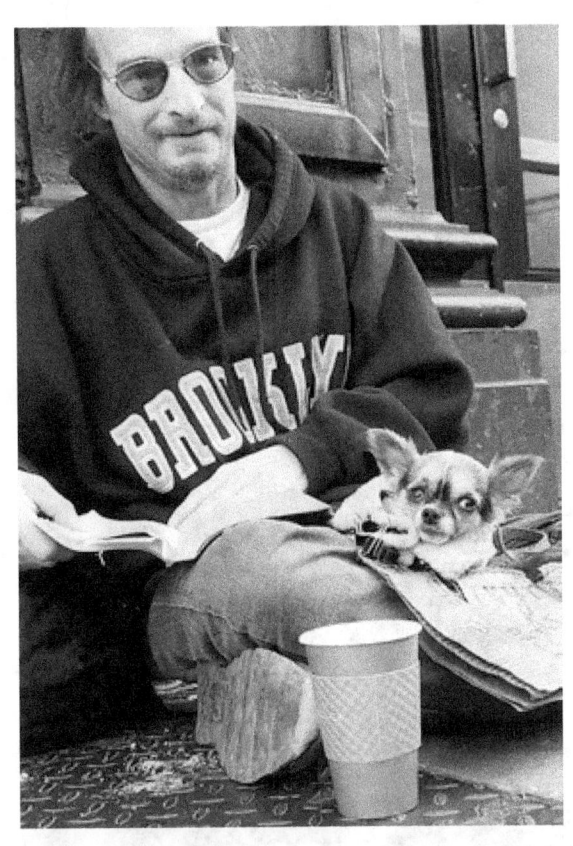
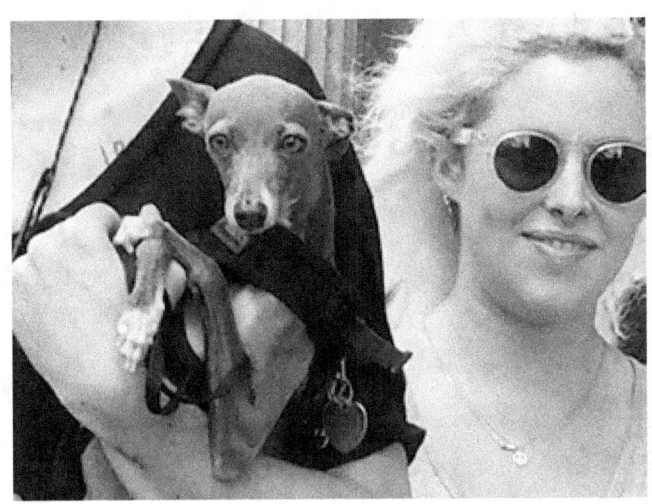

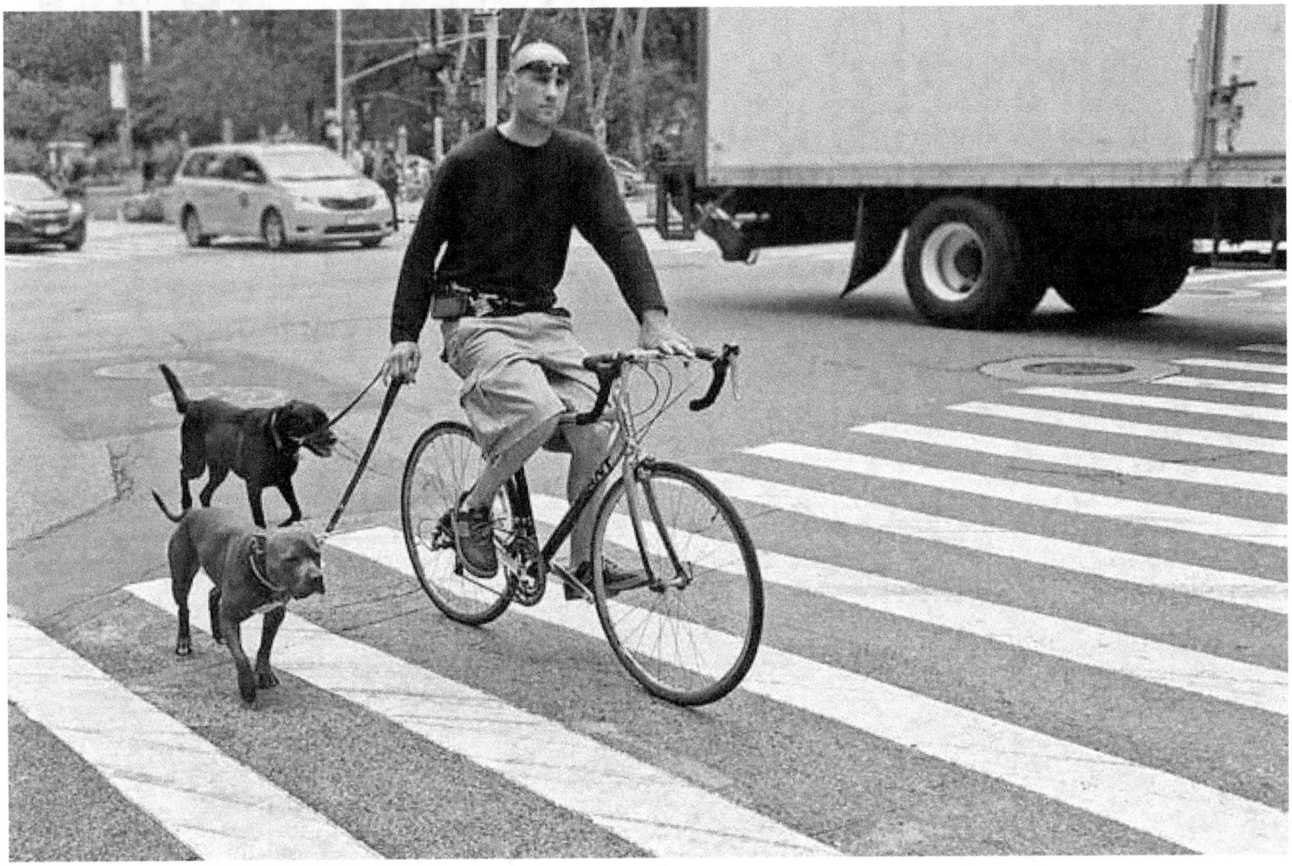

P.E.T.A. saves the pigeons

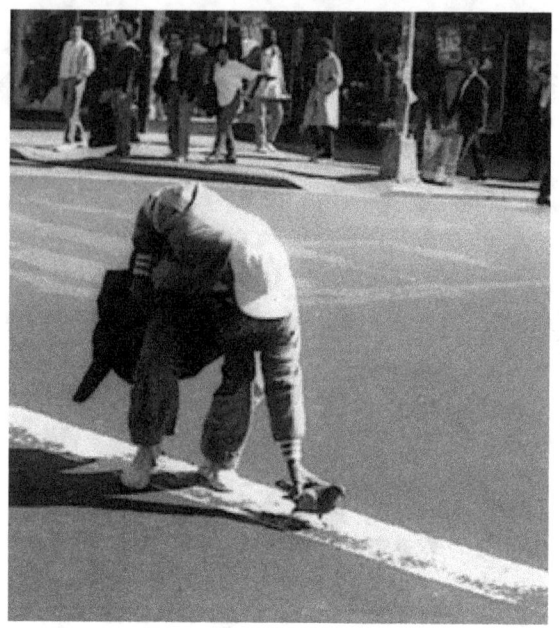

The city discovered that every year 19,000 baby pigeons were run over by cars while crossing the street. A group calling themselves P.E.T.A. (People for the Ethical Treatment of Anything) volunteered to teach these pigeons how to cross the street safely. "We must stop the slaughter of the innocents," a spokesman said. During the first year, twenty-seven of these volunteers were struck and killed by cars and dozens injured. When asked if it was worth this human toll, to save a bunch of pigeons, a spokesman said, "Absolutely, because pigeons are people too." Rather than having so many volunteers from P.E.T.A. killed, the city decided to incarcerate all of the pigeons in the city for their own safety.

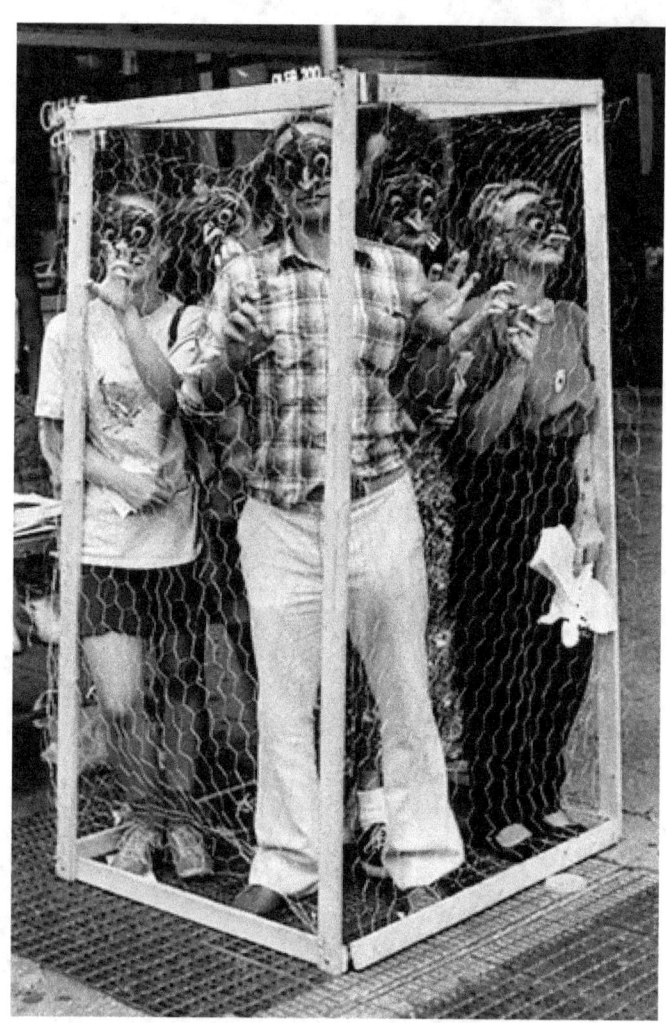

Let my pigeons go

Activists from P.E.T.A., wear pigeon masks inside a pigeon coop to call attention to the plight of the imprisoned pigeons. The president of P.E.T.A., Mr. Jacob Moses held an emotional press-conference, with tears in his eyes Moses said, "Let my pigeons go."

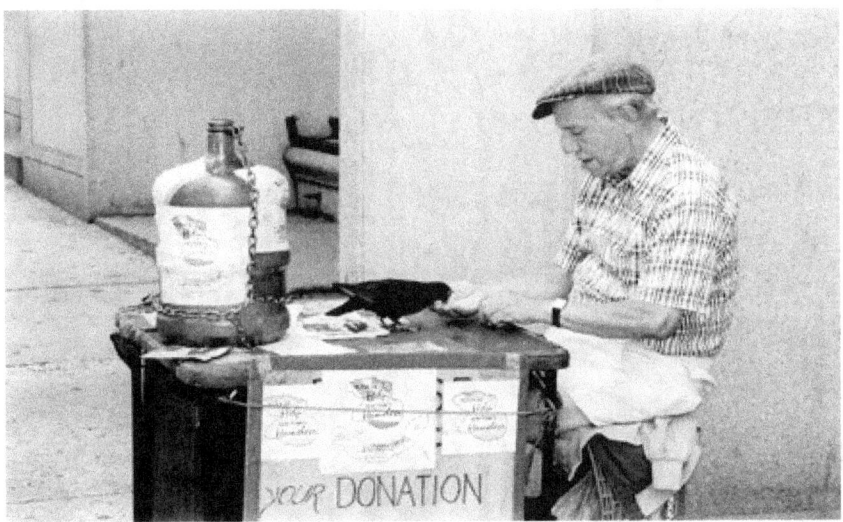

The treasurer of P.E.T.A., Mr. Leo Bloom, dispenses aid to an imprisoned pigeon. The case went all the way to the supreme court where the ruling was in favor of freeing the pigeons.

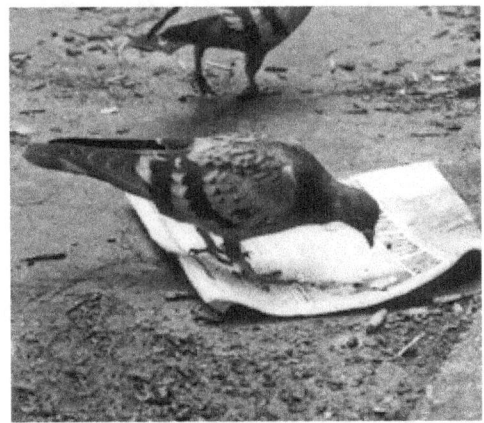

A concerned pigeon follows the case in the papers.

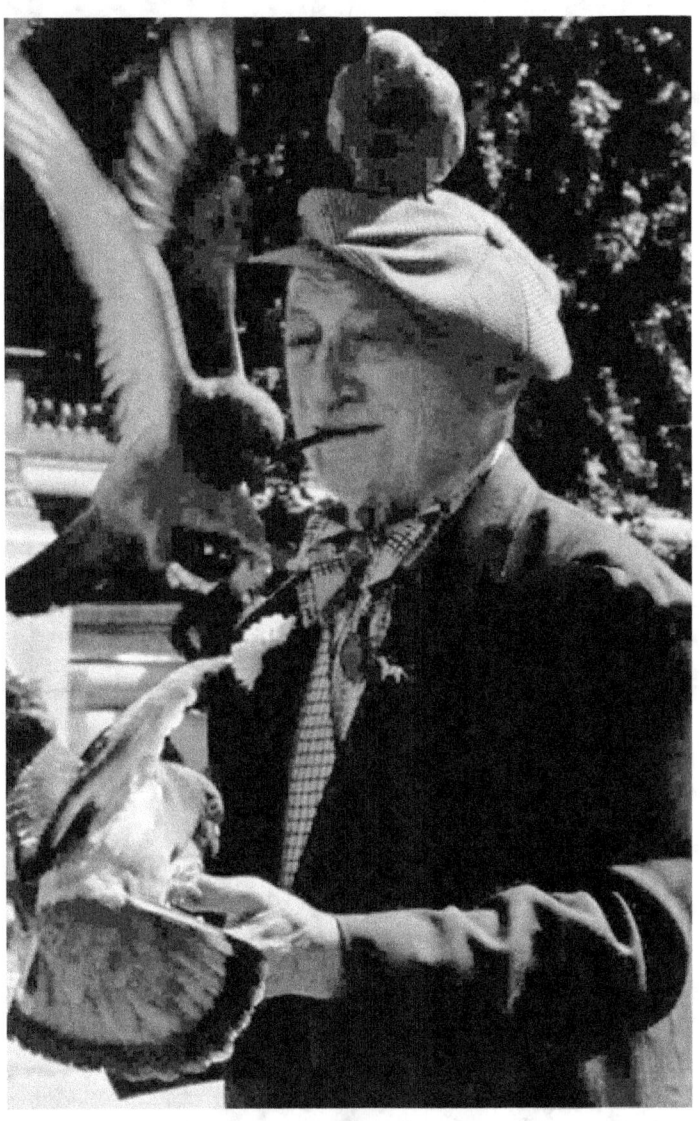

Mr. Melvin Lipschitz, a vice-president of P.E.T.A. celebrates with some pigeons after the favorable court ruling.

Chapter 20
The little man in the traffic light

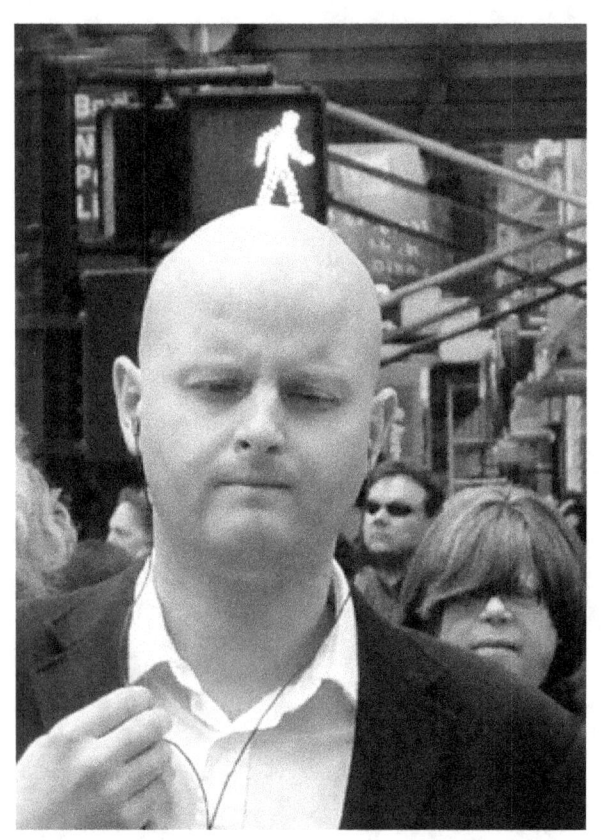
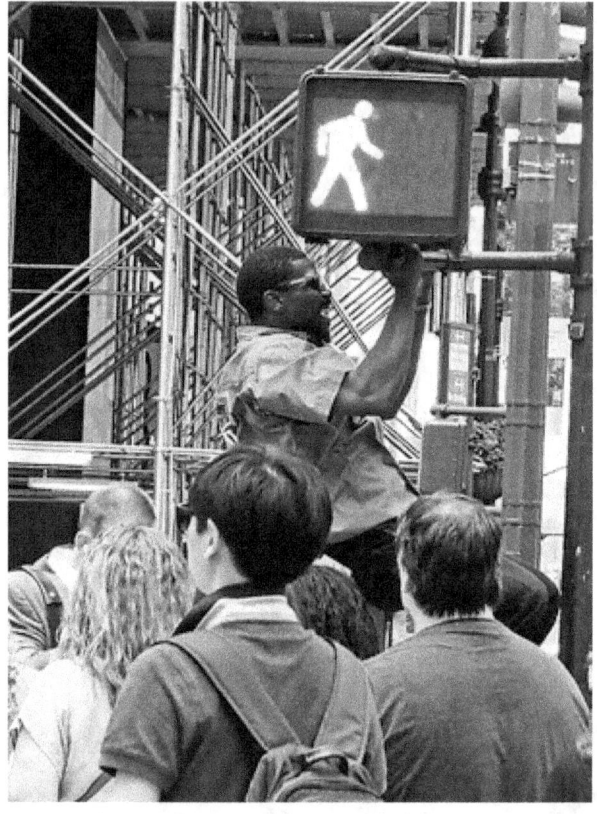
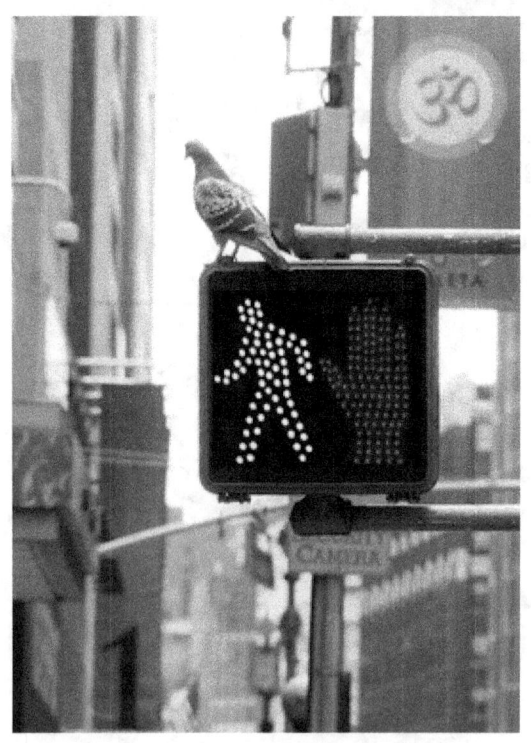
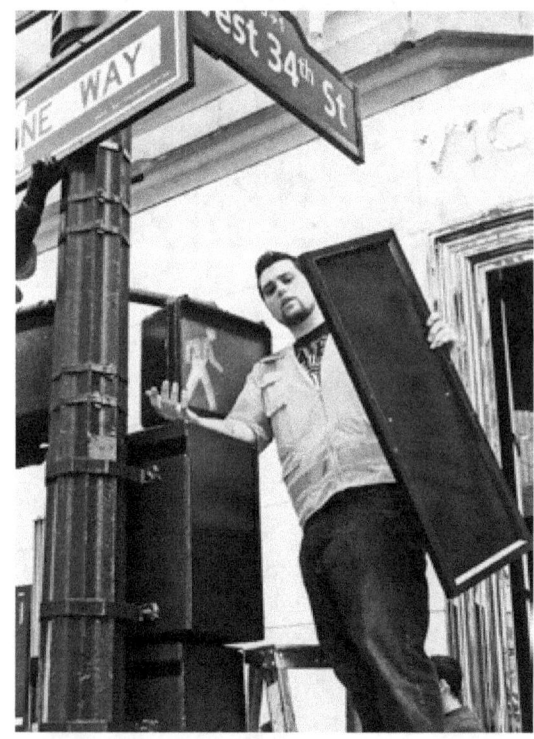

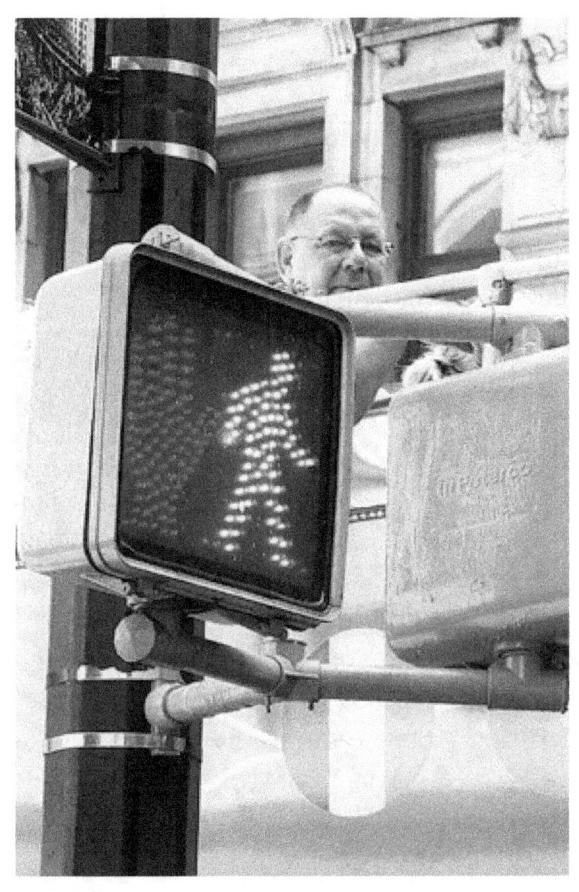
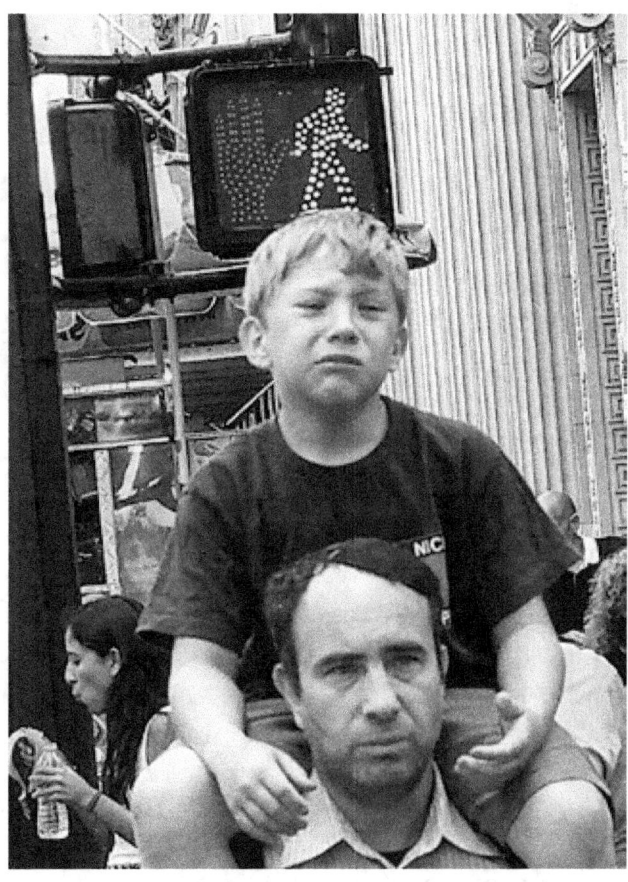
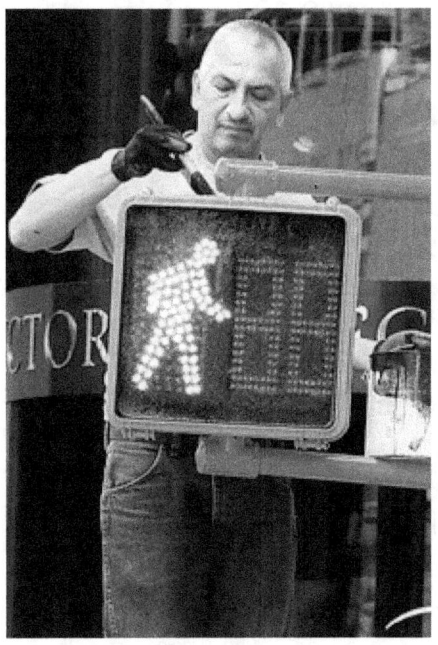
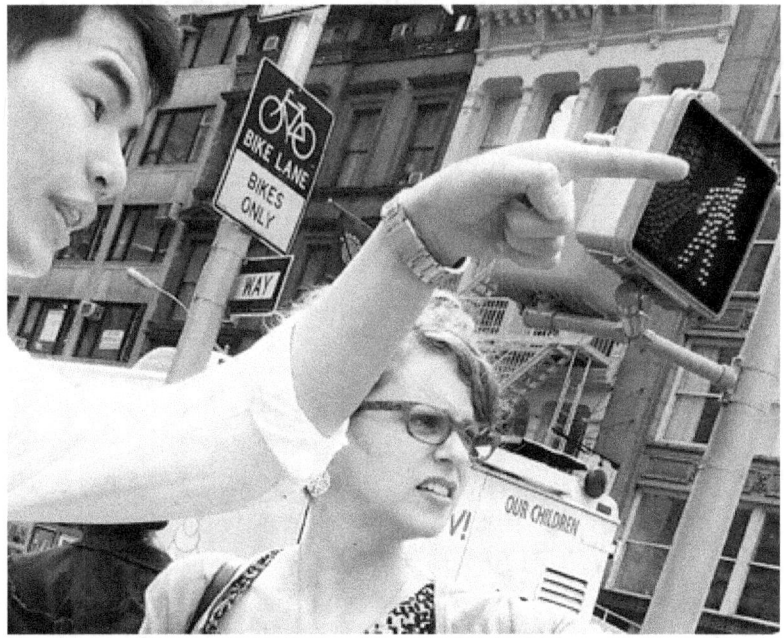

Chapter 21 — *Five more stories*

True stories from the used furniture store

Except for one year, I never worked more than eight hours a week, in my entire life. You can do that when you don't have a wife and kids to feed. That one year I spent working in my fathers used furniture store. It was located in a section of Brooklyn where I grew up. Over the years the neighborhood had changed, with the arrival of large numbers of immigrants from Jamaica and Russia. The Jamaicans were usually well-off, while the Russians were as poor as church mice. I felt sorry for the Russians, they came from a place that was short of everything, and now found themselves in a land of plenty. The problem was, they couldn't afford any of the beautiful things that were all around them.

I was sitting in the store one day, when a middle-aged Russian lady walks in and starts to browse. I had seen her before. She had her eye on a mahogany desk that was made in Italy. It came with seven leaves so it could be turned into a dinner table in seconds. It was a very unusual piece, and I was instructed by my father to stay firm on the price. She circled the desk several times, then asked "how much?" I" said four ninety- five." She made a face and then said "Why so much?" "Why not four fifty?" I said "No, the price is firm." She grumbled something under her breath and walked out.

She returned the next day, and we went thru the same routine. Then she said "My friends warned me not to come to America, the greedy capitalists will exploit you" "I'm not a greedy capitalist, I said I'm just an honest businessman trying to make a profit." I tried to remain polite, but I found myself getting pretty sarcastic. "You see, in this country, I have to make what is called 'a profit' if I want to stay in business. I know that's a foreign concept to you, but perhaps if the people in Russia learned how to make 'a profit' maybe the place wouldn't be coming apart at the seams. And maybe they wouldn't be leaving in droves." She looked at me as if I had insulted Lenin himself. She let loose with a long string of invectives in Russian, and stormed out, slamming the door for good effect! "Well, I won't be seeing her anymore," I said to myself.

She returned the very next day, all smiles. She apologized for her behavior the day before. I said "No problem" Then she announced that she would buy the desk. She had a friend with her, who had a car, and he would bring it home for her. I said "the price is four ninety-five, right?" "Yes, she said, four ninety- five." Her friend, Boris, was a big guy, and he helped me load the desk with all the leaves onto his station wagon. Then I said "Let's go inside, I don't like to handle money on the street." So I sat at my desk, and as I was making out the receipt, she proudly places a five dollar bill on my desk. I looked at it, and said to her "what's this?" "Five dollars, she said, I get 5 cents change." I really don't remember what I did or said after that. I think I retreated into an escape hatch in the back of my mind. I remember asking God what I did to deserve this, what transgression was I guilty of? Why do you send such crazy people into my store to drive me nuts? She brought me back to reality, by waving a hand in front of my eyes. "Are you OK?" She asked. "Yes, I said, but there seems to be a misunderstanding." "The desk is not four dollars and ninety-five cents, it's four HUNDRED and ninety five dollars!" Her jaw dropped, her eyes bulged, "HUNDRED?" She stammered "DOLLARS?" She gasped. Her friend placed a chair behind her, he was trying his hardest not to laugh. "Misha, I told you, it sounded too good to be true" he said. Well, at least I knew her name now. She sat down and stared-off into space. I thought she was going to cry.

Suddenly she jumped up and said "The sign, the sign said 495." She ran to where the desk used to be and removed the sign from the wall that said 495. She shoved it under my nose and said "Look, It says 495, there is no decimal point, how is anyone supposed to know how much it is?" I said "You are right, there isn't any decimal point, I took it for granted that people would know the right price, apparently I was wrong." Then it occurred to me that this whole situation, might not be, what it appeared to be. This naïve old lady might actually be a con-artist! And now my expensive desk was in her station wagon. If they decided to just drive off, there was little I could do about it. So I went outside and wrote down the license plate number, now driving away would be a little more complicated. Then I went back to my desk and put a decimal point on the sign in the right place. Boris and I then dragged the desk back into the store.

Misha just sat there with tears streaming down her cheeks. "What am I going to tell my daughter, I told her I was going to bring her a desk today." "Misha, I said, I want you to like your new country, I'm going to show you that not all Americans are greedy capitalists." I brought her into the back room, where we kept all of the un-finished furniture. I showed her a desk and chair set that wasn't refurnished yet and said "This set is solid wood, it is quality furniture. We haven't worked on it yet, but your daughter could do it herself. It would make a nice project for a rainy day." She looked at it and said "it's nice." I said "Yes it is, and when she re-finishes it, it will be beautiful. And I'm going to give this set to you for the same price we paid for it, twenty dollars, I'm not making one cent profit" She said "You would do this for me?" "Yes" I said. She said something to Boris and he took out his wallet and handed her a twenty dollar bill. She looked at the bill for a second, then extended it towards me hesitantly, then withdrew it. "Why twenty dollars," she said, "why not ten?"

Uncle Vinny

When I was in my early teens, one of my favorite pass times was to play a game called Conflict. It was a very simple, stylized war game that was something like chess. There were little cannons, battleships, and airplanes, which you would maneuver around the board with the goal of capturing your opponent's home base. I would play it for hours on my front porch, with some friends from down the block. Every day around 5:30pm, my uncle Vinny would walk by on his way home from work. He was a big shot on Wall Street and made a lot of money. He was thin and short and looked a little like Johnny Carson. I liked uncle Vinny, he was always nice to me. His own kids however, called him "der Fuhrer" because he was a strict disciplinarian. He was also so tight with money that his wife would say that he "squeaked when he walked."

One day he came up to us on the stoop while we were playing and asked us what we were doing. I gave him a brief summary of the game and he seemed intrigued. He read the rules on the back of the box and then said "I got winners." After I beat my friend Frankie, uncle Vinny took his place at the board and we began to play. For a first time player, he didn't do too badly. I could tell that he would get very good at it with a little practice. Of course I won, so we shook hands and then he said "I'll see you tomorrow." The next day we played again and this time it was much closer, he was learning fast. Our third game went badly for me at first, but my experience got me through. Uncle Vinny did not seem happy. The thought of losing to a fourteen year old boy, three times, did not sit well with him. He was a big shot at work, he was a successful stockbroker, and he was used to winning.

The next week uncle Vinny left work a half hour early so we would have more time to play. I beat him two games in a row in what were now becoming very tense, close games. We would have had a third game but his wife yelled from across the street that his dinner was getting cold. The next day my aunt called me and asked me what I was doing to uncle Vinny! He's in a rotten mood all the time, he keeps snapping at the kids. It's that game you're playing with him! Nicholas, do me a favor please, just once, let him win." I can't do that Aunt Mary, he'll know, and that will make things worse." "Don't worry I said, he's getting better every day, It's just a matter of time before he wins on his own." "I hope you're right she said, he's driving us crazy." The next few days were a disaster for uncle Vinny. He lost every game by a hair. Now it was his daughter who pleaded with me to let him win. "He's obsessed with that game, Nicholas, please let him win, he's reading all kinds of books about strategy and warfare." "I want to go away next week with my girlfriends, I have to ask him for money, if he's in a bad mood, he won't give it to me, you know how cheap he is." "Nicholas, she said, I'll give you twenty dollars if you let him win." It was a tempting offer, twenty dollars was a lot of money. In those days a slice of pizza was 15 cents, but I just couldn't do it.

    The next day when uncle Vinny sat down opposite me I knew right away that something was different. Maybe it was the look in his eye, a sense of determination that I had not seen in him before. Right from the start he began to systematically dismember my forces! There were no master strokes or grand plays, just a series of perfectly timed, precisely executed attacks that left me reeling! No matter what I did, he had an answer for it. It was like he could read my mind. I had no doubt that this time he was going to win. My back was to the wall. His forces had my home base surrounded. All he had to do was sail one of his battleships into my home port and he would win! But first he had to get passed the minefields that guarded the entrance to my harbor. All he had to do was roll two dice and not get "snake eyes." The chances of rolling snake eyes was only one in thirty- six, so the game was as good as won! He picked up the dice and cupped them in his hands. He blew on them and rattled them around, taking his time, letting the suspense build up. He had a sly grin on his face. This was the moment he had been waiting for, for weeks. He was going to put this snot nosed 14 year old kid in his place, once and for all! He rolled the dice…and they bounced, and careened, and ricochet off one another, guided by the laws of physics, or, as some believe, the fickle finger of fate! They seemed to move in slow- motion, reluctant to come to a halt and deliver their verdict, but they finally did, and came up-- snake-eyes!

    Uncle Vinny screamed—"Fuck you -Fuck this - Fuck this game" as he knocked the board over, sending the pieces flying in all directions! His face was beet red, his eyes bulged out, the veins in his neck were throbbing, I thought he was going to have a heart attack right there! He knocked over three cans of soda on purpose. Then he stood up and kicked my cat! "This is Bullshit" he screamed "I need this shit?" "I need this stupid fucking game?" He put on his jacket and stormed off, screaming obscenities all the way home! Then my phone rang, It was his wife, "WHAT---did you do to Uncle Vinny?"

    Uncle Vinny and I made up eventually, but we never played Conflict again. His wife said it was bad for his blood pressure. He lived to be a little old man, dying at the age of 92.

Women with aliases

In the space of six years, I had three lady friends with aliases. What are the odds of that happening? I didn't go looking for them, they just happened. Let me say this, if a woman has multiple names, she is probably either trying to hide a shady past, or is up to no good, or is crazy. My lady friends were all three.

One of them was a real doozy. She was an intimidatingly beautiful brunette. She had gorgeous almond shaped eyes and high cheekbones. Her perfectly straight nose looked like it was chiseled by Michael- Angelo himself. Her luscious lips were made to be kissed, and to tell lies. Her name was Betsy, and her father was a very rich and powerful man. I will not reveal his name here. I can do without the lawsuit. I met her in a small, blue collar neighborhood bar. When she walked in, the whole place fell silent, and everyone just stared at her. She was that stunning! She looked like she just stepped off the cover of Vogue or Harper's Bazaar. She walked the full length of the bar, as if it were the catwalk. Then she turned around and passed many empty seats until she got to the one that was beside me. She sat down and explained that she chose this seat because I was the least intimidating person in the place. I replied that I wasn't sure if that was compliment or an insult. She laughed, and we started talking. We talked for about an hour and the impression I got was that she was very bright and well educated, but not very well read. She didn't seem to be up to speed on current events. She asked me to help her home with some small packages she had. When I walked out with her, everyone's eyebrows raised. I walked her to her door and thanked her for the interesting conversation. Then I returned to the bar. When I walked in everyone wanted to know why I was back so soon. What happened? Didn't you even make a pass at her? "Nah, she's way out of my league "I said. "What are you stupid, you should have gone for it, the girl obviously liked you" The consensus was that I was nuts. The next day she returned and again she sat next to me. This time I was determined not to sell myself short. Betsy and I began to have a very strange and torrid affair. She was unlike any woman I had ever known.

Betsy was a few years older than me, and a few inches taller. She also dressed more "uptown" than me. When we were in public, most people assumed that we were just friends. Strange men were constantly coming- on to her right in front of me, as if I wasn't there! She would let them go on with their passes for about five minutes, until they asked for her number. Then she would point to me and say "Well, ask my boyfriend if it's alright." Then they would say "Oh, are you two together?" She would then laugh hysterically. To her, it was all a game. Sometimes, if we were quarreling, she would make these embarrassing episodes happen deliberately. She could be very sadistic that way. Betsy was a woman of mystery. Everything about her was puzzling. She never seemed to have full time job, yet she always had plenty of money. She would disappear for weeks at a time, and then pop-up suddenly and ask me out to dinner. She would often call me at the last minute and ask me to meet her somewhere. Then she would pull up in a strange car, driven by a strange man, and tell me that it was her uncle! She had so many different uncles that I lost track of them. When I asked her what she did for a living, she was vague. The best I could figure was that she was some sort of saleswoman, selling some sort of service. She was not allowed to talk about it because it was a trade secret. Then one day somebody waved to her from across the street and called her Linda! I said to myself, oh no, not another one. She explained that Linda was a stage name she used to use when she was an actress. Great, now she was an actress!

    The first time I went to her apartment, the mystery only deepened. She had on her kitchen wall a long list of men's names along with their phone numbers. She explained that they were her business associates. On her kitchen table was one of the earliest telephone answering machines in the country. It was a huge reel to reel tape recorder that was hooked up to her phone. I asked her why, when I called her, I didn't get her answering machine. She explained that that was a different phone. So now she had two different phones in her home. That was unheard off at the time. The enigmatic nature of her lifestyle only increased my curiosity about her. I began to stalk her! I waited outside her place and began to follow her from a safe distance. I followed her all the way into the city on the subway. She went into Beth-Israel medical center. I wondered if she was sick. The next week she confided to me that she had to have a minor operation to remove an "abdominal obstruction." After the operation I went to see her in the hospital. I met one of her cousins there and on the way out she said "It's too bad Betsey didn't want to keep the baby." Baby! What baby, I thought she had an obstruction of some kind! I felt so stupid. This whole thing was getting to be too much.

    One of Betsy's stranger habits was to drink little vials of orange juice at all different times of the day. She said it was because she had a vitamin C deficiency. She would carry them in her pocketbook. I told this to a friend of mine and he started laughing. "You idiot" he said, "That's not orange juice. It's probably methadone." "What's methadone?" I asked. "It's a medicine that heroin addicts take when they're trying to kick the habit." "You mean she's a junkie"? "Probably" he said. I couldn't believe it! So, I asked her about it over dinner one night, and she admitted that she was indeed a heroin addict. She paid the tab with a credit card and when the waiter returned it he said "thank you Paula." I asked her "why did he call you Paula?" "Oh, that's just a business name that I use for tax purposes."

So far, I knew she had at least three aliases. I knew from past experiences that this was not a good sign. She had a regular source of income, but didn't seem to have a real job. She had had an abortion plus she was a heroin addict. I was also catching her in all kinds of lies. I had to decide if I was going to continue with this thing or not. I knew I wasn't in love with her, but she looked so damned good on my arm. She was a real trophy! Then she vanished again. I didn't hear from her for two weeks. Then I get a long-distance call from her. She was in Canada. She claimed that there was some misunderstanding with the police there, and that she needed five hundred dollars right away. I asked her to put the police on the phone. She said that they were too busy to talk, so I called them myself. They said that they had my friend Betsy under arrest, if that was her real name. It seems she had I.D.s for half a dozen people on her, and they weren't sure who she was. They also said that they had arrested her for passing bad checks. And for prostitution!

When that cop said the word "prostitution," everything fell into place. It was like finding the missing piece to a puzzle. Suddenly everything made perfect sense. All the evidence was there, in plain sight, but I was just too blind to see it. Betsy was a high-priced call-girl. I decided that this was as good a time as ever to end this thing. Then, at the last moment, I had second thoughts. I really liked Betsy and considered her a friend. Was this the right thing to do, to abandon her in a moment of crisis? Then the policeman, sensing my hesitation, said, "By the way, she was with another man who was acting as her pimp, when she was arrested." That brought me back to reality. I said "Please tell her that I can't send her any money." He said "smart move." I didn't have the guts to tell her myself. She would never forgive me for that.

Several weeks later, I was sitting in the bar where I had met Betsy. I was on my third "scotch on the rocks" when suddenly the whole place fell silent. Then someone tapped me on the shoulder, I turned around. It was her. She was as gorgeous as ever. I was very aware that everyone was watching us. I remember thinking that no one should be allowed to be this beautiful. Women this stunning only cause trouble. They always have, and they always will. Men have been killing each other for such women since the beginning of time.

Helen of Troy must have looked like her, the face that launched a thousand ships. I just smiled and said "hello." She looked at me thru those huge, almond shaped eyes. How many men were enslaved by those eyes? She just stood there, staring. I could see a tear well up and make its way down that beautiful cheek, past those lips that told a thousand lies, past that perfect chin. Then she whispered "I thought we were friends." She turned around and walked away. I never saw her again.

The joys of tripping children on purpose

I was on the "F" train, on my way into the city. I took out the Times from my bag and folded it correctly so it wouldn't take up too much room. A stop or two later, a young mother and her son get on and sit opposite me. This kid is about five or six years old, and after a while he gets restless. So what does he do, he starts to twirl around the pole that's between us. He goes around once and clips my paper with his shoulder. So I move over about half a foot to give him more room. He comes around again and he still clips my paper, so I slide over some more. As he comes by again, he still hits my paper, almost knocking it out of my hands. I shoot him a look that said "knock it off" He gave me a look that said "you can't tell me what to do, you're not my father." And meanwhile, his mother is just sitting there, pretending that she doesn't see what's going on. Now, if I were a mature adult, I would have gotten up and moved to another seat entirely, but I am not. And if his mother was a mature adult, she would have told him to sit down, but she did not. So he comes around again, and this time his hand is extended. He's demanding more space! He must think I'm a schmuck. As he comes by, I stick my foot out and he trips over it, and he hits the floor with a satisfying thud. He lets out a wail, and his mother jumps up and says "you did that on purpose" "I did not" I said, but the smile on my face said otherwise. She picked him up and said "Parker, are you alright, sweetie"? Parker, what a stupid name, I knew it had to be one of those dopey, yuppie names. They both looked at me like I was some kind of monster. I didn't care, I just sat there with a big smirk on my face. It felt so good. I was reminded of the old saying that went: "old age and treachery will always beat youth and exuberance."

On being robbed at knifepoint

When I was in my thirties, I lived in a neighborhood of Brooklyn called Park Slope. It was filled with old brownstones that were in great demand by the up-and-coming yuppies who were flooding into the area. The "gentrification" of Park Slope was just about complete. However, the neighborhoods adjacent to it were still mostly low-income areas with high crime rates. At that time the city was going thru a crime wave that was getting worse every year and life in New York was becoming unbearable. Every day you heard about someone else you knew getting mugged or burglarized. Having your car broken into was so commonplace that it wasn't even worth talking about. And then the "crack epidemic" began, and it got even worse. People were getting mugged at 8am in the morning on their way to work.

I was having a few drinks in my favorite hang-out just two blocks from my place. I was dreading the walk home because I knew it could be dangerous. On my way out one of the guys said to me "watch out for Leroy" It was the standard warning that we used in the bar, and everyone knew what it meant. I began walking up the block and noticed that one of the street lights was out. This created a dark zone which I knew to be wary of. I scanned the street up ahead, looking for suspicious characters, especially young black men. If I was going to "get hit" it would probably be one of them! I was half way home now, just half a block to go and I remember saying to myself "this is no way to live" I felt like a hunted animal in the jungle I was just a few steps from my front door now, keys in hand, when I saw him. He appeared out of nowhere, from behind a parked car. He was a young black man, about 16 years old. As he ran towards me, he asked me if I had the time. I said 3: am, even though I knew it was much earlier. I guess I thought he would just turn around and go home if he thought it was that late. He did no such thing. He was almost upon me when I saw what was in his right hand. It was a stiletto with a long thin blade which gleamed in the night. He came right up to me with the knife held low at his side, but at a threatening angle. "Give me your money" he said. "No problem, you're the boss" I said. He was nervous. I could see his hands trembling. He looked to me like a real amateur at this. He was acting alone, never a good idea. So, I reached into my pocket and took out all the cash I had on me, 15 dollars. The very fact that he let me go into my own pocket was another sign that he was new at this. If I had had a gun in my pocket, he would have been dead! He looked at the money and said "I need more," "that's all I got" I said. I was worried he would get agitated and do something stupid. He pointed to the keys in my hand and told me to open the door. "No way" I said, As I grabbed one of the garbage can covers that were right there to use as a shield.

Then I took another one to use as a weapon! If need be, I was ready to do battle with him, right there, like two gladiators. Under no condition I was going to let him into my home. He stood there for a second and sized up the situation. Maybe it was the crazy look in my eyes, or the smell of booze on my breath that made him back off. Whatever it was, he made the right decision and took off. I went inside and opened a beer and tried to relax. Overall, I got away light. I only lost 15 dollars and didn't get hurt, plus I would have something to talk about tomorrow.

Chapter 22

The future

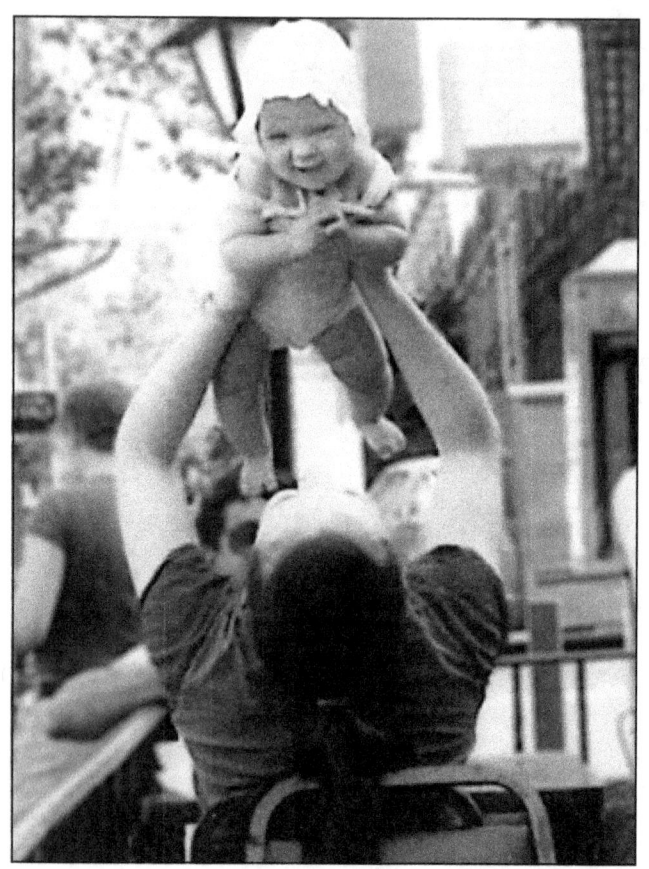

Father and daughter, Park Slope, Brooklyn.

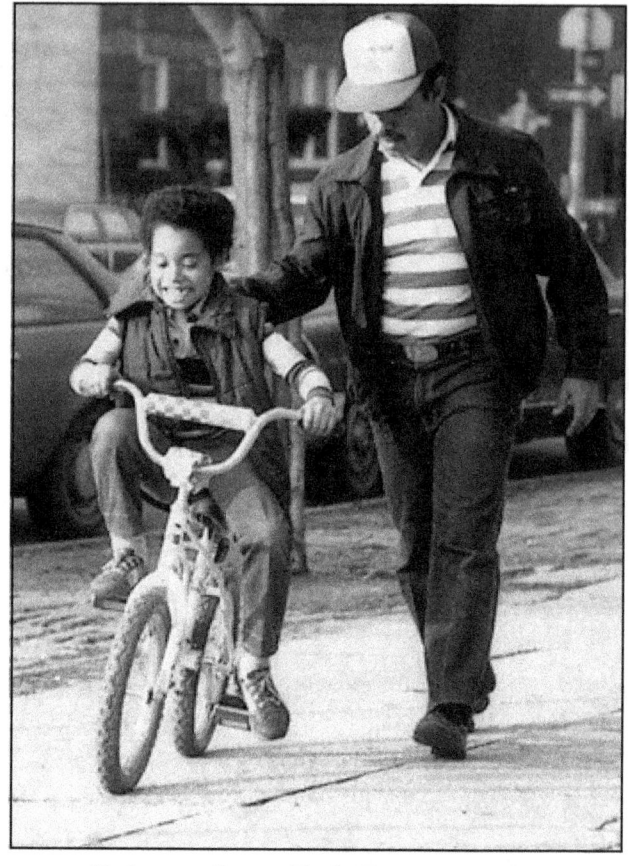

Father and son, Park Slope, Brooklyn.

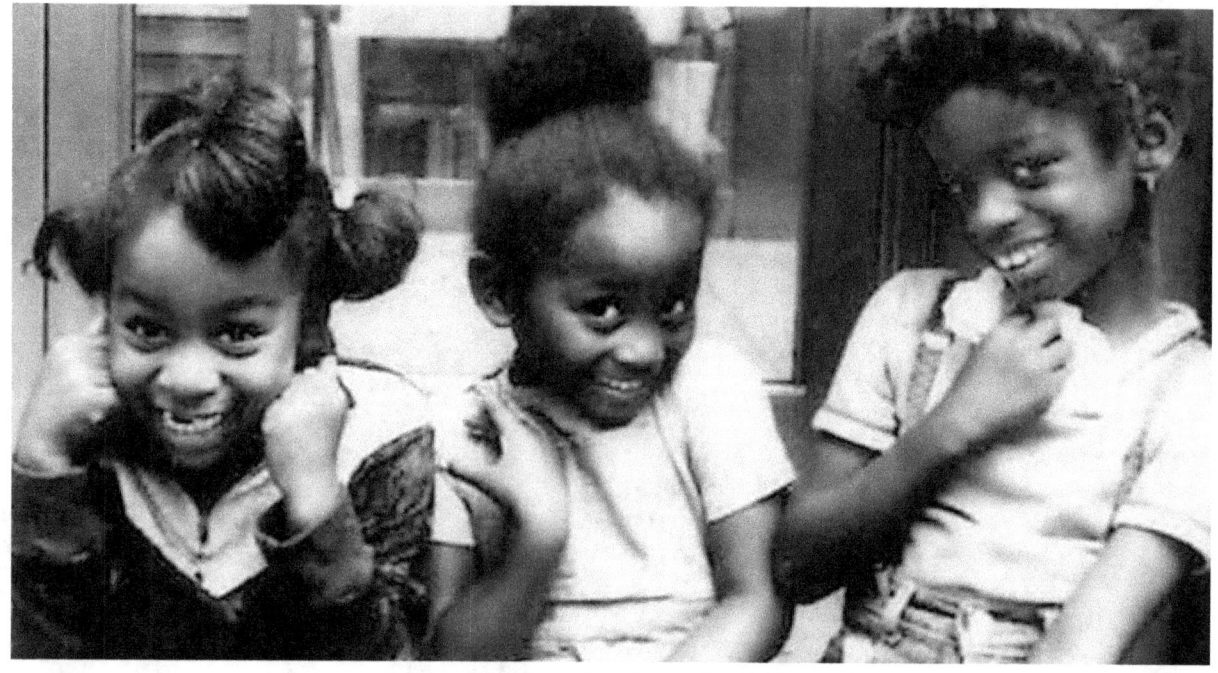

Three cuties from Brooklyn.

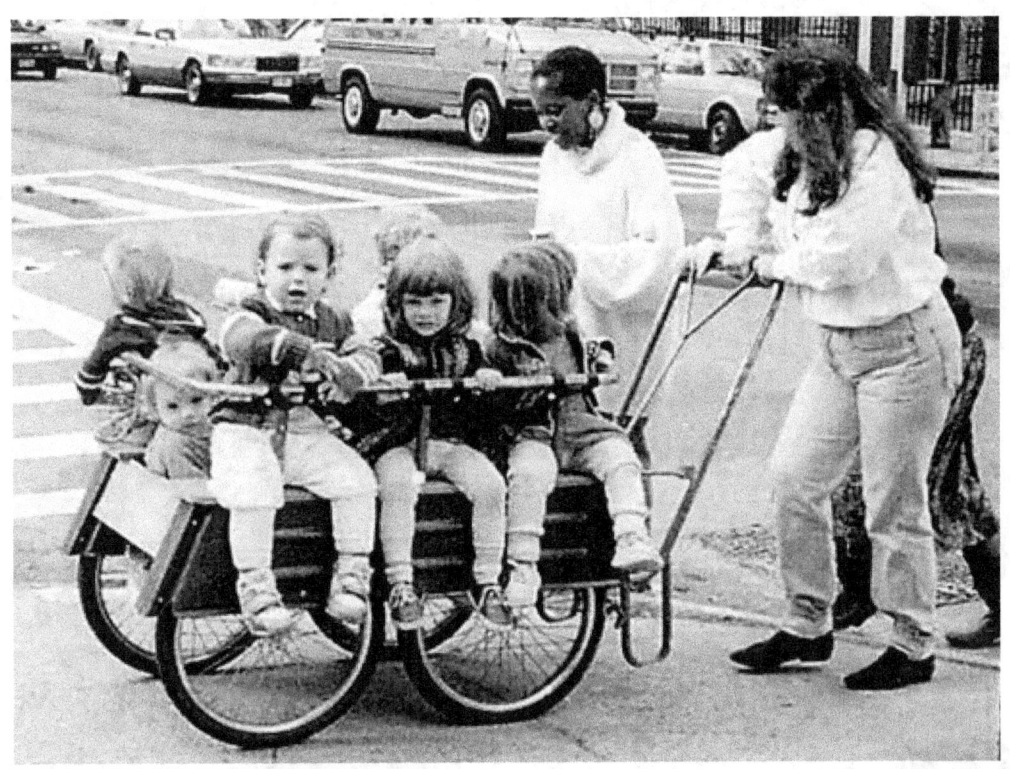
The baby-buggy in Park Slope, Brooklyn.

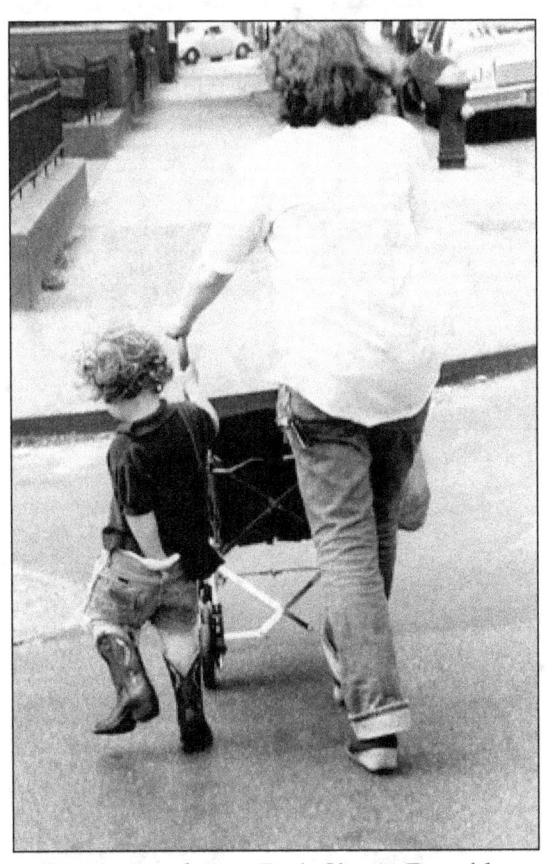
Mother and son, Park Slope, Brooklyn.

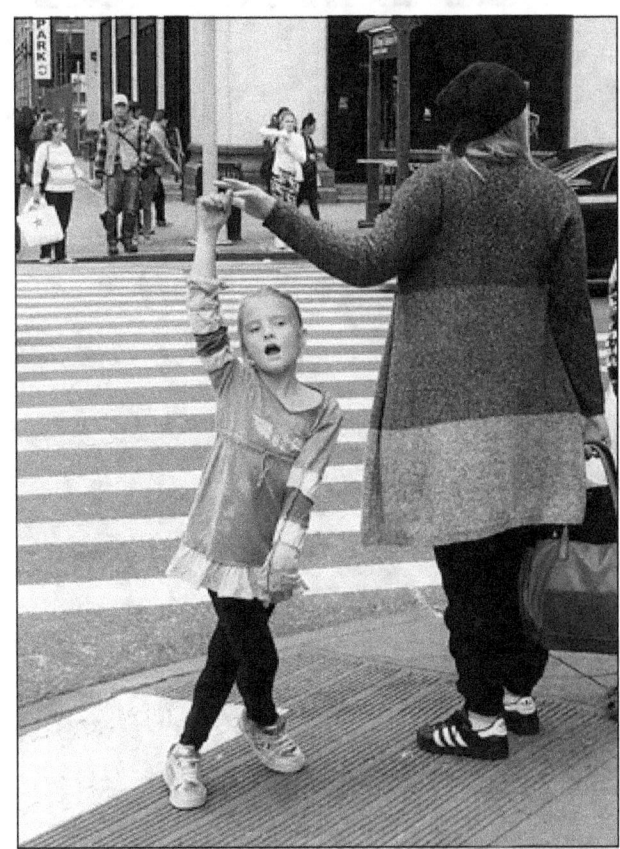

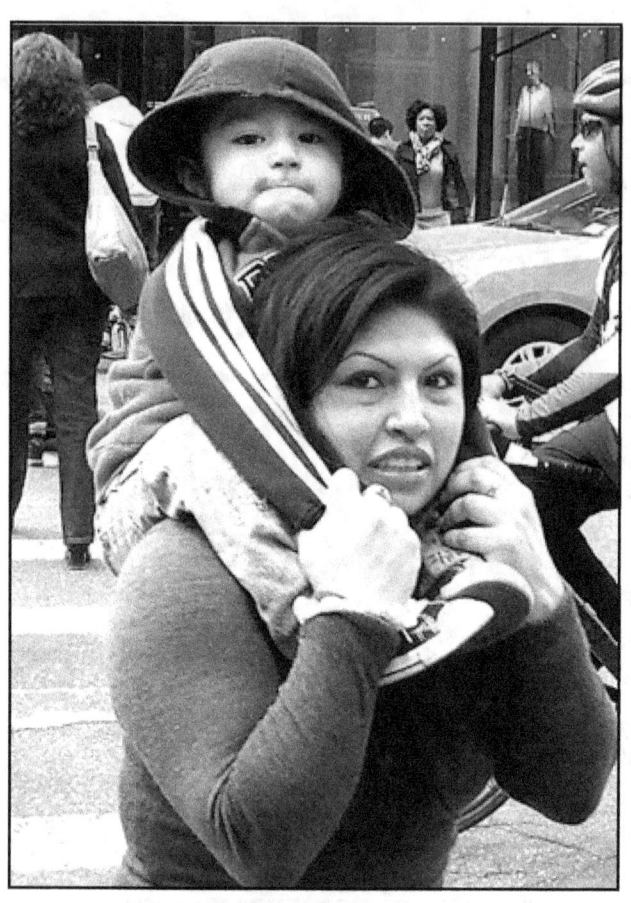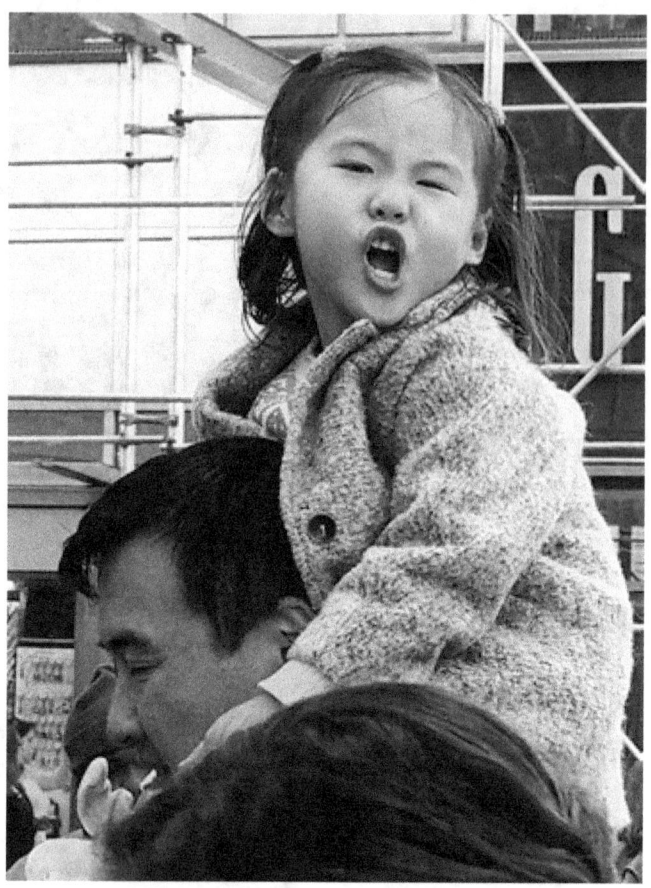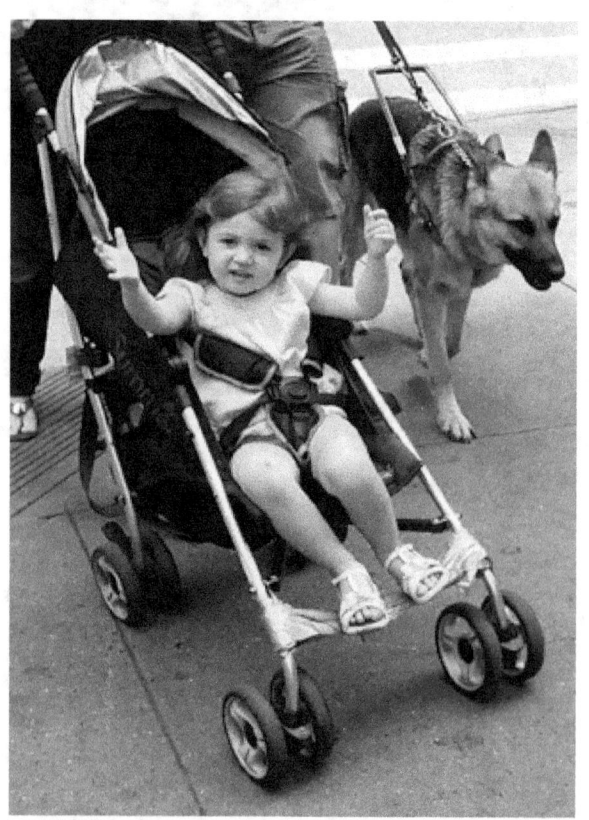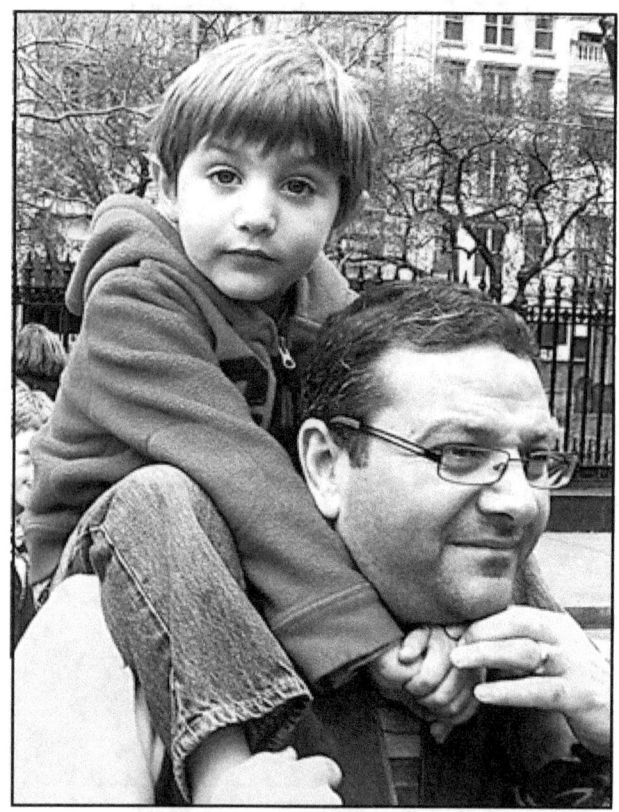

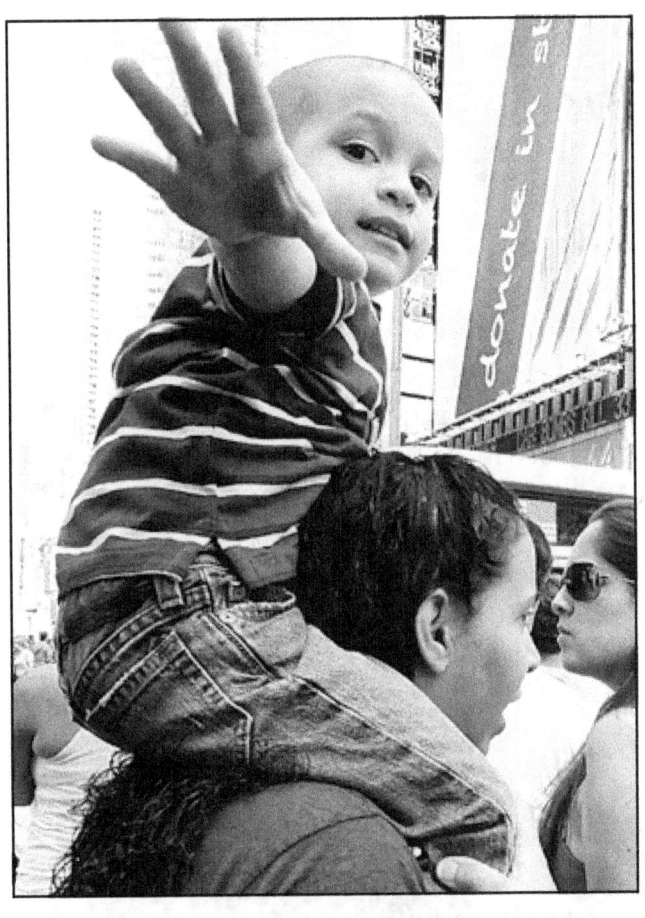
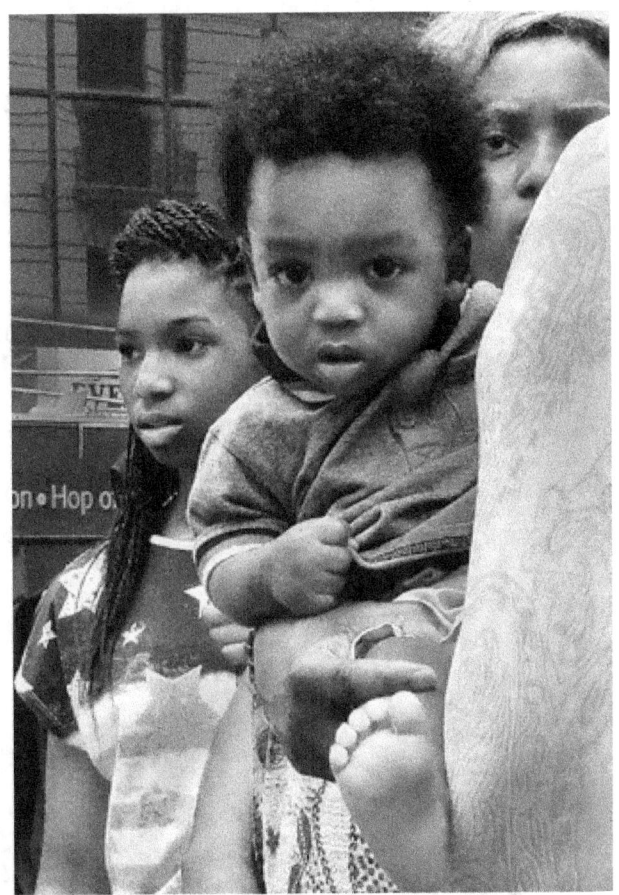
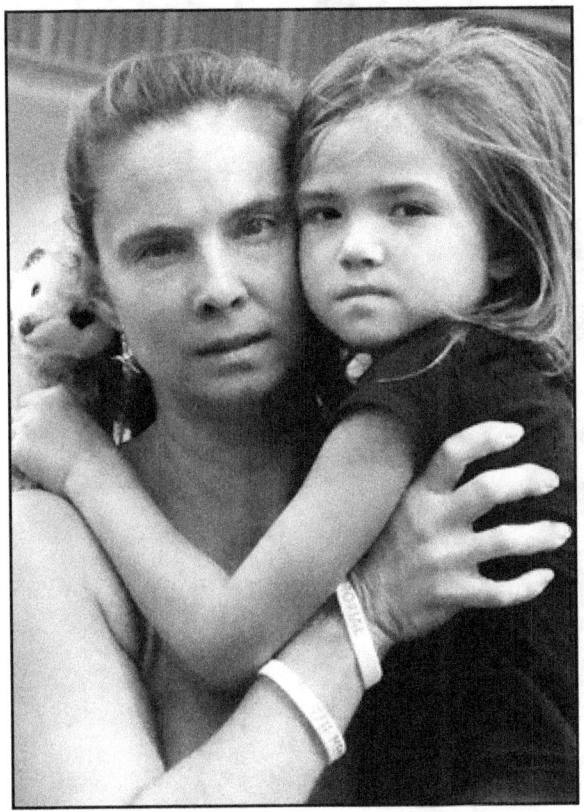
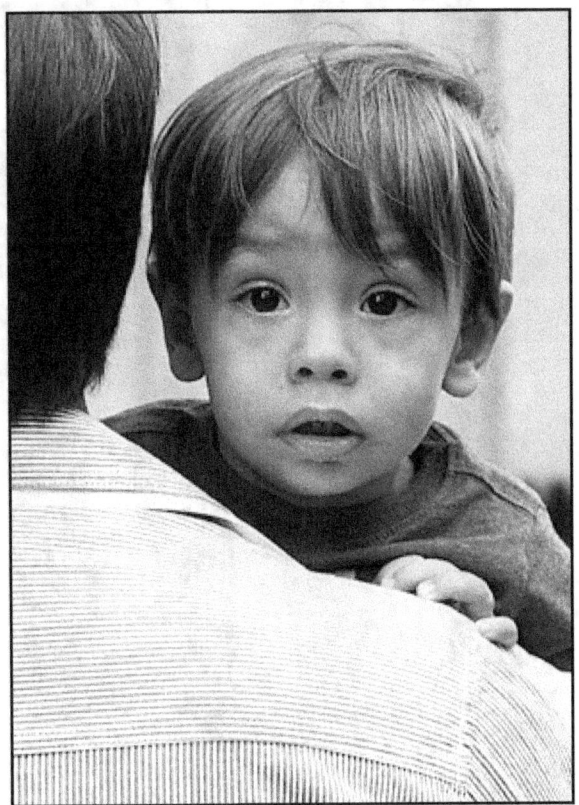

Chapter 23 *End Piece*

The incredible shrinking mayor

He was the savior of New York. He made the city safe again. After 9/11 he was hailed as "America's Mayor." Then he started hanging out with Donald Trump. Inevitably, some of the slime covering Trump rubbed off onto him. Now, like so many of Trump's associates, he is under criminal investigation. When he entered Yankee Stadium recently, he was booed by the entire crowd!

www.ingramcontent.com/pod-product-compliance
Lightning Source LLC
Chambersburg PA
CBHW062323220526
45469CB00008B/2603